HOLT

Decisions for Health

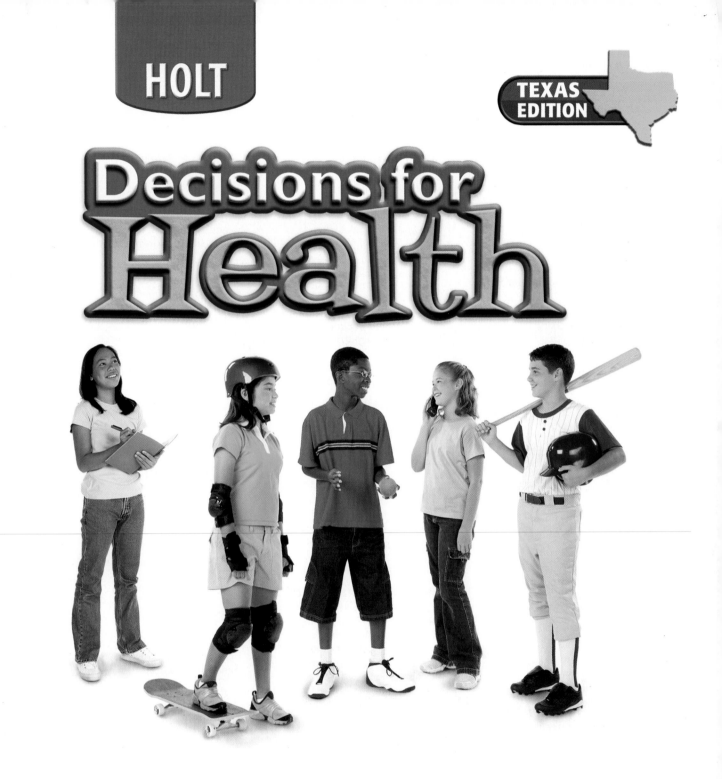

HOLT, RINEHART AND WINSTON

A Harcourt Education Company

Orlando • **Austin** • New York • San Diego • Toronto • London

Acknowledgments

Contributing Authors

Kate Cronan, M.D.
Chief, Division of Emergency Medicine
Alfred I. duPont Hospital for Children
Wilmington, Delaware

Sharon Deutschlander
Department of Health and Physical Education
Indiana University of Pennsylvania
Indiana, Pennsylvania

William E. Dunscombe, Jr.
Associate Professor of Biology
Chairman, Department of Biology
Union County College
Cranford, New Jersey

Efrain Garza Fuentes, Ed.D.
Director, Patient and Family Services
Childrens Hospital Los Angeles
Los Angeles, California

Patricia J. Harned, Ph.D.
Director of Character Development and Research
Ethics Resource Center
Washington, D.C.

Craig P. Henderson, LCSW, MDIV
Therapist
Youth Services of Tulsa
Tulsa, Oklahoma
Trainer
National Resource Center for Youth Services
Norman, Oklahoma

Peter Katona, M.D., FACP
Associate Professor of Clinical Medicine, Infectious Disease Division, Department of Medicine
UCLA School of Medicine
Los Angeles, California

Linda Klingaman, Ph.D.
Professor
Indiana University of Pennsylvania
Indiana, Pennsylvania

Joshua Mann, M.D., M.P.H.
Clinical Assistant Professor, Department of Family and Preventive Medicine
University of South Carolina School of Medicine
Columbia, South Carolina

Kweethai Chin Neill, Ph.D., C.H.E.S., FASHA
Assistant Professor, Department of Kinesiology, Health Promotion, and Recreation
University of North Texas
Denton, Texas

Stephen E. Stork, Ed.D., C.H.E.S.
Assistant Professor
Department of Kinesiology, Health Promotion, and Recreation
University of North Texas
Denton, Texas

Keith Verner, Ph.D.
Chief, Division of Developmental Pediatrics and Learning
Director, Center for Science and Health Education
Associate Professor of Pediatrics
Associate Professor of Education
Penn State Children's Hospital, Pennsylvania State University
Hershey, Pennsylvania

Contributing Writers

Presentation Series Development

Carol Badran, M.P.H.
Health Educator
San Francisco Department of Public Health
San Francisco, California

Pirette McKamey
Teacher
Thurgood Marshall Academic High School
San Francisco, California

Academic Reviewers

John Caprio, Ph.D.
George C. Kent Professor
Department of Biological
  Sciences
Louisiana State University
Baton Rouge, Louisiana

**William B. Cissell, M.S.P.H.,
Ph.D., C.H.E.S.**
Professor of Health Studies
Department of Health Studies
Texas Woman's University
Denton, Texas

Joe Crim, Ph.D.
*Professor and Head Biological
  Sciences Department*
University of Georgia
Athens, Georgia

Susan B. Dickey, Ph.D., R.N.
*Associate Professor, Pediatric
  Nursing*
College of Allied Health
  Professionals
Temple University
Philadelphia, Pennsylvania

Stephen Dion
Associate Professor
Sport Fitness
Salem College
Salem, Massachusetts

Ronald Feldman, Ph.D.
*Ruth Harris Ottman Centennial
  Professor for the Advancement
  of Social Work Education*
*Director, Center for the Study of
  Social Work Practice*
Columbia University
New York, New York

William Guggino, Ph.D.
Professor of Physiology
The Johns Hopkins University
  School of Medicine
Baltimore, Maryland

**Kathryn Hilgenkamp, Ed.D.,
C.H.E.S.**
*Assistant Professor, Community
  Health and Nutrition*
University of Northern
  Colorado
Greeley, Colorado

Cynthia Kuhn, Ph.D.
*Professor of Pharmacology and
  Cancer Biology*
Duke University Medical Center
Duke University
Durham, North Carolina

**John B. Lowe, M.P.H., Dr.P.H.,
F.A.H.P.A.**
Professor and Head
Department of Community and
  Behavioral Health
College of Public Health
The University of Iowa
Iowa City, Iowa

**Leslie Mayrand, Ph.D., R.N.,
C.N.S.**
Professor of Nursing
Pediatrics and Adolescent
  Medicine
Angelo State University
San Angelo, Texas

Karen E. McConnell, Ph.D.
Assistant Professor
School of Physical Education
Pacific Lutheran University
Tacoma, Washington

Clyde B. McCoy, Ph.D.
Professor and Chair
Department of Epidemiology
  and Public Health
University of Miami School
  of Medicine
Miami, Florida

Hal Pickett, Psy.D.
*Assistant Professor of
  Psychiatry*
Department of Psychiatry
University of Minnesota
  Medical School
Minneapolis, Minnesota

Philip Posner, Ph.D.
*Professor and Scholar in
  Physiology*
College of Medicine
Florida State University
Tallahassee, Florida

John Rohwer, Ph.D.
Professor
Department of Health Sciences
Bethel College
St. Paul, Minnesota

Susan R. Schmidt, Ph.D.
Postdoctoral Psychology Fellow
Center on Child Abuse and
  Neglect
The University of Oklahoma
  Health Sciences Center
Oklahoma City, Oklahoma

Fred Seaman, Ph.D.
*Research Scientist, Phamacology
  and Toxicology*
Department of Pharmacy
The University of Texas
Austin, Texas

**Stephen B. Springer, Ed.D.,
L.P.C., C.P.M.**
*Director of Occupational
  Education*
Southwest Texas State
  University
San Marcos, Texas

Richard Storey, Ph.D.
Professor of Biology
Colorado College
Colorado Springs, Colorado

Marianne Suarez, Ph.D.
Postdoctoral Psychology Fellow
Center on Child Abuse and
  Neglect
The University of Oklahoma
  Health Sciences Center
Oklahoma City, Oklahoma

Josey Templeton, Ed.D.
Associate Professor
Department of Health, Exercise,
  and Sports Medicine
The Citadel, The Military
  College of South Carolina
Charleston, South Carolina

Martin Van Dyke, Ph.D.
Professor of Chemistry Emeritus
Front Range Community
  College
Westminster, Colorado

Graham Watts, Ph.D.
*Assistant Professor of Health
  and Safety*
The University of Indiana
Bloomington, Indiana

Acknowledgments continued on page 402.

Contents
in Brief

Chapters

Contents

Myth: Only girls develop eating disorders.

Fact: Go to page 73 to get the facts.

Myth: Some families never have problems.

Fact: Go to page 91 to get the facts.

CHAPTER
6

Coping with Conflict and Stress 108

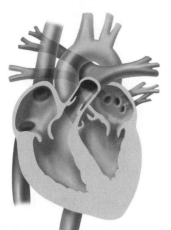

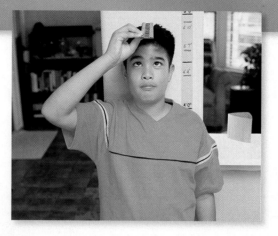

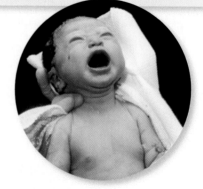

Myth & Fact

Myth: You can always tell when you or someone else has an STD.

Fact: Go to page 225 to get the facts.

Myth: No pain, no gain.

Fact: Go to page 252 to get the facts.

Myth: Taking more medicine than the recommended amount will make it work faster.

Fact: Go to page 286 to get the facts.

Myth & Fact

Myth: Smokeless tobacco is safer than cigarettes because none of the nicotine is inhaled into the lungs.

Fact: Go to page 308 to get the facts.

Appendix

Activities

Hands-on ACTIVITY

LIFE SKILLS ACTIVITY

CROSS-DISCIPLINE ACTIVITY

Life Skills IN ACTION

How to Use Your Textbook

Your Roadmap for Success with *Decisions for Health*

Read the Objectives

The objectives, which are listed under the **What You'll Do** head, tell you what you'll need to know.

STUDY TIP Reread the objectives when studying for a test to be sure you know the material.

Study the Key Terms

Key Terms are listed for each lesson under the **Terms to Learn** head. Learn the definitions of these terms because you will most likely be tested on them. Use the glossary to locate definitions quickly.

STUDY TIP If you don't understand a definition, reread the page where the term is introduced. The surrounding text should help make the definition easier to understand.

Start Off Write

Start Off Write questions, which appear at the beginning of each lesson, help you to begin thinking about the topic covered in the lesson.

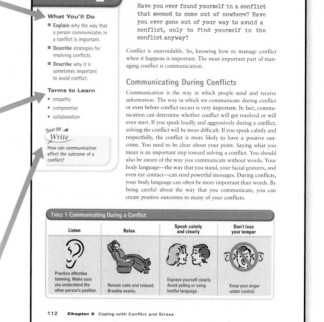

Take Notes and Get Organized

Keep a health notebook so that you are ready to take notes when your teacher reviews the material in class. Keep your assignments in this notebook so that you can review them when studying for the chapter test.

Be Resourceful, Use the Web

Internet Connect boxes in your textbook take you to resources that you can use for health projects, reports, and research papers. Go to **scilinks.org/health** and type in the HealthLinks code to get information on a topic.

Maintained by the National Science Teachers Association

Visit **go.hrw.com**
Find worksheets, *Current Health* magazine articles online, and other materials that go with your textbook at **go.hrw.com**. Click on the textbook icon and the table of contents to see all of the resources for each chapter.

Use the Illustrations and Photos

Art shows complex ideas and processes. Learn to analyze the art so that you better understand the material you read in the text.

Tables and graphs display important information in an organized way to help you see relationships.

A picture is worth a thousand words. Look at the photographs to see relevant examples of health concepts you are reading about.

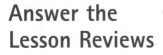

Answer the Lesson Reviews

Lesson Reviews test your knowledge over the main points of the lesson. Critical Thinking items challenge you to think about the material in greater depth and to find connections that you infer from the text.

STUDY TIP When you can't answer a question, reread the lesson. The answer is usually there.

Do Your Homework

Your teacher will assign Study Guide worksheets to help you understand and remember the material in the chapter.

STUDY TIP Answering the items in the Chapter Review will prepare you for the chapter test. Don't try to answer the questions without reading the text and reviewing your class notes. A little preparation up front will make your homework assignments a lot easier.

Visit Holt Online Learning
If your teacher gives you a special password to log onto the **Holt Online Learning** site, you'll find your complete textbook on the Web. In addition, you'll find some great learning tools and practice quizzes. You'll be able to see how well you know the material from your textbook.

Holt Online Learning
For more information go to:
www.hrw.com

Visit CNN Student News®
You'll find up-to-date events in science at **cnnstudentnews.com**.

Health and Wellness

Check out
Current Health
articles related to this chapter by
visiting **go.hrw.com**. Just type in
the keyword **HD4CH01**.

" I am really **looking forward** to this school year. I made first chair in **band,** and I made the **baseball** team, too. And best of all, I still have all of **my friends** from last year. **"**

Health IQ

Answer the following multiple-choice questions to find out what you already know about health and wellness. When you've finished this chapter, you'll have the opportunity to change your answers based on what you've learned.

1. **Doing which of the following would most help your physical health?**
   a. expressing your feelings to a friend
   b. balancing your social life with schoolwork
   c. getting 8 hours of sleep a night
   d. using self-control ⊛ **6.A**

2. **All of the following will help improve your social health EXCEPT**
   a. sharing your feelings with your friends.
   b. showing respect toward your family and friends.
   c. being considerate of others.
   d. solving problems without a lot of difficulty. ⊛ **6.A**

3. **Being able to cope with the demands of daily life is a sign of good**
   a. physical health.
   b. emotional health.
   c. mental health.
   d. social health. ⊛ **6.A**

4. **Getting an annual physical exam is**
   a. preventive healthcare.
   b. a healthy attitude.
   c. positive life skills.
   d. good hygiene. ⊛ **6.A**

5. **The life skill that involves giving thought to the value and quality of a product is**
   a. coping.
   b. making good decisions.
   c. being a wise consumer.
   d. communicating effectively. ⊛ **1.E**

6. **The life skill that gives you something to work toward and keeps you focused is**
   a. assessing your health.
   b. setting goals.
   c. practicing wellness.
   d. communicating effectively.

ANSWERS: 1. c; 2. d; 3. c; 4. a; 5. c; 6. b

What You'll Do

■ **Identify** the four parts of health. ✪ 6.A

■ **Explain** how the four parts of health affect your wellness. ✪ 6.A

Terms to Learn

• health

• wellness

Start Off
Write

What are some ways that you can take care of your health?

What Is Health?

When school started, Sofia joined a sports team. Sofia was surprised to find that, instead of being tired, she felt better and had more energy because she was more active.

Sofia discovered that sports are not only fun but they are also really good for your health. **Health** is the condition of your physical, emotional, mental, and social well-being. Good health starts with making good choices. And good choices lead to good health habits.

Your Physical Health

When you think of health, you probably think about your physical health. Your *physical health* is the part of your health that deals with the condition of your body. Things that you can do to maintain your physical health include the following:

• eating balanced meals

• engaging in physical activity

• getting 8 hours of sleep every night

• maintaining good hygiene (*Hygiene* is the practice of keeping yourself clean. For example, washing your hands before eating is good hygiene.)

• avoiding alcohol, drugs, and tobacco ✪ 6.A

Figure 1 In-line skating is fun, and it is one way to stay physically active and healthy.

Figure 2 Your family is an important part of your life. Getting along with your family can improve your emotional health.

Your Emotional Health

How do you let other people know that you are sad or angry? *Emotional health* is the way in which you express your feelings. Sharing your feelings with other people is important for your emotional health. People who are emotionally healthy usually do the following:

- express their emotions in healthy ways
- deal with sadness and ask for help if they need to
- accept both their strengths and weaknesses

Even emotionally healthy adolescents find that their moods change a lot. These mood changes are a normal part of growing up. And growing up means you may have additional responsibilities both at home and at school. Sometimes, having more responsibilities can cause you stress and make you feel emotional. Talk to your parents or another trusted adult about your feelings and concerns. ⭐ 6.A

Your Mental Health

Solving problems is one part of good mental health. The way that you cope with the demands of daily life is called your *mental health*. People who have good mental health usually have the following characteristics:

- the ability to handle stress effectively and to solve problems.
- openness to new ideas and new ways of doing things
- the ability to adjust to change ⭐ 6.A

Health Journal

Write in your Health Journal about a time in which your family helped you deal with being sad or angry. What, in particular, did they do that helped you the most?

Figure 3 Being with your friends and feeling accepted are necessary for your social health.

Your Social Health

How well you get along with other people says something about your social health. *Social health* is the way you interact with people. People around you, especially your friends and family, give you a sense of belonging. By learning and practicing social skills, you can improve how well you get along with others. And how well you get along with others is important to your overall sense of well-being. How are your social skills? To find out, ask yourself the following:

• Are you considerate of other people?

• Do you show respect to other people?

• Are you dependable?

• Do you support your friends when they make good choices?

• Do you share your feelings with your friends? ⊛ 6.A

LIFE SKILLS ACTIVITY

MAKING GOOD DECISIONS

You are at a party with several of your friends. Everyone is having a great time until two of your classmates get into an argument. It seems that a fight might even start. Role-play this situation with a group of classmates. Discuss what you and your friends could do to prevent the argument from becoming a fight.
⊛ 6.A

What Is Wellness?

The four parts of your health are equally important to your over-all wellness. **Wellness** is a state of good health that is achieved by balancing your physical, emotional, mental, and social health. To keep your health balanced, do the following things:

- Stay physically healthy by taking care of your body.
- Stay mentally healthy by dealing with stress appropriately.
- Stay emotionally healthy by expressing your feelings in a healthy way.
- Stay socially healthy by being considerate of others. ⊛ 6.A

Figure 4 Find out how your wellness rates by taking this quiz.

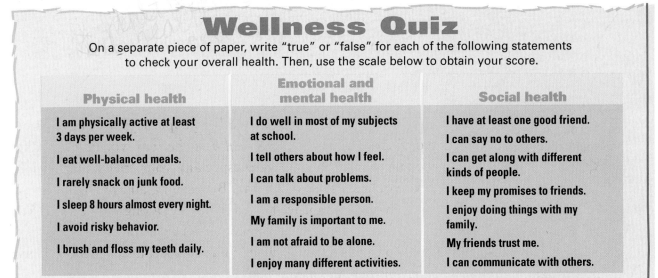

Wellness Quiz

On a separate piece of paper, write "true" or "false" for each of the following statements to check your overall health. Then, use the scale below to obtain your score.

Physical health	Emotional and mental health	Social health
I am physically active at least 3 days per week.	I do well in most of my subjects at school.	I have at least one good friend.
I eat well-balanced meals.	I tell others about how I feel.	I can say no to others.
I rarely snack on junk food.	I can talk about problems.	I can get along with different kinds of people.
I sleep 8 hours almost every night.	I am a responsible person.	I keep my promises to friends.
I avoid risky behavior.	My family is important to me.	I enjoy doing things with my family.
I brush and floss my teeth daily.	I am not afraid to be alone.	My friends trust me.
	I enjoy many different activities.	I can communicate with others.

Give yourself 1 point for every question that you answered "true." A score of 6 or 7 in any area indicates excellent health in that area. If you scored below 4 in an area, you probably need to improve that part of your overall health.

Your Health Magazine 10

⊛ 6.A

Lesson Review

Using Vocabulary

1. Define the term *wellness*.

Understanding Concepts

2. Describe the four parts of health. ⊛ 6.A

3. Explain why the four parts of health must be balanced to achieve wellness. ⊛ 6.A

Critical Thinking

4. Identifying Relationships Emotional and mental health are sometimes confused with each other. Explain how these two parts of health differ. ⊛ 6.A

5. Analyzing Ideas You have lost interest in activities that you once enjoyed. What part or parts of your health are out of balance? Explain your answer. ⊛ 6.A

What Influences Your Health?

What You'll Do

- **Explain** how heredity influences your health. ⭐ 6.A

- **Explain** how the environment affects your health. ⭐ 6.A

Terms to Learn

- heredity
- environment

Start Off
Write

Describe how your environment can have a positive effect on your health.

After Robert's family moved from a ranch to a large city, Robert started coughing a lot and his eyes were always itchy. His doctor said the pollutants in the air might be the cause of his allergies.

Anyone who has ever moved has had to adjust to his or her new surroundings. And new surroundings can often affect your health. In this lesson, you will learn about two things that have a major influence on your health: your heredity and your environment.

Who You Are

You have characteristics, or traits, that you inherited from your parents. For example, you may look more like your mom than your dad. This similarity is due to heredity. **Heredity** is the passing of traits from a parent to a child. These traits determine your physical features. For example, the color of your eyes, hair, and skin are physical traits that can be passed from your parents to you. Even some diseases, such as sickle cell anemia, are inherited. Sickle cell anemia causes the red blood cells to become shaped in such a way that small blood clots form and cause pain. Some diseases, such as diabetes, are affected by both heredity and other factors, such as diet. ⭐ 6.A

Figure 5 Family members often resemble each other because physical traits are passed from generation to generation.

Figure 6 Your environment is made up of everything around you. Your school, home, and friends are just a few of the things that make up your environment.

What Is Around You?

Like Robert's health, your health can also be affected by your environment. The **environment** is all of the living and nonliving things around you. And as you know, you can't control some things in your environment. For example, one of the main causes of health problems, especially respiratory problems, is air pollution. Air pollution can trigger asthma, which is a lung disease, and can contribute to allergies. Secondhand smoke is another form of air pollution that can be difficult to avoid.

You may be aware that your environment can affect your physical health. But you may not realize that your environment can also affect other parts of your health. For example, noise pollution can make it hard to concentrate and thus affects your mental health. ⭐ 6.A

STUDY TIP *for better reading*

Organizing Information
Make a chart with two columns. Title one column "Environment," and title the other column "Heredity." List three things in each column that are influenced by your environment or your heredity.

Lesson Review

Using Vocabulary

1. What is heredity?

2. Define *environment*.

Understanding Concepts

3. Explain how heredity can affect your health. ⭐ 6.A

Critical Thinking

4. Making Inferences What are three things in your environment that can affect your health? Can you control any of these things? Explain your answer. ⭐ 6.A

5. Analyzing Viewpoints Which do you think has a larger role in influencing your health: heredity or environment? Explain your reasons. ⭐ 6.A

Healthy Attitudes

What You'll Do

- **Explain** the relationship between your lifestyle and your health. ⭐ 6.A
- **Explain** what you can do to take control of your health. ⭐ 1.F; 6.A
- **Describe** how you can make responsible choices about your health. ⭐ 1.F; 6.A

Terms to Learn

- lifestyle
- attitude
- preventive healthcare

Start Off
Write

What are two things you could do to improve your health?

> Alejandro had overslept. He had time to either make breakfast for himself or walk his dog if he wanted to get to school on time. He chose to walk his dog and grab a cereal bar.

Everyone has mornings when nothing seems to go right. But even on those mornings, you will want to make the best choices for your health. In this lesson, you will learn the importance of making choices that will keep you healthy.

Healthy Living

The choices that you make reflect your lifestyle. A **lifestyle** is a set of behaviors by which you live your life. A healthy lifestyle begins with having a good attitude. Your **attitude** is the way in which you act, think, or feel that causes you to make certain choices. A good attitude allows you to make choices that are good for you and your health. ⭐ 6.A

Controlling Your Health

You have the ability to control much of your health. If one part of your health isn't as good as it should be, make a decision to improve that part of your health. For example, if you're feeling tired, you could decide to get more sleep. But don't ignore the other parts of your health while you are trying to improve one part. Remember that all four parts of your health are equally important for overall wellness. If you aren't sure how to improve a certain part of your health, talk to your parents or to a trusted adult for advice. ⭐ 6.A; 6.B

Figure 7 These are just some of the things that contribute to a healthy lifestyle. What other things could you add?

Figure 8 Vision problems often can be found with an eye exam, which is an example of preventive healthcare.

Being Responsible

You have things that you are responsible for right now. And as you get older, you will be expected to have more responsibilities, both at home and at school. As you get older, you become more responsible for taking care of yourself. Taking care of yourself involves practicing preventive healthcare. **Preventive healthcare** is taking steps to prevent illness and accidents before they happen. For example, going to the doctor for regular exams is preventive healthcare.

However, preventive healthcare involves more than yearly checkups. For example, when you eat right, avoid risky behavior, and buckle your seat belt, you are protecting yourself from possible illness or injury. The choices that you make today are the start of new health habits. You should form good health habits now because bad health habits can be very difficult to break. ⊛ 1.G; 6.B

Health Journal

Think of a personal decision that you made this year that is an example of acting responsibly. Write your decision in your journal, and explain why you made that decision.

Lesson Review

Using Vocabulary

1. What is a healthy attitude? ⊛ 6.A

2. Define the term *lifestyle* in your own words.

Understanding Concepts

3. Explain why preventive healthcare is important, and give three examples of it. ⊛ 1.F; 1.G

4. What are two things that you can do to take control of your health? ⊛ 1.F; 1.G; 6.B

Critical Thinking

5. Analyzing Ideas What is the relationship between attitude and lifestyle? How do attitude and lifestyle affect your health? ⊛ 6.A

Life Skills to Improve Your Health

What You'll Do

- **Identify** the nine life skills that can improve your health. ⊛ 10; 11
- **Identify** four ways that using life skills can help you. ⊛ 10; 11
- **Explain** how you can check your progress in learning these skills. ⊛ 10; 11

Terms to Learn

- life skills

Start Off
Write

Which life skills are important to you and your health?

A group of popular older teens has asked Miguel to go to a party. He knows that some members of the group use alcohol and tobacco. Miguel doesn't want to do those things, but he isn't sure how to say no.

Like Miguel, you may someday find yourself in a difficult situation. This lesson will teach you skills that will help you deal with difficult situations and that can protect your health.

The Life Skills

As you get older you will have to deal with many new situations. Life skills can help you in these situations. **Life skills** are skills that help you deal with situations that can affect your health. Table 1 defines each of the nine life skills. As you read through this textbook, you will continue to learn about the life skills and how to use them. Each chapter will provide you with more opportunities to practice using the life skills.

Figure 9 Communicating effectively is one of the life skills that will help you now and throughout your life.

TABLE 1 The Nine Life Skills

Assessing your health	evaluating each of the four parts of your health and assessing your health behaviors
Making good decisions	making choices that are healthy and responsible
Setting goals	aiming for something that will give you a sense of accomplishment and achievement, such as breaking bad habits or planning your future
Using refusal skills	saying no to things that you don't want to do as well as avoiding dangerous situations
Communicating effectively	avoiding misunderstandings by expressing your feelings in a healthy way
Coping	dealing with problems and emotions in an effective way
Evaluating media messages	judging the accuracy of advertising and other media messages
Practicing wellness	practicing good health habits, such as getting plenty of exercise and eating good foods
Being a wise consumer	comparing different products and services for value and quality

SOCIAL STUDIES ACTIVITY

Have interested students research and write a report about the goals that Franklin D. Roosevelt had in mind when he began many of his projects during the Great Depression of the 1930s.

Hands-on ACTIVITY

ANALYZING ADVERTISEMENTS

1. For one week, find as many advertisements for a certain kind of product, such as shampoo, as you can.

2. Paste at least five of your ads onto poster board, and number each ad.

3. Study each ad carefully. Try to determine the message of each ad.

Analysis

1. Make a table that has five columns and enough rows for every ad that you brought to class. Title the columns "Eye appeal," "Target age group," "Claims," "Hidden message," and "Believability."

✪ 8.A; 10.A; 10.B; 10.C; 11.A; 11.B; 11.D; 11.E

2. Analyze each ad, and fill in each column with your findings. While you are analyzing the ads, ask yourself the following questions:

- What first caught your eye? (This is called eye appeal.)
- What is the age of the person in the ad? What age group does each ad seem to be targeting?
- What does each ad promise or claim that the product can do?
- Are there hidden messages in the ad?
- How believable is the claim of each ad?

3. Summarize your findings by writing a paragraph about how advertisements convey their messages to consumers.

Using the Life Skills

When you start using a new skill, you may feel uncomfortable at first. As with any new skill, you will have to practice these nine life skills before you feel comfortable using them. But with regular practice, using these skills will soon feel very natural. And before you know it, you will have mastered the nine life skills. Understanding how each of these skills can help you will make learning them easier. Life skills can help you do the following things:

- make a decision or set a goal
- say no to someone
- express your feelings to other people
- practice good health habits
- cope with problems and emotions
- become a better consumer ✪ 11

Checking Your Progress

After you have been using the life skills for a while, you should step back and check your progress. The following are examples of questions you may want to ask yourself to check your progress in using the life skills:

- Which skills do I use most often?
- Which life skills do I feel comfortable using?
- Which skills do I still need help with?

As you check your progress, look for areas in which you have improved. Also, look at areas where you can still improve. If you find that you are having problems using a particular skill, you may want to talk to your teacher or to your parents. These adults probably use many of these skills every day, and they can give you helpful advice. ✪ 11

Figure 10 Life skills will help you make decisions that are in your best interest, such as choosing a healthy snack.

Life Skills and Staying Healthy

Staying healthy takes some effort. But knowing how and when to use the life skills will make staying healthy easier. Think about how you will use the life skills when you face a problem. If you plan ahead, you will find it much easier to deal with problems when they arise. For example, play out a certain scene in your mind ahead of time, and if that situation arises, you will know what to do. Sometimes, it may help to practice certain situations with a friend. Remember that your goal is to keep all parts of your health balanced. And the life skills that you are learning right now will help you assess and improve all of the areas of your health. When your health is balanced, you will feel good physically, emotionally, mentally, and socially. And feeling good is what wellness is all about.

⭐ 10; 11

Figure 11 Using life skills will help you be happy and well–adjusted.

Lesson Review

Using Vocabulary

1. What is a life skill? ⭐ 10

Understanding Concepts

2. Explain why the life skills are important to learn and use. ⭐ 11

3. Describe how you can check your progress in learning the life skills.

4. Explain how practicing a life skill with a friend can help you when you face a real problem. ⭐ 10; 11

Critical Thinking

5. Analyzing Ideas Your friends became upset that you chose not to go to the game Friday night. What life skills could help you say no? Explain your answer. ⭐ 11

6. Applying Concepts Your family is moving to another state. You are upset because you have gone to the same school since the first grade and you will miss your friends. Which life skill would help you, and how would you apply it? ⭐ 11

Chapter Summary

■ The four parts of your health are physical, emotional, social, and mental health. ■ Physical activity, a balanced diet, and plenty of sleep are needed for good physical health. ■ Liking and accepting yourself is a sign of good emotional health. ■ Good mental health helps you deal with daily problems effectively. ■ Good social health is getting along well with other people. ■ Wellness is having all parts of your health balanced. ■ Your health is influenced by your heredity and your environment. ■ Your lifestyle and attitude affect your health. ■ Life skills help you deal with situations that can affect your health. To be healthy and happy, you need to make the life skills a part of your everyday life.

Using Vocabulary

For each sentence, fill in the blank with the proper word from the word bank provided below.

hygiene
environment
preventive healthcare
lifestyle
wellness
health assessment

heredity
refusal skills
health
attitude
life skills

1 All the people and things around you make up your ___.

2 ___ is having your physical, emotional, mental, and social health in balance.

3 ___ is the passing down of traits from parents to offspring.

4 The set of behaviors that guide the way you live your life is your ___.

5 Taking steps to prevent illness from happening is ___.

6 A quiz that allows you to rate your wellness is a(n) ___.

7 Your state of mind that guides your choices is your ___.

8 Brushing your teeth and bathing regularly is part of good ___. ⊛ 6.A

Understanding Concepts

9 What are five things you can do to stay physically healthy?

10 Identify three things that you can do to improve your emotional health.

11 What are three signs of good mental health? ⊛ 6.A

12 Give an example of an inherited trait that can be passed from parents to their offspring. ⊛ 6.B

13 Explain how the environment affects your health. ⊛ 1.B; 6.B

14 Identify three health decisions you make every day. ⊛ 6.B

15 Explain what you can do to practice preventive healthcare.

16 What are the nine life skills that can guide you to better health? ⊛ 11

17 List four examples of how life skills can help you. ⊛ 2.A

Critical Thinking

Applying Concepts

18 You are having trouble concentrating in school, and you are not learning new concepts and solving problems as well as you used to do. What part of your health do you need to improve? How can you make this part of your health better? ★ 6.A

19 How does preventive healthcare improve your physical health? Do you think there are any preventive healthcare measures that you can take to improve other parts of your health? Explain your answer. ★ 1.G

20 A friend of yours is trying to decide which bike to buy. Which life skills would be helpful for your friend to use in making a choice?

21 School is out for the summer, and you have just moved into a new neighborhood. You are sad because you miss your friends. What part of your health do you need to improve? What can you do to improve this part of your health?

Making Good Decisions

22 You are getting ready to go somewhere in a car with your friends. You start putting your seat belt on, and one of your friends starts making fun of you for wearing your seat belt. How would you respond to your friend? ★ 11.B

23 You see an advertisement for a new sports drink. The ad says that the drink will make you stronger and help you to run faster. How would you decide whether or not to buy the sports drink? What would you base your decision on?
★ 6; 11

24 Your best friend missed 2 days of school and has asked if she can copy your math homework for those days. You would like to help her, but you don't feel right about cheating. What should you do?
★ 10.A; 11.B

Interpreting Graphics

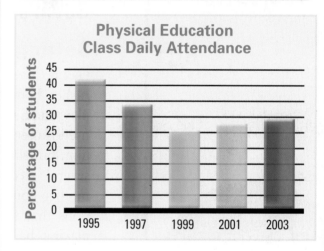

Physical Education Class Daily Attendance

Use the figure above to answer questions 25–27. ★ M: 6.10D; 6.11A

25 What is the general trend in the number of students attending physical education classes daily between 1995 and 2003?

26 What is the percentage of students that attended physical education class in 1999?

27 What year had the highest number of students attending physical education class?

Reading Checkup

Take a minute to review your answers to the Health IQ questions at the beginning of this chapter. How has reading this chapter improved your Health IQ?

Assessing Your Health

Assessing your health means evaluating each of the four parts of your health and examining your behaviors. By assessing your health regularly, you will know what your strengths and weaknesses are and will be able to take steps to improve your health. Complete the following activity to improve your ability to assess your health.

Gavin's Game Playing

ACT 1

Setting the Scene

Gavin loves playing video games. He rushes home from school every day to play, and he plays for hours. A few of his friends used to come over to play with him, but they haven't been over for several weeks. One day, Gavin's mother comes home and mentions that she saw his friends playing ball in the park. She asks him why he isn't playing with them. Gavin tells her that they didn't ask him to play.

★ 1.F

The 4 Steps of Assessing Your Health

1. Choose the part of your health you want to assess.
2. List your strengths and weaknesses.
3. Describe how your behaviors may contribute to your weaknesses.
4. Develop a plan to address your weaknesses.

Guided Practice

Practice with a Friend

Form a group of three. Have one person play the role of Gavin and another person play the role of Gavin's mother. Have the third person be an observer. Walking through each of the four steps of assessing your health, role-play a conversation between Gavin and his mother. In the conversation, Gavin should discuss how his game playing is affecting his social health. The observer will take notes, which will include observations about what the person playing Gavin did well and suggestions of ways to improve. Stop after each step to evaluate the process.

Independent Practice

Check Yourself

After you have completed the guided practice, go through Act 1 again without stopping at each step. Answer the questions below to review what you did.

1. How might Gavin's video game playing affect the four parts of his health?

2. What is one of Gavin's weaknesses in his social health?

3. Describe a plan that Gavin might use to address the weaknesses in his social health.

4. What is a weakness in your social health? ⭐ 1.F

On Your Own

Several weeks later, Gavin is spending more time playing with his friends. He still likes to play his video games but always invites his friends to join him when he wants to play. One day, while Gavin is playing ball, he notices that he becomes tired and out of breath very easily. He starts to wonder if he is out of shape after spending so much time sitting in front of the TV. Make a poster showing how Gavin could use the four steps of assessing your health to develop a plan to improve his physical health.

⭐ 1.B; 1.F

Making Good Decisions

Check out
Current Health
articles related to this chapter by
visiting **go.hrw.com**. Just type in
the keyword **HD4CH02**.

> **“** I feel that **I don't have a say** in anything I do! **My parents** want me to do one thing, and **my friends** want me to **do something else.**
>
> I just don't know what to do. I want to obey my parents, but I don't always know how to say no to my friends. **”**

Health IQ

PRE-READING

Answer the following multiple-choice questions to find out what you already know about making decisions. When you've finished this chapter, you'll have the opportunity to change your answers based on what you've learned.

1. Which of the following statements about consequences is correct?

a. All consequences are good.

b. All consequences are bad.

c. Consequences can be good or bad.

d. Consequences happen only when goals are not reached.

2. Which of the following is NOT a source for your values?

a. your religion

b. your culture

c. your traditions

d. your friends

3. Which of the following is a long-term goal?

a. making an A on a test

b. getting into college

c. finishing your homework

d. cleaning up your room

4. Where does peer pressure come from?

a. adults you don't know

b. older kids

c. adults who break the rules

d. kids your age who want you to do something ✪ **11.C**

5. Which statement about goals is NOT true?

a. You can have only one goal at a time.

b. You can change your goals at any time.

c. Your goals can be short- or long-term goals.

d. You can chart your progress toward a goal.

6. Which statement is true about decisions?

a. All decisions are difficult to make.

b. Good decisions are always easy to make.

c. There is only one good decision for any situation.

d. Good decisions are responsible decisions.

ANSWERS: 1. c; 2. d; 3. b; 4. d; 5. a; 6. d

You Are a Decision Maker!

What You'll Do

- **Describe** what a good decision is. ⭐ 11

- **Identify** three things that influence your decision making. ⭐ 7.A; 8.A

- **Explain** the difference between positive, neutral, and negative consequences.

Terms to Learn

- good decision
- consequence

Start Off
Write

Are all consequences bad? Explain.

It was Marcia's worst fear. While taking a test, Marcia saw two friends sharing answers. She knows if she tells the teacher, her friends will hate her. But if she keeps quiet, she'll hate herself. What should she do?

Let's face it. Sometimes, you have to make choices that you don't know how to make. Still, you have to do something! Being in control means that you make your own choices. You make choices every day. In this lesson, you'll learn how to make the best choices.

What Is a Good Decision?

You're faced with many situations in which you need to figure out what to do. You have to make decisions. A *decision* is a choice that is made. Every day, you make decisions that only you can make. You decide what to wear, how to act, and what to say. No one can make you behave badly, make you break rules, or make you be rude. A **good decision** is a decision in which you have carefully considered the outcome of each choice. When making a decision, you want to make the best choice possible. Good decisions are responsible decisions. They are decisions that you will be proud of having made.

Health Journal

Keep a record of your daily decisions for a week. Your first entry will be to list three or four decisions you made yesterday. What or who influenced your decisions?

Figure 1 Sometimes, even a simple decision, such as what to wear, can be difficult.

What Influences Your Decisions?

There are many influences in your life. An *influence* is something or someone that makes you want to choose one thing over another. Your friends, family, and even the media send messages to you about how you should behave. You want to have positive influences around you. These are influences that can help you and other people. ⭐ 6.A, 7.A; 8.A

What Are the Consequences of Your Decisions?

When you make a decision, there is a result. A **consequence** is the result of an action you take. Sometimes, a consequence happens right away and doesn't last long. For example, if you smoke one cigarette, you might cough for a few minutes. Coughing is a *short-term consequence*. What happens if you continue to smoke? You might develop lung disease in the future. The disease would be a *long-term consequence*. Even if you decided that you would never smoke, there would still be a consequence. You would likely stay healthy. Every decision has a consequence. The consequence can be positive, neutral, or negative. Positive consequences help you or other people. Negative consequences do harm to you or other people. Neutral consequences neither help nor hurt you or other people. ⭐ 1.C

Figure 2 A consequence of failing a class is being suspended from school sports teams.

Lesson Review

Using Vocabulary

1. In your own words, explain what a good decision is. ⭐ 11

2. Define the term *consequence*, and given an example of a short-term consequence and a long-term consequence.

Understanding Concepts

3. Explain the difference between positive, neutral, and negative consequences.

Critical Thinking

4. **Identifying Relationships** List three people or things that are important influences in your life. How do these people or things influence you? ⭐ 7.A, 8.A

Lesson 2

Six Simple Steps to Good Decisions

What You'll Do

- **Identify** six steps useful in making good decisions. ⭐ 7.A
- **Describe** how your values are influences on your decisions.
- **Explain** the importance of predicting consequences. ⭐ 1.C; 11

Terms to Learn

- values
- option
- brainstorming

Start Off
Write

Why is it important to list your options before making a decision?

> Tom hoped that he passed his science class. But when he opened his report card, his hopes were dashed. He decided right then to study and work harder. Tom is now determined to improve his grade.

Like Tom, you can do better. In fact, when you make good decisions, many problems will be solved. If you learn to use the six steps shown in Figure 3, you will become better at making good decisions.

Identify the Problem

Identifying the problem can be the most difficult step in making a decision. For example, what problems do you face when a friend offers you a drink of alcohol? An obvious problem is how to say no. But the basic problem is whether you should drink alcohol. You know that drinking alcohol is illegal and can get you in trouble. If you worry about the wrong problem, you won't make the best decision. When you know the real problem, you can begin to figure out what decision to make.

Figure 3 Making good decisions is easier when you follow these six steps.

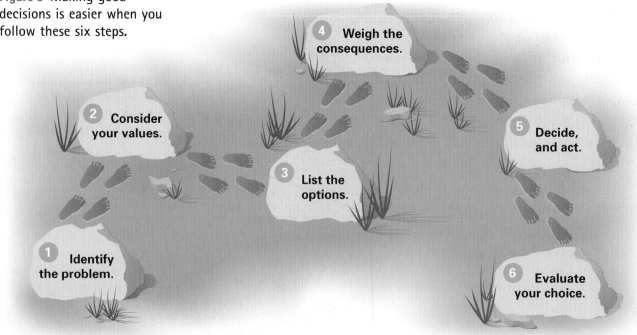

Consider Your Values

The next step to making good decisions is to think about how your values relate to the problem. **Values** are beliefs that you consider to be of great importance. Good values include honesty and responsibility. Values represent the kind of person you want to be. For example, if you value being honest, you will decide not to cheat on a test if the opportunity arises. Values come from your traditions, culture, background, and religion. To identify your values, think of the beliefs that have guided your family over the years. Talk to your parents, and find out their ideas about values.

Values can help you develop a good character. *Character* is the way a person thinks, feels, and acts. Character based on good values will help you make good decisions.

Remember that many things can influence your decisions. Values influence your decisions by reminding you of what's important. Decisions based on good values almost always lead to good results. ★ 6.A; 7.A; 8.A

LIFE SKILLS ACTIVITY

MAKING GOOD DECISIONS

Maria recently enrolled in a new school and doesn't know anyone. When Gwen and Robin asked her to go shopping with them, she was thrilled. However, in the store dressing room, Gwen and Robin began to plan how they were going to shoplift a pair of jeans. What should Maria do? What will influence her the most?

List the Options

There is always more than one way to solve a problem. You have options. An **option** is one of several choices that you can make. You have now identified the problem and thought about your values. Now, think of ways to handle the problem. The best way to list all of your options is by brainstorming.

Brainstorming is thinking of all of the possible ways to carry out your decision. Suppose your friend asks you to skip class with her. But you value the trust of your parents and teachers. Skipping class may put that trust at risk. What are your options? You could say no. You could tell your friend that you will meet her after class. If you aren't sure what to do, talk to your parents. The next time this problem happens, you will be prepared. ★ 10; 11

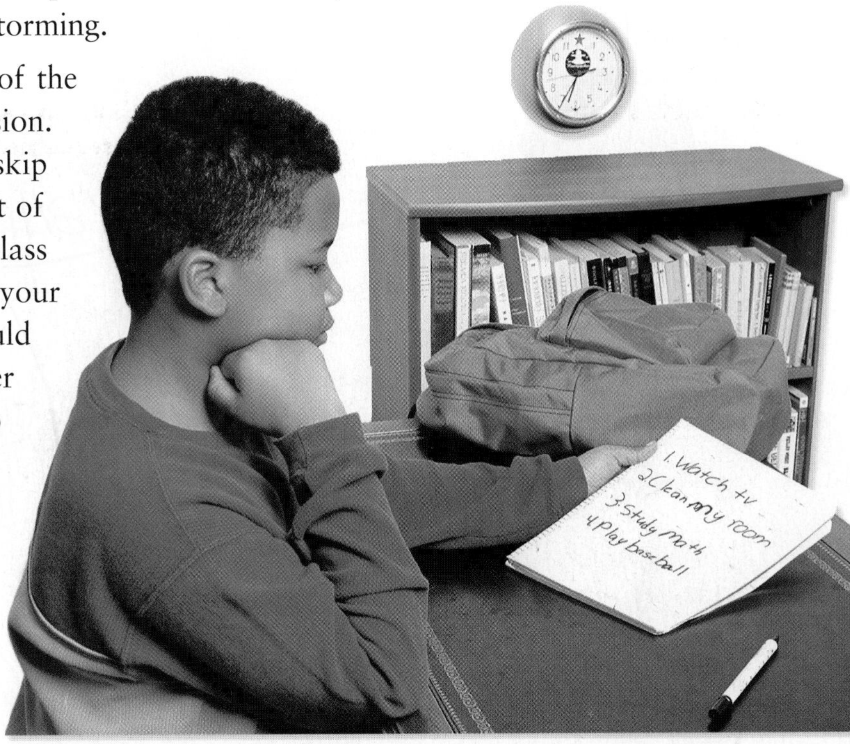

Figure 4 Writing your options may help you see things more clearly.

Weigh the Consequences

You have listed your options. Now decide which option is best. To do this, picture what would happen if you chose each option. Think of the example at the beginning of the chapter. What should Tom do if his friends asked him to go to the movies the night before his science test? He has been working hard, but he thinks that he needs one more night to review. Tom values self-discipline, so he probably should say no. What are the consequences of this option? Tom would do well on his test, which would guarantee that he would pass the class. What would the consequences be if he chose to go to the movies? He might keep his friends from getting mad at him, but he might fail his test and disappoint his parents. You must predict the consequences of each option. Which consequences are good? Which consequences are bad? Which consequences have the best result? Answering these questions will help you make good decisions. ⊛ 1.C

Myth: A consequence always means something negative.

Fact: Many consequences have positive rewards.

Decide, and Act

You've thought through your options and weighed the consequences. Think about which option will bring about the best consequences for you and for others. Choose the option that represents your values. Take time to choose wisely. You can't always be sure that your choice will have good results. Sometimes doing what you believe in will make your friends angry with you. But if you believe that you made the correct choice, then you are probably making a good decision. Remember that no matter which option you choose, the option is something that you have thought about and acted on with the best intentions. ⊛ 10.C

Figure 5 This student's decision to study math will most likely have positive consequences.

Evaluate Your Choice

What would you do if you made a choice and your friends made fun of you? Did you make a bad decision? After all, your friends laughed at you and you felt really dumb! But you cannot measure the value of your choices just by how you feel. You may face many of the same problems over and over again. That is why you need to know if the choices you make are good decisions! Once you've acted on a decision, you should stand back and look at your results. Ask yourself the following questions: Did I uphold my values? Do my parents approve of my choice? Do I feel good about my actions? If you answer yes to these questions, you've probably made a good decision! If you answered no to any of these questions, it's probably not too late to change your mind. You can repeat the process and make a different choice. Even if you can't make a different choice, you can learn from your mistake! Try not to repeat the same mistake. Think about what you will do differently next time. ⭐ 1.C

Health Journal

Evaluate a decision that you made recently. List the pros and cons of your choice. Would you make the same choice next time?

Figure 6 Evaluate your decision by looking at both the pros and cons.

My Choice: I chose to spend more of my time studying math.

Pros	Cons
I am passing math.	I spend less time with my friends.
I am off academic probation.	I missed Geoff's big party.
I am back on the football team.	

Lesson Review

Using Vocabulary

1. Define the term *values.*

2. Define the term *option.*

3. What is brainstorming?

Understanding Concepts

4. Explain why you must predict the consequences of your decisions. ⭐ 1.C; 11

5. Values are an influence on your decisions. Explain this statement, and give an example. ⭐ 7.A

Critical Thinking

6. Making Predictions Identify six steps to making good decisions. Which ones would be difficult for you to carry out? Explain your answer. ⭐ 7.A

🔗 **internet** connect

www.scilinks.org/health

Topic: Smoking and Health

HealthLinks code: HD4090

HEALTH LINKS Maintained by the National Science Teachers Association

Facing Pressure

It was the party of the year, and you were invited. You felt great. You were hanging out with the cool crowd. Then, someone pulled out some cigarettes and offered one to you. Everyone was looking at you.

What You'll Do

- **Distinguish** between positive and negative peer pressure. ✪ 7.A; 11.C
- **List** five refusal skills. ✪ 11.B
- **Explain** the importance of a support system. ✪ 6.A; 7.A

Terms to Learn

- peer pressure
- refusal skill
- assertiveness
- support system

Start Off
Write

How does assertiveness help you handle peer pressure?

Dealing with your peers can be very difficult. A *peer* is someone who is about the same age as you and with whom you interact. In this lesson, you'll learn ways to deal with your peers and with the pressures they put on you.

Dealing with Peer Pressure

Peer pressure is the feeling that you should do something because your friends want you to. You may face peer pressure when a friend dares you to drink alcohol or begs you to join a club. Peer pressure can be positive or negative. *Positive peer pressure* can help you make the right decisions. For example, if your friends are on the honor roll, you may study harder to be like them. On the other hand, *negative peer pressure* can keep you from doing the right thing. The key to dealing with negative peer pressure is to have a plan in place before you have to face a problem.

A **refusal skill** is a strategy you can use to avoid doing something that you don't want to do. Refusal skills can help you handle negative peer pressure. One skill may work better than another for you in some situations. You may find that you are comfortable using one skill but have trouble using other skills. But the more you practice refusal skills, the easier it will be to use them. Figure 7 lists five important refusal skills that will help you learn to deal with peer pressure. ✪ 7.A; 11.B; 11.C

Figure 7 Use these refusal skills when you face negative peer pressure.

RefusalSkills
Are Ways To Say No

▸ **Avoid dangerous situations.**
▸ **Say "No!"**
▸ **Stand your ground.**
▸ **Stay focused on the issue.**
▸ **Walk away.**

Avoiding Dangerous Situations

The easiest way for you to stay out of a bad situation is to avoid it in the first place. You already know some situations that might lead to trouble. Going to a friend's house when his or her parents aren't around, cutting school, or staying out past curfew are examples of bad situations. Before you agree to be in one of these situations, picture what might go wrong if you say yes. You will probably have a feeling that something bad might happen. Will the consequences of your decision hurt you or someone else? Will you regret this decision? If you answer yes to either of these questions, you should avoid the situation. ⭐ 1.C; 6.A; 11.B

Saying No

Refusal skills have to do with learning how to say no. It seems like saying no might be a hard thing to do, but you already know how to do it. You know how to say no to your brother or sister when they want to borrow your clothes or a video game. You know how to say no when your parents ask if you want to eat a food you don't like for dinner. Refusing to give in to negative peer pressure isn't any different. Saying no to peer pressure means using the same skills in tough situations that you use when you refuse foods that you don't like. You not only have to say no but also have to show that you mean no. To show someone that you really mean no, face the person and calmly, but firmly, say no. ⭐ 11.B

Brain Food

Former First Lady Nancy Reagan is credited with coining the phrase, "Just say no." She said the phrase in 1984 when she was talking about peer pressure with students at Peralta Year Round School in Oakland, California.

Figure 8 Sometimes, the best way to avoid a dangerous situation is to walk away.

COPING

Work in a group to think of situations in which other students may need the help of a support system. For example, think about a situation in which a student's parents are getting a divorce. What could you say to support this student?

Standing Your Ground

Sometimes, saying no once will not be enough. Your friends might not like hearing you say no. They might keep pressuring you and hoping that you'll give in. You must be assertive. **Assertiveness** is the self-confidence to defend your thoughts, feelings, or beliefs in a way that is honest, respectful, and not harmful to anyone. Stand your ground, and show your peers that you really mean no. To stand your ground, repeat yourself and use a firm voice. You may need to say no in more than one way. You can say, "I don't want to do that" or "That is something I will not do." It doesn't matter how you refuse as long as you remember that your decision to say no is worth defending.

⭐ 7.D; 10.B; 10.C

Staying Focused on the Issue

When you give in to pressure, you are letting someone else decide what you should do. Remember your values. When you give in to pressure, you risk losing those values. Say no to smoking if you value your health. You know smoking will hurt your lungs. You should also say no if you value staying out of trouble. Smoking is illegal if you are under 18 years old. Whatever your reason for saying no, stay focused on it. ⭐ 10.C

Figure 9 Sometimes, you have to stand your ground when dealing with peer pressure.

Walking Away

When you say no, you are refusing to let people or situations control you. But sometimes saying no is not enough. Sometimes, the best decision is to leave. You do not need to make excuses to your friends. You may have already used several other refusal skills. So, remember that you can always walk away! You don't have to prove anything.

⭐ 7.C; 10.C; 11.C

Supporting Other People

Refusing to do things with your friends can be very hard. But you are not the only person who has a hard time figuring out how to say no. Your friends feel the same way! It takes a lot of courage to stand up and say no to people who want you to do things that will hurt you. That's why it helps to have a support system. A **support system** is a group of people, such as friends and family, who promise to help each other during tough situations. Make a pact with your friends that you will support each other during difficult times no matter how hard life gets. Help each other identify the values that are important to each of you. When you support your friends, you are creating positive peer pressure. That's true friendship! ★ 10.A

Figure 10 Having a friend to support you and your decisions makes you a stronger person.

Lesson Review

Using Vocabulary

1. Define *peer pressure*. ★ 11.C

2. Identify the five refusal skills. ★ 11.B

3. What is assertiveness? ★ 10.B

4. Describe a support system.

Understanding Concepts

5. Explain the difference between positive and negative peer pressure. ★ 7.A; 11.C

6. Why is having a support system important? ★ 6.A; 7.A

Critical Thinking

7. Using Refusal Skills Think of a situation in which you would need to use your refusal skills. Describe the situation, and write a plan about how you would deal with the situation. Include in your plan three people who would make up your support system. ★ 11.B

▣ internet connect
www.scilinks.org/health
Topic: Communication Skills
HealthLinks code: HD4022

HEALTH LINKS. Maintained by the National Science Teachers Association

Goals

What You'll Do

- **Distinguish** between short-term goals and long-term goals. ⭐ 11.E
- **Explain** how achieving goals can improve your self-esteem. ⭐ 11.E
- **Explain** how goals improve your relationships with other people and your community. ⭐ 11.E
- **Describe** the relationship between goals and success. ⭐ 11.E

Terms to Learn

- goal
- self-esteem
- success

Start Off *Write*

Why do you think having goals is important?

Anna wants to be part of the varsity track team. She has been training for weeks now and has been keeping a record of her times. She is very encouraged because she is getting faster every day.

Anna is learning a very important lesson. Things worth doing don't come easily. Reaching a goal takes work. A **goal** is something that you work toward and hope to achieve. In this lesson, you will read about the reasons for setting goals and ways to successfully reach your goals.

Types of Goals

When you woke up this morning, you may have thought about how you wanted your school day to be. Goals such as getting to school on time, talking to friends at lunch, and turning in all of your homework are examples of short-term goals. *Short-term goals* don't take long to reach. They can be reached in a short time. For example, finishing your homework in time to watch a TV show is a short-term goal. Other goals, such as getting into college after high school, are long-term goals. Long-term goals are built from short-term goals. *Long-term goals* can sometimes take years to reach. ⭐ 11.E

Figure 11 Achieving a Long-Term Goal

Start a dog walking business. Walk dogs to earn money.

Earn money to buy a used saxophone.

Buy a used saxophone to join the school band.

Join the school band to achieve your long-term goal.

Figure 12 This teen may set a goal to become an astronaut.

Why Set Goals?

What would happen if you never set any goals? You would not have many responsibilities. But, you wouldn't have many challenges to meet either. Life would become very boring after a while. Think about how your life would be different if you never tried out for the choir, the tennis team, or some other activity that you enjoy. Having goals means the difference between living your life and letting life happen to you. When you set goals, you have a sense of purpose. Goals help your self-esteem. **Self-esteem** is the way you value, respect, and feel confident about yourself. If you feel good about yourself and things you have done, you have good self-esteem. When you reach a goal, your self-esteem increases and you gain a sense of accomplishment. An *accomplishment* is a task that you have successfully completed. This feeling will motivate you to keep going. Having a purpose will also help you feel better about yourself. ⭐ 11.E

Goals and Relationships

Goals aren't only for individuals. Goals can strengthen relationships between people. For example, your family has goals. Your parents want to earn money to pay the bills. They want to take care of you and your brothers and sisters. They want to teach you responsibility by asking you to do chores. They have a goal to teach you about rules when they discipline you. You have goals in your friendships, too. You set goals when you make a promise to each other to stay friends and not to keep secrets from each other. You have goals when you practice together so you can both make the baseball or softball team. In healthy relationships, friends support each other and help each other reach goals. ⭐ 11.A; 11.E

Health Journal

Write a journal entry that describes one of your long-term goals. What short-term goals have you set to help you achieve your long-term goal?

Figure 13 How are the goals of these students helping the community?

Goals and the Community

Communities are groups that are made up of many people that have similar interests. Often, people in a community will work toward the same goal. Sometimes, their goal may be to help the entire community. They may work together to keep their neighborhood clean. Sometimes, the goal of a community may be to help certain people. Members of the community may take food to the sick and elderly. Or they may collect warm clothing for needy children during the holidays. What kind of goals would you like to see at work in your community? ✪ 11.A; 11.E

Defining Success

How will you know when you've reached success? Will millions of people know your name? Will you be able to change people's lives by making one decision? Some people think of success as having fame, money, or power. But actually, **success** is the achievement of a goal. You will be successful when you reach your goals.

Hands-on ACTIVITY

SUCCESS

1. Work in groups of two. Interview one adult and one student.

2. Ask each person to define what success means to him or her. For example, does success mean completing college, getting married, or having a career?

Analysis

1. Categorize the class results into four or five major areas, such as family, education, wealth, or community.

2. Determine the number of responses for each major area, and illustrate the results by making a pie graph. What does success mean to most of the people your class interviewed?

The Path to Success!

Do you ever think about what your dream job would be? At the same time, do you wonder if you could ever do that job? With effort and determination, you can do just about anything that you want to do. The key is to make a decision to reach that goal! Some of your dreams will become your long-term goals. Remember that long-term goals are made of short-term goals.

Figure 14 It is never too early to start working on your long-term goals.

Suppose that you are thinking about the day you will graduate from high school. You will need to reach many short-term goals before that day. You will need to talk to your counselor about the kinds of classes to take. You will want to prepare for your classes by studying hard. There will be exams that you will have to pass. Although the day you graduate may seem a long time from now, you should begin preparing early. Keep your goals in sight. Stay away from things that will prevent you from reaching your goal. Drugs, alcohol, and negative peer pressure can keep you from being successful. If you fail at one of the goals along the way to your long-term goal, don't give up. Learn from your mistakes, and try again. Successful people find a way to keep going. You can, too! ⭐ 11.A; 11.C; 11.E

Lesson Review

Using Vocabulary

1. Define the term *goal*.

2. Explain what self-esteem is.

Understanding Concepts

3. Compare short-term goals with long-term goals. ⭐ 11.E

4. How does reaching your goal improve your self-esteem? ⭐ 11.E

5. How do goals improve your relationships with your friends and your community?

6. Explain the relationship between goals and success. ⭐ 11.A; 11.C; 11.E

Critical Thinking

7. **Making Predictions** Think of a long-term goal that you have. What are some short-term goals that will help you meet your long-term goal? ⭐ 11.A; 11.E

Choosing and Reaching Your Goals

What You'll Do

■ **Describe** how your interests and values influence your goals. ✷ 6.A

■ **Identify** four resources available for working toward one's goal. ✷ 6.A; 7.A

■ **Explain** the importance of measuring and rewarding your progress towards meeting a goal.

■ **Explain** why changing goals is sometimes okay. ✷ 6.A

Terms to Learn

• interest
• resource
• mentor

Start Off
Write

How do rewards help you achieve your goals?

Leslie had always been interested in dolphins. She hoped that someday she could work as a trainer. For now, she spends a lot of her time reading and learning about dolphins and their behavior.

Leslie has a goal that she wants to reach. For now her steps are small. Eventually, she will build on those activities. In this lesson, you'll learn about the ways you can choose goals, work towards goals, and measure your progress along the way to success.

What Are Your Interests?

The goals you reach will be the ones in which you have an interest. An **interest** is something that you enjoy and want to learn more about. Have you ever thought about starting a new hobby? Maybe you would like to try painting or photography. You may have an interest in those things. Find ways to learn about your interests. Take a class at your school. Call your community center for information on classes offered there. Think of goals you might have because of your interests. These are goals you will want to reach.

Figure 15 Explore your interests. You may find a new, exciting hobby.

What Is Important to You?

If you are going to reach your goals, they will have to be important to you. You must have an interest in your goals. But your values should be an influence on your goals, too. Build your goals around both your interests and your values. For example, imagine that you have an interest in cooking. But you want to learn to cook balanced meals because you value good health. By learning to cook nutritious meals, you are pursuing an interest and upholding your values. This activity is important to you because it includes both your interest and your values. You are more likely to reach goals based on your interests and values.

⭐ 6.A

What Resources Do You Need?

What do you have to do to buy a pair of jeans? First, you need to find a pair that you like and that fits you. You also need money to buy jeans. Money is a resource. A **resource** is something you use to help you. Resources are all around you. Resources can be money, knowledge, people, or skills. For example, the Internet is a good resource for information. Another resource is a mentor. A **mentor** is a person who can give you good advice. If you have an interest in cooking, your mother or father could be a mentor. She or he probably has experience with cooking and may be happy to give you advice. If you have an interest in playing tennis, one resource might be the local parks where tennis lessons are taught. Whatever your interest is, be creative. Use the resources that are available to you. ⭐ 7.A; 11.A

LIFE SKILLS ACTIVITY

SETTING GOALS

Identify a career that interests you. What interests do you have that relate to this career? What long-term and short-term goals can you set to prepare for this career?

Figure 16 Examples of Resources

Parents and teachers can give you information or help you find useful information.

Books and encyclopedias found at your local library, are excellent references.

The Internet can provide you with many sources of current information.

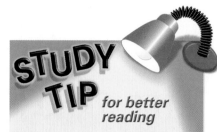
Measure Your Progress

Reaching goals can take a long time. So, you should measure your progress along the way. *Progress* is a step toward your goal. Progress is often slow, and you won't be able to see it on a daily basis unless you measure it. For example, if your goal is to run a 6-minute mile, you might not notice your daily progress. Keeping track of your time during each mile you run is one way to measure your progress. How you measure your progress depends on the goal. First, list the steps that you need to take to reach your goal. Then, make a chart that shows each step. As you complete each step, fill in the chart. If a chart doesn't work, find another way to measure your progress. Some activities might only need to be measured every 2 weeks, rather than daily. The important thing is to keep track of your improvement so that you stay focused on your goal.

Reward Your Success!

Reward yourself when you make progress toward your goal. A *reward* is a prize you give yourself for accomplishing a task. When you're working toward a long-term goal, you should reward yourself for accomplishing each step that leads to your goal. Use your chart to mark when you will earn a reward. Share your success with your parents and your friends. Let them help you with your reward. For example, do something fun with friends and family if you get good grades on your report card. Decide in advance what reward you will earn. You will find that you will start working harder to get that reward! But the best reward is knowing that you're closer to your goal.

Figure 17 A trip to an amusement park can be a fun reward for accomplishing a long-term goal.

Changing Your Goals

As you get older, your interests may change. Changing your goals is okay as long as you are changing them for the right reasons. Ask yourself the following questions to decide whether you are still on the right path.

- Does the idea of reaching my goal make me happy?

- Am I doing well at what I do?

- Am I upholding my values through my goals?

- Is there something else I would rather be doing?

Your answers to these questions will help you decide if you should change your goals. You can always take a different direction.

Write a short story about a teenager who is thinking about changing his or her goals.

Conflict: Do I play the guitar, or do I stay in track?

I do not have time to do both.

1. *Am I still interested in playing the guitar?*

2. *I am better at track than I am at playing the guitar.*

3. *physical fitness is very important to me.*

Figure 18 Write down your interests and values when deciding to change your goals. This tip will help keep you focused.

Lesson Review

Using Vocabulary

1. Define the term *interest*.

2. Explain what a resource is. Identify four resources. ⊛ 6.A; 7.A

3. Describe what a mentor does.

Understanding Concepts

4. Why should you think about your interests and values when you set goals? ⊛ 6.A

5. Why should you measure your progress towards a goal?

6. Why do goals sometimes change? ⊛ 6.A

Critical Thinking

7. Analyzing Ideas What is one of your goals right now? Under what circumstances would you have to change this goal? What interests did you have that influenced you to set this goal?

Chapter Summary

■ A good decision is one in which you have carefully considered the outcome of each choice. ■ There are many influences on your decisions. ■ A consequence is the result of a decision. ■ There are six steps to making good decisions. ■ Peer pressure is a feeling that you should do something your friends want you to do. ■ Refusal skills are ways to avoid doing something you don't want to do. ■ A support system is made up of family and friends who can help you deal with negative pressure. ■ A goal is something that you try to achieve. ■ Setting goals improves your self-esteem. ■ Goals reflect your values and your interests. ■ Success is the achievement of your goals.

Using Vocabulary

For each sentence, fill in the blank with the proper word from the word bank provided below.

consequence	goals
interests	mentor
peer pressure	refusal skills
resource	success
support system	values

1 Doing something just because everyone does it is an example of ___.

2 Solving crossword puzzles might be considered one of your ___.

3 Someone who helps you find the resources to reach your goals is a ___.

4 Different ways to say no are also called ___.

5 Reaching your goals is a measure of ___.

6 If you want to find books about fishing, the library would be a good ___.

7 Friends who help you make good decisions are part of your ___.

8 Beliefs you consider important are your ___.

Understanding Concepts

9 What are the six steps to making good decisions?

10 List three possible short-term goals for a long-term goal of making better grades.

11 List five of your interests. ★ 6.A

12 Name one of your interests, and identify three resources that would help you learn more about your interest. ★ 6.A

13 How can you show someone that you mean no? ★ 7.E; 11.B

14 What is a reward, and how does it help you reach your goal?

15 Why is it important to set goals?

16 What should you do if you realize that a goal you are working toward is not what you really want?

17 How can a support system help you when you face pressure? ★ 6.A; 7.A; 11.C

Critical Thinking

Analyzing Ideas

18 You have been given an assignment for a big class project. You have broken the project down into three steps: doing research, writing a paper, and making a class presentation. How would you use rewards to help you finish your class project?

19 You and several of your friends have decided to set up a support system to help each other accomplish the goals that you have set. However, your friends think that one of your goals is impossible. What should you do? ⭐ 7.A; 11.A

20 What should you do if you evaluate a decision that you made and decide that it was not the best choice you could have made?

Making Good Decisions

21 Your best friend tells you that she has been sneaking alcohol from her house and bringing it to school. She claims it makes her school day more fun. However, you have seen her sleeping in class and you know her grades have also been going down. You don't know whether to risk losing her friendship by telling her counselor or to ignore the situation and hope she soon realizes what she is doing is unhealthy. What should you do? ⭐ 7.E

22 One of your friends wants you to skip class and go to the mall. What are the consequences of your actions? What other people would be affected by your decision? What would be the consequences for the other people? ⭐ 7.A

23 You are with some of your friends, and one of them offers you a cigarette. You tell them you don't want to start smoking, but they keep on teasing and harassing you. What should you do? ⭐ 7.E; 11.B

24 Use what you have learned in this chapter to set a personal goal. Write your goal, and make an action plan by using the Health Behavior Contract for making good decisions and using refusal skills. You can find the Health Behavior Contract at go.hrw.com. Just type in the keyword HD4HBC01.

Name _____ Class _____ Date _____

Health Behavior Contract
Making Good Decisions

My Goals: I, _____, will accomplish one or more of the following goals:
I will use the six-step method for making decisions.
I will work toward one long-term goal.
I will practice at least one refusal skill.
Other: _____

My Reasons: By using the six-step method of decision making, I will make better choices. I will also improve my ability to set short-term and long-term goals. By using refusal skills, I will make more-responsible decisions.
Other: _____

My Values: Personal values that will help me meet my goals are
_____
_____
_____

My Plan: The actions I will take to meet my goals are
_____
_____

Evaluation: I will use my Health Journal to keep a log of actions I took to fulfill this contract. After 1 month, I will evaluate my goals. I will adjust my plan if my goals are not being met. If my goals are being met, I will consider setting additional goals.

Signed _____

Date _____

Reading Checkup

Take a minute to review your answers to the Health IQ questions at the beginning of this chapter. How has reading this chapter improved your Health IQ?

Setting Goals

A goal is something that you work toward and hope to achieve. Setting goals is important because goals give you a sense of purpose and achieving goals improves your self-esteem. Complete the following activity to learn how to set and achieve goals.

Allison's Goal

Setting the Scene

ACT 1

Allison's drama class is planning a field trip to see a play in another city. Any student that wants to go has to contribute a certain amount of money to help pay for the trip. Allison really wants to go on the trip, but her parents tell her that she must try to raise the money herself. Allison thinks that she can earn enough money if she starts a baby-sitting service.

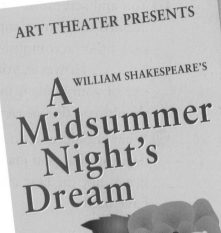

ART THEATER PRESENTS

WILLIAM SHAKESPEARE'S

A Midsummer Night's Dream

The 5 Steps of Setting Goals

1. Consider your interests and values.
2. Choose goals that include your interests and values.
3. If necessary, break down long-term goals into several short-term goals.
4. Measure your progress.
5. Reward your success.

Guided Practice

Practice with a Friend

Form a group of two. Have one person play the role of Allison, and have the second person be an observer. Walking through each of the five steps of setting goals, role-play Allison setting and working toward her goal of earning money for her field trip. The observer will take notes, which will include observations about what the person playing Allison did well and suggestions of ways to improve. Stop after each step to evaluate the process.

Independent Practice

Check Yourself

After you have completed the guided practice, go through Act 1 again without stopping at each step. Answer the questions below to review what you did.

1. Allison decided to start a baby-sitting service. What interests and values might have influenced her decision?

2. What is Allison's long-term goal? What are some short-term goals that might help her reach her long-term goal?

3. How can Allison measure her progress toward her goal?

4. What is one of your long-term goals? What are some short-term goals that might help you reach that goal?

On Your Own

Allison was able to earn enough money to go on the field trip. After she saw the play, Allison decided that she wants to be an actress when she is older. Allison told her drama teacher her plans, and he suggested that in addition to acting classes, she should take some singing and dancing classes. Allison is a good dancer, but she does not sing very well. Make an outline that shows how Allison could use the five steps of setting goals to improve her singing skills.

CHAPTER 3

Self-Esteem

Check out **Current Health®** articles related to this chapter by visiting go.hrw.com. Just type in the keyword **HD4CH03**.

Lessons

> **"** At first, I was **excited** that Shanna and her **friends** wanted to **hang out with me.** But after they asked me to skip class with them, I realized that I wouldn't feel right doing something that was wrong just to fit in. **"**

Health IQ

PRE-READING

Answer the following multiple-choice questions to find out what you already know about self-esteem. When you've finished this chapter, you'll have the opportunity to change your answers based on what you've learned.

1. **Which of the following is a characteristic of a person who has high self-esteem?**
   a. feelings of worthlessness
   b. acceptance of himself or herself
   c. low levels of confidence
   d. none of the above ⭐ **6.A**

2. **The media can influence your self-esteem. The media includes**
   a. TV.
   b. magazines.
   c. music videos.
   d. All of the above ⭐ **8.A**

3. **Self-esteem is**
   a. how you see your body.
   b. a measure of how much you value and respect yourself.
   c. the way you see yourself.
   d. a measure of how popular you are.

4. **Which of the following might help you build healthy self-esteem?**
   a. setting a goal
   b. helping others
   c. focusing on your strengths
   d. all of the above ⭐ **6.A**

5. **Having integrity means that you are**
   a. popular at school.
   b. affected by negative peer pressure.
   c. very intelligent.
   d. honest with yourself and others.

6. **Acting on your values and thoughts without making other people feel bad shows**
   a. assertiveness.
   b. self-respect.
   c. your self-concept.
   d. peer pressure.

Self-Esteem and You

What You'll Do

- **Explain** how self-esteem affects your life. ✸ 6.A
- **Identify** the characteristics of high self-esteem and low self-esteem. ✸ 6.A
- **Identify** five influences on self-esteem. ✸ 6.A

Terms to Learn

- self-esteem

Start Off
Write

How can your peers affect your self-esteem?

> Samantha is not very good at soccer, but she tries very hard. Even though she did not score a goal in the game today, she helped her team score one. And her team won the game!

Samantha has healthy self-esteem. She knows that she may not be the best soccer player. But she is not afraid to play on the team. Samantha feels good about herself because she helped her teammates succeed.

How You Feel About Yourself

Your level of self-esteem is a large part of your personality. **Self-esteem** is a measure of how much you value, respect, and feel confident about yourself. You can think of self-esteem as how much you like yourself.

There are many levels of self-esteem. People who generally feel good about themselves have high self-esteem. People who have low self-esteem don't feel good about themselves. No one has high self-esteem all the time. It is normal to have high self-esteem sometimes and to have low self-esteem at other times. Having a healthy level of self-esteem is important. People who have healthy self-esteem are between high and low levels of self-esteem.

Your level of self-esteem affects how you face new situations. It affects your relationships with other people. Your level of self-esteem affects how you make decisions. Finally, your self-esteem affects your success at the things you do, including how well you do in school. If you have healthy self-esteem, you will be more likely to do well in the things you do. Even if you do not fully succeed, you will be able to deal with disappointment better than if you have low self-esteem. ✸ 6.A

Figure 1 Shannon did not win the race, but she feels good about herself because she tried very hard. Shannon has healthy self-esteem.

Figure 2 Jennie had never played the flute before. But, she had the confidence to try something new.

High Self-Esteem

People who have a high level of self-esteem share many characteristics. For example, people who have high self-esteem feel good about themselves. They know their strengths, and they know their weaknesses. They accept who they are. Most importantly, they like themselves. People who have high self-esteem are comfortable with their personality. They are comfortable with their physical appearance. People who have high self-esteem usually do not depend on the opinions of others to feel good about themselves. They do not let negative comments from others affect them too much. They are confident in themselves and they are more likely to choose behaviors that are healthy.

Low Self-Esteem

People who have low self-esteem also share certain traits. People who have low self-esteem do not feel very good about themselves. People who have low self-esteem are affected deeply by what others say to them. They also have a low level of confidence. Sometimes, people who have low self-esteem are not happy with their physical appearance. They may not be comfortable with their personality. Often, people who have low self-esteem don't practice healthy behaviors.

Many people have parts of their personality that they don't like. You may find yourself feeling this way. However, as you grow as a person, your self-esteem changes. This chapter will help you learn more about building a healthy level of self-esteem.
⭐ 1.D; 6.A

SETTING GOALS

Write down one thing that you want to learn to do but that you are afraid to try. Figure out three things you can do to get started. Write down when you would like to achieve this goal.

Health Journal

Think of a person who has positively influenced your self-esteem. Write a letter to this person in your health journal. Describe the situation in which the person helped you, and explain how he or she helped you.

How People Affect Your Self-Esteem

Your level of self-esteem changes as you grow emotionally. As your self-esteem develops, it is influenced by many factors. Some of these factors include your family, friends, teachers, and coaches.

Your family is a large influence on your self-esteem. The way your family acts toward you and the amount of support your family gives you can affect your self-esteem. Your family is usually a good source of encouragement, which can help you build high self-esteem.

Your friends can also influence your self-esteem. Friends who encourage and support each other help build high self-esteem. Your peers also have an effect on your self-esteem. Sometimes, peers may tease you or bully you. These actions may hurt your self-esteem if you let them.

Your teachers and coaches may influence your self-esteem as well. Teachers and coaches often support and encourage teens to succeed. By encouraging you, they can boost your self-esteem.

The person who influences your self-esteem the most is you. You can decide how much you respect and value yourself. You can also decide to focus on your strengths and to encourage yourself.
⭐ 6.A; 7.A

Figure 3 Teachers are very encouraging and can help boost your self-esteem.

The Media and Your Self-Esteem

The media can affect your self-esteem. The media includes TV, magazines, movies, and music videos. The media tends to show only people who are very successful and unusually attractive. Some people compare themselves to the people they see in the media. If someone is not comfortable with his or her body, he or she may develop an unhealthy body image.

Your **body image** is the way you see and imagine your body. Your body image can affect your self-esteem. If you don't feel good about your body, you probably won't feel good about yourself. If you understand that the media shows only a certain body type, you will be less likely to have an unhealthy body image. So, your body image will not negatively affect your self-esteem. ✪ 1.D; 8.A

Figure 4 Knowing that the media is not always realistic can help you have healthy self-esteem.

Lesson Review

Using Vocabulary

1. How does self-esteem affect your life? ✪ 6.A; 7.A

Understanding Concepts

2. Name five factors that influence your self-esteem. ✪ 1.D; 6.A; 7.A; 8.A

3. Explain the difference between high self-esteem and low self-esteem.

Critical Thinking

4. Making Inferences How would having a healthy level of self-esteem help you overcome the fact that you did not get a part in the school play? ✪ 6.A

Lesson 2 Your Self-Concept

What You'll Do

- **Describe** how self-concept and self-esteem are different. ★ 6.A
- **Identify** three areas of self-concept.

Terms to Learn

- self-concept

Start Off Write

How does self-concept develop?

Tai gets good grades in math. He has a group of good friends, but he doesn't think he is very popular at school. He also thinks that he doesn't do as well in gym as his classmates do.

Tai sees himself as a good student who has good friends. He realizes that he may not be as popular as some of his peers or be a star athlete. But he sees himself as person who has many strengths. The way Tai sees himself is called his *self-concept.*

What Is Self-Concept?

Self-concept is a part of self-esteem. **Self-concept** is the way you imagine and see yourself as a person. Self-concept is different from self-esteem. Your self-concept is the way you see yourself in comparison to other people. But your self-esteem is how you feel about yourself. For example, you may see yourself as an artist. You see yourself as an artist because you like to draw and paint. This image of yourself is your self-concept. You feel good about yourself because you can draw and paint well. This feeling is your self-esteem.

Your self-concept can affect your self-esteem. Suppose you think that you are not very good at science. This self-concept leads you to feel bad about yourself. This self-concept can lower your self-esteem. In this case, your self-concept affected your self-esteem in a negative way. Having a positive self-concept will help you keep a healthy level of self-esteem. ★ 6.A

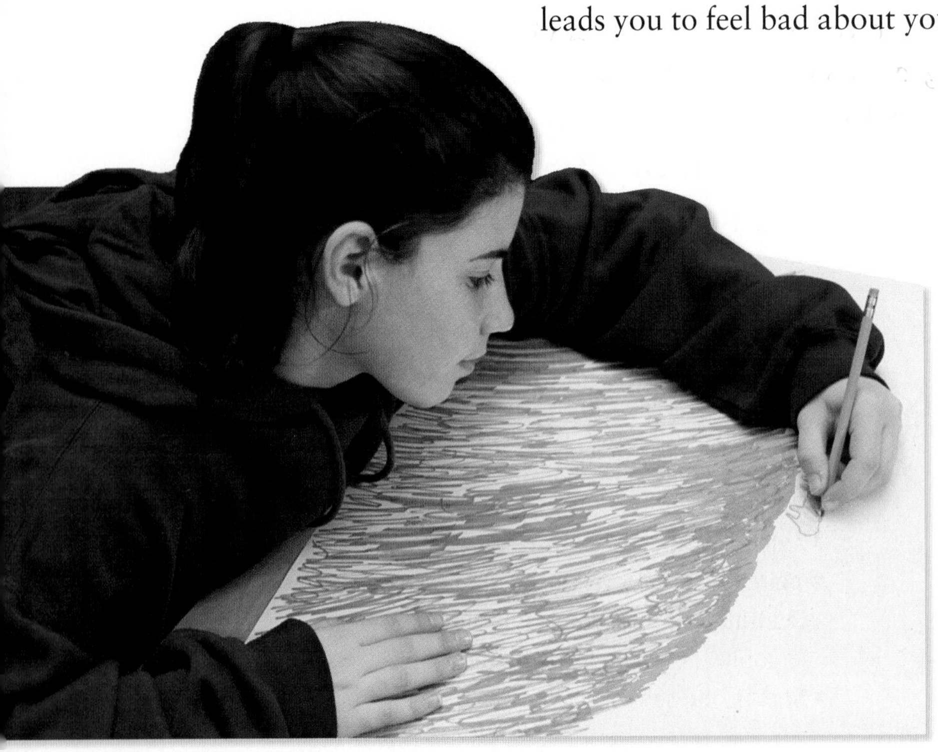

Figure 5 Allison sees herself as an artist because she likes to paint and draw. This image of herself is her self-concept.

How Self-Concept Develops

Your overall self-concept develops from different areas of your personality. Three important areas include your academic self-concept, your physical self-concept, and your social self-concept.

Your academic self-concept is how you see yourself as a student. You may compare yourself to other students at school. In some classes, you may feel that you are a good student. In other classes, you may not feel the same way. The way you see yourself as a student is your academic self-concept.

Your physical self-concept is how you see your physical abilities. You may see yourself as being a very good athlete. Or you may see yourself as an average athlete.

Your social self-concept is how you see yourself in your relationships. Your social self-concept is how you see yourself as a friend, as a peer, as a brother or sister, and as a son or daughter. For example, you may see yourself as a very good friend. But sometimes you may think you could be nicer to your siblings.

These three important areas of self-concept form your overall self-concept. As you grow emotionally, your overall self-concept will change. Having a positive self-concept will help you have healthy self-esteem. ⭐ 1.D; 6.A; 8.A

Figure 6 Rafael does not think he is the best athlete. But he sees himself as a good student and a great friend. His overall self-concept is positive.

Lesson Review

Using Vocabulary

1. In your own words, define the term *self-concept*.

Understanding Concepts

2. How is self-concept different from self-esteem? ⭐ 6.A

3. What are three areas of self-concept? ⭐ 6.A

Critical Thinking

4. Making Inferences How would having a negative self-concept affect your self-esteem? ⭐ 6.A

5. Analyzing Ideas Jason sees himself as a good athlete. However, sometimes, he does not feel good about himself. How can Jason use his positive physical self-concept to boost his self-esteem? ⭐ 6.A

Building Self-Esteem

Eric has a hard time fitting in at school. He doesn't have many friends, and this makes him feel bad about himself. Last week, a classmate asked Eric if she could copy his homework.

Eric let his classmate copy his homework. Now he feels terrible because he knows he did something wrong. Eric wonders how he can feel better and build healthier self-esteem.

Three Keys to Healthy Self-Esteem

Your actions affect the way you feel about yourself. You can learn to have healthy self-esteem by building good character. There are three key ways to build good character and healthy self-esteem. These keys are having integrity, respecting yourself, and being assertive.

Your integrity is your honesty to yourself and others. Integrity is your ability to take responsibility for your actions. Eric didn't really want his classmate to copy his homework. In this case, Eric had trouble being honest with himself.

You must respect yourself to have healthy self-esteem. Respecting yourself means knowing what is right for you and what is wrong for you. You are respecting yourself if you refuse to join an activity that you know is wrong. Sometimes, it is hard to refuse things, especially if you are trying to make friends. But you will feel better about yourself if you respect yourself.

Finally, being assertive can help you build healthy self-esteem. Being assertive means acting on your thoughts and values in an honest, respectful way. Being assertive also means having confidence in yourself. You are being assertive when you communicate your feelings without making other people feel bad. You may need help in developing the three keys to healthy self-esteem. This lesson will give you some strategies to help you develop these areas.

★ 10.C; 11.B

What You'll Do

■ **Identify** three keys to healthy self-esteem. ★ 10.C; 11.B

■ **Identify** seven ways to build healthy self-esteem.

Start Off ✐
Write

What can you do to build healthy self-esteem?

Figure 7 Doing the right thing, such as refusing tobacco, may not always be the popular choice. But it will help you develop healthy self-esteem.

Seven Ways to Healthy Self-Esteem

Here are seven ways to help you build your self-esteem.

Get to know yourself. Getting to know yourself is an easy way to build self-esteem. Think about who you are as a person. Perhaps you like to ride bikes but dislike playing basketball. Maybe you think that you are a good reader but that you could improve your math skills. What kinds of things do you like? What kinds of things don't you like? What are your strengths, or positive qualities? What are your weaknesses? These are good questions to ask yourself. These questions will help you get to know yourself better. When you know yourself, developing integrity will be easier. If you know yourself, you will be able to respect yourself and to be assertive. So, knowing yourself can help you build healthy self-esteem.

Accept yourself. After getting to know yourself, the next step to building a healthy self-esteem is accepting yourself. You must accept your strengths and your weaknesses. You must accept that you like certain things and don't like other things. Accepting yourself means that you don't want to change your personality too much.

Accepting yourself may include accepting your appearance. Everyone has parts of their appearance that they like and parts that they dislike. For example, a friend of yours may not like her nose, but she likes her hair. Once you accept yourself, you will be able to feel good about yourself. Accepting yourself will help you build healthy self-esteem. ⭐ 10.C; 11.B

Things I do well
- swim
- listen
- draw

Things I would like to do
- volunteer at a nursing home
- learn to play the guitar
- make an "A" in history class

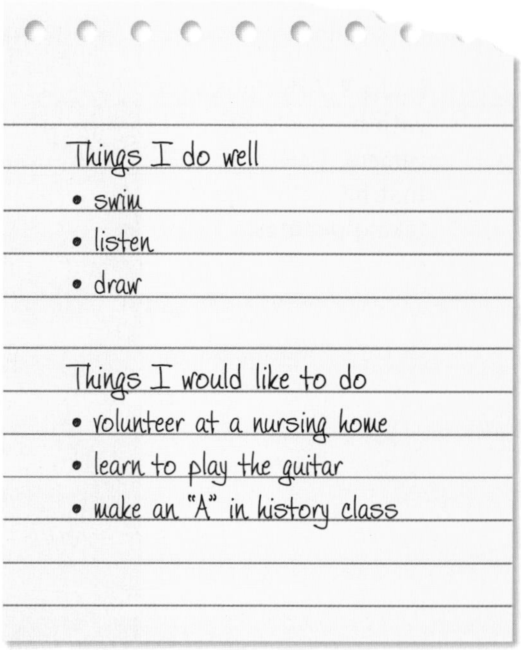

Figure 8 Trying new things is one way to get to know yourself better.

Hands-on ACTIVITY

SELL YOURSELF!

1. Make a list of your likes and dislikes. Then, make a list of your strengths. Finally, make a list of your weaknesses that you would like to improve.

2. Using your lists, posterboard, markers, construction paper, and magazine cutouts, create a billboard that describes you. Use the billboard to advertise yourself.

3. Create a commercial using your billboard, and present your commercial to the class.

Analysis

1. What did you use to describe your strengths? Was it hard to describe the weaknesses you wanted to improve?

2. After creating your billboard and commercial, do you feel more confident about yourself? Explain your answer.

Figure 9 After playing with his dad's old camera, Tyler realized that he really enjoys taking pictures.

Hong's friend Andy is a negative influence on Hong's self-esteem. Write a skit or story describing why Andy is hurting Hong's self-esteem. Be sure to describe a positive way in which Hong copes with her situation.

Be good at something. Another way to build self-esteem is to be good at something. Think of the things you like to do. Do you have any hobbies? Are you good at a certain sport? Choose an activity you would like to do well. In your free time, concentrate on practicing the activity you have chosen. If you like what you are doing, you will probably become better at it. Knowing that you are good at your activity will help you feel good about yourself. Being good at your activity will help you build healthy self-esteem.

Set a goal. Setting goals for yourself can help you build self-esteem. Following a plan to reach a goal will give you a sense of accomplishment. Start by setting a small goal. After you feel more confident about setting and reaching small goals, you can set bigger goals. You may have to stretch yourself to reach these bigger goals. By setting goals and reaching for them, you will find your strengths. As a result of finding your strengths, you will build self-esteem.

Be positive. Did you know that you can build self-esteem by being your own personal cheerleader? Thinking positive thoughts is a good way to build self-esteem. Positive thoughts also build confidence. Imagine that you are nervous about a test. You can say to yourself, "I studied for this test, and I know I can do well. I can do it!" Encouraging yourself will help you feel more confident. ✪ 6.A; 10.C

Figure 10 Sarah tried out for the school band. She did not get to be part of the band, but not being in the band allowed her to try out for the school play.

Turn problems into challenges. Imagine that you tried out for the swim team and didn't make the team. Not making the swim team may be disappointing. However, you may choose to see it as a challenge instead. Your challenge can be to try harder for next year. And now you have an opportunity to to be on the debate team! Looking at problems as challenges will help you deal with disappointments in a positive way. Having a positive attitude helps you build self-esteem.

Do something for others. Helping people who need help is a good way to build self-esteem. Taking part in volunteer work also helps build character. Volunteering allows you to share your strengths with other people. You could volunteer at a local charity. Or you could take part in a food or clothing drive. You could also volunteer at a nursing home. Volunteering can help you feel good about yourself. It can build confidence and self-esteem. ⭐ 6.A

> **Health Journal**
>
> Describe a time in which you experienced a disappointment. If this situation happened again, how would you turn the disappointment into a challenge?

Lesson Review

Understanding Concepts

1. How does knowing yourself help you build self-esteem? ⭐ 6.A

2. How can volunteer work build confidence and self-esteem?

3. Describe three keys to having healthy self-esteem. ⭐ 10.C; 11.B

Critical Thinking

4. **Using Refusal Skills** Imagine that a classmate pressured you to skip class with him. What would you say to your classmate? How will your answer reflect your character and your self-esteem? ⭐ 10.C; 11.B

🔲 internet connect

www.scilinks.org/health
Topic: Building Healthy Self-Esteem
HealthLinks code: HD4020

HEALTH LINKS Maintained by the National Science Teachers Association

Chapter Summary

■ Self-esteem is how much you like yourself as a person. Self-esteem includes how much you value yourself and how you feel about yourself. ■ Self-esteem affects your relationships with other people and how you face new situations. ■ Five influences on your self-esteem include family, friends, teachers, coaches, and the media. ■ Self-concept is how you see yourself. Three areas of self-concept are academic self-concept, social self-concept, and physical self-concept. ■ Three keys to healthy self-esteem include having integrity, respecting yourself, and being assertive.

Using Vocabulary

For each pair of terms, describe how the meanings of the terms differ.

1 self-esteem/self-concept

2 body image/self-esteem

For each sentence, fill in the blank with the proper word from the word bank provided below.

self-esteem	self-concept
body image	

3 ___ is how you much you like yourself and how you feel about yourself as a person.

4 How you see and imagine your body is your ___.

5 How you see yourself as a person is called your ___.

Understanding Concepts

6 What are the characteristics of a person who has high self-esteem?

7 What is academic self-concept?

8 How can your friends be a positive or negative influence on your self-esteem? ★ 7.A; 11.C

9 What is physical self-concept?

10 List seven ways to build self-esteem. ★ 10.C; 11.B

11 What does having integrity mean? Give an example.

12 Discovering your strengths and weaknesses, or getting to know yourself, can help you build healthy self-esteem. Explain why this may be true. ★ 6.A

13 Explain how setting a goal can help boost your self-esteem.

14 What does being assertive mean? Give an example. ★ 10.C

15 What are the characteristics of a person with low self-esteem? ★ 1.D; 6.A

16 How can the following actions help you build a healthy self-esteem?

a. accepting yourself

b. developing a hobby

c. being positive

d. looking at problems as challenges and not as disappointments ★ 6.A

Critical Thinking

Applying Concepts

17 Why is it healthier to have high self-esteem than to have low self-esteem?

18 Luke enjoys playing football. This year, Luke really wanted to play football. Luke tried out for the football team, but he didn't make it. Now, he is a little disappointed. Explain how Luke may turn this disappointment into a challenge. ⭐ 6.A

19 Explain how a classmate who teases you can affect your self-esteem. ⭐ 6.A; 7.A

20 How does your overall self-concept develop?

Making Good Decisions

21 Use what you have learned in this chapter to set a personal goal. Write your goal, and make an action plan by using the Health Behavior Contract for building healthy self-esteem. You can find the Health Behavior Contract at go.hrw.com. Just type in the keyword HD4HBC02.

Name _____ Class _____ Date _____
(Health Behavior Contract)
Self-Esteem

My Goals: I, _____, will accomplish one or more of the following goals:
I will build a higher self-esteem.
I will focus on my strengths.
I will make a plan to improve my weaknesses.
Other: _____

My Reasons: By building a healthy self-esteem, I will improve my overall confidence and attitude, and I will feel good about myself as a person.
Other: _____

My Values: Personal values that will help me meet my goals are
_____
_____

My Plan: The actions I will take to meet my goals are
_____
_____

Evaluation: I will use my Health Journal to keep a log of actions I took to fulfill this contract. After 1 month, I will evaluate my goals. I will adjust my plan if my goals are not being met. If my goals are being met, I will consider setting additional goals.
Signed _____
Date _____

Interpreting Graphics

How Students Feel About Themselves

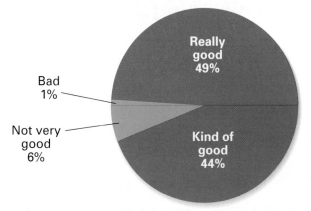

Really good 49%
Bad 1%
Not very good 6%
Kind of good 44%

Use the figure above to answer questions 22–25. ⭐ M: 6.10D; 6.11A

22 Imagine that a survey was taken at a local middle school in your city. The pie chart above shows how the students at the middle school feel about themselves. According to the chart, do most students have high self-esteem or low self-esteem?

23 What percentage of students may have low or unhealthy self-esteem?

24 If 300 students completed this survey, how many students feel "Really good" about themselves?

25 If 300 students completed this survey, how many students feel "Not very good" about themselves?

Reading Checkup

Take a minute to review your answers to the Health IQ questions at the beginning of this chapter. How has reading this chapter improved your Health IQ?

Life Skills IN ACTION

Communicating Effectively

Have you ever been in a bad situation that was made worse because of poor communication? Or maybe you have difficulty understanding others or being understood. You can avoid misunderstandings by expressing your feelings in a healthy way, which is communicating effectively. Complete the following activity to develop effective communication skills.

Teasing Troubles

ACT 1

Setting the Scene

Daniel has new braces. He doesn't like them—they feel uncomfortable and he thinks they make him look funny. The day after he got the braces, his classmates started teasing him about them. Since then, several classmates—including some of his friends—have been calling him Metal-Mouth and Jaws. The teasing makes Daniel feel bad, and he wishes his classmates would stop teasing him.

⭐ 1.D; 6.A; 10.C; 11.B

The 4 Steps of Communicating Effectively

1. Express yourself calmly and clearly.
2. Choose your words carefully.
3. Use open body language.
4. Use active listening.

Guided Practice

Practice with a Friend

Form a group of three. Have one person play the role of Daniel and another person play the role of one of Daniel's classmates. Have the third person be an observer. Walking through each of the four steps of communicating effectively, role-play Daniel telling his classmate to stop teasing him. The classmate should use active listening when Daniel speaks. The observer will take notes, which will include observations about what the person playing Daniel did well and suggestions of ways to improve. Stop after each step to evaluate the process.

Independent Practice

Check Yourself

After you have completed the guided practice, go through Act 1 again without stopping at each step. Answer the questions below to review what you did.

1. Why is it important for Daniel to express himself calmly and clearly when confronting his classmate?

2. What body gestures should Daniel use to show open body language?

3. How will active listening help Daniel's classmate understand Daniel's views?

4. Why should Daniel use active listening?

5. How can healthy communication help Daniel's self-esteem?

On Your Own

After Daniel talked to some of his classmates, they stopped teasing him about his braces. A few weeks later, Daniel learns that several of his friends have had their feelings hurt by teasing. Daniel decides to teach his friends how to stop others from teasing. Imagine you are Daniel and make a pamphlet that explains how to use the four steps of communicating effectively to stop others from teasing.

⭐ 6.A; 11.B; 11.C

Body Image

Lessons

Check out
Current Health
articles related to this chapter by
visiting **go.hrw.com**. Just type in
the keyword **HD4CH04**.

> **""** I usually **feel pretty good** about **myself**. But sometimes I feel **uncomfortable** around my friends. I feel like they all look better than I do. I feel bad when I think that I am not thin enough to wear cool clothes. How can I make myself feel better? **""**

Health IQ

PRE-READING

Answer the following true/false questions to find out what you already know about body image and eating disorders. When you've finished this chapter, you'll have the opportunity to change your answers based on what you've learned.

1. Exercising too much is bad for you. ⊛ 1.B

2. You can improve how you feel about your body by eating well and staying physically active. ⊛ 1.B

3. Eating disorders affect only girls and women. ⊛ 1.D

4. Your body image is important only when you are at school. ⊛ 1.D

5. Your body image affects how you face new challenges. ⊛ 1.D

6. Following fad diets is not harmful to your health. ⊛ 1.A

7. A person with a healthy body image wants to change their body in some way. ⊛ 1.D

8. The photographs you see on TV and in magazines influence your body image. ⊛ 8.A

9. Eating disorders are only a phase, and most people don't suffer from them for a long time. ⊛ 1.D

10. Being realistic about your body can help you have a healthy body image. ⊛ 1.D

11. Dieting is an unhealthy eating behavior. ⊛ 1.A

12. Staying physically active can help you maintain a healthy weight. ⊛ 1.F

ANSWERS: 1. true; 2. true; 3. false; 4. false; 5. true; 6. false; 7. false; 8. true; 9. false; 10. true; 11. true; 12. true

An Image of Yourself

Sachiko was getting frustrated. She had put on three different outfits before leaving for school. Still, she couldn't find an outfit that looked good on her.

Many teens, boys and girls, have had days like Sachiko's. Most likely, Sachiko looked fine in all of her outfits. It was how she saw herself that made her change her clothes several times.

What You'll Do

- **Explain** why body image is important. ✪ 1.D; 6.A
- **Compare** healthy body image with unhealthy body image. ✪ 1.D

Terms to Learn

- body image

Start Off
Write

How can your body image affect your life?

How You See Yourself

Many teens feel confused about their appearance at one time or another. Such feelings are a normal part of becoming an adult. The way you see yourself, the way you feel about your appearance, and your level of comfort with your body is called your **body image.** Your body image is very important. How you feel about your body can affect the way you deal with many situations. If you feel comfortable with your body, you will be more likely to have confidence when you are faced with new challenges. If you are uncomfortable with your body, you may feel like changing how your body looks. These feelings can lead to some unhealthy behaviors. ✪ 1.D

Figure 1 It is very common to be confused about how you should look, especially in middle school.

Age 5   Age 7   Age 9   Age 11

Healthy Body Image

A healthy body image means that a person feels good about the way he or she looks. People who have a healthy body image are comfortable with their appearance. They accept their bodies, and they don't feel the need to change anything about their bodies. People who have a healthy body image are not easily influenced by what people say about their appearance or by what they see on TV or in magazines. Accepting and feeling good about your appearance helps you build healthy self-esteem. Having a healthy body image can help you feel confident in new situations. ✪ 6.A; 8.A; 11.C

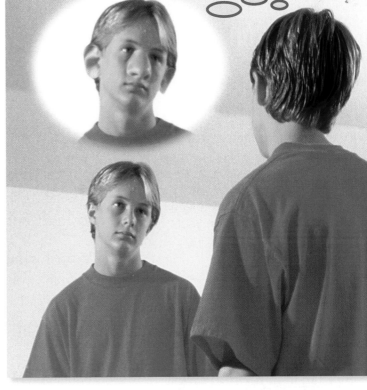

Figure 2 Erik thinks his nose and ears are too big. But in reality they are not. Erik may have an unhealthy body image.

Unhealthy Body Image

An unhealthy body image means that a person is not comfortable with the way that he or she looks. People who have an unhealthy body image tend to compare themselves with others. They want to change the way they look. And people who have an unhealthy body image might take part in unhealthy behaviors. These behaviors include fad dieting and eating disorders. Also, people who have an unhealthy body image may develop low self-esteem. Low self-esteem may cause them to avoid their friends because they don't feel good enough for their friends. Or they may become less active in class, which can hurt their grades. ✪ 1.D

Lesson Review

Using Vocabulary

1. In your own words, define *body image*. ✪ 1.D

Understanding Concepts

2. Why is having a healthy body image important? ✪ 1.D; 6.A

3. What are some characteristics of having an unhealthy body image? ✪ 1.D

Critical Thinking

4. **Analyzing Viewpoints** Both Megan and Julie have curly hair. Megan doesn't like her hair, and she spends a lot of time trying to straighten her hair. Julie, however, got a haircut that makes her curly hair look really good. Which of these girls has a healthy body image? ✪ 1.D; 6.A

Influences on Body Image

What You'll Do

- **Identify** four factors that influence body image. ⭐ 1.D; 6.A; 7.A; 8.A
- **Explain** how people in your life can be both positive and negative influences on your body image. ⭐ 1.D; 6.A; 7.A

Start Off
Write

How can your peers influence your body image?

Sarah is athletic, and her friends often call her a tomboy. Although Sarah enjoys sports, being called a tomboy makes her feel uncomfortable, especially around the other girls at school.

Sarah's friends may be affecting her body image. Sometimes other people's comments affect your own thoughts about your body. Almost anyone can affect your body image—even people in magazines and on TV.

Your Family and Your Body Image

Your body image began to develop when you were a baby. It will continue to develop as you grow older. All of your life, your body image is affected by the people around you. Right now, your family can be the largest influence on your body image. Your family is a great source of positive support. When they say good things about your appearance, they help you feel good about your body. However, sometimes your family may say things about your body that hurt your feelings. Most likely, your family is not trying to hurt your feelings. But these comments can hurt your body image—especially if you are already uncomfortable with your body. ⭐ 1.D; 6.A; 7.A

Figure 3 Spending time with your family can be a positive influence on your body image.

People at Your School

People at your school also affect your body image. These people include your friends, peers, teachers, and coaches.

- **Friends** Your friends can be good influences on your body image if they support you when you feel uncomfortable with your body. However, a friend may criticize the way you look without realizing it. If you already feel uncomfortable about your body, these comments could hurt your body image.

- **Peers** Peers are people you know who are your age. Your peers may take part in teasing or bullying. When a peer says something negative about your appearance, your body image may be hurt. If you have a healthy body image, negative comments from peers will not bother you very much.

- **Teachers** Your teachers may also affect your body image. Teachers encourage you to be successful at schoolwork. However, like anyone else, a teacher may say something about your appearance that makes you feel bad.

- **Coaches** Coaches help and encourage you to be successful at physical activities. In some sports, however, your physical characteristics may affect how well you play. A coach may make a comment about your body that hurts your feelings. For example, a coach may tell you to gain weight to fit into a certain weight class for a wrestling meet. If this happens, keep in mind that your coach does not mean to hurt your feelings. Being comfortable with your body will keep your feelings from getting hurt by such comments. ⭐ 6.A; 7.A

Figure 4 Your friends can help you build a healthy body image by providing encouragement when you are feeling unsure about yourself.

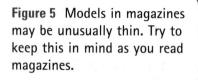

Figure 5 Models in magazines may be unusually thin. Try to keep this in mind as you read magazines.

Magazines

You may realize that you are influenced by the people around you. You talk to these people every day. Sometimes, they say things that make you feel good. Other times, they may make you feel pretty bad. It may be harder for you to see that you are influenced by magazines, too.

Many magazines have teen models. The girls are often very thin. The boys are often very muscular. Teens' bodies are changing all of the time. And many teens feel confused about how they are supposed to look. Some teens may look at magazines and think that they should look like those models. They may start to feel fat, weak, or ugly. But just look around you. Do the students in your class look like those models? How many of the girls are really that thin? How many of the boys have big muscles? Probably very few do. These unrealistic images can hurt a teen's body image. ⊛ 8.A

Hands-on ACTIVITY

HEALTHY IMAGES

1. Using a variety of teen magazines, cut out pictures of teens who look healthy.

2. Then, cut out pictures of teens who are made to look unusually thin or muscular.

Analysis

1. Which types of magazines had more photographs of typical people than photographs of unusually thin or muscular people?

2. How many photographs of typical people did you find? How many photographs of thin or muscular people did you find?

3. In your own words, explain why the photographs in magazines may have an influence on a person's body image. ⊛ 6.A; 8.A

Television and Body Image

Like the models in magazines, the people we see on TV are unusually thin or muscular. Often, teens compare themselves with the people they see on TV. These teens find that they don't look like the people they see on TV. Then, the teens may want to change their bodies. People come in all shapes and sizes. But people on TV are not typical. They may be unusually pretty, thin, or muscular. Seeing the people on TV can hurt a person's body image.

If you find that you compare yourself with the people you see on TV, remember that these people are made to look a certain way. Remember that many techniques are used to enhance the way people look on TV. If you have a healthy body image, you won't compare yourself as much. And even if you do compare yourself, you won't want to change your body. ⊛ 8.A

SOCIAL STUDIES ACTIVITY

Different cultures idealize different body types for men and women. Research the body types that are considered beautiful for several cultures. How do the idealized body types compare to each other?

Figure 6 Teens who have an unhealthy body image may want to change their bodies to look like the people they see on TV.

Lesson Review

Understanding Concepts

1. Explain how your family can be a positive influence on your body image. ⊛ 1.D; 6.A; 7.A

2. How can your friends and peers be a positive influence on your body image? How can they be a negative influence on your body image? ⊛ 1.D; 6.A; 7.A

3. What are four factors that affect your body image? ⊛ 1.D; 6.A; 7.A; 8.A

Critical Thinking

4. **Analyzing Viewpoints** Why is a teen who has a healthy body image less likely to be negatively influenced by friends, peers, magazines, and TV? ⊛ 8.A

Building a Healthy Body Image

Reena felt like everyone was staring at her when she arrived at Cristina's party. Everyone was wearing shorts, but Reena was wearing jeans. Reena thinks her legs have a funny shape, and she doesn't like people to see them.

Have you ever felt the way Reena does about herself? It could be your hair, skin, arms, legs, or height—almost anything—that you don't like. Most people would like to change something about their body. Sometimes, people even think that they aren't "normal."

What Is Normal, Anyway?

You may find yourself asking this question a lot. But there is no such thing as "normal." Teens come in many shapes and sizes. There are certain factors that affect the size and shape of your body. How you look has a lot to do with how your parents look. How you look also has to do with your ethnicity. Accepting your body is an important part of building a healthy body image. Practicing good nutrition and staying active also help you build a healthy body image. A healthy body image can give you more confidence. Reena's body image was pretty low at Cristina's party. If she had felt better about herself and her body, she may have had more fun. ⊛ 1.D; 2.B

Figure 7 There is no such thing as "normal." People come in all shapes and sizes.

In small groups, use pictures of your classmates, brothers, sisters, parents, and other family members to create a poster. Then, using photographs from magazines, create a second poster. Finally, make a list of the similarities and differences between the two posters.

Be Realistic

The first step to having a healthy body image is to understand what a healthy body image means. A healthy body image means being comfortable with your body and your appearance. Being comfortable with yourself will help you be comfortable with other people. It will also help you face the many challenges in your life.

The second step to having a healthy body image is to be realistic about your body. You have to learn to accept your body. To accept your body, you need to be realistic about your size and weight. Every person has a different healthy weight range. Your healthy weight range depends on how tall you are and on the size of your body frame.

The body mass index is a tool that can help you find your healthy weight range. A person's body mass index is a number that describes his or her weight in relation to height. You can find a table of these numbers in the appendix of this book. ⭐ 1.D

Figure 8 Joe is realistic about his body and is comfortable with his appearance. He has a healthy body image.

Figure 9 Practicing good nutrition is one way to build a healthy body image.

Eat Well, Feel Well

When you practice good nutrition, you are taking care of your body. Taking care of your body is a good way to build a healthy body image. Eating well helps you feel good because you are doing something good for your body. Eating healthy foods will give you the energy to stay active. A healthy diet will also help you keep a healthy weight. The table below shows you some tips for making good nutritional choices. ⭐ **1.B; 6.A**

TABLE 1 Tips for Eating Well	
Eat a lot of fresh fruits and vegetables every day.	Include fruits and vegetables in each meal that you eat. Try having a piece of fruit at breakfast and at lunch. Also, try eating bananas, apples, oranges, or raisins for snacks.
Drink plenty of water every day.	Water helps keep your body functioning properly. Make sure to drink at least 8 to 10 glasses of water each day. If you play sports, you should drink more than 10 glasses a day.
Eat foods low in fat.	Eating too many fatty foods can lead to weight gain. These foods include french fries and potato chips. Sweets such as donuts and pastries are also high in fat.
Eat foods low in sugar.	Foods that are high in sugar are often high in Calories. Sugary foods include candy bars, hard candies, cakes, and cookies.
Eat foods low in salt.	Eating foods that are high in salt can make you feel sluggish. These foods include salty snacks, such as potato or corn chips. Many fast foods are also high in salt.

Move That Body!

Another way to build a healthy body image is to be physically active. Regular physical activity helps you feel comfortable with your body. Being active also helps you maintain a healthy weight.

Many teens don't like to play sports, which is OK. There are many other ways to be active. Sometimes, you may not even notice that you're exercising. Playing outside with your friends is a great way to be active. You can also be active by walking to school, riding your bicycle, raking leaves, or walking your dog. And don't forget that activities such as dancing, in-line skating, or even helping to clean the house are good ways to stay active, too! ⭐ 1.F; 6.A

Health Journal

How do you stay physically active? In your Health Journal, write down 2 or 3 physical activities that you enjoy. Then, make a list of physical activities that you would like to try. Make a plan to try one of these activities soon.
⭐ 1.F; 6.A

Figure 10 You don't have to join a sports team to be active. You can be active while playing with your friends.

Lesson Review

Understanding Concepts

1. Describe two factors that affect the size and shape of your body. ⭐ 1.D; 2.B
2. Name three ways to build a healthy body image. ⭐ 1.D; 1.F
3. How does eating well help your body image? ⭐ 1.B
4. List three ways to be physically active without playing a sport. ⭐ 1.F

Critical Thinking

5. **Analyzing Ideas** How does being realistic help you build a better body image? Why is building a healthy body image important? ⭐ 1.D; 6.A

Lesson 4

Eating Disorders

What You'll Do

- **Explain** how unhealthy eating behaviors may affect a person's health. ★ 1.B; 1.D
- **Describe** a fad diet. ★ 1.A
- **Give** three examples of eating disorders. ★ 1.D
- **Summarize** two strategies for giving and getting help for an eating disorder. ★ 1.D; 11.A

Terms to Learn

- eating disorder
- anorexia nervosa
- bulimia nervosa
- binge eating disorder

Start Off Write

Why should you be suspicious of fad diets?

Andy is not very comfortable with his appearance. In fact, he thinks he is too skinny. Andy saw an advertisement on TV for a muscle-building pill that will help him gain weight quickly.

Often, when someone has an unhealthy body image, he or she may try to change something about his or her body. In this case, Andy wants to take pills to help him gain weight. Do you think this decision is a healthy choice for Andy?

Unhealthy Eating Behavior

Although many people feel uncomfortable with their bodies at some point, some people may feel so bad that they develop unhealthy eating behaviors. These people may try to change their bodies. They may go on a diet, skip meals, take diet pills, or even eat large amounts of food at one time. These actions are called *unhealthy eating behaviors.*

Unhealthy eating behaviors can affect a person's growth and development. They can also develop into eating disorders, which are diseases that can be very dangerous to a person's health.

A healthy body image can prevent a person from practicing unhealthy eating behaviors. However, learning about some common unhealthy eating behaviors and eating disorders is important. Many teens don't realize how dangerous these behaviors can be. Knowing your healthy weight range and being comfortable with your body size and shape can prevent you from taking part in unhealthy eating behaviors.

★ 1.A; 1.B; 1.D

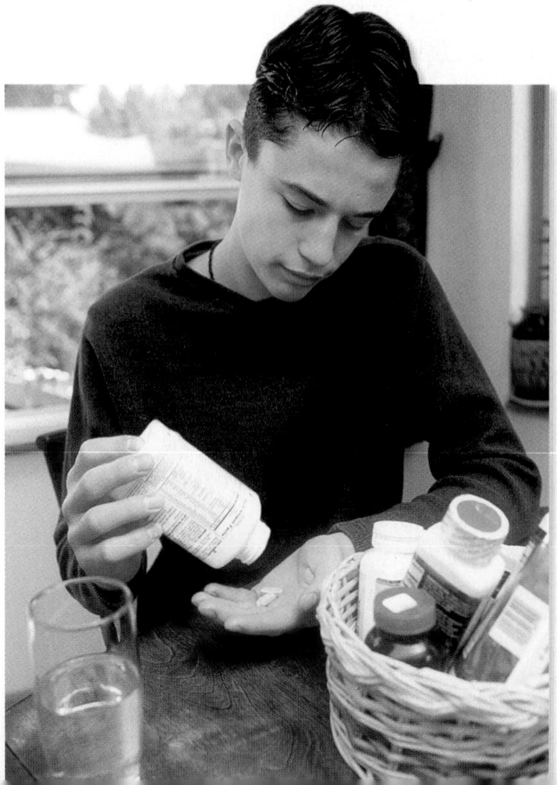

Figure 11 Taking pills that claim to change your body is an unhealthy eating behavior.

Fad Diets

You may have seen ads on TV or billboards that say, "Lose 30 pounds in 30 days!" This promise is a sure sign of a fad diet. A *fad diet* is an eating plan that promises quick weight loss with very little effort. Fad diets usually require you to buy special products from the company selling the diet. These products can range from pills to special drinks or powdered shakes.

Fad diets can be dangerous. Many fad diets require you to eat in unhealthy ways. These diets often do not provide the nutrients that your body needs to stay healthy. People who do lose weight on a fad diet usually gain all of the weight back once they stop following the diet. Fad diets do not work over time. If you are worried about your weight, check with your family doctor to see if you have a weight problem. Together, you and your doctor can create an eating plan that is right for you. ⍟ 1.A; 1.D

Figure 12 When it sounds too good to be true, it probably is!

What Is an Eating Disorder?

You have probably heard of eating disorders, but you may not know exactly what they are. An **eating disorder** is a disease in which a person is overly concerned with his or her body weight and shape. Eating disorders affect thousands of people in the United States each year. Eating disorders affect people of all ethnicities, all income levels, and both genders. Most of these people are women and girls. However, men and boys are also affected. People with eating disorders are usually very unhappy with how they look. They constantly worry about their weight. They may also suffer from depression and anxiety. Eating disorders can be cured with the help of a doctor. Unfortunately, without medical help, a person can die from an eating disorder. ⍟ 1.D

Myth: Only girls develop eating disorders.

Fact: Eating disorders affect girls, boys, women, and men of all cultures. ⍟ 1.D

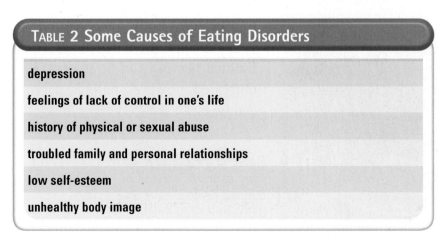

TABLE 2 Some Causes of Eating Disorders

depression
feelings of lack of control in one's life
history of physical or sexual abuse
troubled family and personal relationships
low self-esteem
unhealthy body image

Anorexia Nervosa

Anorexia nervosa is a serious and potentially life-threatening eating disorder. **Anorexia nervosa** is an eating disorder in which a person stops eating food because he or she is obsessed with being thin. People who have anorexia nervosa think they are fat even though they may already be very thin. In addition, they are very afraid of being or becoming fat. So, they starve themselves in order to stay as thin as possible. Over time, people who suffer from anorexia nervosa will become very thin. They may also suffer from symptoms such as dry skin, brittle nails, and hair loss. Fortunately, anorexia nervosa can be treated. If left untreated, however, this eating disorder may cause permanent damage to a person's organs. A person may even starve to death. ⊛ 1.D

Bulimia Nervosa

People who suffer from bulimia nervosa are afraid of gaining weight, but they do not starve themselves. **Bulimia nervosa** is an eating disorder in which a person eats large amounts of food at one time and then gets rid of the food before the body can digest it. Eating a large amount of food at one time is called *bingeing*. After bingeing, people who suffer from this disorder feel ashamed that they ate so much food. They are also afraid they will gain weight. So, they try to get rid of the food by *purging*. They purge by making themselves vomit or by taking laxatives (LAKS uh tivs) or diuretics (DIE you RET iks). Laxatives are drugs that make you have a bowel movement. Diuretics are drugs that make you urinate. Sometimes, people who suffer from bulimia nervosa may also over-exercise to burn the extra Calories from the food they eat. The cycle of bingeing and purging is very harmful to a person's body, and eventually it will damage many body systems. Bulimia nervosa can be treated. Left untreated, however, bulimia nervosa can be fatal. ⊛ 1.D

Brain Food

Studies show that 42 percent of 1st through 3rd grade girls want to be thinner. The studies also show that 81 percent of 10-year-old girls and boys are afraid of being fat.

Figure 13 People who suffer from anorexia nervosa or bulimia nervosa have a very unhealthy body image.

Binge Eating

Some people eat too much food. **Binge eating disorder** is an eating disorder in which a person has difficulty controlling how much food he or she eats. People who suffer from binge eating disorder do not purge. They often feel ashamed after they binge. A person with this disease may suffer from depression. People who have binge eating disorder often become overweight. If they do not get help, people who have this disorder may become *obese,* which means "extremely overweight." They may develop health problems that stem from being obese. These problems include high blood pressure and heart problems. ⭐ 1.D

Giving and Getting Help

Here are some tips to get help if you feel you or a friend may have unhealthy eating behaviors or an eating disorder.

- **If you are concerned about your eating behavior, tell someone.** Talk to a parent or another trusted adult. Also, talk to a professional who understands eating behaviors, such as a doctor or counselor. Once you decide to talk to someone, choose a time and a place where you can talk in private. Then, share your feelings. Explain to this person what you are going through. Together, you can plan a way to get well.

- **If you are concerned for a friend, be honest with him or her.** Talk openly with your friend about your concerns. Be caring, and understand that your friend may be scared. Also, tell a trusted adult, such as a parent or a counselor, about your concerns. ⭐ 10.A; 11.A

Lesson Review

Using Vocabulary

1. What is an eating disorder? ⭐ 1.D

2. What is anorexia nervosa? ⭐ 1.D

Understanding Concepts

3. Describe a fad diet. ⭐ 1.A; 1.B

4. Explain how unhealthy eating behaviors may affect a person's health. ⭐ 1.A; 1.B; 1.D

Critical Thinking

5. Making Good Decisions You notice that your friend has become very concerned about her weight and body shape. Recently, she has been skipping lunch. What do you think may be wrong? What will you do? ⭐ 1.D; 10.A; 11.A

6. Analyzing Concepts How can a negative body image lead to an eating disorder? ⭐ 6.A

Chapter Summary

■ Body image is the way that you see and imagine your body. Your body image is important because it affects the way you face new challenges. ■ Factors that affect your body image include your family, friends, peers, teachers, coaches, and the media. ■ The people in your life can be both positive and negative influences on your body image. ■ You can build and keep a healthy body image by sharing your feelings, eating healthy foods, and staying physically active. ■ Unhealthy eating behaviors are unhealthy changes in your diet. Unhealthy eating behaviors include taking weight-gain products, skipping meals, and following fad diets to lose weight. ■ Eating disorders are diseases and require medical attention. Anorexia nervosa, bulimia nervosa, and binge eating disorder are examples of eating disorders. ■ If you or a friend has an eating disorder, getting help is the most important thing to do.

Using Vocabulary

For each pair of terms, describe how the meanings of the terms differ.

1 anorexia nervosa/bulimia nervosa

2 bulimia nervosa/binge eating disorder

For each sentence, fill in the blank with the proper word from the word bank provided below.

anorexia nervosa	binge eating disorder
eating disorder	body image
bulimia nervosa	

3 ___ is an illness in which a person eats a large amount of food and then purges the food from his or her body.

4 A(n) ___ is an illness in which a person is overly concerned about his or her weight and body size.

5 How you see and imagine your body is your ___.

6 An illness in which a person has difficulty controlling how much he or she eats but does not purge is called ___.

Understanding Concepts

7 What are some factors that influence your body image? ✪ 1.D; 6.A; 8.A

8 How can being realistic help you build a healthy body image? ✪ 6.A

9 Describe the differences between a person with a healthy body image and a person with an unhealthy body image.

10 How can people in your life be both positive and negative influences on your body image? ✪ 6.A; 7.A

11 What is a fad diet? ✪ 1.A; 1.B

12 Give three examples of eating disorders. How are these diseases alike? How are these diseases different? ✪ 1.D

13 Describe one way to build a healthy body image. ✪ 6.A

Critical Thinking

Analyzing Viewpoints

14 Emily thinks that she should look like the models she sees in magazines. She does not feel that she is thin enough to be popular in school. She has started taking diet pills to lose weight. What kind of body image does Emily have? Describe how you can encourage Emily to change how she feels about her body. ⭐ 1.A; 1.B; 1.D

15 Tim and Wyley are on the wrestling team at school. Next week, they are competing against your school's biggest rival. Tim suggests to Wyley that they start using a product called Muscle Grow. Tim thinks that this product will help them beat the other team. Wyley thinks that using Muscle Grow could be dangerous to their health. Tim tells Wyley that the Muscle Grow can't hurt them if they use it for only 1 week. If you could give Tim and Wyley advice about using Muscle Grow, what would you tell them? ⭐ 1.A; 1.D; 10.A

Making Good Decisions

16 Your friend Alicia has become worried about her body shape and size. She has started dieting regularly. At lunch, she eats only a few French fries or a small cup of frozen yogurt. You notice that Alicia has lost a great deal of weight in a short time. You are worried that Alicia may have an eating disorder. What two steps could you take to help Alicia? ⭐ 1.B; 7.A; 10.A; 11.A

Interpreting Graphics

Survey of High School Teens

	Male students	Female students
Total number of students	215	235
Number of students with anorexia nervosa	2	11
Number of students with bulimia nervosa	3	15
Number of students with binge eating disorder	9	5

Use the table above to answer questions 17–20. ⭐ M: 6.10D; 6.11A

17 Your local newspaper published an article about the number of students in your neighborhood high school who have eating disorders. The article provided the table above. What percentage of students suffer from eating disorders?

18 How many female students suffer from an eating disorder?

19 What percentage of students suffer from binge eating disorder?

20 How many more females than males have eating disorders?

Reading Checkup

Take a minute to review your answers to the Health IQ questions at the beginning of this chapter. How has reading this chapter improved your Health IQ?

Life Skills IN ACTION

Evaluating Media Messages

You receive media messages every day. These messages are on TV, the Internet, the radio, and in newspapers and magazines. With so many messages, it is important to know how to evaluate them. Evaluating media messages means being able to judge the accuracy of a message. Complete the following activity to improve your skills in evaluating media messages.

Skin Deep

Setting the Scene

Shannon and Leigh Ann enjoy looking at fashion magazines. One day, while looking at the new *In Fad*, Leigh Ann says that she wishes she could be as thin as the models in the magazine. She then tells Shannon that she wants to go on a diet so she can look like the models. Shannon thinks that Leigh Ann is not being very wise and that Leigh Ann needs to be realistic about having a healthy weight. ★ 8.A

The 5 Steps of Evaluating Media Messages

ACT 1

1. Examine the appeal of the message.
2. Identify the values projected by the message.
3. Consider what the source has to gain by getting you to believe the message.
4. Try to determine the reliability of the source.
5. Based on the information you gather, evaluate the message.

Guided Practice

Practice with a Friend

Form a group of three. Have one person play the role of Shannon and another person play the role of Leigh Ann. Have the third person be an observer. Walking through each of the five steps of evaluating media messages, role-play Shannon and Leigh Ann's evaluation of the magazine's message. The observer will take notes, which will include observations about what the people playing Shannon and Leigh Ann did well and suggestions of ways to improve. Stop after each step to evaluate the process. ★ 1.D

Independent Practice

Check Yourself

After you have completed the guided practice, go through Act 1 again without stopping at each step. Answer the questions below to review what you did.

1. What is the appeal of the fashion magazine?

2. What are the values projected by the magazine?

3. How can Shannon convince Leigh Ann that a fashion magazine is not the most reliable source for ideal weight? ⭐ 10.A

4. What are other media sources that project the same appeal and values as fashion magazines? ⭐ 8.A

ACT 2 — On Your Own

A few days later, Shannon and Leigh Ann are watching TV. A music video comes on that shows a girl driving an expensive car. The girl appears to be very popular. Write a skit about how Shannon and Leigh Ann could evaluate the video's message. Be sure to include each of the five steps of evaluating media messages. ⭐ 8.A

Friends and Family

Check out
Current Health
articles related to this chapter by
visiting **go.hrw.com**. Just type in
the keyword **HD4CH05**.

"Beth was **such a pest** when she was little. Once, she **dumped glue** on all of the keys of our piano. By the time we found out, **every key** was stuck.

So, when Mom gave me the responsibility of watching Beth every day before supper, I wasn't happy. But Beth is not a bad kid. She just has a lot of energy and likes attention. We usually have fun. I just have to keep her away from glue. "

Health IQ

PRE-READING

Answer the following multiple-choice questions to find out what you already know about relationships. When you've finished this chapter, you'll have the opportunity to change your answers based on what you've learned.

1. Which of the following shows body language?
a. your hands
b. your face
c. the way you stand
d. all of the above ⭐ 10.A

2. Assertiveness is
a. only used by adults.
b. a respectful way of behaving.
c. a way of not expressing your true feelings.
d. rude. ⭐ 7.E; 10.A; 10.B

3. Abuse is
a. sometimes the victim's fault.
b. always the victim's fault.
c. never the victim's fault.
d. All of the above

4. The best way to cope with abuse is to
a. tell a trusted adult as soon as possible.
b. wait and tell someone if the abuse happens again.
c. wait until someone asks about it.
d. keep it a secret. ⭐ 5.G; 5.H

5. Leadership is
a. bossing people around.
b. guiding people responsibly.
c. something only adults do.
d. expressing your feelings loudly.

6. Which statement about affection is NOT true?
a. Abstinence is one way to show affection among teens.
b. People should always show affection the same way to everyone.
c. People should never offer affection in a way that is unwelcome.
d. You can show affection to your family and friends. ⭐ 10.D

ANSWERS: 1. d; 2. b; 3. c; 4. a; 5. b; 6. b

Relationship Skills

Your physical health has to do with your body. Your emotional health has to do with your feelings. Your social health has to do with your relationships. But what is a relationship?

What You'll Do

- **Describe** six skills of good speaking and listening. ⭐ 7.E
- **Describe** the three kinds of body language. ⭐ 7.E
- **Distinguish** between assertive, aggressive, and passive behavior. ⭐ 7.E; 10
- **Explain** how tolerance and empathy help build relationships. ⭐ 10.A; 10.B

Terms to Learn

- relationship
- communication
- body language
- behavior
- empathy
- tolerance

Start Off *Write*

How can you tell if a friend is disappointed?

A **relationship** is a social or emotional connection between people. Families, friendships, and teams all require healthy relationships. We build healthy relationships by using social skills, such as good communication. **Communication** is sending and receiving messages clearly. Good communication helps people in relationships know and understand each other.

Speaking and Listening

When you are talking to someone, it's important to be clear. Think carefully before you speak. Plan what you want to say. Make sure that your tone matches your message. Look at people when you are talking to them. Speak clearly and directly. Ask questions to be sure you are understood.

When you are listening, pay attention to the speaker. Look at the speaker's face, and show that you are interested. Allow the speaker to finish sentences without interruption. Nod when you understand. Ask questions when you don't understand. Good listeners also try to learn from what they hear. ⭐ 7.E; 10

Figure 1 These friends can't communicate until they are both paying attention to each other.

Happy

Angry

Sad

Figure 2 Your hands, face, and the way you stand change to express different moods and feelings.

Body Language

Could a friend tell just by looking at you after a game if your team won or lost? Your friend may know from your body language. **Body language** is a way of communicating by using the look on your face, the action of your hands, and the way you stand.

Here are three ways your body communicates:

- **The Look on Your Face** People who are happy often smile. People who have wide eyes and arched eyebrows may be showing that they are surprised. People who are gritting their teeth and scowling may be angry. People who are tired may have trouble keeping their eyes open.

- **The Action of Your Hands** People who are clenching their fists may be angry. People who are clapping may be happy or excited. Someone who is putting a hand around an ear may want you to speak louder. People sometimes put their face in their hands when they are frustrated.

- **The Way You Stand** People who feel confident may stand up straight and hold their head up. People who feel sad may slouch and hang their head.

We communicate best when our words and body language express the same information. Sometimes, a person's body language and words send different messages. If a person scowls, grits her teeth, and yells, "I'm fine!" you may wonder what she really means. If you get a mixed message, ask the person to explain it to you. ⭐ 7.E; 10

Behavior

Your behavior is also a method of communication. Your **behavior** is how you choose to act. An important word in this definition is *choose*. You are responsible for choosing your behavior. You have the ability to respond to most situations in many ways, so choose your behavior wisely.

Your behavior tells people a lot about you and your feelings. For example, when you take out the trash without being asked, you send the message that you care about your family and are responsible. Good behavior helps build good relationships.

⭐ 10.A

Kinds of Behavior

There are three basic kinds of behavior:

- Passive behavior is not acting on your thoughts, feelings, or beliefs. For example, not speaking up when something is wrong is passive behavior.

- Assertive behavior is acting on your thoughts, feelings, or beliefs in a way that is honest, respectful, and not harmful to anyone. For example, respectfully speaking up when something is wrong is assertive behavior.

- Aggressive behavior is acting on your thoughts, feelings, or beliefs in a way that is not respectful to those who have different thoughts, feelings, or beliefs. For example, pushing someone who upsets you is aggressive behavior.

Assertive behavior is often the best choice for communicating respect and understanding. Assertiveness lets people know what is important to you. It also respects what is important to others.

⭐ 10.A; 10.B; 10.C

LIFE SKILLS ACTIVITY

COMMUNICATING EFFECTIVELY

Role-play using assertive behavior in the following scenarios:

- Someone interrupts you while you are trying to explain your project idea.

- A waiter brings you the wrong food.

- Your friend asks you to let him cut in line.

Figure 3 Every situation has a range of possible responses. Assertive behavior is often an effective choice.

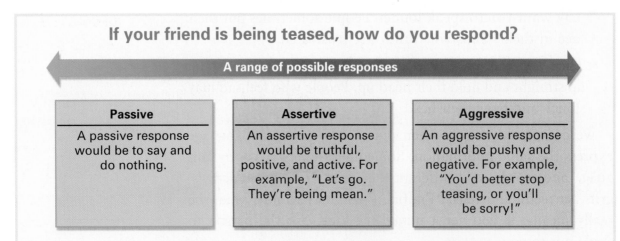

If your friend is being teased, how do you respond?

A range of possible responses

Passive	Assertive	Aggressive
A passive response would be to say and do nothing.	An assertive response would be truthful, positive, and active. For example, "Let's go. They're being mean."	An aggressive response would be pushy and negative. For example, "You'd better stop teasing, or you'll be sorry!"

Empathy

Empathy (EM puh thee) is a way to improve communication and relationships. **Empathy** is understanding and sharing another person's feelings. You can learn about another's feelings by listening carefully and noticing body language. Also pay attention to the person's behavior. If you get a sense that a person is having strong feelings, you may want to check it out with him or her. For example, if you are talking with a new student in your school who seems afraid, try asking, "Is it scary to be in a new school?" Try to imagine what that would feel like. You won't feel exactly what the other person is feeling. But understanding another person's feelings helps you both communicate better. ✪ 10.A

Tolerance

Some of your relationships will be with people who do not think, believe, or act in the same way you do. **Tolerance** (TAHL uhr uhns) is the ability to put differences aside and accept people as they are. Tolerance helps us work together and share our skills. You can show tolerance by

- listening carefully to many points of view

- being respectful, even when you don't agree with someone

- looking past differences to see what people have in common
  ✪ 10.A; 10.B

Figure 4 A person with a broken arm might have trouble carrying books or a lunch tray. Empathy can help you understand and help that person.

🔲 **internet** connect ▤

www.scilinks.org/health
Topic: Communication Skills
HealthLinks code: HD4022

HEA|TH Maintained by the
LINKS℠ National Science
        Teachers Association

Lesson Review

Using Vocabulary

1. Identify three forms of body language. ✪ 7.E; 10.A

Understanding Concepts

2. Explain how to show empathy. ✪ 7.E; 10.A

3. List six good speaking skills. ✪ 10.A

4. List six good listening skills.

5. Identify three ways to show tolerance. ✪ 10.B

Critical Thinking

6. **Applying Concepts** Raj sees a sixth-grade boy push a first grader out of a school bus seat so that he can sit there. The first grader is sad but does not do anything. Raj is angry. What would be an example of an assertive response from Raj? What kinds of behaviors do the other two students show? ✪ 10.B

Family Relationships

Last summer, Gustavo's grandfather taught Gustavo how to make toasted cheese sandwiches, fix a bike chain, and tell when tomatoes in the garden are ripe. Last Saturday, Gustavo helped his younger brother, Damian, fix his bike chain. Then, they washed up and made lunch.

Like Gustavo, you may learn and teach in your family relationships. Your family teaches you your language and your values and teaches you how to get along as part of a group. Family members should care for and respect each other. But they don't always agree. Family members sometimes disagree and respond differently to problems. The members of a family have different roles, and every role is important. But keeping family relationships healthy is everybody's job. ★ 7.A

Kinds of Families

There are many kinds of families. Some families have two parents. Some families have one parent. Couples can be a family without having children. New families are made when a person who has been married before gets married to someone else. The new couple and all of their children form a *blended family*. *Extended families* can include grandparents, aunts, uncles, and cousins.

What You'll Do

- **Describe** five kinds of families. ★ 7.A

- **Explain** the roles of children and adults in families. ★ 7.A

- **Explain** why children's roles may be different in different families. ★ 7.A

- **Describe** six ways you can help your family function smoothly. ★ 7.A; 7.E

- **Identify** three ways to show support and five ways to show affection in a family. ★ 10.A; 10.D

Terms to Learn

- support
- affection

Start Off
Write

How do people in families care for each other?

Roles

Running a household is a lot of work. So everyone in a family has a role to play, and everyone's role is important. Adults make rules and make sure everyone is safe. They are responsible for providing the family with the basic things a family needs, such as food and housing. They teach children values and help them learn to be responsible.

Children's roles change over time. Your role in your family has probably changed as you have gotten older and have learned to do more. Right now, you probably have chores such as helping to do the dishes or laundry. Your role in your family will probably continue to change as your family's needs change and as you grow older and more responsible. ★ 7.A; 7.E

Health Journal

In your Health Journal, keep track of the things you do to help your family. List the roles you have. Write down the roles you would like to have. How can you add those roles?

Different Families, Different Roles

Different families have different needs. So, the roles for both children and adults can vary from family to family. Your role in your family may be very different from the roles your friends have in their families. Your parents may give you different jobs to do than your friends have. Each family is organized around its needs. For example, children whose parents both work outside the home may have more jobs around the house than other children do. If a friend has a pet or a yard and you do not, your friend may have responsibilities for those things that you don't have. ★ 7.A; 7.E

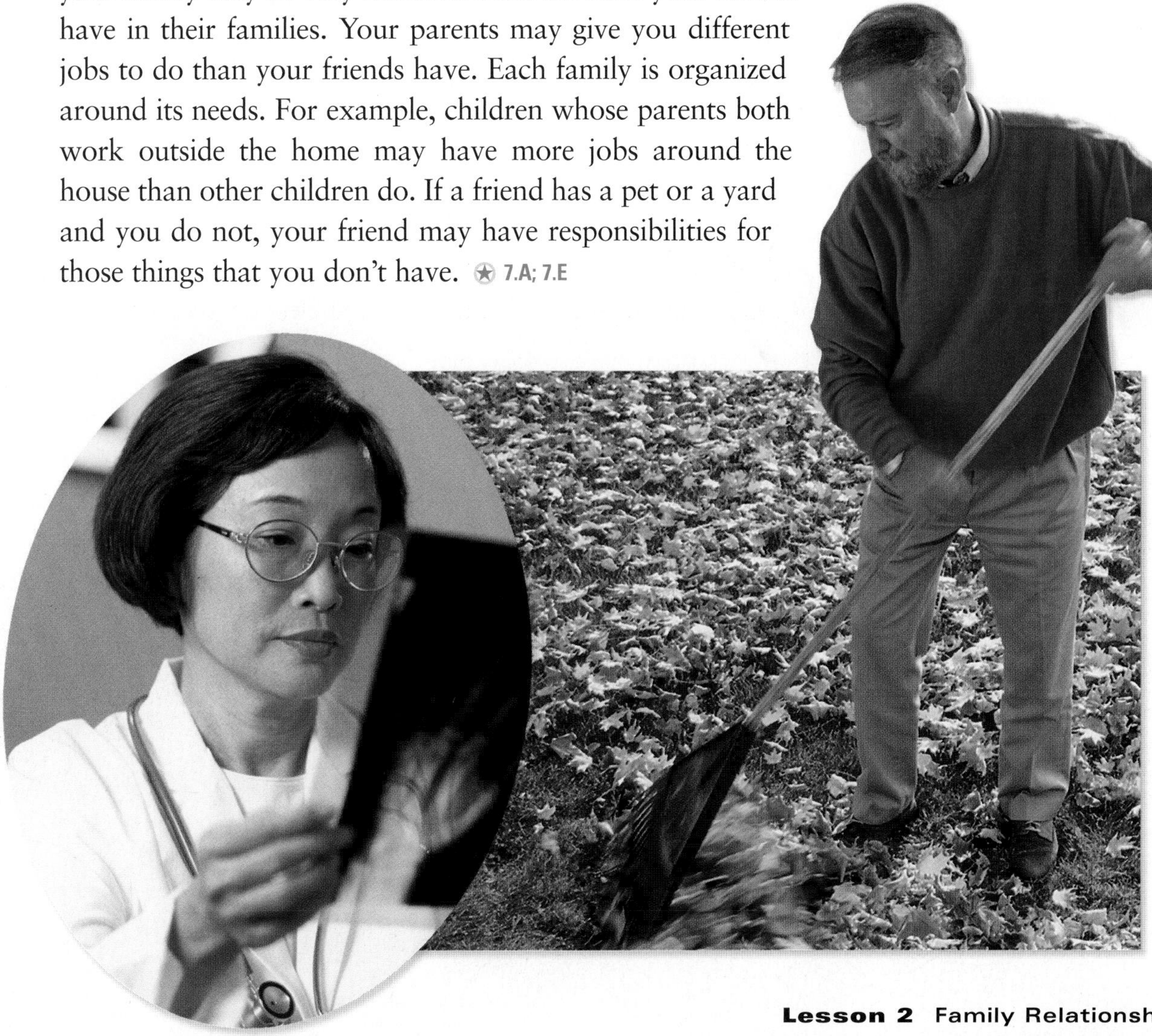

Figure 5 Children and adults have different responsibilities in families. But everyone's responsibilities are important.

Functioning Smoothly

The way you behave in your family affects the other members. For a family to function smoothly, all members have to care about the others and take their roles seriously.

How can you help your family function smoothly?

- Show respect for others in your family by politely asking for things or telling them your ideas.
- Tell adult family members about problems you see. For example, if your older sister drives the car dangerously, tell your parents. Your sister may be upset you told, but you may prevent her from hurting herself or others.
- Help your brothers and sisters. For example, offer to help a younger brother or sister with schoolwork or a project.
- Do your chores without being reminded.
- Be sensitive to others' needs and feelings.
- Spend time having fun and relaxing with your family.

The members of your family are individuals. They will not always think or act exactly alike. Appreciating the differences in each other strengthens your family. ✪ 7.A; 7.E; 10.A

Figure 6 Supporting your family can include helping a brother or sister.

Supporting Each Other

Adults provide most of the support for a family by making sure the family has food, clothing, housing, and leadership. But you can give some support, too. **Support** is helping when help is needed. You can support your family by

- being a good listener
- showing your brothers and sisters that you care about their concerns and activities
- taking part in family events, traditions, and celebrations
  ⭐ 7.E

Figure 7 Supporting family members is one way to keep your family strong.

Showing Affection

Showing affection helps family members care for each other. **Affection** is a feeling of liking or fondness. When you show your family members that you feel affection and love for them, you help them know they are valuable to you. You can tell them in person that you love them, or you can express your feelings in writing. You can show your love by treating them the way you would like to be treated. Your relationship with your family is probably the most important bond you have. Showing your family members that you love them lets them know how important they are to you. ⭐ 10.D

Lesson Review

Using Vocabulary

1. What is support? What are three ways you can support your family? ⭐ 10.A; 10.D

Understanding Concepts

2. Describe five kinds of families. ⭐ 7.A

3. List five ways of showing love and affection to your family. ⭐ 10.D

4. Identify six ways you can help your family function smoothly. ⭐ 7.E; 10.A; 10.D

5. Why does the role of children vary from family to family? ⭐ 7.A

Critical Thinking

6. Making Inferences Juan's responsibilities at home include vacuuming, taking out the trash, and making his bed. Laura's responsibilities include setting rules and providing for the health and safety of her family. What can you infer about Juan and Laura? ⭐ 7.E

Facing Family Problems

Katie's older brother, Allen, argues with their stepfather almost every day. Lately, the arguments are getting louder. Katie would like the shouting to stop.

What You'll Do

- **List** five difficult changes that families face. ⭐ 7.A
- **Describe** two ways to settle a minor family conflict. ⭐ 7.C; 7.E; 9.A
- **Describe** two serious problems that families face. ⭐ 7.A
- **Identify** a way to cope with serious problems. ⭐ 7.E; 9.A; 9.B; 11.A

Terms to Learn

- family conflict
- abuse
- neglect

Start Off *Write*

What is a good way to cope with a difficult change?

Katie's family has a problem, but her family is not alone. Every family has problems sometimes. Dealing with problems in your family is a skill you can learn. Often, identifying a minor problem early can help manage the problem and keep it from becoming a major problem later. Families can work through many kinds of problems together. Major problems may require help from outside the family.

Difficult Changes

Some problems arise because of changes in a family. The illness or death of a family member, moving to a new city, losing a job, and divorce can all disrupt a family. After these difficult changes happen, family members may feel sad or angry.

One of the best ways to cope with difficult changes is to talk about them. Talking about how these changes affect each member of a family can help the family see the problem from everybody's viewpoint. Sometimes, it helps to learn that other people feel the way you feel. Or it may help to learn that other people have feelings you didn't know they had. ⭐ 7.A; 9.A

Figure 8 One of the best ways to cope with problems and stress is to address them as soon as possible.

Family Conflicts

Another kind of problem that families face is a family conflict. A **family conflict** is any clash of ideas or interests within a family. Conflicts can be major or minor. Major conflicts include loud arguments, such as the ones between Allen and his stepfather. Major conflicts and adult conflicts are not your responsibility and should be handled by adults. But you can learn to work on minor conflicts you may have with your brothers and sisters.

To manage a minor conflict, use the following steps:

1. Allow time for each person in a conflict to calm down.

2. Then, allow each person in the conflict to tell his or her point of view. Remind each person in the conflict to practice good listening skills.

3. After everyone has spoken, identify the problems.

4. Try to find an answer everyone can agree on.

⭐ 7.C; 7.E; 9.B, 10.B; 10.C

Myth: Some families never have problems.

Fact: All families go through times of change and difficulty.

Family Meetings

Family meetings can also help you work on problems and prevent conflicts. Family meetings give family members time to meet and speak together. At family meetings, everyone should act and speak respectfully and should listen carefully. It may be helpful for someone to write down a list of things to talk about so that the meeting can stay on track. A list also helps keep the meeting short. If you meet regularly, your family can follow up on problems that were brought up at earlier meetings to see if the problems are being resolved. ⭐ 7.C; 7.E; 9.B, 10.B

Figure 9 Family meetings can help keep conflicts from growing into bigger problems.

Figure 10 Talking with counselors can help people cope with serious problems.

Serious Problems

Not all problems are minor. Anytime a problem puts someone in danger, the problem is major and serious. Abuse (uh BYOOS) and neglect (ni GLECKT) are two examples of serious problems.

- **Abuse** is treating someone in a harmful or offensive way physically, emotionally, or sexually. Abuse is always wrong.

- **Neglect** is the failure of a parent or other responsible adult to provide a child basic care, such as food, clothing, or shelter. Neglect is always wrong.

Abuse and neglect can cause serious harm or death. All types of abuse and neglect are dangerous problems that must be stopped as soon as possible. ⭐ 9.B

Coping with Serious Problems

Living in a household with abuse or neglect is hard. Sometimes, victims of abuse think that they are the reason someone is abusive. Some victims believe they are neglected or abused because they don't deserve to be treated well. But victims never cause people to become abusive. Furthermore, a young person alone probably cannot stop a person from behaving that way. So, it is important for victims of abuse to get help. Perhaps they can talk to another member of their family about the problem. If they cannot talk to someone in their family, they can talk to a guidance counselor or one of their teachers. School officials know how to get students in touch with people who help victims of abuse. ⭐ 7.G; 9.A; 9.B; 11.A

SOCIAL STUDIES ACTIVITY

What resources in your community help families with their problems? Use the library or Internet to research resources in your community for various kinds of family problems. Write a report about one of the agencies you learn about and the kinds of services it provides.
⭐ 9.B

Getting Help

Help is available for people who have to cope with serious problems. Victims of abuse and neglect can live in safety, but only if the people who can help know about the problem. If you or someone you know has a serious problem, tell a trusted adult as soon as possible. A list of people who can help is included below.

⭐ 11.A

Figure 11 A lot of people are ready to help.

We're Here to Help

Guidance

Abuse and neglect are serious problems. One of the best ways to handle serious problems is to talk about them with a trusted adult, such as a(n):

- adult family member
- teacher
- coach
- guidance counselor
- neighbor
- youth group leader
- religious leader
- doctor or nurse
- social worker
- police officer
- firefighter

Any of these people can help you. If the first person you tell doesn't help you, keep trying until someone does.

Lesson Review

Using Vocabulary

1. What is family conflict? ⭐ 7.A

Understanding Concepts

2. Identify two ways to settle a minor family conflict. ⭐ 7.C; 7.E; 9.A

3. Describe two serious problems that families face. ⭐ 7.A; 9.B

4. What are five difficult changes that families face? ⭐ 7.A

5. Identify a way to cope with abuse or neglect in a family. ⭐ 7.B; 7.E; 9.B; 11.A

Critical Thinking

6. **Identifying Relationships** Why is it a good idea to turn off radios and televisions during a family meeting? ⭐ 11.E

7. **Making Good Decisions** When Pat's grandfather went into the hospital, Pat felt scared. What might Pat do to cope? ⭐ 9.A; 11.A

🔲 **internet** connect

www.scilinks.org/health
Topic: Abuse and Violence
HealthLinks code: HD4003

HEALTH LINKS Maintained by the National Science Teachers Association

Friendship

What You'll Do

- **List** six questions that can help you identify people who may make good friends. ⭐ 7.A
- **List** three questions that can help you identify bad relationships. ⭐ 7.A
- **Identify** two benefits of positive peer pressure. ⭐ 7.A

Terms to Learn

- friendship

Start Off
Write

Is peer pressure always bad? Explain your answer. ⭐ 7.A

> Emilia has been lonely since she moved 6 months ago. She misses her old school and her old home. But mostly she misses her friends. Making new friends is harder than she thought it would be.

Like Emilia, you would probably miss your friends if you moved away. Besides your family, your friends are probably the most important people in your life. So, keeping friendships healthy is important, too. A **friendship** is a relationship between people who enjoy being together and who care about each other. The number of friends that you have is not important. It is important that the friends you do have help keep you healthy and safe.

Friendship and Character

Good friends like each other and treat each other well. Friends enjoy keeping each other company. They use good communication skills to talk about ideas and goals. And by doing activities together, they learn new things and grow closer.

Good friends also demonstrate good character. They look out for one another's safety. They know what is important to each other. They share or respect each other's beliefs and values. They are friends not only when friendship is easy. They are dependable and loyal during difficult times, too. ⭐ 6.A; 7.A

Figure 12 Good friends like being together and doing things together.

Making Friends

Friends who like and care about you can help you stay safe and healthy. But how do you meet people who can become good friends? Sometimes, people meet and become friends because they live near each other or are in classes together. Sometimes, people meet friends through other friends. One of the best ways to meet friends is to take part in projects and activities at school or in your community. By taking part in activities you enjoy, you can meet other people who enjoy those activities, too.

After you meet someone, how can you tell if that person may make a good friend for you? Ask yourself the following questions:

- Does this person share or respect my values?
- Do I enjoy being with this person?
- Does this person accept me and like me?
- Do my parents trust this person?
- Does this person have qualities that I think are important?
- Will this person and I have a chance to spend time together?

If the answer to each of these questions is yes, the person is likely to be a good friend to you. If you answer no to some of these questions, think about finding other people to be friends with. ✷ 6.A; 7.A

Health Journal

Imagine that a person moves into your neighborhood and will be going to your school. In your Health Journal, write how he or she could make friends there. What teams, clubs, and organizations might help this person make friends?

Figure 13 One way to meet new friends is to take part in activities.

TABLE 1 A Summary of Refusal Skills

Avoid dangerous situations.

Say "No," verbally and with body language.

Stand your ground!

Stay focused on the issue.

Walk away from unhealthy situations.

Bad Relationships

Some relationships are not good. How can you spot a bad relationship? One feature of most bad relationships is negative peer pressure. *Negative peer pressure* is encouragement to do things that could cause harm. The following questions can help you identify bad relationships:

- Does this person hurt me or threaten to hurt me?

- Does this person try to control me, keep me away from other friends, or ask me to hurt others?

- Does this person encourage me to act against my values?

If you answered yes to any of these questions about a relationship, talk to your parents so that they can help you resolve the problem. Using the refusal skills in the table above can also help you stay safe in relationships and resist negative peer pressure.

⭐ 7.A; 7.B; 7.E

STUDY TIP *for better reading*

Organizing Information
Make a list of refusal skills. For each refusal skill, list a situation in which you would use that skill.

Hands-on ACTIVITY

FRIENDSHIP SURVEY

1. Create a survey about friendship. Include questions such as the following:
   - What qualities do you value in your friends?
   - How do your friends help keep you healthy?

2. Gather answers for each question. Record all of the answers without using names.

3. For each question create a bar graph that shows the range of answers given.

Analysis

1. Which answers were given most often?

2. Which answers were given least often?

3. What did this survey teach you about friendships?

Positive Peer Pressure

Not all peer pressure is negative. You can create positive peer pressure by showing good character. *Positive peer pressure* is encouragement to stick to values and achieve goals. Positive peer pressure is helpful in two ways. First, it can help friends challenge each other to do their best.

Using positive peer pressure can also keep a risky situation from resulting in a bad choice. Speak up if you think a friend has made a bad decision or an unhealthy choice. Help him or her make a better one. Sometimes, it takes an idea from only one person to help another be strong and stay on track. For example, if a friend decides to pick on someone, tell him or her that teasing is wrong. Being honest takes courage. But honesty can be the most important part of friendship. ⭐ 5.H; 7.E

MAKING GOOD DECISIONS

Role play using positive peer pressure to help in the following scenes. You discover that your friend

- has stolen candy from a store
- is preparing to cheat on an upcoming test
- is planning to sneak into a movie without paying

Figure 14 Helping a friend study is one example of positive peer pressure.

Lesson Review

Using Vocabulary

1. What is friendship? ⭐ 7.A

Understanding Concepts

2. List six questions that can help you identify good friends. ⭐ 7.A

3. List three questions that can help identify bad relationships. ⭐ 7.A

4. Explain two benefits of positive peer pressure. ⭐ 6.A

Critical Thinking

5. Applying Concepts Yolanda loves playing soccer, but she wants to quit the soccer team because she is not allowed to play every minute of every game. What could Yolanda's friends say to her about her decision to quit the team? ⭐ 7.E

Improving Friendships

Becky likes group projects. She enjoys meeting new people. She likes planning. She enjoys learning new skills. Most of all, Becky likes becoming better friends with people by working together.

How can working together on a project help make friendships stronger? When you work together, you learn the importance of good communication, and you learn to trust people's strengths. Working together can help you learn to get along, take charge, and respect the people around you.

Showing Respect

Friends often have many things in common. But friends are still individual people who have their own ideas and goals. Sometimes, friends disagree. Accepting the differences in your friends is a way to show them that you respect them and like them for who they really are, not because they are just like you.

Respect can also help you learn about people from other backgrounds and cultures. The world is large, and there are many ways of living in it. Learning to appreciate differences in people and cultures helps you respect people from many backgrounds. By respecting and understanding the views of people from many backgrounds, you can learn to look at the world in new ways. Understanding the world from many points of view can help you find more ways to solve problems. ✪ 6.A; 7.B; 10.A

What You'll Do

- **Explain** two benefits of respecting people. ✪ 10.A
- **Describe** three ways you can lead by example. ✪ 10.A
- **Explain** how cooperation helps you reach goals. ✪ 7.A
- **Explain** the difference between friendship and popularity. ✪ 7.A

Terms to Learn

- leadership
- cooperation

Start Off
Write

How can you make good friendships even better?

Figure 15 Respecting differences among your peers opens your world to different cultures and ideas.

Showing Leadership

Sometimes, being a good friend means you have to be a leader. **Leadership** is guiding others in a responsible way. Leadership is not "bossing people around." Good leaders set a good example for others to follow whenever an example is needed.

You can be a leader by

- using refusal skills to show others how to handle negative peer pressure
- demonstrating respect
- developing a plan to solve a problem

Leadership takes practice. The more chances you have to practice being a leader, the better leader you will become. ⭐ 10.A

Myth: It's easy to be a leader because everyone else does the work.

Fact: Good leadership is hard work.

Leading Projects

Most projects need a good leader. Project leaders first break a big project into smaller jobs. Then, they manage the smaller parts so that all the work gets done.

For example, if you wanted to lead a car wash for a fundraiser, you may break the project into smaller jobs such as advertising, washing, and collecting money. After you have identified the jobs in a project, you can make a plan to get the jobs done in order. You could help people as they work on the project, show people how to work together, and thank them when the project is over. ⭐ 10.A

(**Figure 16**) Some Jobs in a Car Wash

Advertising   Washing   Collecting money

Working Together

Even if a project has a great leader, the work will not get done unless people agree to work together. **Cooperation** (koh AHP uhr AY shuhn) is working with others to reach a goal. Sharing the work among many people allows each person to gain from other people's skills. For example, when working on a car wash, you may find that one person is good at making posters and another likes keeping track of money. Both skills are valuable, so both people are important to the goal. And both people can learn from each other. Cooperation is a skill that does more than get jobs done. It helps you learn and grow socially. ✪ 7.E; 10.A

Cooperating in Friendships

Friendships gain from cooperation, too. You and your friends have skills and talents that you can use to help each other. For example, you can help each other study for classes, learn the lines of a play, or practice a sport. Friends who work together can reach larger goals by helping each other than either friend could reach alone.

Cooperation helps make a friendship stronger by showing your friends that you want them to succeed. It shows that you are willing to spend time and effort to help them reach their goals. ✪ 7.A

Figure 17 Cooperation helps get jobs done faster and helps you learn and grow.

Supporting Your Friends

Sticking to your values can be hard when you think you are alone. Doing what is right is often easier if you know that your friends will support you even if others do not. How can you and your friends support each other? You can talk together regularly about decisions you are making. You can also offer suggestions when friends ask for help. And you can stand by your friends when they say no to negative peer pressure.

Sticking to your values may not always make you popular. Every day, you get the message that being popular is important. And being liked does feel good. But popularity is often based on things you cannot control. Friendship is based on values and respect. The support of one good friend is more valuable than being popular. Popularity can change quickly. But a good friend will support you even during hard times, when you need help the most. ✪ 10.A; 10.C

Teen: My best friend is starting to hang out with some people who ask her to lie to her parents about where she is going and what she is doing. How can I be a good friend to her?

Expert: Stick to your values, and encourage your friend to stick to hers, too. Encourage your friend to be honest with her parents and with you. Tell her that you care about her and are concerned for her safety.

Lesson Review

Using Vocabulary

1. What is leadership? List three ways you can lead by example. ✪ 7.A; 10.A

Understanding Concepts

2. Explain the difference between friendship and popularity. ✪ 7.A

3. Explain how cooperation helps you reach goals. ✪ 7.A; 10.A

4. Explain two benefits of respect. ✪ 6.A

Critical Thinking

5. Identifying Relationships How do cooperation and leadership help solve problems? Can you have cooperation without leadership? Can you have leadership without cooperation? Explain your answers. ✪ 7.A; 10.A

Healthy Affection

Showing your friends that you like them is an important part of friendship. Choosing healthy ways to show your friends that you like them helps you strengthen your friendships.

What You'll Do

- **Describe** eight healthy ways to show affection to friends. ⊛ 10.D

Terms to Learn

- affection
- abstinence

Start Off Write

What are three ways you could show affection to a friend in the hospital?

Affection is a feeling of liking or fondness. People who feel affection for one another can show it in many ways. The ways people show affection vary from person to person and from culture to culture.

Showing Affection

There are many healthy ways for you to show affection for your friends, such as

- smiling or speaking cheerfully
- complimenting
- telling the person how much you like his or her company
- sending a kind card or letter
- making a kind phone call
- patting your friend on the back
- showing empathy

When you show affection, make sure your message is clear, understood, and respectful. Never offer affection in a way that is unwelcome. For example, some people don't want to be touched. Don't touch them, even if you think a hug would show affection. Respecting their choice not to be touched also shows you care about them. ⊛ 10.D

Figure 19 A nice card is one way to show someone that you care.

Choosing Abstinence

Another way to show affection respectfully is to choose sexual abstinence (AB stuh nuhns). **Abstinence** is refusing to take part in an activity that puts your health or the health of others at risk. For example, abstinence from smoking helps protect your health and the health of the people around you. Abstinence from sexual activity prevents pregnancy and keeps you safe from some diseases. Teens who choose sexual abstinence live safer, healthier lives.
⭐ 5.I

Figure 20 Real friends show affection respectfully.

Refusal Skills

You may face negative peer pressure to begin sexual activity. Using the refusal skills listed below will help you maintain abstinence.

- Avoid situations that put you at risk.
- Say "No!" whenever you need to.
- Stand your ground.
- Stay focused on the issue.
- Walk away if someone asks you to do anything you think is risky or wrong.

Support your friends in their abstinence, too. Support shows that you care. ⭐ 11.B

Myth: Your behavior is controlled by other people.

Fact: You are responsible for choosing your behavior.

Lesson Review

Using Vocabulary

1. What is affection? ⭐ 10.D

2. Define *abstinence.* ⭐ 5.I; 10.D

Understanding Concepts

3. Describe eight healthy ways to show affection. ⭐ 10.D

4. John's dog has died of old age. What can Sarah do to show John that she cares about his feelings? ⭐ 10.A; 10.E

Critical Thinking

5. Identifying Relationships Negative peer pressure can challenge your decision to choose abstinence. How can positive peer pressure help you maintain abstinence? ⭐ 5.I; 11.C

☑ **internet** connect

www.scilinks.org/health

Topic: Abstinence

HealthLinks code: HD4002

HEALTH LINKS. Maintained by the National Science Teachers Association

5 CHAPTER REVIEW

Chapter Summary

■ Healthy relationships require good communication skills and healthy behavior. ■ Working together as a family requires taking roles seriously. ■ When the family has problems, the family should work on those problems. ■ Serious problems should be reported to a trusted adult as soon as possible. ■ Positive friendships are healthy relationships between people who have similar interests and values. Friends support each other. They also show each other cooperation and leadership. ■ Bad relationships are risky. ■ Healthy relationships benefit from sharing affection. ■ Sexual abstinence is the only sure way to avoid pregnancy and some diseases.

Using Vocabulary

For each pair of terms, describe how the meanings of the terms differ.

1 empathy/tolerance

2 support/neglect

For each sentence, fill in the blank with the proper word from the word bank provided below.

abstinence	body language
support	leadership
cooperation	behavior
friendship	

3 The way you choose to act is called your ___.

4 ___ means not taking part in unsafe behavior.

5 Offering guidance to others in an organized, responsible way shows ___.

6 Working together toward a goal and using the strengths of each person to reach that goal requires ___.

7 You send messages with your face, hands, and the way you stand through ___.

8 ___ is giving help when help is needed.

Understanding Concepts

9 Distinguish between passive, aggressive, and assertive behavior. ⭐ 10

10 Explain the roles of children and adults in families. ⭐ 7.A

11 What is a blended family? ⭐ 7.A

12 Describe some steps that can help manage a small conflict. ⭐ 7.C

13 Describe the benefits of abstinence from sexual activity. ⭐ 5.I

14 How can you resist negative peer pressure? ⭐ 7.B

15 How can empathy and tolerance help relationships? ⭐ 10.A

16 Describe how you can show your family your love. ⭐ 10.D

17 Why may your friend's role in his or her family differ from your role in yours? ⭐ 9.A

18 Describe a way to cope with a serious problem, such as abuse or neglect. ⭐ 9.B

19 Why does your role in your family change over time? ⭐ 7.A

20 What are two difficult changes that families face? ⭐ 9.B

Critical Thinking

Applying Concepts

21 Kevin likes belonging to the school band and playing the trumpet. But Kevin has decided to quit playing his trumpet because the director scolded him for not practicing. How can Kevin's friends use positive peer pressure to help him? ⭐ 10.B

22 Because of a disagreement, Beth's brother and sister are not talking to each other. They each ask Beth to join them in not speaking to the other person. Describe a way Beth can handle this situation. ⭐ 9.A

23 Malik has decided to lead the bake sale for his class fundraiser. How may Malik provide good leadership for this project? ⭐ 7.E

24 Bart was frustrated by his math homework. He became very angry and wanted to yell and throw his book. Instead of throwing his book, he called his friend Melissa and asked for help. What kind of behavior did Bart originally want to use? What kind did he choose instead? ⭐ 10.C

Making Good Decisions

25 Emily's friend Karen called Emily on the phone to invite her over. Karen's voice sounded happy on the phone. When Emily got to Karen's house, Karen still sounded happy, but she was slouching in her chair and had a worried look on her face. Emily was confused about how Karen was feeling. What could Emily do to help her understand how Karen was really feeling? ⭐ 7.E; 10.A

26 Calvin recently moved to a new town and has met another student, Darnell. Darnell seemed like a good friend at first, but now he makes fun of Calvin and tells him not to spend time with any of his other friends. What should Calvin do? ⭐ 10.B

27 Helene tried out for a part in a play, but she did not get the part. Describe passive, assertive, and aggressive responses to this situation. ⭐ 7.C

Interpreting Graphics

Two Examples of Body Language

Example A	Example B
hands on hips	hands clapping
face frowning, head hanging down	face smiling
body slouching	standing tall

Use the table above to answer questions 28–29.

28 What message do you read from the information in example A?

29 What message do you read from the information in example B?

Reading Checkup

Take a minute to review your answers to the Health IQ questions at the beginning of this chapter. How has reading this chapter improved your Health IQ?

Communicating Effectively

Have you ever been in a bad situation that was made worse because of poor communication? Or maybe you have difficulty understanding others or being understood. You can avoid misunderstandings by expressing your feelings in a healthy way, which is communicating effectively. Complete the following activity to develop effective communication skills.

Tony and Casey's Conflict

ACT 1

Setting the Scene

Tony and Casey have a lawn-mowing business. On the weekends, their neighbors pay them to mow and edge their lawns as well as rake leaves, pull weeds, and prune bushes. Lately, Tony has been annoyed with Casey because Tony doesn't feel like Casey takes care of their tools. Casey never cleans the tools after he uses them and some of them are starting to rust. Tony wants to talk with Casey, but he doesn't want to hurt their friendship.

The 4 Steps of Communicating Effectively

1. Express yourself calmly and clearly.
2. Choose your words carefully.
3. Use open body language.
4. Use active listening.

Guided Practice

Practice with a Friend

Form a group of three. Have one person play the role of Tony and another person play the role of Casey. Have the third person be an observer. Walking through each of the four steps of communicating effectively, role-play Tony telling Casey what is bothering him. The observer will take notes, which will include observations about what the people playing Tony and Casey did well and suggestions of ways to improve. Stop after each step to evaluate the process. ★ 7.E; 10.A

Independent Practice

Check Yourself

After you have completed the guided practice, go through Act 1 again without stopping at each step. Answer the questions below to review what you did.

1. Why should Tony choose his words carefully? ⊛ 7.E

2. What kind of body language should Casey use when listening to Tony? Give some examples. ⊛ 7.E

3. How can Casey and Tony resolve their conflict? Explain your answer. ⊛ 7.C

4. Describe a time when you had a conflict with one of your friends. In what ways did you communicate effectively? How could you have improved the way you communicated?

On Your Own

The next weekend, Tony and Casey get a call from one of their neighbors. The neighbor is mad because Tony and Casey forgot to pull the weeds in her yard. Write a short story about how Tony and Casey could use the four steps of communicating effectively to deal with the angry neighbor.

Coping with Conflict and Stress

Check out
Current Health
articles related to this chapter by
visiting **go.hrw.com**. Just type in
the keyword **HD4CH06**.

> **"I** had a lot going on at **school**. I was on the **soccer** team and the **swimming** team. I was also acting in the **school play**. On top of all that, I was taking some really hard classes. One day, I started having really bad headaches. I started getting them every day. When I went to the doctor, she said that my headaches might be caused by stress. **"**

PRE-READING

Answer the following true/false questions to find out what you already know about stress and conflict. When you've finished this chapter, you'll have the opportunity to change your answers based on what you've learned.

1. Stress and conflict are the same thing. ✪ 10.F

2. Conflict usually happens only at school.

3. Physical activity is a good way to relieve stress. ✪ 1.F; 10.G

4. Stress causes only emotional problems and never causes physical problems. ✪ 10.F; 10.G

5. Some stressful situations can be avoided.

6. Talking with someone about stress can relieve stress. ✪ 1.H

7. Anger always leads to violence.

8. Mediation means ignoring a problem until it goes away. ✪ 7.C

9. If you are mad at someone, it is always best to confront the person immediately.

10. Anger is usually the result of other emotions, such as frustration or fear.

11. Telling on others is always wrong.

12. A conflict will end however it ends. There is nothing you can do to change the outcome. ✪ 5.G

13. A person can be in conflict with himself or herself.

14. Compromise and collaboration are the same thing. ✪ 5.G; 7.C

ANSWERS: 1. false; 2. false; 3. true; 4. false; 5. true; 6. true; 7. false; 8. false; 9. false; 10. true; 11. false; 12. false; 13. true; 14. false

What Is Conflict?

No matter who you are, you have experienced conflict at some point in your life. Everyone's idea of conflict is different. But what is conflict really?

Conflict is any situation in which ideas or interests go against one another. Conflict is not always bad. If conflicts are resolved in a healthy way, they can help us learn and grow. If conflicts are not solved, they can result in headaches, lack of sleep, emotional problems, and even violence. There are two kinds of conflict: internal conflict and external conflict.

Internal Conflict

Have you ever had a hard time deciding between two things? It may sound strange that a person can be in conflict with himself or herself. However, that is exactly what happens every time you have to decide between two or more things. Conflict with yourself is called **internal conflict.** Even simple decisions can create internal conflict. Often, the expectations of others, such as teachers, parents, and peers, can make simple internal conflicts more difficult. For this reason, it is very important to develop skills for making the right decisions as well as skills for solving conflicts. ⊛ 5.G; 6.A

What You'll Do

- **Explain** what conflict is. ⊛ 5.G; 6.A
- **Describe** the difference between internal conflict and external conflict. ⊛ 6.A

Terms to Learn

- conflict
- internal conflict
- external conflict

Start Off
Write

Can a person be in conflict with himself or herself? Explain.

Figure 1 You experience internal conflict whenever you choose between two things, such as studying or hanging out with friends.

External Conflict

At some point in your life, you have had an argument or disagreement with another person. Conflict that happens with another person or group of people is called **external conflict.** External conflict can happen almost anywhere. You can experience external conflict at school, in your community, or even at home. Conflict often arises between people and groups because of different values and beliefs. We have all seen how external conflict can arise between nations and political groups. However, the conflicts that affect us most are the ones that we encounter every day. These conflicts may include an argument between you and your parents, a fight with a classmate, or a disagreement with a friend over which movie to see. There can be many reasons for a conflict to exist. Some of these reasons may be good reasons. Some of these reasons may be bad reasons. However, most external conflicts can be solved with healthy, open, honest communication. ⊛ 5.G; 6.A; 7.C

Figure 2 External conflict can happen in many places, such as with a teacher at school.

Lesson Review

Using Vocabulary

1. What is conflict? ⊛ 5.G; 6.A

2. What is the difference between internal and external conflict? ⊛ 6.A

Understanding Concepts

3. What are some of the reasons that external conflict happens? What are some of the reasons that internal conflict happens? ⊛ 5.G; 6.A

Critical Thinking

4. Making Good Decisions Imagine that you are trying to decide whether to study or to go out with friends. How might the expectations of others make this decision more difficult? ⊛ 5.G; 6.A

5. Analyzing Ideas Which type of conflict do you think is more difficult to solve: internal conflict or external conflict? Explain. ⊛ 6.A

Managing Conflict

Have you ever found yourself in a conflict that seemed to come out of nowhere? Have you ever gone out of your way to avoid a conflict, only to find yourself in the conflict anyway?

What You'll Do

- **Explain** why the way that a person communicates in a conflict is important.
  ⭐ 7.C; 7.E; 10.A; 10.B; 10.C
- **Describe** strategies for resolving conflicts. ⭐ 7.C; 7.E
- **Describe** why it is sometimes important to avoid conflict. ⭐ 7.C

Terms to Learn

- empathy
- compromise
- collaboration

Start Off
Write

How can communication affect the outcome of a conflict?

Conflict is unavoidable. So, knowing how to manage conflict when it happens is important. The most important part of managing conflict is communication.

Communicating During Conflicts

Communication is the way in which people send and receive information. The way in which we communicate during conflict or even before conflict occurs is very important. In fact, communication can determine whether conflict will get resolved or will even start. If you speak loudly and aggressively during a conflict, solving the conflict will be more difficult. If you speak calmly and respectfully, the conflict is more likely to have a positive outcome. You need to be clear about your point. Saying what you mean is an important step toward solving a conflict. You should also be aware of the way you communicate without words. Your body language—the way that you stand, your facial gestures, and even eye contact—can send powerful messages. During conflicts, your body language can often be more important than words. By being careful about the way that you communicate, you can create positive outcomes to many of your conflicts. ⭐ 7.C; 7.E; 10.A; 10.B; 10.C

TABLE 1 Communicating During a Conflict			
Listen	**Relax**	**Speak calmly and clearly**	**Don't lose your temper**
Practice effective listening. Make sure you understand the other person's position.	Remain calm and relaxed. Breathe evenly.	Express yourself clearly. Avoid yelling or using hurtful language.	Keep your anger under control.

Resolving Conflicts

The longer a conflict continues, the worse it can get. The people in the conflict may get more and more upset. They may become less likely to work out a solution to the conflict. That is why it is important to address conflict when it arises and to work with everyone involved to reach a solution. This process is called conflict resolution. *Conflict resolution* (REZ oh LOO shuhn) is the process of finding a solution to a conflict with which everybody involved in the conflict agrees. If one person simply gets his or her way, then the conflict has not been resolved even though it may be over.

There are three ways that a conflict can end. The first and best is a win-win situation. In this type of situation, everyone involved in the conflict is pleased with the solution. In a win-lose situation, one side is pleased with the solution, but the other side is not. In a lose-lose situation, neither side is pleased with the outcome of the conflict.

✪ 5.H; 7.E; 10.B; 10.C

Empathy

To resolve a conflict, both sides must be willing to understand the other side's point of view. This understanding is called *empathy*. **Empathy** (EM puh thee) is the ability to understand or identify with the ideas or feelings of another person or group. Empathy doesn't mean always agreeing. It simply means that you attempt to "put yourself in others' shoes" and try to understand why others feel the way they do. Understanding why the other person or people feel a certain way can make it much easier to resolve a conflict. The more that each person in a conflict can understand the others, the more opportunities there will be to develop win-win solutions. When we focus only on our own feelings and desires, conflicts end in win-lose or lose-lose situations.

✪ 5.H; 7.C; 10.A; 10.B; 10.C

◄ win-win solution

► win-lose solution

◄ lose-lose solution

Figure 3 A conflict can end in several different ways. These ways include win–win situations, win–lose situations, and lose–lose situations.

Negotiation

When conflicts arise, finding a solution that makes both sides happy can be difficult. That is why it is important to discuss conflict and to work with others to reach a conclusion that is positive for everyone. To do this, the people involved talk about what they want, which things are most important to them, and what sacrifices they are willing to make. This process of give and take is called *negotiation*. Negotiation (NI goh shee AY shuhn) is the first step in resolving any conflict.

⍟ 5.G; 5.H; 7.C; 7.E; 10.A; 10.E

Compromise and Collaboration

When we negotiate to resolve conflict, we are usually trying to achieve one of two things: compromise or collaboration. **Compromise** (KAHM pruh MIEZ) is a solution to a conflict in which both sides give things to come to an agreement. For example, imagine two people are arguing over which toppings to get on their pizza. One person wants pepperoni. The other person wants green olives. A compromise would be deciding to order pepperoni this week and green olives next week.

Another way to resolve conflict is called *collaboration*. **Collaboration** (kuh LAB uh RAY shuhn) is a solution to a conflict in which both parties get what they want without having to give up anything important. Imagine the same two people in the pizza example above. Collaboration in that situation would be deciding to order a pizza that had both pepperoni and green olives on it. By working together to compromise or collaborate, the two parties in a conflict can resolve a conflict in a way that is positive for both sides. ⍟ 5.G; 5.H; 7.C; 7.E; 10.A; 10.E

LIFE SKILLS ACTIVITY

COMMUNICATING EFFECTIVELY

Choose a partner in your class. Together, make up a conflict that might occur between two friends. Choose who will play each part. Go through the steps needed to resolve the "conflict." Be careful to watch the way you communicate with one another, including your body language.

Figure 4 By using skills such as compromise or collaboration, you can resolve conflicts in a way that pleases everyone involved.

Walking Away

A final strategy for dealing with conflict is simply walking away from conflict. Sometimes you have to decide whether it is worth your time and energy to be in certain conflicts. This is often called "picking your battles." Believe it or not, some people actually like conflict. These people will work hard at keeping conflict around them. It is wise to avoid conflict with these people, because even if one conflict is resolved, another one will often quickly appear.

Walking away from conflict or "picking your battles" doesn't always mean avoiding conflict. There can be many reasons to walk away from a conflict. Sometimes, it is not the right place or time to deal with the conflict. In this case, you should try to resolve the conflict at a later time. For example, if you get into a conflict with a friend during lunch, it is probably not a good idea to talk about the conflict after you return to class. You may need to wait until after class to further discuss the problem.

Finally, many conflicts can lead to violence. It is important to know when a conflict might turn violent and to walk away from conflicts that could become violent.

⭐ 5.G; 5.H; 7.C; 10.B; 10.C; 11.B

STUDY TIP *for better reading*

Reviewing Information
When you have finished reading this lesson on managing conflict, write an outline that describes the different strategies for managing conflict.

Figure 5 Sometimes, it is smart to walk away from a conflict that is unnecessary or out of control.

Lesson Review

Using Vocabulary

1. What is empathy? ⭐ 10.A

Understanding Concepts

2. Why is the way that you communicate in a conflict important?
⭐ 7.C; 7.E; 10.A; 10.B; 10.C

3. Describe four strategies for resolving conflicts.
⭐ 7.C; 7.E; 10.A; 10.B; 10.C

4. Why is it important to avoid unnecessary conflict? ⭐ 5.G

Critical Thinking

5. Making Inferences If you can sometimes avoid unnecessary conflicts, why not simply avoid all conflicts? ⭐ 11.D

🖸 **internet** connect

www.scilinks.org/health
Topic: Communication Skills
HealthLinks code: HD4022

HEALTH LINKS Maintained by the National Science Teachers Association

Anger

You can probably think of one time in the last week when you were angry about something. Anger happens often in life, and different people get angry about different things. But what is anger, and what causes it?

Anger is a strong negative feeling toward someone or something that is caused by a sense of being hurt or wronged. Everyone has feelings of anger. Anger is a normal human emotion, and anger is neither good nor bad. Anger can be caused by almost anything. However, it is usually the result of events that happen in your life or the result of your reaction to the behavior of other people.
⭐ 6.A; 7.A

Anger at Events

Can you think of a recent event that made you angry? Perhaps it was a game that you lost. Maybe it was a concert that you wanted to go to but couldn't. Maybe it was something bad that you read about in the newspaper or saw on television. Many everyday events can cause strong emotions. Sometimes these emotions can lead to anger.

Usually, anger at events happens when things don't turn out the way you expected. Anger is a natural response to negative situations. But often the things that make you angry are events that are beyond your control. Losing your temper or staying angry for a long time isn't going to change what happened. Instead, you should look at what has happened and try to find a way to make something positive out of it. For example, if you don't get to go to a concert, find a friend and listen to some music at your house instead. Many events in your life may cause you to become angry. Knowing how to handle your anger at negative events will make you much happier.
⭐ 6.A; 10.C

What You'll Do

- **Discuss** how events can cause anger. ⭐ 7.A
- **Describe** how the actions of others can cause anger. ⭐ 7.A
- **Explain** the importance of resolving anger at yourself. ⭐ 6.A; 7.A

Terms to Learn

- anger

Start Off *Write*

How can events lead to anger?

Figure 6 Anger can be a result of events that are out of your control, like a cancelled concert.

Aalok, age 13
"I get really angry when someone talks really loud on a cell phone in public places."

Gerritt, age 12
"It makes me angry when somebody doesn't listen to me."

Brandy, age 10
"I get angry when somebody takes one of my ideas and says that it's her idea."

Preston, age 15
"I think it is so rude when somebody chews his gum really loud or eats with his mouth open."

Kelli, age 13
"I get angry when somebody interrupts me while I'm talking."

Matthew, age 13
"It drives me crazy when my sister bosses me around."

Anger with Others

Have you ever become angry because of something that someone else has done? At times, the things other people do can cause angry feelings. Sometimes, other people do things on purpose to make us angry, such as teasing you or calling you names. If somebody is teasing you or calling you names, you should ask that person to stop. Talk to the person and try to work out the problem together in a healthy way. If that doesn't work, try ignoring the person. Usually, the reason a person teases you is to make you angry. If you get angry, then the person teasing you has won.

Other times, you may become angry because you feel like others are rude to you or insensitive to your feelings. You can also get angry when you feel that you are being neglected or ignored. Often, the people who are upsetting you don't even know that they are doing so. If you become angry as a result of somebody's behavior, you should tell that person that his or her behavior is upsetting to you. Then you can work together to solve the problem. ⭐ 7.A; 7.B; 10.C

Figure 7 The behaviors of others can make us angry. Different behaviors can also make different people angry.

Health Journal

Look at Figure 7. Do any of the things that make these teens feel angry make you feel angry, too? Write down at least five things that other people do that anger you. Have you ever told the people who do these things how you feel? What could you do to keep from becoming so angry at these things?

⭐ 7.A; 10.B; 10.C

Figure 8 You should always be careful to notice how your behavior is affecting others. These two teens don't realize that they are disturbing others.

Take a Look at Yourself

Sometimes, your behavior might cause someone else to feel angry. For this reason, you should always look at your own behavior to make sure that it is not upsetting the people around you. For example, if you are talking loudly with a friend in a public place, you may not realize that you are angering people around you. However, if you are aware of your environment and the effect of your behavior on others, you can avoid this type of situation. ⊛ 6.B; 10.A; 10.B; 10.C

Anger Turned Inward

It is easy to see how you can become angry at events or angry with others. However, you may not realize that sometimes you can become angry with yourself. Have you ever failed a test or lost a game? Afterward, you may have felt angry because you knew that you could have done better. This feeling is anger turned inward. Usually, you become angry with yourself because you feel that you have failed or made a mistake. Sometimes, you may blame others or become angry with others when you don't realize that you are actually angry with yourself. For example, when you fail a test, your first reaction might be to blame the teacher. However, when you realize you should have studied more, you might realize that you are angry only with yourself. ⊛ 6.A; 10.C

Forgiving Yourself

Dealing with being angry at yourself is often more difficult than dealing with anger with others. When you are angry with somebody else, you can talk to him or her about it. Then, you can work together to solve the problem. Solving the problem can be much more difficult when you are angry with yourself. You may be embarassed to talk with somebody else about your own mistakes and failures. However, talking with someone else can help you resolve your anger. Staying angry with yourself can lead to many emotional problems, including depression and low self-esteem. Sometimes people can get so angry with themselves that they can become violent and attempt to harm themselves.

When you are angry with yourself over a mistake you have made, you may want to look at why the mistake happened. Then you can make plans for how not to make the same mistake next time. That way, a mistake turns into a positive learning experience. If you continue to be angry with yourself over a long period of time or if you find that you are often angry with yourself, you should talk to a parent or trusted adult. You shouldn't be embarrassed. Remember that everybody makes mistakes. Sometimes, we just need a little help in dealing with the feelings that our mistakes can cause. ⭐ 5.H; 11.A

Figure 9 If you do not resolve anger with yourself, the result may be depression or other emotional problems.

Lesson Review

Understanding Concepts

1. What are some events that can cause angry feelings? ⭐ 6.A; 7.A

2. How can the actions or behaviors of others result in you becoming angry? ⭐ 6.A; 7.A

3. Why is resolving feelings of anger with yourself important? ⭐ 6.A; 7.A

Critical Thinking

4. **Making Inferences** Why is it nearly impossible to avoid anger that is the result of events or of the behavior of others? ⭐ 6.A; 7.A

5. **Analyzing Ideas** Name three events that could result in you becoming angry with yourself. Do not mention events that were mentioned in the text. ⭐ 6.A; 7.A

Managing Anger

What You'll Do

- **Describe** how anger can lead to violence. ⭐ 6.A; 7.A

- **Describe** the signs that violence is about to happen.

- **Describe** how anger can affect relationships. ⭐ 6.A; 7.A; 7.B

Terms to Learn

- violence

Start Off
Write

What could happen if you don't manage your anger well?

> Derek's sister had promised that she would take Derek to the football game. At the last minute, Derek's sister said that she couldn't go. Derek got very angry and said hurtful things to his sister. Derek's sister's feelings were very hurt, and now Derek wishes he could take back all of the things he said.

If Derek had managed his anger well, his relationship with his sister might not have been damaged. It can be hard to manage your anger when you are so upset, but there can be serious consequences if you don't. These consequences can include damaged relationships and even violence.

Anger and Relationships

Do you remember the last time you were angry with a parent or sibling or even your teacher? One or more of these people has probably been angry with you too. Regardless of how much you like other people and how close you feel to them, every relationship you have can produce angry feelings. Anger is not always an unhealthy thing. If you manage your anger well, your relationships can improve. By sharing the feelings behind your anger, you can better understand other people and grow closer to other people. If you do not manage your anger, it can damage or ruin your relationships. ⭐ 5.H; 7.A; 7.B; 7.E

Figure 10 You probably have many relationships in your life. All of these relationships can cause conflict and anger from time to time.

Anger and Violence

When the people in a conflict are angry, violence is more likely to happen. Violence is using physical force to hurt someone or to cause damage. Violence does not always happen when people are angry. However, if anger is not managed, violence is often the result. Usually, there are many emotions that cause anger. These emotions include loneliness, sadness, and frustration. If these emotions are not addressed, they continue to build and cause anger. Eventually, this anger can spill over into violence. It is important to be aware of your own feelings so you can address anger and the emotions that cause it before violence occurs. ★ 6.A; 7.E; 10.C

Predicting Violence

Often, you can tell when your own anger begins to get out of control. Hopefully, you can stop yourself from becoming violent. However, predicting when other people or persons are about to become violent is more difficult. By looking for signs that others might become violent, you may be able to protect yourself from violence. The first signs that violence may happen are verbal signs. A person who is about to become violent often yells or uses profanity. His or her words are usually angry and threatening. The person might even make a direct verbal threat against a person or a group of people. There are also physical signs that a person is about to become violent. A person who is becoming violent will often move into your personal space. The person's body language will be tense. His or her fist may be clenched, and his or her facial expressions may show anger. ★ 6.A; 7.A

Health Journal

Have you ever gotten so angry that you said something that you wish you had not said? Has anybody ever said something hurtful to you because he or she was angry? Write about what happened and how you felt. ★ 6.A

Figure 11 Anger is often the result of many emotions building up, like water filling a cup. If anger is not dealt with, it can turn into violence.

Fear

Frustration

Anxiety

Anger

VIOLENCE

The term *truce* is used most often in discussing military conflicts between two governments or groups. Research and write a paper on what *truce* means in a military context, and give examples of how truces have been used in past military conflicts.

Calling a Truce

Some anger in a relationship can be expected and can cause healthy change. However, too much anger can be unhealthy. If anger toward another person seems to last for a long time, you may need to call a truce. Calling a *truce* (TROOS) means taking a break from the conflict to let things cool down. Remember that when you call a truce with somebody, you aren't simply walking away from the conflict. The conflict will still need to be resolved. But resolving the conflict will be easier when both sides have had a chance to calm down. ✪ 5.H; 7.B; 10.C

Going Too Far

In some cases, failing to manage anger may have consequences. Anger that is not managed can cause many problems in our relationships. These problems can include bitterness or hurt feelings. Anger can also cause problems in getting along with our parents or teachers. If anger is not managed but is allowed to continue, it can ruin relationships permanently. Expressing anger in an unhealthy way can also have other consequences. These consequences might include getting grounded, losing privileges, or being disciplined at school. If anger turns into violence, the consequences might even include trouble with the police. Remember that anger can be healthy and can cause positive changes. However, when anger is not managed, it can be very destructive and can even turn into violence. ✪ 5.H; 10.C

Figure 12 If anger is not managed, it can lead to violence.

Preventing Violence

If you are aware that someone is making threats, you should always tell a parent or trusted adult. You read or hear about a lot of violence in the news every day. Much of this violence could have been prevented if people had reported threats or aggressive behavior before the violence happened. By being aware of clues that violence might happen and by taking the proper steps to report threats or to get away from potentially violent situations, you can help prevent violence. ✪ 5.H; 10.C; 11.A

Figure 13 Always report threats of violence to a trusted adult.

MAKING GOOD DECISIONS

Imagine that you are talking with a friend about an argument he had with a classmate. Your friend is still very angry. He tells you that tomorrow he is going to bring his brother's hunting knife to school to scare the classmate that he was arguing with. You don't think that your friend is serious, but you know that he is very angry, and you know that his brother does have a hunting knife at home. What should you do? What might happen if you tell a teacher what your friend said? What might happen if you don't tell a teacher? ✪ 5.G; 5.H; 10.C; 11.A

Lesson Review

Using Vocabulary
1. What is anger?

2. What is violence?

Understanding Concepts
3. How does anger lead to violence? ✪ 5.H

4. What are some negative things that can happen in any of our relationships if anger is not resolved? ✪ 6.A; 7.A

5. Name two types of signs that violence is about to happen, and give one example of each type. ✪ 5.G; 5.H

Critical Thinking
6. Applying Concepts Does calling a truce mean that a conflict is over? What might be the benefits of calling a truce? What might the benefits or dangers be of continuing the conflict? ✪ 5.G; 6.A; 7.A; 7.B

Lesson 5

Expressing Anger

What You'll Do

- **Explain** the importance of expressing anger properly.
  ⭐ 5.G; 5.H; 7.A; 7.B
- **Describe** three healthy ways to express anger.
  ⭐ 7.B; 7.C; 10.A; 10.C
- **Identify** three unhealthy ways to express anger.
  ⭐ 5.H; 7.C; 10.A; 10.C
- **Explain** that other factors can affect the way we express anger. ⭐ 7.A; 7.B; 7.E; 10.A; 10.B

Start Off

Write

How can you express your anger in a healthy way?

Andrea's friend Corey borrowed some clothes and wouldn't give them back. Andrea yelled at Corey and said some mean things. Now Corey won't talk to Andrea, and Andrea may never get her clothes back.

If Andrea had expressed her anger in a different way, she might have been able to keep her clothes and her friend.

The Way You Express Anger Is Important

As you learned earlier, anger is a natural response to many situations. Because anger is a natural response, it is not good or bad. However, the way that you express your anger can be healthy or unhealthy. If anger is expressed in an unhealthy way it can make others angry and can force a conflict to end negatively. If anger is expressed in a healthy way, the conflict may end in a positive way. Often, expressing anger in a healthy way can be difficult. However, making sure that a conflict ends well is worth the effort. ⭐ 5.H; 7.B; 7.C; 10.C

Figure 14 The way in which anger is expressed can determine whether a conflict ends positively or negatively.

Steven cuts in front of Joel in the cafeteria line.

Joel tells Steven that he thinks that it was rude to cut in line, and that Steven should go to the back of the line.

Steven goes to the back of the line.

Joel gets angry and pushes Steven.

Joel and Steven both end up in the principal's office.

Healthy Expressions of Anger

When you are angry, you are less able to think calmly about the things you say or do. That is why when you are in a conflict, you have to make more of an effort to remember the healthy ways to express your anger.

When you are in a conflict, you express yourself with your words and with your body. You should be careful to use your words in a calm way to tell the other person why you are angry. Do not use threatening or aggressive language. The more you share your feelings and the less you use name-calling, threats, and yelling, the better chance you have of being listened to. You should say what you think should be done to fix the conflict.

You should also be aware of the way that you express your anger with your body. Keep a little bit of distance from the other person in a conflict. If you are too much in someone's personal space, you may seem threatening or aggressive. Also be careful not to clench your fist or make any other threatening movements.

⊛ 5.H; 10.A; 10.C

Figure 15 Expressing anger in a healthy way, such as having a calm discussion, makes resolving conflicts much easier.

Watch Your Words

Remember that the way that you express your anger will often determine how the other person in a conflict expresses his or her anger. When you are calm and express your anger in a healthy way, getting what you need out of a conflict is much easier. For example, imagine that you and a friend are arguing over a book that your friend borrowed from you. If you yell at your friend and call him a thief, he will most likely yell and call you names as well. You may damage your friendship, and you probably won't get your book back. Instead, try telling your friend "It is upsetting me that you haven't given back the book you borrowed. Can we talk about it?" Your friend will see that you are upset and will be more willing to work out a solution.

⊛ 5.H; 7.E; 10.A; 10.C

Health Journal

Think about the last time that you were very angry. Why were you so angry? How could you have better expressed your anger? Write about your experience in your Health Journal.

⊛ 10.A; 10.C

Unhealthy Expressions of Anger

Sometimes, it is acceptable to be loud or aggressive depending on the situation. For example, it may be all right to be loud while you are watching a football game. It may also be all right to be aggressive while you are playing basketball.

However, being loud or aggressive is not appropriate in most social situations. This is especially true when you are angry or in a conflict. Expressing anger in an unhealthy way during a conflict decreases the chance that the problem will be solved. It also increases the risk that the situation will turn violent. The more aggressive and angrier you appear during a conflict, the greater the chance that the other person or people will become angry and aggressive.

Some of the unhealthy ways in which anger is often expressed are in loud or aggressive speech, name-calling, and threats. Another unhealthy expression of anger is threatening or aggressive body language, such as invading somebody else's personal space. The unhealthiest way to express anger is through violence. Violence is never useful. In addition to making any conflict much worse, violence can have more serious consequences. These can include suspension from school or trouble with the police.

If you are in a conflict and the other person uses unhealthy expressions of anger, remain calm. This may be difficult. If you don't think you can remain calm, walk away and try to resolve the conflict later. Doing so will help you avoid violence.

✹ 10.A; 10.B; 10.C

Figure 16 Yelling and pointing your finger, like the teen in this picture, are unhealthy ways to express anger.

Figure 17 Getting the right amount of sleep and eating properly can put you in a good mood. Being in a good mood can make you less likely to get angry or to express anger in an unhealthy way.

Staying Cool

Have you ever felt as if you were angrier or more likely to act aggressively on a certain day or at a certain time? Sometimes, our moods are caused by things that we can control. For example, you may have noticed that when you stay up too late, you are in a bad mood the next day. There are certain things that you can do to make yourself less likely to express your anger in an unhealthy way. First, make sure that you are getting enough rest. If you are getting tired or irritable in the middle of the day, you may need to go to bed earlier. Also, your body needs a healthy diet and regular exercise. Eating too much sugar or exercising too little can cause changes in your mood that may lead to anger. By taking care of your body, you can make sure that you are able to think clearly and calmly and to express your anger well. ⭐ 5.H; 10.C

Lesson Review

Understanding Concepts

1. Why is the way in which you express your anger important? ⭐ 5.G; 5.H; 7.A; 7.B

2. What are three healthy ways to express anger? ⭐ 7.B; 7.C; 10.A; 10.C

3. What are three unhealthy ways to express anger? ⭐ 5.H; 10.A; 10.C

Critical Thinking

4. Making Inferences How do other factors, such as eating poorly or getting too little sleep, affect how we express anger? ⭐ 7.A; 7.B; 7.E; 10.A; 10.C

What Is Stress?

What You'll Do

- **Explain** what stress is. ✪ 10.F
- **Describe** the negative effects of stress on a person. ✪ 10.F
- **Explain** how stress can have a positive effect on a person. ✪ 10.F

Terms to Learn

- stress

Start Off
Write

Can stress affect your physical health? Explain.

Charles has a test in math in a week. He is very worried about how he is going to do. He has had trouble sleeping and has been getting upset easily because of his worrying. What is causing Charles's problems?

Charles's problems are a result of stress. **Stress** is a physical and emotional response that is the result of a new or uncomfortable situation. Depending on how we deal with it, stress can have a positive or negative effect on our lives. ✪ 10.F

Everybody Has Stress

Everybody experiences some stress in his or her life. The amount of stress a person experiences can vary from day to day. Some days, a person may feel overwhelmed by the amount of stress in his or her life. But on other days, the same person may not experience very much stress. You have little or no control over the amount of stress in your life. However, you do have control over how you manage your stress. If it is managed properly, stress can be something that drives you to succeed and grow. If it is managed poorly, stress can cause serious physical, mental, or emotional problems. ✪ 10.F

Figure 18 Everybody experiences stress. Even a famous athlete, like Natalie Williams, experiences stress when she is competing.

What Is Negative Stress?

Negative stress is stress that results in problems in your life. Sometimes, negative stress is the result of a negative situation, such as an illness or injury. These types of situations are often beyond your control and can happen at any time. That is why it is important to recognize and know how to manage negative stress when it arises.

Another way that negative stress can happen is by managing stress poorly. For example, the stress caused by taking a math test is not necessarily negative. However, if you get so worried about the test that you cannot study, the stress can quickly become negative.

Often, you can learn something from dealing with negative stress in your life. For example, attending a new school can be frightening and uncomfortable. However, this experience can help you cope with other major changes later in life. Remember that you don't have to let negative stress become a bigger problem than necessary. Do not dwell on the negative stress in your life. Remember that almost every problem has a solution. Every bad time will pass eventually if you confront your problems and work to solve them. ⭐ 10.F

Figure 19 Dwelling too much on the negative stress in your life can cause your problems to become even greater.

The Signs of Negative Stress

It is possible to deal with negative stress in a healthy way if you recognize the signs of negative stress. You may recognize things that cause negative stress. But you may not always recognize what this stress is doing to you physically and emotionally. Physically, stress may make you feel tired. If you have too much stress, you may experience health problems. These problems can include stomachaches, headaches, hair loss, and even heart problems. Negative stress can also cause serious emotional problems, including nervousness, restlessness, and sadness. These problems can lead to more serious problems, such as depression or suicide. By recognizing the signs of negative stress in your life, you will know when you need help. A trusted adult can give you advice on how to deal with your negative stress. ⭐ 10.F

Myth: Health problems caused by stress aren't serious.

Fact: The way you respond to stress can cause many serious and lifelong problems, such as high blood pressure and heart problems.

What Is Positive Stress?

While much of the stress we experience is negative, some stress is positive. Positive stress is stress that pushes you to do better or to grow. If you've ever been in a sporting event or contest, you've probably experienced positive stress. The stress you feel while competing can lead you to perform better. Pressure to do well in school can also be positive. It can push you to get better grades.

Positive stress sometimes results from happy events that lead to changes in a person's life. Examples of this type of event include vacations, the birth of a new brother or sister, and school graduations. If you experience this type of event, focus on your happiness—not on the changes. Doing so will help you enjoy the events more. ✪ 6.A; 10.F

Figure 20 The stress that results from trying to do well in school is positive stress. However, too much stress, even positive stress, can have a negative effect.

Recognizing Positive Stress

Often, positive stress can lead to increased performance, energy, and even excitement. You feel a different type of stress when you are trying to achieve a higher grade than when you are faced with trying to avoid a lower grade. Similarly, there is a difference between the stress of gaining a new sister and the stress of losing a grandparent.

It is important to recognize the sources of stress in your life that are positive. And make sure that these do not become sources of negative stress. Although positive stress can be a very good thing in your life, positive stress can have negative effects if there is too much of it in your life. If you are always being pushed to win or compete, for instance, you can develop some of the same symptoms that are caused by negative stress. ✪ 10.F

Health Journal

Think about your own life. What are some things that increase your stress? Write about the sources of stress in your life. Do you think that the stress in your life is positive or negative stress? Explain.
✪ 6.A; 10.G

STRESS TEST

For each of the following statements, record how often you have experienced that situation. 1=Never; 2=Almost Never; 3=Sometimes; 4=Often; 5=Very often or always (DO NOT WRITE IN BOOK)

1. feeling angry or frustrated
2. feeling lonely
3. feeling pressure to perform well at school
4. feeling pressure to perform well in sports
5. feeling behind in schoolwork
6. fighting with friends
7. fighting with parents or caretakers
8. worrying
9. losing your temper
10. suffering headaches
11. feeling tired
12. experiencing stomach pain

For the following list of events, check off every event that has happened to you in the last 12 months. Then, record the number of points next to each event that has happened to you. (DO NOT WRITE IN BOOK)

1. starting at a new school (6)
2. failing a class or an important exam (3)
3. parents divorcing (10)
4. joining a sports team (2)
5. losing at an important competition (3)
6. death of a close friend or relative (8)
7. large increase in number of arguments with friends or family members (5)
8. birth of new brother or sister (5)
9. serious injury or illness (6)
10. moving to a new town or city (7)
11. being teased or bullied regularly (5)

Now add up your score, and measure your results against the following scale:

12–40   **Low to moderate stress:** You are experiencing little stress in your life. It is good that you are not dealing with a lot of negative stress. Be sure that you are not missing out on activities that can cause positive stress.

41–90   **Average stress:** You are experiencing an average amount of stress. Look at your answers for this test. Where did most of your points come from? Keep an eye on these sources of stress, and be sure that they do not start causing too much negative stress in your life.

91–120   **Stressed out!:** You have too much stress in your life. Talk to a parent or trusted adult about the results of this test, and see what you can do to reduce the level of stress in your life. Do this before the stress causes you many serious problems.   ⊛ 10.F; 10.G

Lesson Review

Using Vocabulary

1. What is stress? ⊛ 10.F

2. What effects can negative stress have on a person? ⊛ 6.A; 7.A; 10.F

3. How can stress positively affect a person? ⊛ 10.F

Critical Thinking

4. Identifying Relationships Is all stress either positive or negative? Is it possible for stress to be positive and negative? Explain your answer. ⊛ 10.F; 10.G

Sources of Stress

Portia's family just moved to a new city, and Portia has just started at a new school. Portia is feeling a lot of new emotions, including fear, anxiety, and loneliness. These emotions are causing a lot of stress in Portia's life.

Although stress can be caused by almost anything, it is usually a response to new or uncomfortable emotions or a response to an unexpected or uncomfortable event. In Portia's case, stress is being caused by the event of moving and the emotions that have resulted from it. ✪ 10.G

Stressful Emotions

Stress is caused by how you react to situations and by your feelings about them. New or uncomfortable situations can cause many different emotions. Depending on the situation, these emotions can be positive or negative. For example, if you are competing in an important game, you might feel excitement or anxiety. On the other hand, if a loved one dies, you may feel sadness or anger. The way that your body responds to your emotions is what causes stress.

It is very important to deal with stressful emotions before they become a problem. Stressful emotions are perfectly normal, but if they are not addressed, they can lead to serious physical and mental problems. ✪ 10.E; 10.G

TABLE 2 Common Teen Stressors

Common stressors	Possible emotions caused by stress
Schoolwork	fear of failing, anger at doing poorly, pride at doing well, and frustration at amount or difficulty of work
Relationships with friends	affection toward friends, fear of upsetting friends, anger or frustration caused by fighting with friends, and jealousy caused by friends' relationships with others
Relationships with family members	frustration or anger at having to follow rules, and anger or jealousy caused by arguing or competing with siblings
Competing on a sports or academic team	fear of performing poorly, frustration at performing poorly, and pride at performing well ✪ 10.G

What Causes Stressful Emotions?

Stressful emotions can be the result of several things. Sometimes, stressful emotions come from our relationships with other people. For example, you may feel a lot of stressful emotions after having a disagreement with another person. Expectations that others have for you and your performance can also result in many stressful emotions. For example, if you play on a sports team, you may feel stressful emotions because your parents, the coach, and your teammates all expect you to play well.

Events in our lives are another source of stressful emotions. The death of someone close to you, changing schools, or competing in a sport are just some of the events that can cause stressful emotions. Most often, the events that cause us stress are things that are beyond our control. These events can happen at any time. If you don't know how to deal with stressful emotions as they arise, you can quickly find yourself with way too much stress. Knowing how to manage stressful emotions can lessen the impact that stress has on your life.
⊛ 10.F; 10.G

Figure 21 Big changes, such as moving to a new city or town, can cause a great deal of stress.

Lesson Review

Understanding Concepts

1. In your own words, describe how emotions can lead to stress. ⊛ 10.G

2. What are three examples of events that can result in stressful emotions? ⊛ 10.F; 10.G

Critical Thinking

3. Making Inferences Why might you feel more stress after an argument with somebody close to you than after an argument with a stranger? ⊛ 10.F; 10.G

Managing Stress

Melissa has a lot of stress in her life, and she is beginning to have stomachaches because of it. Is there anything that she can do to avoid having stress in her life?

What You'll Do

- **Describe** two ways to prevent stressful situations. ⭐ 1.H
- **Discuss** how stress can be controlled by talking about it. ⭐ 1.H
- **Describe** how stress can be controlled through physical activity. ⭐ 1.F
- **Describe** how stress can be controlled through creative activity. ⭐ 1.H

Start Off ✎

Write

How do you control the stress in your life?

The bad news is that nobody can avoid stress. However, the good news is that there are many things you can do to manage your stress and to prevent many stressful situations.

Preventing Stressful Situations

Not all stress can be avoided, but some of it can be prevented. Recognizing stressful situations before they happen can be difficult. Doing so requires practice. The older you get, the easier it may become to recognize and prevent stressful situations. If you have been in a situation that was stressful, remember how you dealt with it. Think about what you might do differently if a similar situation arises. If possible, stay out of situations that have caused you a lot of stress in the past. For example, if you know that going camping makes you uncomfortable and nervous, then don't go camping. Planning ahead can also keep certain situations from becoming stressful. For example, have you ever taken a test for which you did not feel well prepared? Next time, if you begin studying earlier, you might be able to prevent this stress. ⭐ 1.H

Figure 22 By planning ahead, you can sometimes prevent stressful situations, such as having to study all night for a test.

Figure 23 Stress can often be relieved by simply talking to somebody, such as a parent or trusted adult, about the stress.

Talk About It

While it may seem simple, talking to someone is one of the easiest ways to deal with stress. Sometimes problems can seem bigger if you keep them to yourself. Sharing your feelings can reduce or even get rid of your stress. As soon as you talk to somebody about your problems, the problems may suddenly seem not as bad.

Other times, you may need the help of others to solve the problems that cause your stress. Somebody else may be able to think of a solution that you had not considered. It doesn't always matter whom you choose to talk to. The important thing is that you trust the people to whom you turn for advice. As you begin to form relationships, you will learn which people you trust and to which people you feel comfortable talking. The people to whom you might talk include parents, siblings, or other trusted friends or adults. ✪ 1.H; 11.A

LIFE SKILLS ACTIVITY

MAKING GOOD DECISIONS

Imagine that you are on a sports or academic team. You really enjoy the team, but lately, the team's coach has been putting a lot of pressure on you to improve. The extra practice time is taking away from your studies. You realize that being on this team is causing a lot of stress and anxiety in your life. How can you manage this stress and anxiety? ✪ 1.H; 10.E

Hands-on ACTIVITY

STRESS SURVEY

1. Pick 10 people that you know. Be sure to pick both peers and adults.

2. Ask each person to rate his or her stress on a scale of 1 to 10. Ask each person how many hours of exercise he or she gets every week. Ask each person what his or her largest source of stress is.

3. Make a chart showing each person's name, age, and answers to the three questions.

Analysis

1. Look at your chart. Do people who exercise more also have less stress? Why do you think your results turned out the way they did?

Reducing Stress Through Physical Activity

Another way to reduce stress is through physical activity. When you think of physical activity, you might immediately think of running, jumping, lifting, and sweating. These types of activities are great for relieving stress. However, there are many other ways to be physically active and to reduce stress. You might take a walk, go swimming, or ride a bicycle. Whatever activity you choose should take your mind and energy away from the cause of your stress. The activity should also be enjoyable. If you do not enjoy running, then the time you spend running may not help to relieve your stress.

Remember that physical activity is only a way to manage stress. Stress can be removed only by facing and solving the problems that cause it. Physical activity will never make stress go away entirely. When you are finished exercising, the problems that were causing your stress will still be there. However, after physical activity, your body and your mind will be refreshed. As a result, you will cope better with the problems that are causing your stress. ⭐ 1.B; 1.F; 1.H

Figure 24 Physical activity can reduce stress. If you are trying to reduce stress, be sure to pick an activity that you enjoy.

Be Creative!

When looking for ways to reduce stress in your life, you should rely on your creative side as well as on your physical abilities. While you can certainly reduce stress by running around the block or playing soccer, you should also have non-physical ways to relax. For example, you might write in a journal, draw or paint, write poetry, doodle, or listen to or play music. All of these activities take your mind off stressful situations. Some of these activities, especially journal writing, can actually help you work through some of the problems that cause stress. However, most of these activities are intended to take your mind off stress. Again, these activities aren't necessarily going to make stressful situations go away. However, they may give you a break from stress so that you are refreshed. When you are refreshed, you will be better able to manage your stress.

The next time you are in a stressful situation, try different ways to reduce your stress. This will help you determine which method of controlling stress works best for you. ⭐ 1.H

Figure 25 Creative activities, such as writing in a journal, can help you relieve stress.

Lesson Review

Understanding Concepts

1. Is it possible to prevent stressful situations? If so, how? ⭐ 1.F; 1.H

2. What are two benefits of talking about stress? ⭐ 1.H

3. How does physical activity help you deal with stress? ⭐ 1.F; 1.H

4. How can creative activities help you relieve stress? ⭐ 1.F.; 1.H

Critical Thinking

5. Making Good Decisions You are feeling a lot of stress, and you think some physical activity might help. You could go running, which is a lot of exercise but not much fun to you, or take a walk in the park, which is fun but not much exercise. Which activity do you think will be better for reducing stress? Explain. ⭐ 1.B.; 1.F; 1.H

Chapter Summary

■ Conflict is any clash of ideas or interests. Conflicts can be internal or external. ■ The way in which you communicate during a conflict can determine if the conflict ends positively or negatively. ■ Conflicts can be resolved in several different ways. ■ Anger is a strong feeling that can be caused by a sense of being hurt or wronged. ■ Anger is neither positive nor negative, but the way it is expressed can be healthy or unhealthy. ■ Resolving anger before it results in violence is important. ■ Stress is a response to a new or uncomfortable situation. Stress can be positive or negative. ■ It is important to manage stress so that it does not result in serious problems. ■ Stress can be managed by talking to someone, through physical activity, or through a creative outlet.

Using Vocabulary

For each pair of terms, describe how the meanings of the terms differ.

1 internal conflict/external conflict

2 compromise/collaboration

3 positive stress/negative stress

For each sentence, fill in the blank with the proper word from the word bank provided below.

conflict	violence
negotiation	stress
anger	empathy

4 ___ is a clash of ideas or interests.

5 ___ is a physical harm that one person does to another on purpose.

6 ___ is a response to a new or uncomfortable situation.

7 The ability to understand or identify with another person's ideas or feelings is called ___.

Understanding Concepts

8 Why does external conflict arise? Give two examples of external conflict. ⭐ 6.A; 7A

9 What are three possible outcomes of a conflict? Explain each one. ⭐ 5.G; 5.H; 7.A

10 Why might you want to walk away from a conflict? ⭐ 5.G; 5.H; 7.A; 10.A; 10.C

11 How can anger turn into violence? ⭐ 5.H

12 Why is it bad to stay angry at yourself for a long period of time or to be angry at yourself often? What should you do if you are often angry with yourself? ⭐ 10.F; 11.A

13 Name three unhealthy ways of expressing your anger, and give an example of each. ⭐ 10.A; 10.C

14 What are some physical and emotional symptoms that you might experience if you are feeling too much stress? How can you avoid them? ⭐ 1.B; 1.H; 10.F

15 What are two consequences of managing anger poorly? ⭐ 5.H; 7.A; 10.F; 10.G

Critical Thinking

Applying Concepts

16 In this chapter, you learned several different ways of managing stress. What benefits might creative ways of relieving stress have that physical ways of reducing stress do not? What benefits might physical ways of relieving stress have that creative ways do not? ⭐ 1.F

17 Imagine that you are having a conflict with somebody. She begins to raise her voice until she is yelling. She then pokes you in the chest and calls you a nasty name. Do you think that this conflict might become violent? What should you do? ⭐ 5.G; 5.H; 10.A; 10.B; 10.C

Making Good Decisions

18 Your friend Maggie wants to return a pair of shoes to the store. When she gets to the store, the clerk tells her that he will not take them back. Maggie becomes very angry and begins acting aggressively and talking loudly. Is Maggie's reaction a good way to solve the conflict? What would you recommend that she do differently? ⭐ 1.H; 5.G; 5.H

19 Imagine that you have several tests coming up at school. You are studying a lot, and you feel as if these tests are causing negative stress in your life. What can you do to turn this negative stress into positive stress? ⭐ 1.H

Interpreting Graphics

Sources of Stress in Kim's Life

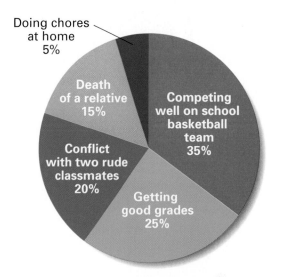

The figure above shows the different sources of stress in the life of an eighth-grade student named Kim. Use this figure to answer questions 20–24. ⭐ M: 6.3A; 6.10D; 6.11A

20 What is Kim's greatest source of stress?

21 What percentage of the stress in Kim's life is negative?

22 What percentage of the stress in Kim's life is positive?

23 What percentage of Kim's stress is not school related?

24 Write down each of the sources of stress in Kim's life, from the most important to the least important, and write whether the stress is negative or positive.

Reading Checkup

Take a minute to review your answers to the Health IQ questions at the beginning of this chapter. How has reading this chapter improved your Health IQ?

Life Skills IN ACTION

Coping

At times, everyone faces setbacks, disappointments, or other troubles. To deal with these problems, you have to learn how to cope. Coping is dealing with problems and emotions in an effective way. Complete the following activity to develop your coping skills.

Stressed Out!

ACT 1

Setting the Scene

Sondra just started 6th grade. She likes her classes, but she can't seem to find enough time to do all of her homework. Sondra thinks her classes are much harder than the classes she took last year. She worries that she will not be able to earn good grades in all of her classes, and she feels stressed. ⭐ 6.A; 10.G

The 5 Steps of Coping

1. Identify the problem.
2. Identify your emotions.
3. Use positive self-talk.
4. Find ways to resolve the problem.
5. Talk to others to receive support.

Guided Practice

Practice with a Friend

Form a group of two. Have one person play the role of Sondra, and have the second person be an observer. Walking through each of the five steps of coping, role-play Sondra dealing with the stress resulting from her schoolwork. The observer will take notes, which will include observations about what the person playing Sondra did well and suggestions of ways to improve. Stop after each step to evaluate the process. ⭐ 1.H; 10.E

Check Yourself

After you have completed the guided practice, go through Act 1 again without stopping at each step. Answer the questions below to review what you did.

1. What emotions could Sondra be feeling? How do those emotions contribute to her stress?

2. What are some ways that Sondra could solve her problem? ⊛ **1.H**

3. Who could Sondra talk to about her problem? ⊛ **11.A**

4. What do you do to cope when you feel stressed? ⊛ **1.H**

ACT 2

On Your Own

After a few weeks, Sondra works out a study schedule that helps her stay on top of all of her classes. She no longer feels stressed by her classes. At soccer practice one day, Sondra's coach tells her that she will play goalie in the biggest game of the season. The coach says that Sondra is a good goalie and that the team will be counting on her to do well in the game. Sondra feels proud but also nervous. Draw a comic strip that shows how Sondra could use the five steps of coping to deal with her nervousness.

Caring for Your Body

Check out
Current Health
articles related to this chapter by
visiting **go.hrw.com**. Just type in
the keyword **HD4CH07**.

Lessons

"My toothache was really intense. The pain was **sharp** and **sudden.** I had to go to the **dentist right away.** Now, I brush and floss my teeth every day. I never want to feel pain like that again!**"**

Health IQ

PRE-READING

Answer the following true/false questions to find out what you already know about caring for your body. When you've finished this chapter, you'll have the opportunity to change your answers based on what you've learned.

1. The outer layer of your skin is made of dead cells.

2. Acne is an inflammation of the skin.

3. Hair helps you sense the world around you.

4. The flap of skin around a fingernail is called the cornea.

5. The dentin of your tooth is the hardest substance in the body.

6. You should brush your teeth a few times per week.

7. You should floss your teeth every day.

8. Tiny bones in your ears enable you to hear.

9. Only adults are healthcare consumers.

10. You should change your toothbrush every few months.

11. Figuring out the unit price can help you find the best price for a particular product.

12. Smart shoppers gather as much information as they can before they buy.

13. Loud sounds can damage your ears.

14. Fingernails and hair are made of the same material.

15. Dandruff is made by tiny insects.

16. Stress can make acne worse.

ANSWERS: 1. true; 2. true; 3. true; 4. false; 5. false; 6. false; 7. true; 8. true; 9. false; 10. true; 11. true; 12. true; 13. true; 14. true; 15. false; 16. true

Caring for Your Skin

What You'll Do

- **Describe** the structure and function of skin. ⊛ 2.A

- **Explain** how to care for your skin. ⊛ 1.C

Terms to Learn

- epidermis
- dermis
- acne

Start Off
Write

How does your skin help you stay healthy?

Taking care of your physical health means caring for your body. Learning how different body parts work helps you learn how to take care of them. For example, when you know how your skin works, you know how to care for it better.

Your skin helps you stay healthy. Skin may look like a simple covering. But your skin is a complex organ that has many jobs.

You're Covered!

Your skin is made up of two basic layers. The **epidermis** (EP uh DUHR mis) is the outer layer of skin. The outermost cells of the epidermis are dead. The layer of living cells below the epidermis is called the **dermis** (DUHR mis). Together, these layers protect you from germs that could enter your body. So, when your skin is punctured or cut, you risk getting an infection. Your skin also contains nerve endings, pores, hairs, and sweat glands. Nerves give you a sense of touch. Sweat from pores helps cool you off and eliminates some wastes. The layer of fat under the skin helps keep you warm. Oil glands make oil that helps keep your skin soft and flexible. Sometimes, the glands make too much oil, and the pores can get clogged. **Acne** is an inflammation of the skin that happens when pores get clogged with dirt and oil. The bumps that develop from acne are called *pimples*. ⊛ 1.C; 2.A

Figure 1 The Parts of Your Skin

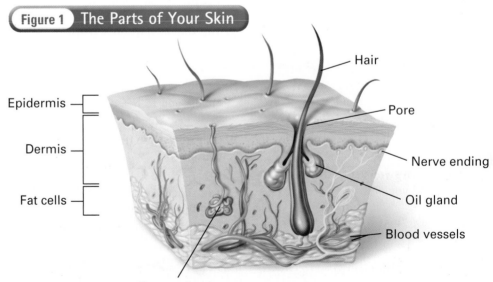

Epidermis

Dermis

Fat cells

Hair

Pore

Nerve ending

Oil gland

Blood vessels

Sweat gland

Caring for Your Skin

To care for your skin, wash it thoroughly and often. Washing skin gets rid of dirt, sweat, and bacteria. When you sweat, the bacteria on your skin multiply. When bacteria multiply, they can cause body odor. Showering every day and after physical activity can keep bacteria under control. Treat the skin on your face gently. This skin is very sensitive. Use warm (not hot) water and mild soap. Use your hands or a soft cloth.

Be especially gentle with skin that has acne. Don't squeeze or disrupt pimples. Stress may make acne worse. So, relieving stress in healthy ways can help keep acne under control. Get plenty of rest. Foods don't cause acne. But eating a balanced diet and drinking plenty of water helps your skin get the nutrients it needs to stay healthy.

Acne is not the only skin problem. The sun can harm your skin. Always keep your skin safe from getting too much sun. Avoid the strong sunlight in the middle of the day (from about 10:00 A.M. until 2:00 P.M.). When you are outside, use plenty of sunscreen that has a skin protection factor of at least 15. Also, wear clothing that protects you from the sun. For example, wearing a hat can protect your face, ears, and neck from strong sunlight. ✪ 1.C

Figure 2 Sunscreen helps protect your skin from the harmful rays of the sun.

SCIENCE ACTIVITY

Use colored pencils to draw and label the diagram of the skin. Under each label, write what each part of the skin does.

Lesson Review

Using Vocabulary

1. Define *acne*. ✪ 2.A

Understanding Concepts

2. Name the different structures and layers of your skin. ✪ 2.A

3. Describe four functions of skin. ✪ 2.A

4. Explain how to clean your skin. ✪ 1.C; 2.A

Critical Thinking

5. Making Inferences Alex is going swimming. His sunscreen is not waterproof. What should he do to protect himself from the harmful rays of the sun after he swims? ✪ 1.C

Caring for Your Hair and Nails

What You'll Do

- **Describe** two functions of hair. ✪ 2.A
- **Explain** how to care for your hair and nails. ✪ 1.C
- **Describe** two functions of fingernails. ✪ 2.A

Terms to Learn

- dandruff
- head lice
- cuticle

Start Off

Write

Why is it a bad idea to bite your nails?

How would you describe what you look like? What features make you look like you? One of those features is probably the color and style of your hair.

Hair

Hair grows from *follicles* (FAHL i kuhlz) on almost every part of your skin. Hair is made of a material called *keratin* (KER uh tin). Keratin's strength allows hair to stick out from the surface of the skin. Because hair sticks out, it can help you in two ways.

First, hair traps air near your skin. This layer of air works as insulation and keeps you warm. Hair also helps you sense the world around you. When something touches a hair on your skin, the nerve endings near the base of the hair let you know something is close to you. Gently touch your eyelash to see how hair can help your sense of touch. ✪ 2.A

Hair Care

Keeping your hair neat and clean helps it stay healthy. Trimming and brushing your hair helps keep it neat. Use a soft brush, and brush your hair gently. Wash your hair at least twice a week. Use mild shampoos and warm water so that you do not hurt or dry out your scalp. A dry scalp can make flaky, dried clumps of dead cells, which are called **dandruff** (DAN druhf).

Another common hair problem is head lice. **Head lice** are small insects that live on the scalp and suck blood. Lice lay eggs on hair shafts. Special shampoos can help a person get rid of lice. But it's best to avoid lice in the first place. Don't share hats, combs, brushes, or any other items that can transfer lice to you. ✪ 1.C

Figure 3 Keeping your hair neat and clean helps your hair stay healthy.

Figure 4 Nails should be trimmed neatly.

Nails

Your nails grow from nail beds. Nail beds begin under your skin, between the base of your nail and the knuckle closest to it. Like your hair, your nails are made of keratin. But in your nails, the keratin forms hard layers. Because nails are hard, they help protect the sensitive ends of your fingers and toes. Fingernails help with everyday tasks, too. Picking up a pin or scratching an itch is easier because you have fingernails. ⭐ 2.A

The **cuticle** (KYOOT i kuhl) is a thin flap of skin around the nail. Sometimes, the cuticle becomes dry and cracks. The cracking can be painful. Using lotion on your hands can help you keep your cuticles soft and healthy.

Nail Care

Keeping your fingernails and toenails cleaned and trimmed is important. Germs and dirt collect under nails. Even when you cannot see bugs and bacteria, they are there! When washing your hands, carefully clean underneath your fingernails with a brush. When you bathe, make sure your toenails are clean.

Because germs collect under your nails, biting your fingernails is unhealthy. Instead, use a nail clipper or a pair of nail scissors to trim your nails. When clipping your nails, trim them neatly. ⭐ 1.C

STUDY TIP *for better reading*

Reviewing Information
Trace your hand on a piece of paper. Draw your fingernails. Label your nails and cuticles.

Lesson Review

Using Vocabulary

1. Define *cuticle*.

Understanding Concepts

2. Describe two common hair problems. ⭐ 1.C

3. Describe two functions of hair. ⭐ 2.A

4. Describe good hair and nail care. ⭐ 1.C

5. Describe two functions of fingernails. ⭐ 2.A

Critical Thinking

6. Identifying Relationships Describe two ways that hair and nails are similar. Describe two ways that they differ.

Lesson 3 Caring for Your Teeth

What You'll Do

- **Describe** the structure and function of teeth. ⊛ 2.A
- **Identify** two minor problems of teeth. ⊛ 1.C
- **Describe** how a cavity forms. ⊛ 1.C
- **Describe** effective dental care. ⊛ 1.A; 1.C

Terms to Learn

- plaque
- cavity

Start Off
Write

How does a cavity form?

Karen held the soccer ball tightly. She blocked the shot despite getting kicked in the chin. Later, she was glad that she had worn her mouth guard. Imagining herself without front teeth was scary.

Karen is smart to take care of her teeth. You should care for yours, too. If you lose a permanent tooth, it won't grow back. When you were about 6 or 7 years old, you began losing your baby teeth, and your permanent teeth began to grow in. By age 14 or so, you will have 28 permanent teeth. You may get 4 more teeth (called *wisdom teeth*) when you are about 20.

Structure and Function of Teeth

When you look at your teeth, you see only the part that grows out of your gums. This shiny, white portion of the tooth is called the *crown*. It is white and hard because it is covered by enamel (e NAM uhl), the hardest substance in your body. You can learn the parts of the tooth by studying the figure below.

As you know, teeth are very important for chewing. Imagine trying to bite into an apple without your teeth. Teeth are also helpful when you speak. Notice how both your tongue and lips touch your teeth when you say the words "fine teeth"! ⊛ 2.A

Figure 5 The Parts of Your Teeth

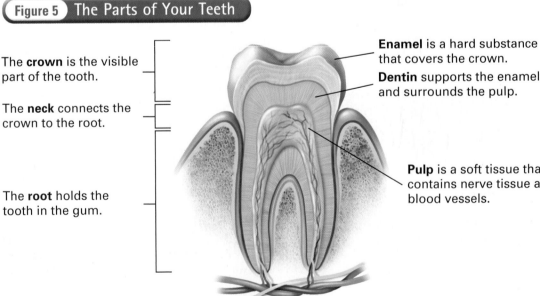

The **crown** is the visible part of the tooth.

The **neck** connects the crown to the root.

The **root** holds the tooth in the gum.

Enamel is a hard substance that covers the crown.

Dentin supports the enamel and surrounds the pulp.

Pulp is a soft tissue that contains nerve tissue and blood vessels.

Tooth and Gum Problems

You should take care of problems with your teeth and gums as soon as possible. If you do not, small problems can become big ones. Check your gums regularly by looking at them in the mirror. Your gums should be bright pink and free from sores.

One of the most common tooth problems is plaque (PLAK). **Plaque** is a mixture of bacteria, saliva, and food particles. It is very sticky and binds to the enamel of your teeth. The bacteria and acid found in plaque can cause bad breath and even worse—cavities! ✷ 1.C

Dental Cavities

A **cavity** is a hole in your tooth that is made by acids. A cavity begins when plaque forms on your tooth. The bacteria in the plaque make acids from food particles. The plaque holds the acids very close to the enamel of the tooth. Even though the enamel is very tough, the acids eventually eat through it and make a hole. This process is called tooth decay. You probably won't feel anything at first. However, the hole in the enamel can enlarge and go deeper into the tooth. As the decay continues through the dentin (DEN tin), the hole eventually reaches the pulp. The cavity now reaches from the surface of the tooth all the way to the sensitive nerves inside. When the acids that made the hole touch the nerves in the pulp, you get a toothache. If you have a toothache, visit a dentist right away. ✷ 1.C

Figure 6 | Tooth Decay

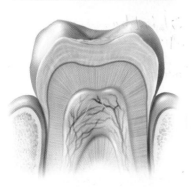

Step 1
Bacteria in plaque make acids.

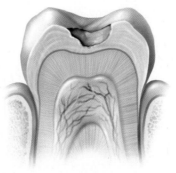

Step 2
The acids make a hole in the enamel. The hole is called a cavity.

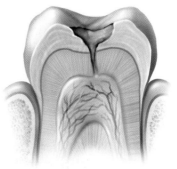

Step 3
If the cavity enlarges, it can reach the nerves in the pulp and cause a toothache.

How to Brush Your Teeth

One way to avoid cavities is to brush properly. Brushing helps get rid of plaque before it binds tightly to your teeth. If possible, brush your teeth after each meal. Brushing your teeth helps get rid of trapped food particles before the bacteria in your mouth can use the food to make acids. If you can't brush after each meal, brush at least twice a day. Brush once after breakfast and once before bed. When you brush, move the toothbrush up and down and back and forth. Be sure to get in between your teeth where food particles and plaque tend to build up. Also, be sure to brush your gums to ensure that they stay healthy, too. ✪ 1.C

How to Floss Your Teeth

No matter how good you are at brushing your teeth, it is almost impossible to get all of the food particles out from between them. These hard-to-reach areas are a perfect place for plaque to form. As a result, cavities often form on the surfaces between teeth. To get your teeth really clean, you should floss once a day. Flossing is easy. Simply grab 12 to 18 inches of dental floss, wrap a few inches around one finger finger of each hand, and pull tight. Slip the floss between two teeth, and move it up and down and back and forth on each inner surface of each tooth. Go slightly below gum level to reach the trapped plaque and bacteria. If you floss between all of your teeth, you will be rewarded with healthy teeth and gums. ✪ 1.C

Health Journal

In your Health Journal, write down your dental care for 1 week. Be sure to include when you eat, when you brush, how long you brush, and when you floss. Do you think you are spending enough time caring for your teeth? Explain your answer.

Figure 7 When you floss your teeth, move the floss gently up and down and back and forth to remove food trapped between teeth.

Keeping Your Teeth for Life!

The best way to prevent cavities is to brush and floss properly. Use a toothpaste that contains fluoride (FLAWR IED) and that is recommended by the American Dental Association. Use a toothbrush with soft bristles, and replace it every few months. Your diet is also an important part of good dental health. Eat plenty of fresh fruits and vegetables. Drinking milk and eating yogurt and cheese helps provide calcium (KAL see uhm), a mineral needed for strong teeth. Avoid eating too many sweets. Soft, gooey foods that stick to your teeth are especially likely to promote cavities. ✪ 1.C

Also, even though your teeth are the hardest part of your body, if they are not protected, they can break or chip. Don't use your teeth to pry things open. And be sure to wear a mouth guard when you play sports.

Visit your dentist regularly. Mention any problems that you have been having with your teeth, and listen to the advice that your dentist gives you. Caring for your teeth will help you keep them for life! ✪ 1.G

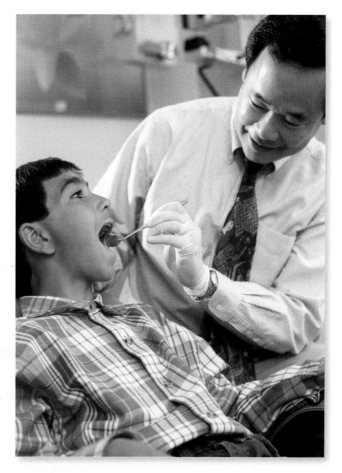

Figure 8 Visiting the dentist is part of good tooth care.

Lesson Review

Using Vocabulary

1. What is a cavity?
2. Define *plaque*.

Understanding Concepts

3. Describe the structure and function of teeth. ✪ 2.A
4. Identify two common tooth problems. ✪ 1.C
5. Describe how a cavity forms. ✪ 1.C
6. Describe effective dental care. ✪ 1.C; 1.G
7. Explain how to floss and why flossing is a good idea, even if you brush regularly. ✪ 1.C

Critical Thinking

8. **Identifying Relationships** Sticky foods contribute to cavities. Why might crunchy vegetables, such as raw carrots, help fight cavities? ✪ 1.A; 1.C

📶 **internet** connect ▤

www.scilinks.org/health
Topic: Teeth
HealthLinks code: HD4098

HEALTH LINKS Maintained by the National Science Teachers Association

Caring for Your Eyes

What You'll Do

- **Identify** the parts of the eye. ⊛ 2.A
- **Explain** how the eye works. ⊛ 2.A
- **Describe** five ways to take care of your eyes. ⊛ 1.C; 1.G

Terms to Learn

- cornea
- iris
- pupil
- lens
- retina

Start Off
Write

Why should you wear eye protection when you work with hand tools?

Mary Beth's new glasses help Mary Beth see better. Good vision is important. Your eyes sense the color, shape, and movement of the world around you. You depend on your eyes to recognize your friend's face, see a ball thrown to you, and watch movies.

How Eyes Work

Your eyes are covered by your eyelids. Your eyelids protect your eyes and bathe them in tears to remove dust and harmful bacteria. Light first passes through the **cornea** (KAWR nee uh), the clear, protective structure at the front of the eye. The **iris** (IE ris) is the colorful part of the eye. It controls the amount of light that enters by opening and closing the pupil (PYOO puhl). The **pupil** is a hole in the iris. The pupil gets bigger in low light and smaller in bright light. The **lens** focuses the light on the retina (RET'n uh) at the back of the eye. The **retina** is the part of the eye that contains millions of light-sensitive cells that detect the energy from the light. These cells convert light energy into nerve signals that are sent along the *optic nerve* to the brain. The brain processes the nerve signals into the images that you see. ⊛ 2.A

Figure 9 The Parts of Your Eye

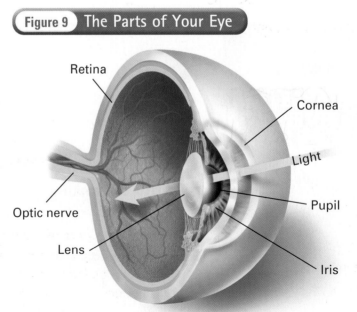

Retina
Cornea
Light
Optic nerve
Pupil
Lens
Iris

TABLE 1 Common Eye Problems

Condition	What is the difficulty?	What can be done?
Nearsightedness (NIR SIET id nis)	seeing things at a distance	glasses or contact lenses; surgery is an option for adults
Farsightedness (FAHR SIET id nis)	seeing things up close	glasses or contact lenses
Astigmatism (uh STIG muh TIZ uhm)	seeing things clearly	glasses or contact lenses
Colorblindness	telling the difference between certain colors	no treatment; person adjusts to condition without treatment

Eye Care

Some eye problems, such as those in Table 1, can't be prevented. Other problems can be prevented. Be careful with your eyes. Eyes can be damaged easily. Some ways to protect your eyes are listed below.

- Wear a protective face mask or goggles whenever your eyes could be hit or hurt. Always wear eye protection when working in science labs, when playing sports that could hurt your eyes, or when working with tools.

- Wear sunglasses to prevent eye damage from the sun.

- Don't rub your eyes. Rubbing your eyes can spread germs from your hands to your eyes, which can lead to infection.

- Get regular eye exams, and follow your doctor's advice. If you are supposed to wear glasses, wear them.

- Never wear glasses that are prescribed for someone else.
  ✪ 1.C; 1.G

Lesson Review

Using Vocabulary

1. Name the parts of your eye. ✪ 2.A

Understanding Concepts

2. Explain how eyes work. ✪ 2.A

3. Why should you avoid rubbing your eyes? ✪ 1.C

4. Describe five ways to care for your eyes. ✪ 1.C; 1.G

Critical Thinking

5. **Applying Concepts** What might happen if a cornea were cloudy and not perfectly clear? How would someone's ability to see be affected? ✪ 2.A

🔲 **internet** connect

www.scilinks.org/health
Topic: The Eye
HealthLinks code: HD4038

HEALTH LINKS. Maintained by the National Science Teachers Association

Caring for Your Ears

After the school dance, Wayne could hear ringing in his ears as he waited for a ride home. Wayne likes music, but he was starting to wonder when his hearing would return to normal.

Wayne's hearing returned to normal the next day. But Wayne now knows that he has to care for his ears so that they will work properly.

How You Hear

To care for your ears, you need to know how the ear works. Sound waves are caused by vibrations that travel through solids, liquids, or air. For example, when someone strikes a drum, the drum vibrates. The vibrations of the drum cause the air around the drum to vibrate. The vibrations travel as sound waves through the air. Sound waves enter the outer ear and are funneled into the middle ear through the ear canal. The sound waves cause the eardrum to vibrate. The vibrations in the eardrum move three tiny bones (the hammer, anvil, and stirrup). The vibrations of the ear bones are transferred through a small membrane to the cochlea (KAHK lee uh). The **cochlea** is a tiny, snail-shaped, fluid-filled part of the inner ear. The fluid in the cochlea moves when vibrations come into the inner ear. Cells in the cochlea convert these vibrations into nerve impulses. The nerve impulses are sent to the brain and are processed into recognizable sounds. ⊛ 2.A

Ears help you hear because tiny parts inside your ears vibrate delicately. Loud sounds, such as those made by lawn mowers, jet engines, and loud music make the tiny parts vibrate much too hard. If you expose your ears to loud sounds too often, the tiny parts of your ear can break. Hearing loss may result. ⊛ 1.C; 2.A

Figure 10 The Parts of Your Ear

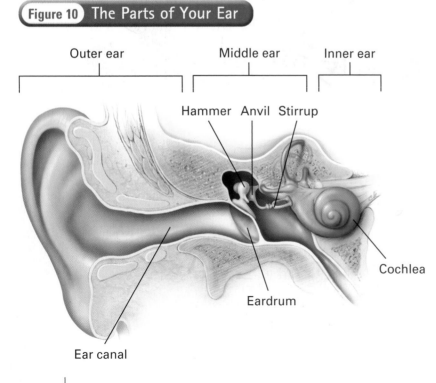

Outer ear   Middle ear   Inner ear

Hammer Anvil Stirrup

Cochlea

Eardrum

Ear canal

Other Hearing Problems

Besides loud sounds, the most common causes of hearing problems are earwax buildup and middle-ear infections. Anything that blocks the ear canal can create hearing problems. Sometimes, earwax builds up and hardens in the canal. This can block the sound waves and prevent the eardrum from vibrating. Infections in the middle ear can cause fluid buildup, which can also prevent the eardrum from vibrating properly. ✪ 1.C

Hearing and Ear Care

The best way to keep your ears healthy and working well is to protect them from loud sounds and to keep them clean. Wear ear protection whenever you are around loud sounds. Don't put anything into your ear canal. Inserting anything into your ear canal can damage your eardrum. ✪ 1.C; 1.G

The best way to clean your ears is in the shower while you are washing your hair. Use your fingers to gently clean your ears. Don't stick your finger in your ear canal. Turn your head to the side to let the shower rinse out the water and wax. Hardened earwax should be removed by a doctor.

Wear Earplugs

Listening to loud music can cause permanent hearing damage. Even rock stars wear earplugs to avoid damaging their hearing!

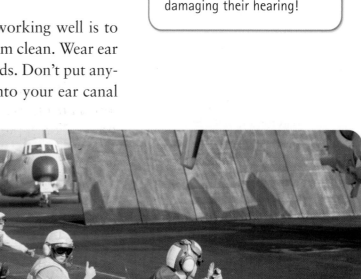

Figure 11 Airplanes make a lot of noise. People who work around them need to protect their ears.

Lesson Review

Using Vocabulary

1. What is a cochlea?

Understanding Concepts

2. Describe how the ear works. ✪ 2.A

3. What are three common things that can cause hearing problems? ✪ 1.C; 2.A

4. Explain good ear care. ✪ 1.C; 1.G

Critical Thinking

5. Making Inferences Loud sounds cause the parts of your ear to vibrate too much. Why do you think some sounds are too soft for you to hear? ✪ 2.A

☑ internet connect

www.scilinks.org/health
Topic: The Ear
HealthLinks code: HD4033

HEALTH LINKS. Maintained by the National Science Teachers Association

Healthcare Resources

Rosa has a cold. She stood in the drugstore with her mother and looked at dozens of cold medicines. She was afraid that by the time they read all of the labels, she would also have a headache!

What You'll Do

- **Describe** three things that influence healthcare purchases. ⊛ 4.A; 6.A; 7.A; 8.A

- **Describe** how to make a careful healthcare purchase. ⊛ 4.A; 4.B

- **Calculate** a unit price. ⊛ 1.E

- **Describe** how to communicate clearly with healthcare providers. ⊛ 1.C; 1.G

- **Explain** how state, local, and federal agencies help keep you healthy. ⊛ 6.

Terms to Learn

- healthcare consumer
- unit price
- healthcare provider

Start Off
Write

Why do you need to communicate clearly with your doctor?

Rosa went to the store to buy cold medicine, so she is a healthcare consumer (kuhn SOOM uhr). A **healthcare consumer** is anyone who pays for healthcare products or services. Healthcare products are things that help you get or stay well. They include medicine, soap, and even sunglasses. Healthcare services include the care of any professional who treats a medical problem or helps you stay well.

Why Do You Buy?

Many factors influence your choice of healthcare products and services. A few of these influences are listed below.

- **Advertising** TV, radio, magazines, and billboards all have ads that try to influence what you buy and use.

- **Tradition** You may choose to buy something because your family has always used it.

- **Peer Pressure** You may buy something because your friends and classmates buy it. ⊛ 4.A; 6.A; 7.A; 8.A

Figure 12 Healthcare products are things that you buy to help yourself stay healthy.

Smart Shopping

Many things can influence you. But a smart consumer gathers a lot of information about a product or service before paying for it. Ask your parents for advice. Talk to healthcare professionals, including doctors, nurses, and pharmacists, and to librarians. Good healthcare products work well, and are endorsed by medical and dental groups. Companies that make good products stand by their products. Watch out for wild claims and quick fixes. If a claim sounds too good to be true, it probably is.
⊛ 1.E; 4.A; 4.B; 8.A

Calculating a Unit Price

Figuring out the unit price of a product can also help you make a good choice. The **unit price** of an item is the cost of the item divided by the amount of the item. For example, two similar mouthwashes may each cost $2.50 a bottle. However, one may have 12 ounces, and the other may have 20 ounces. So, the bigger bottle costs 13¢ per ounce and the other bottle costs about 21¢ per ounce. The bigger bottle has a lower unit price. ⊛ 1.E

BEING A WISE CONSUMER

Collect two or three empty cereal boxes. Using a ruler, calculate the amount of space on each box that advertises the cereal. Calculate the amount of space that tells you nutritional information about the cereal. Compare the two numbers. Explain what you think may be the reasons for the way the space was divided.
⊛ 1.E; M: 6.11A

TABLE 2 Unit Prices

Product	Cost	Amount	Unit price
Toothpaste	$2.89	6.4 ounce tube	45¢ per ounce
Pain reliever	$3.90	300-tablet bottle	1.3¢ per tablet
Dental floss	$2.42	55-yard roll	4.4¢ per yard

Hands-on ACTIVITY

UNIT PRICING

You are trying to decide which of two similar mouthwashes to buy. You have found the following data:

1. Mouthwash A comes in a 20-ounce bottle and costs $1.40.

2. Mouthwash B comes in two sizes, a 20-ounce bottle that costs $1.60 and a 40-ounce bottle that costs $2.40.

Analysis

1. What is the unit price of mouthwash A?

2. What is the unit price of each of the two sizes of mouthwash B?

3. Which is the best price per ounce?

⊛ 1.E; 4.A; M: 6.1A; 6.2C; 6.11A

Healthcare Providers

A **healthcare provider** is any professional who helps people stay healthy. You already know about some kinds of healthcare providers. A dentist checks your teeth. If you have braces, you go to an *orthodontist* (AWR thoh DAHN tist). For medical check ups, your family might go to a general practitioner. A *general practitioner* is a doctor who treats people who have common medical problems. Sometimes, a general practitioner will send a patient to a specialist. A *specialist* is a healthcare provider who is an expert in a particular medical field. Some specialists are doctors, but other healthcare providers, such as pharmacists, can be medical specialists, too.

Talking About Your Health

When you visit your doctor, nurse, or other healthcare provider, you should communicate clearly. The doctor or nurse will examine you. But he or she will also rely on what you say. Don't be shy or embarrassed. Healthcare providers are used to hearing about people's bodies and concerns. You may have questions to ask. Write them down ahead of time, and take them with you. Clearly describe any pain that you feel or problems that you have. Also, describe when and how often you have these problems. For example, if your knee hurts when you climb stairs but not when you walk, say so. Before you leave, be sure you understand what you need to do and how soon you can expect to feel better. ⊛ 1.C; 1.G

LIFE SKILLS ACTIVITY

PRACTICING WELLNESS

With a partner, make a list of reasons why it is important to make regular, periodic visits to healthcare providers such as a doctor or a dentist. Explain why it may be helpful to visit a doctor before you get sick.

⊛ 1.G

Figure 13 When you talk with healthcare providers, be as clear as you can.

Local Healthcare Agencies

Doctors, dentists, and nurses are healthcare providers whom you may see regularly. But many other individuals and services also help keep you healthy. Many state and local governments provide services that protect your health. Some of these services include

- collecting trash and garbage
- treating wastewater
- making sure your drinking water is clean
- inspecting restaurant kitchens
- providing health information
- giving emergency medical care

Figure 14 Some agencies protect your health by making sure that the water supply is clean.

Federal Healthcare Agencies

The federal government and other national organizations also play a role in healthcare. For example, The National Institutes of Health (NIH) conducts research to help develop treatments for diseases. The NIH also makes recommendations to both consumers and healthcare professionals on health-related issues. The Food and Drug Administration (FDA) is responsible for approving both foods and drugs for widespread use. Other federal organizations help people pay for healthcare.

Lesson Review

Using Vocabulary

1. Define *healthcare consumer*.

Understanding Concepts

2. Describe three things that influence consumer decisions. ⭐ 4.A; 6.A; 7.A; 8.A

3. Describe how to make a careful healthcare purchase. ⭐ 4.A; 4.B

4. Explain how to communicate clearly with healthcare providers. ⭐ 1.C; 1.G

5. Explain how state, local, and federal agencies help keep you healthy. ⭐ 6.A

Critical Thinking

6. Making Good Decisions Three bottles of the same kind of hand lotion are for sale at a drugstore. The 14-ounce bottle costs $5.00. The 10-ounce bottle costs $4.00. The 8-ounce bottle costs $3.50. Which bottle has the lowest unit price? ⭐ 1.E

Chapter Summary

■ Cleaning your skin can help you keep your skin healthy. ■ Keeping your hair and nails neat and clean helps you stay healthy. ■ Brush and floss your teeth every day to prevent cavities. ■ Protect your eyes from damage, and schedule regular eye exams. ■ Avoid exposing your ears to loud sounds. ■ Wear ear protection if you must be around loud sounds. ■ Be smart when you shop for healthcare products. Shop carefully, and compare unit prices to find the best value. ■ Local, state, and national agencies provide services that help keep you healthy.

Using Vocabulary

1 Use each of the following terms in a separate sentence: *plaque*, *retina*, and *dandruff*.

For each sentence, fill in the blank with the proper word from the word bank provided below.

head lice	retina
healthcare consumer	cavity
cuticle	cornea
plaque	acne
dandruff	epidermis
pupil	dermis
iris	sound wave
lens	unit price

2 A(n) ___ is made by acids.

3 The ___ is a hole in the iris that changes sizes.

4 Calculating a(n) ___ can help you save money.

5 Pimples are small bumps that develop from ___.

6 The ___ is a skin layer whose outer cells are dead.

7 You can avoid getting ___ by not sharing hats, brushes, or combs.

8 Each fingernail is surrounded by a(n) ___.

9 Brushing and flossing help remove ___.

10 When you describe the color of your eyes, you are describing the ___ of each eye.

Understanding Concepts

11 Explain why plaque is a problem. ★ 1.C; 2.A

12 List three ways to research products before making a healthcare purchase. ★ 4.A; 4.B

13 What is a medical specialist?

14 How may advertisements affect you? ★ 4.A; 8.A

15 How is taking care of your eyes similar to taking care of your ears? ★ 1.C; 2.A

16 How is taking care of your nails similar to taking care of your hair? ★ 2.A

17 Why does wax in your ear affect your hearing?

18 Explain how the Food and Drug Administration helps people stay healthy. ★ 6.A

19 How do local agencies help you stay healthy? ★ 6.A

20 How can writing a list help you talk to healthcare providers? ★ 1.G

21 What does the lens in your eye do?

Identifying Relationships

22 What is the short-term effect of not brushing and flossing your teeth? What is the long-term effect? ⭐ 1.C; 2.A

23 How can keeping your nails clean help keep you healthy? ⭐ 1.C

24 Explain how taking care of your teeth and your ears helps you communicate clearly. ⭐ 2.A

Making Good Decisions

25 One pair of athletic socks costs $2.00 and lasts 3 months. Another pair of athletic socks costs $4.00 and lasts 8 months. Which pair costs less to use? ⭐ 4.A

26 Glenn doesn't brush his teeth or go to the dentist. What could you tell Glenn about the importance of caring for his teeth and getting dental checkups? ⭐ 1.C; 1.G; 2.A

27 You read an ad that says: "Our skin lotion not only will make your skin softer but also will actually make you younger!" List ways to analyze the claims in the ad. How could you research the ad and evaluate its claims? ⭐ 4.A; 4.B

28 The unit price of a healthcare product generally changes with the amount of product in the package. The larger the amount of product in a package is, the lower the unit price of the product. So, buying larger amounts of a product can often save you money. When would buying a product that has the lowest unit price be an unwise decision? ⭐ 1.E; 4.A; 4.B

29 Mark is having trouble hearing in one ear. He thinks wax has hardened in his ear canal. What should Mark do?

30 Kathy is having trouble reading. Kathy thinks that she may need glasses. Kathy's friend, Simone, just got new glasses and offered Kathy her old pair. What should Kathy do? ⭐ 1.C; 11.D

Interpreting Graphics

Shampoo Data

Shampoo	Cost	Amount
Brand X	$1.98	18-ounce bottle
Brand X	$2.64	24-ounce bottle
Brand Y	$2.52	18-ounce bottle
Brand Y	$3.60	30-ounce bottle
Brand Z	$2.70	18-ounce bottle
Brand Z	$3.12	24-ounce bottle

Use the table above to answer questions 31–34. ⭐ M: 6.2C; 6.3A

31 Which bottle of shampoo costs the most?

32 What is the unit price for each bottle of shampoo?

33 Which bottle of shampoo has the highest unit price?

34 Does the larger bottle of brand X have a lower unit price than the smaller bottle of brand X?

Reading Checkup

Take a minute to review your answers to the Health IQ questions at the beginning of this chapter. How has reading this chapter improved your Health IQ?

ACT 1

The 4 Steps of Practicing Wellness

1. **Choose a health behavior you want to improve or change.**

2. **Gather information on how you can improve that health behavior.**

3. **Start using the improved health behavior.**

4. **Evaluate the effects of the health behavior.**

Practicing Wellness

Practicing wellness means practicing good health habits. Positive health behaviors can help prevent injury, illness, disease, and even premature death. Complete the following activity to learn how you can practice wellness.

Elijah's Cavity

Setting the Scene

Elijah's tooth has been hurting for a few weeks. So he isn't surprised when his dentist tells him that he has a cavity. The dentist drills the tooth and fills the cavity. Elijah finds the whole process unpleasant and a little painful. Elijah tells his dentist that he never wants another cavity. ⭐ 1.C

Guided Practice

Practice with a Friend

Form a group of three. Have one person play the role of Elijah and another person play the role of his dentist. Have the third person be an observer. Walking through each of the four steps of practicing wellness, role-play Elijah learning how to improve his dental care. Elijah may speak to his dentist to gather information about dental care. The observer will take notes, which will include observations about what the person playing Elijah did well and suggestions of ways to improve. Stop after each step to evaluate the process.

Check Yourself

After you have completed the guided practice, go through Act 1 again without stopping at each step. Answer the questions below to review what you did.

1. What can Elijah do to improve his dental health? ⊛ 1.C; 1.G

2. Aside from his dentist, where can Elijah find information about how to care for his teeth? ⊛ 4.A; 4.B

3. When caring for your body, which health behaviors do you want to improve? How could you improve them?

ACT 2 ▶ On Your Own

For the next 6 months, Elijah thoroughly cleaned his teeth every day. At his next dentist appointment, Elijah is happy to learn that he has no cavities and that his teeth are in great condition. Elijah realizes that following a daily routine is an easy way to practice good hygiene. He decides to follow a daily routine to keep his skin healthy and to control his acne. Make a poster showing how Elijah can use the four steps of practicing wellness to care for his skin.

Your Body Systems

Lessons

Check out
Current Health
articles related to this chapter by
visiting **go.hrw.com**. Just type in
the keyword **HD4CH08**.

" When I had my **asthma attack,** I had no idea what was happening. I **woke up** in the middle of the night and **couldn't breathe** well at all. My parents took me to the emergency room. The doctor explained that I had a problem with my respiratory system. **"**

Health IQ

PRE-READING

Answer the following multiple-choice questions to find out what you already know about body systems. When you've finished this chapter, you'll have the opportunity to change your answers based on what you've learned.

1. A group of cells that work together for a specific purpose is a(n)
a. body system.
b. organ.
c. cell.
d. tissue.

2. Where does the body make blood cells?
a. in the muscles
b. in the bones
c. in the brain
d. in the stomach

3. Food moves from the mouth to the stomach through the
a. esophagus.
b. small intestine.
c. trachea.
d. lungs.

4. How many chambers are in the human heart?
a. one
b. two
c. four
d. six

5. When cells use energy, ___ is formed as waste.
a. oxygen
b. plasma
c. carbon dioxide
d. calcium

6. Which part of the blood helps a person stop bleeding?
a. white blood cells
b. red blood cells
c. plasma
d. platelets

7. A reflex is
a. an automatic response.
b. a pathway to the brain.
c. one of the five senses.
d. a change outside the body.

ANSWERS: 1. d; 2. b; 3. a; 4. c; 5. c; 6. d; 7. a

Body Systems

Did you know that your small intestine's length is more than three times your height? Your body is full of amazing parts!

Each body part has its own task. But all body parts work together to keep the body alive and healthy.

What Are Body Systems?

Your body is made up of trillions of cells. A **cell** is the basic unit of all living things. Different kinds of cells make up different parts of the body. For example, nerve cells are different than muscle cells. The differences allow each type of cell to do a different job in the body.

A group of similar cells working together is called a **tissue.** For example, muscle cells make up muscle tissue, and nerve cells make up nerve tissue. Each kind of tissue is different.

A group of tissues that work together is called an **organ.** For example, the heart is an organ that is made of muscle tissue. Each organ is responsible for a particular job. The heart's job is to pump blood. But the heart depends on help from other organs to send blood through the body. A group of organs working together to complete a task is called a **body system.**
✪ 2.A

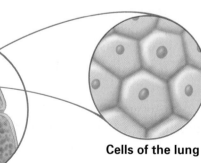

Figure 1 Body systems are made of organs. Organs are made of tissues. Tissues are made of cells.

Lung (Organ)

Lung tissue

Cells of the lung

Respiratory system (Body system)

▶ The **respiratory system** takes in and releases air. As air passes through the vocal chords, it makes sound.

▶ The **skeletal system** supports the body to help it maintain posture while singing.

▶ The **muscular system** shapes the mouth and vocal chords to control words and pitch.

▶ The **nervous system** controls all body systems. It also allows the singer to sense her surroundings. This ability allows her to read the music and listen to the other singers and musicians.

▶ The **circulatory system** carries oxygen and nutrients to give a singer energy.

▶ The **digestive system** gathers nutrients from food. These nutrients are used for energy.

Figure 2 Singing requires body systems to work together.

Body Systems Work Together

Each body system plays a different role in the body. However, the systems work together to make sure that the body maintains homeostasis (HOH mee OH STAY sis). *Homeostasis* is the condition in which the body's internal conditions are at a stable state. For example, a person uses oxygen more quickly during exercise. When the body's level of oxygen decreases, the respiratory and circulatory systems work together to supply more oxygen. These systems speed up so that the amount of oxygen in the body is kept at a healthy level.

Body systems constantly work together. For a person to do anything, several body systems must work together. For example, when a person runs, the respiratory system moves air in and out of the body. The muscular system moves the arms and legs. The skeletal system provides support for the entire body. And none of these systems could function without direction from the nervous system or energy provided by the digestive and circulatory systems. ✪ 2.A

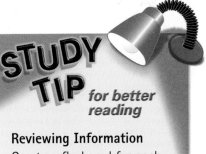

STUDY TIP *for better reading*

Reviewing Information
Create a flashcard for each body system. As you read the chapter, list on the back of each card the system's organs, functions, and some health problems that can occur within the system. Use these flashcards to study each body system.

TABLE 1 Functions of Selected Body Systems

Skeletal system		supports the body
		protects internal organs
		works with muscular system to allow movement
		stores minerals, such as calcium and phosphorus
		produces blood cells
Muscular system		works with the skeletal system to allow movement
		helps maintain posture
		produces heat to help maintain body temperature
		aids in respiration, blood circulation, food movement, emptying the bladder, and functions of the reproductive system
Digestive system		digests foods so that the nutrients can be absorbed into the blood
		stores and releases nutrients
		absorbs nutrients to deliver them to the cells of the body
		eliminates solid waste products from the body
Circulatory system		transports and distributes oxygen, nutrients, and hormones throughout the body
		collects and transports waste products
		transports materials that help fight and prevent disease and that help heal injuries
Respiratory system		exchanges air between the environment and the lungs
		exchanges oxygen and carbon dioxide between the lungs and the blood
		warms and moisturizes air as it comes into the lungs
		filters materials from the air before it enters the lungs
Nervous system		controls the activities of the organs and body systems
		senses through touch, vision, hearing, smell, and taste
		enables the body to respond to changes in the environment
		allows for communication between parts of the body ⍟ 2.A

Body Systems Depend on Each Other

All of the body systems are important. If any one system is not working properly, it affects other body systems. For example, problems in the nervous system can cause problems in other systems. The nervous system controls the activities of all the other body systems. If the nervous system is not working properly, other body systems can lose control. Without direction from the nervous system, your heart and breathing rates could get too slow or too fast. If your muscles do not function properly, running or walking becomes difficult.

Because your body systems are so dependent on each other, caring for each system helps protect the others as well. When the health of one system improves, the health of all the other systems also improves.
★ 2.A

Figure 3 Michael J. Fox educates people about Parkinson's disease, which impairs muscular function by affecting the nervous system.

Health Journal

Write a paragraph about the last time that you had the flu. What happened to your digestive system? Were any other body systems affected?
★ 2.A

Lesson Review

Using Vocabulary

1. How do cells, tissues, and organs form body systems? ★ 2.A

2. Define the term *cell*.

Understanding Concepts

3. What is the difference between a tissue and an organ? Give examples of tissues and of organs. ★ 2.A

4. How do body systems work together? ★ 2.A

Critical Thinking

5. Identifying Relationships Explain what may happen if your circulatory system stops working properly. What problems may occur in the digestive system? What problems may occur in the respiratory system? Can you think of any other body systems that may be affected? ★ 2.A

The Skeletal System

What You'll Do

■ **Describe** the functions of the skeletal system. ⍟ 2.A

■ **Explain** how the skeletal system changes with age.

Terms to Learn

● bone
● bone marrow
● joint

Start Off
Write

How do bones help your body?

> Theo was upset about his broken arm. He wanted to play basketball, but the doctor said Theo's arm would need weeks to heal.

Theo's broken bone will take 4 to 12 weeks to heal. Healing takes a long time because the bone needs to recover and build its strength.

Bones and Joints

A **bone** is an organ of the skeletal system. Bones are hard because they store minerals. This allows bones to protect soft organs and support the body. Inside a bone is soft tissue called **bone marrow.** Bone marrow makes blood cells and stores fat.

A **joint** is a place where two or more bones meet. Bones are held together at joints by tissues called *ligaments* (LIG uh muhnts). Joints allow the body to move in controlled ways.

The skeletal system works with the muscular system to produce movement. Tissues called *tendons* attach muscles to bones. When muscles move, tendons cause the bones to move, too. ⍟ 2.A

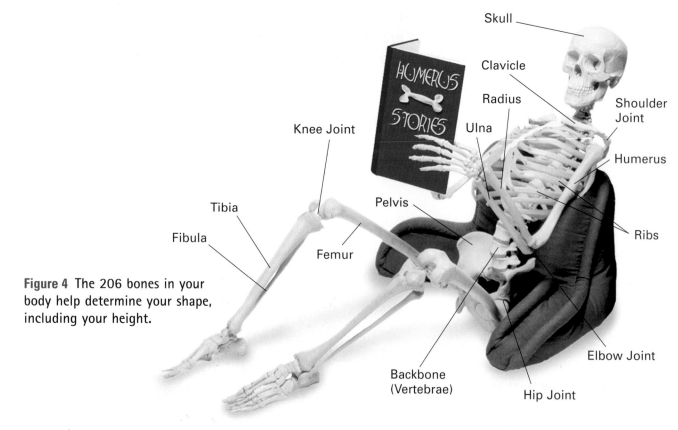

Figure 4 The 206 bones in your body help determine your shape, including your height.

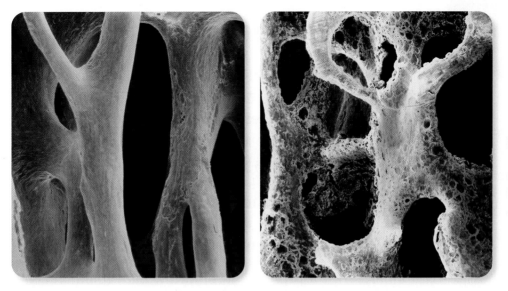

Figure 5 These microscope images show a healthy bone on the left and a bone with osteoporosis on the right.

Bone and Joint Development

Before birth, most of the bones in a baby's body are made of cartilage (KAHRT'l ij). *Cartilage* is a soft, flexible tissue. Cartilage starts changing to bone before a baby is born. The soft tissue hardens and becomes bone tissue as minerals, such as calcium, build up in the bone. This change is not finished until a person is around 18 years old. Even then, some cartilage remains in the body. The joints, nose, and ears use cartilage for flexible support and shape.

Healthy bones stay strong and solid for many years. However, as a person ages, the skeletal system may develop problems. *Osteoporosis* (AHS tee OH puh ROH sis) is a disease in which the bones become weaker. This disease increases a person's risk of breaking bones. *Arthritis* (ahr THRIET is) is irritation of the joints. This problem can occur in young or old people. People who have arthritis often feel pain when moving their joints. ✭ 2.A

SOCIAL STUDIES ACTIVITY

Did you know that some cultures take advantage of the soft cartilage present at birth to shape a baby's bones? For example, the ancient Mayan culture of South America shaped newborns' skulls by pressing boards against their heads. Write a paragraph about why this would work only with newborn children.

Lesson Review

Using Vocabulary

1. Define the term *joint*.

Understanding Concepts

2. What does bone marrow do? ✭ 2.A

3. Explain the functions of the skeletal system. ✭ 2.A

Critical Thinking

4. Making Inferences Calcium is a mineral that is found in several foods and drinks. Calcium makes bones harder. How could eating calcium-rich foods relate to preventing osteoporosis? ✭ 2.A

The Muscular System

Violet really enjoyed hiking yesterday. But she hadn't realized how much it would affect her muscles. Today, her legs ached and hurt when she walked. How could hiking make her feel this way?

What You'll Do

- **Describe** the three different types of muscle.
- **Explain** how muscles work in pairs to produce movement. ⭐ 2.A

Terms to Learn

- skeletal muscle
- smooth muscle
- cardiac muscle

Start Off
Write

Why do muscles work in pairs?

Violet's legs were not used to working so hard. Hiking, like any kind of exercise, requires the use of muscles. When muscles work especially hard, they may ache as they become stronger.

Many Kinds of Muscles

Muscles help the body move. They also provide stability and support to the body. Muscles cause movement and support by *contracting*. When a muscle contracts, its length shortens.

There are three types of muscle tissue. **Skeletal muscle** is muscle that is attached to bones. The figure below shows some of the body's skeletal muscles. When skeletal muscles contract, they pull on bones, causing bone movement. **Smooth muscle** is muscle that forms some internal organs. For example, the stomach is an organ made of smooth muscle. When smooth muscle contracts, it pushes materials through the organ. **Cardiac muscle** is muscle that forms the heart. When the heart muscle contracts, it pumps blood through the body. ⭐ 2.A

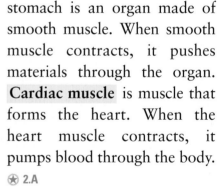

Pectoral muscles

Biceps muscle

Quadriceps muscles

Deltoid muscle

Triceps muscle

Abdominal muscles

Calf muscle

Figure 6 This figure shows some of the skeletal muscles in the human body.

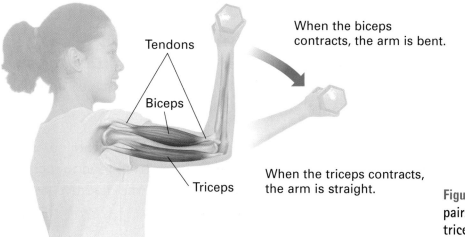

Tendons

Biceps

Triceps

When the biceps contracts, the arm is bent.

When the triceps contracts, the arm is straight.

Figure 7 Muscles work in pairs. Here, the biceps and triceps move the bones of the arm by pulling them in opposite directions.

Muscles and Movement

When skeletal muscles contract, they pull on bones. When a muscle contracts, its two ends are pulled towards its center. If the two ends are attached to different bones, the bones are pulled towards each other. To return to the original position, a different muscle must pull the bone in the other direction.

Most body movements require effort from two different muscles or muscle groups. For example, a muscle called the *biceps* contracts to bend the arm, as shown in the figure above. The biceps pulls the bones in the lower arm such that the arm bends at the joint. But the biceps cannot straighten the arm. A muscle called the *triceps* contracts to straighten the arm. When the triceps contracts, it pulls bones in the lower arm, so the arm straightens. ⊛ 2.A

> **Health Journal**
> Draw a stick figure walking. Circle each joint in the arms and the legs. Write a paragraph explaining how muscles move the bones in one direction and then back in the other direction. Can you circle other joints in other parts of the body?

Lesson Review

Using Vocabulary

1. How do skeletal, smooth, and cardiac muscle differ? ⊛ 2.A

Understanding Concepts

2. How do muscles work with bones to cause the body to move? ⊛ 2.A

Critical Thinking

3. Making Predictions Skeletal muscles are connected to bones by tendons. If bones were not connected to muscles, how would a person's ability to move be affected?

⊛ 2.A

☑ internet connect
www.scilinks.org/health
Topic: Muscle Contraction
HealthLinks code: HD4067

HEALTH LINKS. Maintained by the National Science Teachers Association

The Digestive System

Julia woke up late on the day of her track meet. She was tempted to skip breakfast, but she remembered that her coach said that breakfast is really important.

What You'll Do

■ **Explain** how the body uses food. ⭐ 2.A

■ **Explain** four ways that the body releases waste products. ⭐ 2.A

Terms to Learn

• digestion
• nutrients

Start Off
Write

Why do people need food?

Julia needed breakfast so that she would have enough energy for her track meet. People use the energy from food to fuel their bodies. The body processes food through the digestive system.

Food and Nutrients

As soon as food enters the mouth, the digestive system begins digesting it. **Digestion** is the process of breaking down food into a form your body can use. Most digestion occurs in the stomach and small intestine.

Digestion frees the nutrients from food so that they can be used by the body. **Nutrients** are substances in food that the body needs to work properly. After foods are digested, the blood absorbs the nutrients. The blood delivers nutrients to cells throughout the body. Cells use nutrients to grow, repair themselves, and get energy. ⭐ 2.A

Figure 8 There are several steps in the digestion process.

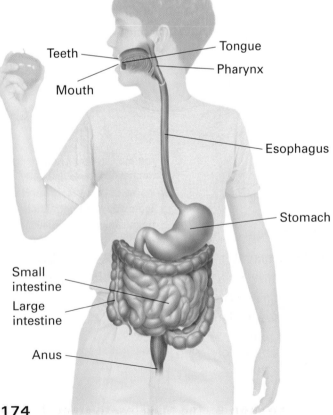

Teeth
Tongue
Pharynx
Mouth

Esophagus

Stomach

Small intestine
Large intestine

Anus

1. Food is chewed and swallowed in the **mouth**. Little digestion occurs here.

2. Food passes through the **pharynx** and **esophagus**. No digestion occurs here.

3. Food enters the **stomach**, where it mixes with stomach juices. Some digestion occurs here.

4. Food enters the **small intestine**, where most nutrients are absorbed. Digestion is completed here.

5. Food waste enters the **large intestine**, where water and salts are absorbed. Then, any remaining food matter leaves the body through the **anus**.

Solid Waste

Most of the nutrients have been removed by the time food material reaches the large intestine. The large intestine absorbs water and salts from the remaining food material. The parts of food that the body cannot use become solid waste. This waste passes through the large intestine and then leaves the body through the anus. ⭐ 2.A

Nondigestive Waste Removal

Digestion is not the only body process that produces and removes waste. When cells use nutrients to get energy, they produce waste products. The blood carries some of these wastes to the kidneys. The kidneys mix wastes with water to form *urine*. Urine is released from the body by the urinary system.

Other waste products are released by the respiratory system. The gas carbon dioxide is a waste that is released from the body when you breathe. The blood carries this gas to the lungs, where it is released into the air.

The skin also helps remove wastes from the body. Sweat glands in the skin remove salt and water by sweating. ⭐ 2.A

Figure 9 Some waste products are removed by sweating, breathing, and urinating.

Lesson Review

Using Vocabulary

1. Define *digestion*.

Understanding Concepts

2. How does the body use food? ⭐ 2.A

3. Where are most nutrients absorbed? ⭐ 2.A

4. How do nutrients reach cells throughout the body? ⭐ 2.A

5. What are four ways that wastes are removed from the body? ⭐ 2.A

Critical Thinking

6. Applying Concepts You know that body systems work together. What body systems work together with the digestive system? ⭐ 2.A

🔗 **internet** connect

www.scilinks.org/health
Topic: Excretory System
HealthLinks code: HD4037

HEALTH
LINKS™ Maintained by the National Science Teachers Association

The Circulatory System

Henry just ran 5 miles, and his heart is pounding. Why is his heart working so hard?

When the body is active, cells use more oxygen and produce more carbon dioxide. Blood carries these products through the body. Henry's heart is beating faster to pump extra blood to and from his cells.

Blood

The circulatory system carries materials through the body in the blood. Blood is made up of plasma, platelets, white blood cells, and red blood cells. Each part of blood has a role in the circulatory system. Plasma is a liquid that is mostly water. The body's cells absorb water from plasma. Platelets help the blood clot if a blood vessel is injured. White blood cells help fight infection and prevent disease. Red blood cells carry oxygen throughout the body.

Blood moves through the body in *blood vessels*, which are hollow tubes of tissue. A blood vessel that carries blood away from the heart is an **artery.** A blood vessel that carries blood to the heart is a **vein.** A **capillary** (KAP uh LER ee) is a tiny blood vessel that carries blood from arteries to veins.

Oxygen is one of many materials that blood carries through the body. Blood also carries nutrients from the stomach and intestines to the body's cells. And blood carries waste products, such as carbon dioxide, away from cells. ✪ 2.A

What You'll Do

- **Trace** the path of blood through the heart. ✪ 2.A
- **Explain** the function of the circulatory system. ✪ 2.A

Terms to Learn

- artery
- vein
- capillary

Start Off
Write

How does the body stop a cut from bleeding?

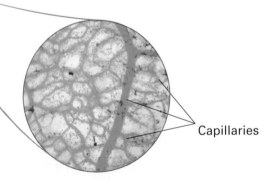

Heart

Blood vessels

Capillaries

Figure 10 Blood vessels carry blood throughout the body.

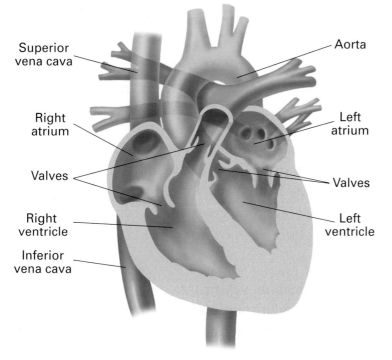

Superior vena cava

Aorta

Right atrium

Left atrium

Valves

Valves

Right ventricle

Left ventricle

Inferior vena cava

Figure 11 The heart has four chambers. Blood flows to the heart through veins. Blood flows away through arteries.

The Heart

The heart muscle contracts to pump blood through the blood vessels. The four chambers of the heart are shown above. The two upper chambers are called the *right atrium* (AY tree uhm) and the *left atrium*. The two lower chambers are called the *right ventricle* (VEN tri kuhl) and the *left ventricle*.

The right ventricle pumps blood to the lungs, where the blood exchanges carbon dioxide for oxygen. The blood then flows to the left atrium. The left atrium pumps the blood to the left ventricle. The left ventricle then pumps the blood to all parts of the body. The body absorbs oxygen from the blood and releases carbon dioxide into the blood. This blood then flows to the right atrium. The right atrium then pumps the blood back to the right ventricle.

⊛ 2.A

Lesson Review

Using Vocabulary

1. What is the difference between an artery, a vein, and a capillary?

Understanding Concepts

2. Trace the path of blood through the heart. ⊛ 2.A

3. Explain the functions of the circulatory system. ⊛ 2.A

Critical Thinking

4. **Applying Concepts** If a man cut his finger, how would platelets help him? What could happen if he had a low number of platelets? ⊛ 2.A

📶 **internet** connect

www.scilinks.org/health
Topic: Blood
HealthLinks code: HD4015

HEALTH LINKS. Maintained by the National Science Teachers Association

The Respiratory System

Bernard took a drink of water that made him cough. What went wrong when he tried to swallow the water?

Bernard's water went down the wrong pipe. If water enters the pipe that carries air to the lungs, a person coughs to force the water out. This pipe is used only to carry air to and from the lungs as part of the respiratory system.

The Path of Air

The respiratory system moves air into and out of the body. Air enters the body through the nose and the mouth and then moves to the *pharynx* (FAR ingks), or throat. Air moves from the throat to the *larynx* (LAR ingks), or voice box. Air then enters the trachea (TRAY kee uh). The **trachea** is the pipe that carries air deep into the body. The lower end of the trachea splits into two branches, called *bronchi* (BRAHNG KIE). The bronchi carry air to and from the two lungs.

A **lung** is a sponge-like organ that allows gases to pass between blood and air. In the lungs, the bronchi branch into smaller tubes called *bronchioles* (BRAHNG kee OHLZ). The bronchioles are covered with tiny air sacs called *alveoli* (al VEE uh LIE). Capillaries surround the alveoli. ⊛ 2.A

What You'll Do

■ **Describe** the breathing process. ⊛ 2.A

■ **Explain** how cells exchange oxygen and carbon dioxide with the air. ⊛ 2.A

Terms to Learn

• trachea
• lung
• diaphragm

Start Off
Write

Why do people have trouble breathing when they have a cold?

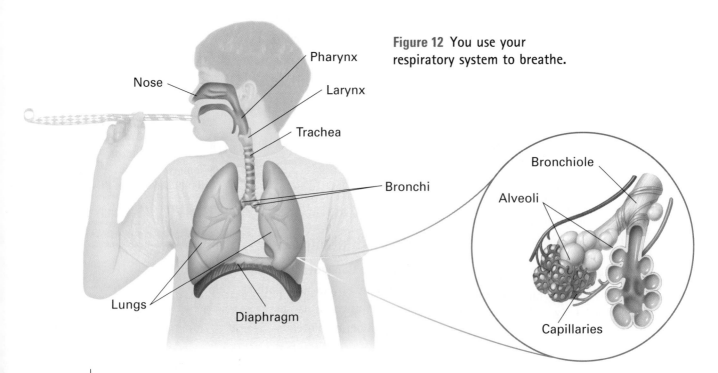

Figure 12 You use your respiratory system to breathe.

Nose

Pharynx

Larynx

Trachea

Bronchi

Lungs

Diaphragm

Bronchiole

Alveoli

Capillaries

Gas Exchange

The lungs and the blood exchange oxygen and carbon dioxide in the alveoli. When air enters the alveoli, the oxygen in the air enters the blood through the capillaries. The blood carries this oxygen to the body's cells. Cells use the oxygen to release the energy in nutrients. This process produces the waste gas carbon dioxide. The blood carries carbon dioxide from the cells to the alveoli. Carbon dioxide leaves the blood through the capillaries. This gas passes into the alveoli as oxygen enters the blood. The carbon dioxide then leaves the body with air released from the lungs. ⭐ 2.A

Figure 13 When you exercise, your body uses more oxygen.

The Breathing Process

Air must move in and out of the lungs for gas to be exchanged in the lungs. Moving air in and out of the lungs is called *breathing*. Breathing involves both *inhalation* (IN huh LAY shuhn) and *exhalation* (EKS huh LAY shuhn). Inhalation is the process in which the air enters the lungs. Exhalation is the process in which the air leaves the lungs. Inhalation occurs when the diaphragm contracts and the rib cage expands. The **diaphragm** is a muscle that separates the chest from the abdomen. When the diaphragm relaxes, it works with other muscles to force air out of the lungs.

When people exercise, they use more oxygen and breathe faster. This rate increase allows the blood to absorb oxygen more quickly during exercise. Using more oxygen produces more carbon dioxide waste. Breathing fast also allows the body to remove this waste quickly. ⭐ 2.A

Lesson Review

Using Vocabulary

1. How are the trachea, lungs, and diaphragm related? ⭐ 2.A

Understanding Concepts

2. Describe the breathing process. ⭐ 2.A
3. Explain how gases are exchanged in the lungs. ⭐ 2.A

Critical Thinking

4. **Applying Concepts** Smoking tobacco for a long time destroys alveoli. How would this destruction affect a person? ⭐ 2.A

5. **Making Predictions** What do you think happens to your breathing rate when you are asleep? Why? ⭐ 2.A

🔲 **internet** connect ▤

www.scilinks.org/health
Topic: Asthma
HealthLinks code: HD4011

HEALTH LINKS Maintained by the National Science Teachers Association

The Nervous System

Rosaura shook her hand in pain. She had accidentally touched a hot pan on the stove. She was lucky that she released the pan so quickly! She let the pan go before even realizing that it had burned her.

How did Rosaura's hand move before she realized the need to move it? Rosaura's nervous system sensed the heat and moved her hand automatically.

Parts of the Nervous System

The nervous system controls all of the body's activities. This system allows different parts of the body to exchange information. It also helps people sense changes inside and outside the body.

The major organ in the nervous system is the **brain.** Different parts of the brain control different body functions, as shown in the figure below. Movement, memory, learning, speaking, and the five senses are controlled by the brain. The senses allow you to see, hear, smell, taste, and feel your surroundings.

The brain is attached to the spinal cord. The **spinal cord** is an organ that carries messages to and from the brain. These messages travel through groups of nerves. A **nerve** is a bundle of cells that conducts messages from one part of the body to another. Messages from the brain go through the spinal cord to nerves that reach other parts of the body. Nerves throughout the body send messages to the brain through the spinal cord. ⊛ 2.A

What You'll Do

■ **Describe** the functions of the nervous system. ⊛ 2.A

■ **Explain** how the nervous system responds to the body's needs. ⊛ 2.A

Terms to Learn

● brain
● spinal cord
● nerve
● reflex

Start Off
Write

What is a reflex reaction?

Brain Food

Your brain is divided into two halves that communicate with each other. Often, the left half controls the right side of your body while the right half controls the left side of your body.

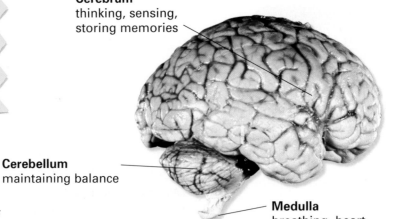

Cerebrum
thinking, sensing, storing memories

Cerebellum
maintaining balance

Medulla
breathing, heart rate, blood pressure

Figure 14 Different parts of the brain control different body functions.

Responding to Stimuli

The nervous system responds to changes. Changes that cause a reaction are called *stimuli*. The eyes, ears, tongue, nose, and skin sense stimuli outside the body and send messages to the brain and spinal cord through nerves. Nerves throughout the body also carry messages about stimuli that occur inside the body.

Sometimes, people react to stimuli after thinking about how to respond. For this kind of response, the brain sends messages through the spinal cord to tell the body how to react. For example, if a person wants to swat a fly, the brain sends a message telling the arm muscle to contract.

In other cases, a person responds to stimuli automatically. For example, heart rate increases automatically when a person exercises. Or, a person can drop a hot pan before realizing it is hot. An automatic response to stimuli is called a **reflex.** In a reflex reaction, messages about stimuli are sent to the spinal cord. The spinal cord then sends a fast response message before the original message even reaches the brain. ⭐ 2.A

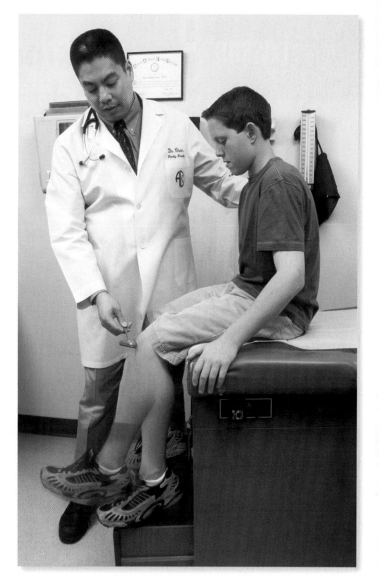

Figure 15 Reflexes help protect the body from harm. This doctor is checking the boy's reflexes.

Lesson Review

Using Vocabulary

1. Define *reflex*. ⭐ 2.A

2. How are the *brain, spinal cord,* and *nerves* related? ⭐ 2.A

Understanding Concepts

3. What are the functions of the nervous system? ⭐ 2.A

4. Explain how the nervous system responds to stimuli. ⭐ 2.A

Critical Thinking

5. **Applying Concepts** When a person's spinal cord is injured, he or she may become paralyzed, or unable to move. Why do you think a spinal cord injury can cause this? ⭐ 2.A

🖪 **internet** connect

www.scilinks.org/health
Topic: Nervous System
Research in Texas
HealthLinks code: HHTX014

HEALTH LINKS Maintained by the National Science Teachers Association

Taking Care of Your Body Systems

What You'll Do

- **Describe** how exercise affects the heart and the lungs. ⭐ 1.B; 1.F; 2.A
- **Explain** how healthy food helps the body systems. ⭐ 1.A; 1.B
- **Explain** how drugs can damage the body systems. ⭐ 2.A; 5.C
- **Discuss** the importance of getting sleep and drinking water. ⭐ 1.B; 2.A

Terms to Learn

- calcium
- sleep

Start Off
Write

Why is water important for your health?

Nina felt exhausted during her basketball game. She had stayed up late studying for a test. And she had only a bag of chips and a soda for lunch. Could these behaviors have affected Nina's game?

Being fit is tough when your body does not get enough sleep or healthy food. These things probably affected Nina's performance at the basketball game. Your body needs proper exercise, food, sleep, and water in order to stay healthy.

Getting Exercise

Your body needs frequent exercise to function properly. Exercise keeps bones, joints, and muscles strong and healthy. Exercise can help prevent osteoporosis. Joints can become more flexible with exercise, decreasing the risk of getting arthritis. Strong muscles can work harder for longer periods of time. This strength allows you to do more things and to do them more easily.

The circulatory and respiratory systems also benefit from exercise. Exercise strengthens the heart, because the heart works faster during exercise. A strong heart can pump blood through the body more easily. Exercise also strengthens the muscles used for breathing. A strong respiratory system allows a person to be active without running out of breath. ⭐ 1.B; 1.F; 2.A

Figure 16 Exercise keeps people healthy, and it can be fun!

Eating Healthy Foods

Food provides nutrients for all of your body systems. The body uses nutrients to grow, get energy, and stay healthy. Eating a variety of healthy foods will provide your body with the right nutrients. Vitamins and minerals from fruits and vegetables help a person grow and function properly. Protein from meat and dairy products helps build strong muscles and tissues. Carbohydrates (KAHR boy HIE drayts) from grains are a good source of energy.

A proper diet can even help prevent some illnesses. For example, eating dairy products and green leafy vegetables is a way to get calcium. **Calcium** is a mineral that makes the bones strong and healthy. Getting enough calcium can help prevent osteoporosis. Proper nutrition allows all of the body systems to function properly. And when all of the systems are healthy, the body has the strength to fight diseases.

⭐ 1.A; 1.B; 2.A

Health Journal

For 1 week, keep track of how many hours you sleep, what foods you eat, how much you exercise, how much water you drink, and how you feel at the end of each day. What health behaviors affect your body most? least? ⭐ 2.A

Figure 17 Healthy food supplies the body with nutrients.

Hands-on ACTIVITY

CHEWING YOUR FOOD

1. Crush an unwrapped piece of hard candy into small pieces. Put the pieces into a glass of water. Put an uncrushed piece of hard candy in another glass of water.

2. At the end of class, check to see if one candy has dissolved more than the other has.

3. Check the glasses again the next day.

Analysis

1. How quickly did each candy dissolve? Did one dissolve more quickly than the other?

2. How does this lab demonstrate the importance of chewing your food to aid digestion?

Avoiding Tobacco and Other Drugs

Tobacco products, alcohol, and illegal drugs can harm every system in your body. Smoking or chewing tobacco damages the respiratory, circulatory, digestive, and nervous systems. Tobacco products increase the risk of getting lung, mouth, throat, and pancreatic cancers.

Drugs can change how the nervous system works. Because of this danger, drugs can affect the entire body. Drugs can alter chemicals in the brain, changing how the brain functions. Drugs can cause the brain to send dangerous messages throughout the body. Sometimes, these messages cause permanent damage or even death. Refusing drugs is an important part of caring for your body systems. ⭐ 5.C; 10.C; 11.B; 11.D

Getting Enough Sleep

Sleep is necessary for both physical and mental health. A person deprived of sleep would die more quickly than a person deprived of food. **Sleep** is a period of reduced awareness during which many body systems rest or slow down. The body repairs and heals injured parts during sleep. Without enough sleep, many organs—especially the brain—will not function correctly.

Scientists do not know exactly what happens to the body when it sleeps. They do not know how sleep helps the body repair itself. But they do know that good sleep is essential for maintaining a healthy body. Good sleep requires a comfortable place to rest. A comfortable bed in a dark, quiet room can help people sleep without being disturbed. ⭐ 1.C; 2.A

LIFE SKILLS ACTIVITY

MAKING GOOD DECISIONS

Do you think it's possible to diet or exercise too much? In groups, brainstorm about how a person could go too far in limiting their diet. Brainstorm about how a person could exercise too much. Then prepare a skit about dieting or exercising too much. The skit should end with someone making a healthy decision about eating and exercise habits. ⭐ 1.C

Figure 18 Quiet, comfortable places allow people to get quality sleep.

Drinking Water

The human body is made up of about 70 percent water. Water helps the body systems function. Without enough water, the body systems cannot do their jobs. For example, the circulatory system depends on water as the major part of blood. A lack of water could decrease the amount of blood in the body.

The digestive system also depends on water. The body uses water in the process of getting nutrients from food. A lack of water could decrease the amount of food that is digested. When less food is digested, fewer nutrients will reach the body's cells. With fewer nutrients, the body cannot get as much energy.

Drinking enough water can prevent many health problems. Most people should drink eight glasses of water each day. This is usually enough to replace the water that is lost by the body. The body loses water during urination, breathing, and sweating. When people sweat a lot because of heat or exercise, they need to drink extra water.

⭐ 1.A; 1.B; 2.A

Dehydration

Dehydration is the condition of not having enough water. It causes severe health risks, including death. It is important to drink enough water, especially when exercising or when the weather is very hot.

Figure 19 People get water from foods in addition to the liquids they drink each day.

Lesson Review

Using Vocabulary

1. Define *calcium*.

Understanding Concepts

2. Why is drinking water important? ⭐ 1.A; 1.B

3. Why is eating healthy foods important? ⭐ 1.A; 1.B

4. What are three body systems that are affected by exercise? ⭐ 1.B; 1.F; 2.A

5. What body systems can be damaged by smoking or using illegal drugs? ⭐ 2.A; 5.C

Critical Thinking

6. Making Good Decisions If you have an important basketball game tomorrow, what should you do to help your body be ready to compete? What should you do throughout the basketball season to improve your overall health? ⭐ 1.A; 2.A

Chapter Summary

■ Cells form tissues. Tissues form organs. Organs form body systems. ■ Body systems work together. ■ The skeletal system supports and protects the body, produces blood cells, and helps the body move. ■ The muscular system provides movement. ■ The digestive system breaks down food to get nutrients. ■ The circulatory system carries materials through the body. ■ The respiratory system gets oxygen from the air and releases carbon dioxide waste. ■ The nervous system controls all other body systems. It also senses changes. ■ Exercise, healthy food, sleep, water, and drug-free habits are important in caring for body systems.

Using Vocabulary

For each pair of terms, describe how the meanings of the terms differ.

❶ cell/tissue

❷ organ/body system

❸ bone/bone marrow

For each sentence, fill in the blank with the proper word from the word bank provided below.

skeletal muscle	digestion
calcium	nerves
capillaries	nutrients
cardiac muscle	joint

❹ A place where two or more bones meet is called a(n) ___.

❺ The body breaks down food to get ___.

❻ In the lungs, oxygen and carbon dioxide are exchanged through ___.

❼ ___ carry messages to and from the brain so a person can respond to stimuli.

❽ Bones are hard because they store minerals, such as ___.

❾ The heart is made of ___.

Understanding Concepts

❿ Why do muscles work in pairs to move the body? ✪ 2.A

⓫ How could playing soccer help the circulatory system? ✪ 1.F; 2.A

⓬ How do cells, tissues, and organs work together in the body? ✪ 2.A

⓭ How do body systems work together when a person is singing? ✪ 2.A

⓮ How could damage to the nervous system affect another body system? ✪ 2.A

⓯ How does the skeletal system protect the body's soft organs? ✪ 2.A

⓰ What are three kinds of muscles?

⓱ Does blood enter the heart through an atrium or through a ventricle? ✪ 2.A

⓲ What does the circulatory system do for the body? ✪ 2.A

⓳ What path does air follow when a person inhales? ✪ 2.A

⓴ How does the nervous system respond to the body's needs? ✪ 2.A

Critical Thinking

Applying Concepts

21 A large number of capillaries are located around the alveoli and around the small intestine. Why do you think there are so many capillaries in these areas of the body? ★ 2.A

22 Anemia is a condition in which the body does not have enough red blood cells in the blood. Why do you think people with anemia often feel tired or low on energy? ★ 2.A

23 During exercise, the body produces and releases increased amounts of carbon dioxide gas. Why do you think this happens? ★ 2.A

24 Smoking may cause cancer of the larynx in some people. Sometimes, a person's larynx must be removed to stop the cancer from spreading through his or her body. What problems might a person have if their larynx is removed? ★ 2.A

Making Good Decisions

25 Imagine that a person tries an illegal drug that changes the chemistry in the brain. How could this change affect the circulatory system? the respiratory system? the muscular system? the digestive system? How could a change in brain chemistry affect a person's thoughts and actions? ★ 2.A; 5.C

26 Your friend Sara just made it to the state dance competition. She tells you that she wants to smoke a cigarette in celebration. You want to help her make a healthy decision not to smoke. What could you tell her about how smoking could affect her ability to compete? ★ 2.A; 11.D

27 You and your family are planning a 4-mile hike through a park. What should you do to prepare for the hike? Remember that you will need energy on the hike. ★ 1.B; 2.A

28 Use what you have learned in this chapter to set a personal goal. Write your goal, and make an action plan by using the Health Behavior Contract for your body systems. You can find the Health Behavior Contract at go.hrw.com. Just type in the keyword HD4HBC03.

Name _____ Class _____ Date _____

Health Behavior Contract
Your Body Systems

My Goals: I, _____, will accomplish one or more of the following goals:
I will exercise three times a week.
I will eat a healthy variety of fruits, vegetables, grains, and dairy products.
I will drink eight glasses of water every day.
Other: _____

My Reasons: By exercising, eating well, and getting plenty of water, I will be giving my body the things that it needs to function properly.
Other: _____

My Values: Personal values that will help me meet my goals are
_____
_____

My Plan: The actions I will take to meet my goals are
_____
_____

Evaluation: I will use my Health Journal to keep a log of actions I took to fulfill this contract. After 1 month, I will evaluate my goals. I will adjust my plan if my goals are not being met. If my goals are being met, I will consider setting additional goals.

Signed _____

Date _____

Reading Checkup

Take a minute to review your answers to the Health IQ questions at the beginning of this chapter. How has reading this chapter improved your Health IQ?

Life Skills IN ACTION

Assessing Your Health

Assessing your health means evaluating each of the four parts of your health and examining your behaviors. By assessing your health regularly, you will know what your strengths and weaknesses are and will be able to take steps to improve your health. Complete the following activity to improve your ability to assess your health.

Manami's Stomachaches

ACT 1

Setting the Scene

Manami loves eating at fast-food restaurants. She goes to one restaurant on her way home from school as often as she can. Manami eats three balanced meals a day, so she thinks it is OK for her to eat a little fast food as an afternoon snack. Lately, Manami has been suffering from stomachaches. She is not sure what causes the stomachaches, but she wants to prevent them.

The 4 Steps of Assessing Your Health

1. Choose the part of your health you want to assess.
2. List your strengths and weaknesses.
3. Describe how your behaviors may contribute to your weaknesses.
4. Develop a plan to address your weaknesses.

Guided Practice

Practice with a Friend

Form a group of two. Have one person play the role of Manami, and have the second person be an observer. Walking through each of the four steps of assessing your health, role-play Manami analyzing her stomach problems. The observer will take notes, which will include observations about what the person playing Manami did well and suggestions of ways to improve. Stop after each step to evaluate the process. ★ 1.A; 1.B

Check Yourself

After you have completed the guided practice, go through Act 1 again without stopping at each step. Answer the questions below to review what you did.

1. What health behaviors contribute to Manami's strengths and weaknesses? ✪ 1.A

2. What can Manami do to address her weaknesses?

3. How might Manami's weaknesses in her physical health affect the other parts of her health? ✪ 2.A

4. What are some of your weaknesses in your physical health? What can you do to improve these weaknesses?

✪ 1.A; 2.A

On Your Own

Manami has stopped going to fast-food restaurants as often, and she hasn't had a stomachache in weeks. After successfully improving the weaknesses in the health of her digestive system, Manami is interested in working on other weaknesses in her physical health. Make an outline that shows how Manami could use the four steps of assessing your health to assess the health of one of her other body systems.

Growth and Development

Check out
Current Health
articles related to this chapter by
visiting go.hrw.com. Just type in
the keyword **HD4CH09**.

> **❝** My little **sister** changes so much every year. She **makes me laugh** at some of the **silly things** she does. But my mom says I used to act exactly the same way when I was my sister's age. **❞**

Health **IQ**

PRE-READING

Answer the following true/false questions to find out what you already know about growth and development. When you've finished this chapter, you'll have the opportunity to change your answers based on what you've learned.

1. Men's bodies are different from women's bodies. ✪ 2.A

2. Older adults have less fulfilling lives than younger people.

3. Most newborn infants learn to crawl within three months of birth.

4. Adolescents go through physical, mental, emotional, and social changes. ✪ 6.A

5. Grief is a process that should be avoided.

6. Everyone starts puberty at the same age. ✪ 2.B; 2.C

7. The menstrual cycle is exactly 28 days for every woman. ✪ 2.D

8. Sperm mature over several months. ✪ 2.B

9. All children grow at the same rate. ✪ 2.B

10. While a fetus is in the mother's uterus, the fetus cannot hear sound or detect light.

11. Health habits of pregnant women affect the health of the fetus. ✪ 11.D

12. Health decisions you make now will not affect you when you are older. ✪ 1.C

13. Males and females make the same type of sex cell. ✪ 2.B

14. During the first year of life, babies triple in weight.

15. Childhood is the longest stage of life.

16. A human pregnancy usually lasts 6 months.

What You'll Do

- **Describe** the structure and function of the male and female reproductive systems. ⊛ 2.A
- **Identify** four ways to protect your reproductive health. ⊛ 1.C; 3.A; 5.I

Terms to Learn

- sperm
- testes
- egg
- ovary
- menstruation

Start Off Write

What are the functions of the male and female reproductive systems?

Human Reproduction

Men's bodies are different from women's bodies in some ways. One difference is in the reproductive organs. Men and women have different reproductive organs because their roles in reproduction are different.

The male and female reproductive systems both make sex cells. A *sex cell* is a parent cell that can join with another sex cell to create a new cell. This new cell contains all the information needed to develop into a new human being. The combination of two sex cells may begin a pregnancy.

The Male Reproductive System

The main function of the male reproductive system is to make and store sperm. **Sperm** are the sex cells made by males. The male reproductive system also makes the hormone *testosterone* (tes TAHS tuhr OHN). Testosterone controls much of the growth and function of the male body.

The parts of the male reproductive system are shown in Figure 1. The **testes** (TES TEEZ) are the organs that make sperm and testosterone. The testes are sometimes called *testicles*. ⊛ 2.A; 2.C

Figure 1 Male Reproductive Organs

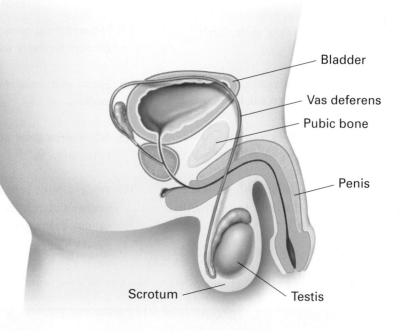

Bladder

Vas deferens

Pubic bone

Penis

Scrotum

Testis

Figure 2 You should talk to your parents or doctor about any concerns you have about your reproductive health.

Sperm Production

Sperm are made in the testes. A healthy adult male makes several million sperm each day. Each sperm cell takes about 70 days to mature. Then, the sperm are carried into the vas deferens. The vas deferens are long tubes that lead to the urethra. The urethra is the tube that runs through the penis. ⊛ 2.A

Caring for the Male Body

Good hygiene is important to protecting your health. You should bathe every day and wear clothes that are not too tight. Watch for anything that seems different about your body. If you are ever concerned about your health, talk to your parent or doctor.

Many boys and men get a fungal infection of the skin called *jock itch*. Jock itch is usually treated by keeping the area clean and dry, avoiding tight clothing, and using an over-the-counter antifungal cream.

Another threat to the reproductive system is sexually transmitted diseases, or STDs. These diseases are spread by sexual activity with an infected person. Sexually transmitted diseases can be prevented by avoiding sexual activity. ⊛ 1.C; 3.A; 5.I

Brain Food

Once they are mature, sperm stay in the male body for about 2 weeks. Then, they degenerate and are absorbed by the body.

Figure 3 Female Reproductive Organs

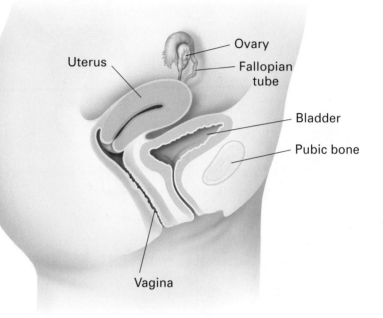

The Female Reproductive System

The female reproductive system has two main functions. The first function is to make the female sex cell called the **egg.** The second function is to carry out a pregnancy.

The female reproductive system is shown in Figure 3. The **ovaries** are the organs that make eggs and the hormones *estrogen* (ES truh juhn) and *progesterone* (pro JES tuhr OHN). These hormones control much of the growth and function of the female body. The *uterus* is the organ that holds a fetus during pregnancy. ✪ 2.A; 2.C

Menstruation

Beginning at puberty, the lining of the uterus thickens every month in preparation for pregnancy. The monthly breakdown and shedding of this lining is called **menstruation** (MEN STRAY shuhn). During this menstrual period, blood and tissue leave the woman's body through the vagina. This bleeding generally lasts 3 to 5 days. The menstrual period is one part of a cycle that lasts about 28 days. This cycle is described in Figure 4. Many young women have menstrual cycles that vary in length from month to month, or are irregular. Usually, menstrual cycles become more regular with age. ✪ 2.D

Figure 4 The Menstrual Cycle

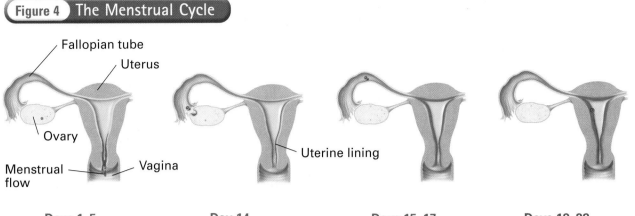

Fallopian tube
Uterus
Ovary
Menstrual flow
Vagina
Uterine lining

Days 1–5
The lining of the uterus is shed through menstruation.
Days 1–13
The egg matures in the ovary.

Day 14
The ovary releases the egg into the fallopian tube. The uterine lining gets thicker.

Days 15–17
The egg travels through the fallopian tube toward the uterus.

Days 18–28
The egg reaches the uterus. If the egg was not fertilized, it will dissolve. Menstruation will begin as the cycle repeats.

Caring for the Female Body

By practicing good hygiene, you can avoid reproductive health problems. Bathe daily, and don't wear clothing that is too tight. Good hygiene is very important during the menstrual period. Tampons and sanitary napkins should be changed every 4 to 6 hours. Many women have menstrual cramping. Cramps can usually be treated with over-the-counter pain relievers. But if the cramps are severe or last a long time, see a doctor. Women should see a doctor at least once a year. Like men, women can also get STDs. To prevent STDs, avoid sexual activity. Abstaining from sex will also prevent unplanned pregnancy. ⍟ 1.C; 2.D; 3.A; 5.I

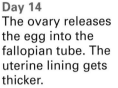

Lesson Review

Understanding Concepts

1. What are the functions of the male reproductive system? ⍟ 2.A

2. What are the functions of the female reproductive system? ⍟ 2.A

3. Describe the typical menstrual cycle. ⍟ 2.A; 2.D

4. Identify four ways to protect your reproductive health. ⍟ 1.C; 3.A; 5.I

Critical Thinking

5. Analyzing Ideas Why is it important to keep the reproductive area clean and dry? ⍟ 1.C; 2.A

6. Identifying Relationships How are the ovaries similar to the testes? How are the ovaries different from the testes? ⍟ 2.A; 2.B

☐ internet connect

www.scilinks.org/health
Topic: Reproductive System
HealthLinks code: HD4081

HEALTH **Maintained by the**
LINKS **National Science**
Teachers Association

Before You Were Born

Tom's older sister is 5 months pregnant. She and her husband came over yesterday to show Tom's family a videotape of her ultrasound. Tom couldn't believe how much the picture looked like a little person!

What You'll Do

- **Summarize** the growth and development of humans before birth. ⭐ 1.A; 5.D

- **Describe** three factors that affect the health of both the mother and fetus.

Terms to Learn

- fertilization
- fetus

Start Off *Write*

How long is the average pregnancy?

During human reproduction, one sperm and one egg come together to form a new human cell in a process called **fertilization** (FUHR t'l uh ZAY shuhn). This new cell grows from one cell into many cells. Eight to 10 days after fertilization, the cells attach to the mother's uterus. Eight weeks after fertilization, the developing human is called a **fetus** (FEET uhs). The fetus remains in the uterus until birth. A baby is born about 9 months or 40 weeks after fertilization.

Caring for the Fetus

Development of a fetus can be affected by many factors. Most things that a mother puts into her body are carried to the fetus. So pregnant women should not use tobacco, alcohol, or other drugs. They should eat well and take vitamins. They should also go to the doctor regularly. A doctor can often identify and prevent many problems that may affect both the mother and fetus. ⭐ 1.A; 5.D

Figure 5 Fetal Development

1 A new cell is formed when an egg is fertilized by a sperm. The new cell multiplies. The cells attach to the mother's uterus.

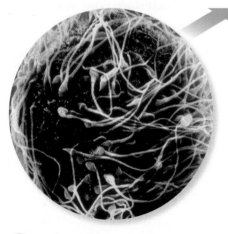

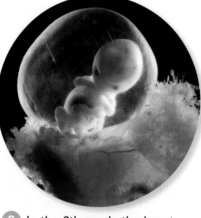

2 In the 6th week, the heart starts to beat. By the 8th week, the internal organs are developing.

3 By 12 weeks, the internal organs are functioning. Arms, legs, and feet have formed.

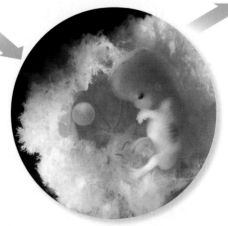

5 By 20 weeks, the fetus has begun to react to sound. By 25 weeks, taste buds have formed. Also, the fetus has eyebrows and eyelashes and opens its eyes. By 27 weeks, the fetus can practice breathing.

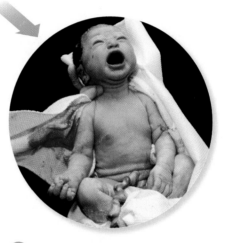

4 At 13 weeks, the fetus can swallow, hiccup, and make a fist. By 14 weeks, the doctor can tell if the fetus is male or female. By 16 weeks, the fetus has begun to move. The mother may not feel these movements right away.

6 At 35 to 40 weeks, the organs are fully functional. The fetus responds to light. During this time, the fetus is getting bigger. A baby born at or after 38 weeks is fully developed.

Lesson Review

Using Vocabulary

1. Define and describe fertilization.

2. What is a fetus?

Understanding Processes

3. Explain why a pregnant woman should eat well and take vitamin pills. Why should she avoid using tobacco, alcohol, and other drugs?
★ 1.A; 1.B; 5.D

4. Summarize how the fetus develops from fertilization to birth.

Critical Thinking

5. Making Inferences Some pregnant women do not visit the doctor regularly during their pregnancy. What effect might this have on the health of the fetus? Explain your answer.
★ 1.C; 1.G; 11.D

☑ internet connect

www.scilinks.org/health
Topic: Before Birth
HealthLinks code: HD4013

HEALTH LINKS. Maintained by the National Science Teachers Association

Infancy and Childhood

Carla has been baby-sitting Tyler for two years. When she started baby-sitting, Tyler had just started walking and could say only a few words. Now, he runs around the house and speaks in sentences!

What You'll Do

- **Summarize** development during infancy and childhood.

Terms to Learn

- infancy
- childhood

Start Off *Write*

How do babies change as they grow into children?

You may remember relatives or friends commenting on how much you have grown. Growth and development happen very rapidly during the early stages of life.

Infancy

The time between birth and 1 year of age is called **infancy.** Many important physical and mental changes happen during infancy. During this time, height and weight increase rapidly. In fact, babies often triple in weight during the first year. The infant gets stronger and begins to control its body. At birth, the infant is basically helpless. A newborn baby cannot even hold its head up straight!

By about 3 months of age, infants can hold their heads up and look around. The infant also recognizes its parents, smiles at them, and enjoys playing with them. By 7 months of age, the infant can roll over and has learned to play with toys. During the next few months, the baby will learn to crawl and then stand. By 1 year of age, most infants have begun cruising. Cruising is walking by leaning on furniture or other objects for support. Some 1-year-old infants have begun walking and many have begun to say a few words.

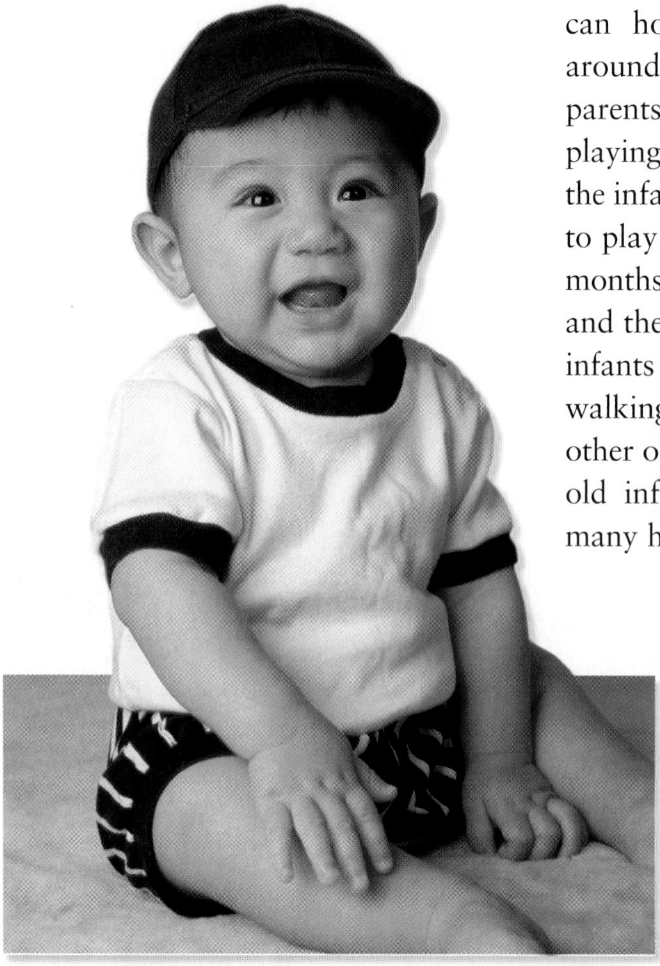

Figure 6 Infants learn to crawl and may begin to walk within the first year of life.

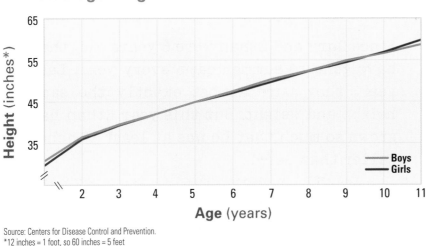

Average Height of Children in the United States

Source: Centers for Disease Control and Prevention.
*12 inches = 1 foot, so 60 inches = 5 feet

Figure 7 This graph shows the average height of boys and girls at different ages.

Childhood Development

The stage of development after infancy is called **childhood.** Childhood is divided into three stages—early, middle, and late. Early childhood is from age 1 to age 3. During early childhood you learned to walk and run. You also started to build with blocks, play make believe, and form short sentences.

Middle childhood is from age 3 to age 5. During middle childhood, you started asking many questions and trying new things. You learned to speak in longer sentences, name colors, and count. You also started to dress and undress yourself.

Late childhood is from age 6 to about age 11. During late childhood, you learn to move more gracefully. You learn to perform complex tasks, such as writing in cursive. You learn to read and write, and to connect different ideas. In late childhood, you become more interested in social relationships.

HOW YOU'VE CHANGED

1. Collect three full-length photos of yourself—one from each stage of childhood.
2. Measure the length of your whole body and the length of your head in each photo.
3. Calculate the ratio of head length to body length for each photo by dividing the head length by the body length.

Analysis

1. Make a graph of the ratio of head length to body length over time.
2. How did the ratio of your head length to your body length change as you grew?

Lesson Review

Using Vocabulary

1. What is the difference between infancy and childhood?

Understanding Concepts

2. How do humans change between infancy and late childhood?

Critical Thinking

3. Making Inferences Why might childhood be divided into three stages? What developments might be used to distinguish one stage from another?

internet connect
www.scilinks.org/health
Topic: Human Development
HealthLinks code: HD4057
HEALTH LINKS. Maintained by the National Science Teachers Association

Adolescence

Since Gary and Ethan were 6 years old, they have gone to summer camp every year. Last year, they were almost exactly the same height and weight. But this year Ethan had grown so much that he was at least 3 inches taller than Gary!

What You'll Do

- **Explain** how hormones affect growth and development. ⭐ 2.C
- **Describe** physical development during adolescence. ⭐ 2.B; 2.C
- **Summarize** the emotional, physical, mental, and social changes that happen during adolescence. ⭐ 2.B; 2.C; 7.A

Terms to Learn

- adolescence
- hormone
- puberty

Start Off Write

What are some changes that happen during adolescence?

What caused Ethan to grow so quickly? Ethan grew quickly because he entered adolescence (AD'l ES'ns). **Adolescence** is the stage of development during which humans grow from childhood to adulthood.

What Controls Growth?

Most body functions, including growth, are controlled by hormones. A **hormone** is a chemical that is made in one part of the body and causes a change in a different part of the body. For example, human growth hormone is made by a gland in your brain and causes your bones and muscles to grow. Hormones are released into your body by the endocrine system.

Hormones that affect your reproductive system are called *sex hormones*. These hormones cause a number of changes in the body. They cause growth spurts in adolescents. One way they do so is by telling your body to make more growth hormones. These hormones cause the shape of your body to change as you get older. Table 1 lists a few hormones and what they do in the body.
⭐ 2.C

TABLE 1 Important Hormones

Hormone	Where it's made	What it does
Thyroxine (thie RAHKS een)	thyroid gland	controls how your body makes and uses energy; helps regulate growth and development
Testosterone	testis	controls much of the growth and function of men's bodies, causes the male body to make sperm
Estrogen	ovary	controls much of the growth and function of women's bodies, causes the female body to release eggs
Epinephrine (ep uh NEF rin)	adrenal gland	makes your heart beat faster and prepares your body to fight or flee when you are frightened or excited
Human growth hormone	pituitary gland	causes your body to grow; causes height and weight growth spurts ⭐ 2.C

Figure 8 Your body can change a lot during a growth spurt. This boy grew several inches in less than a year.

Growth Spurts

Adolescence generally lasts from about age 10 to age 18. It begins a little later for boys than for girls. The most obvious part of adolescence is puberty. **Puberty** is the stage of development when the reproductive system becomes mature. Puberty usually happens between 9 and 15 years of age in girls and between 10 and 16 years of age in boys. During this time, your body makes more sex hormones. Some of these hormones make boys' bodies grow and change until they become men. Other hormones cause girls' bodies to grow and change until they become women.

Greater amounts of sex hormones and growth hormones also lead to growth spurts. Between 11 and 16 years of age, the average girl will grow 12 inches and gain about 40 pounds. By the time she is 16 or 17 years old, she will reach her full adult height. Between 12 and 18 years of age, the average boy grows about 16 inches and gains over 60 pounds. By the time he is 18 or 19 years old, he will reach his full adult height. ⭐ 2.B; 2.C

Brain Food

Girls begin their growth spurt about 1 year earlier than boys do.

Figure 9 Changes in Boys' and Girls' Bodies

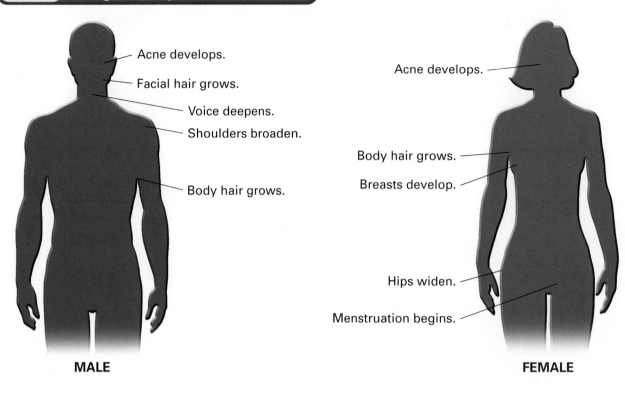

- Acne develops.
- Facial hair grows.
- Voice deepens.
- Shoulders broaden.
- Body hair grows.

MALE

- Acne develops.
- Body hair grows.
- Breasts develop.
- Hips widen.
- Menstruation begins.

FEMALE

Physical Changes

Hormones also cause other physical changes in both boys and girls. These changes show that the person is becoming mature. During puberty, the voices of both boys and girls get deeper. Hair begins to grow in different places on the body. Both boys and girls are likely to get *acne,* or pimples. Acne is a normal part of growing up and is nothing to be embarrassed about. Physical changes may happen rapidly or may take several years. These changes may cause you to feel awkward or self-conscious. But all of these changes are normal, and everyone goes through them. ✪ 2.B; 2.C

Social Changes

Adolescence brings about many social changes as well. Most adolescents are interested in forming friendships with other people their age. You may also become more independent and begin to show more responsibility. Learning to communicate with your parents is very important if you want to gain more independence.

Your teen years are a time when you may become more aware of the world around you. You may develop an interest in political and social issues. As you learn how you fit in to society, you are preparing to be an adult. ✪ 2.B; 2.C

MATH ACTIVITY

Girls reach three-fourths of their adult height by the age of $7\frac{1}{2}$. Boys reach three-fourths of their adult height by age 9. Sandra is $7\frac{1}{2}$ years old and is 4 feet tall. Her brother Sam is 9 years old and is 5 feet tall. How tall will Sandra and Sam be as adults? ✪ M: 6.3.C

Mental and Emotional Changes

You also grow mentally and emotionally during adolescence. The following list describes some of these changes:

- Your ability to understand complex ideas increases. You learn to analyze different situations and decide how to respond. You further develop your personal identity and beliefs.

- You may begin to feel attracted to other people and become interested in romantic relationships.

- You may feel happy one day and sad the next day. These mood swings are common during adolescence.

- You may feel tempted to do unhealthy or unsafe things, such as smoke tobacco, to try to fit in with your friends. But these behaviors can damage your health, and there are better ways to be accepted.

Dealing with the changes of adolescence can be difficult. Talking to your parents and other trusted adults can help you deal with the changes you are going through. ⊛ 2.A; 11.A

Figure 10 Teens explore their identities in many ways, including through music.

Lesson Review

Using Vocabulary

1. Explain the difference between adolescence and puberty. ⊛ 2.B; 2.C

Understanding Concepts

2. List three physical changes that happen to both boys and girls during puberty. ⊛ 2.B; 2.C

3. How do hormones affect growth and development? ⊛ 2.C

Critical Thinking

4. Identifying Relationships How are the mental, emotional, social, and physical changes that happen during puberty related to the health of the adolescent? ⊛ 2.B; 2.C; 7.A

☑ internet connect

www.scilinks.org/health
Topic: Puberty
HealthLinks code: HD4078

HEALTH LINKS Maintained by the National Science Teachers Association

Adulthood, Aging, and Death

What You'll Do

- **Describe** development during adulthood. ⊛ 2.A
- **Explain** how technology has affected life expectancy in the United States. ⊛ 8.A; 8.B
- **List** the stages of grief. ⊛ 10.E

Terms to Learn

- adulthood
- death
- grief

Start Off
Write

How do people change after they reach adulthood?

> Asonda loves animals and wants to be a veterinarian when she's an adult. The local veterinarian, Dr. Carver, offered to let Asonda help out at the office. Now Asonda is working for the vet and planning for her future as an animal doctor.

Asonda is preparing to enter adulthood. **Adulthood** is the period of life that follows adolescence. Although most physical growth stops when you reach adulthood, your life will continue to change. You will be expected to take responsibility for your well-being.

Life as an Adult

Adulthood is the stage of life that lasts the longest. It lasts from about age 18 until death. Most people will be adults for more than 50 years. Because of advancements in medicine, you will likely live much longer than your grandparents or parents.

During adulthood, many people get married, establish a career, and raise children. Marriage is a lifelong union between a husband and a wife. Whether married or not, most adults must balance their families, friends, and careers. These responsibilities allow adults to help other people and to feel useful and productive. ⊛ 2.A

Figure 11 Many adults find happiness in their families and careers.

Aging

Aging is a natural part of life and happens to everyone. *Aging* is a term that describes the changes that happen as adults get older. Aging is affected by things we cannot change, such as heredity. It is also affected by things we can change, such as diet, exercise, and tobacco and drug use. The best way to maintain good health while aging is to focus on factors that you can control.

Many people live very happy lives into old age. By staying healthy, these people are able to enjoy their later years. They continue to do things that interest them, such as traveling and spending time with their families.

Figure 12 Older adults can lead happy and fulfilling lives.

Conditions Associated with Aging

As we get older, our bodies begin to wear out. Some diseases associated with aging are heart disease, osteoporosis, and Alzheimer's (AHLTS HIE murhz) disease. Heart disease damages the heart tissue and may lead to heart attacks. This disease can be deadly.

Osteoporosis is a condition in which bones lose a lot of their mass and strength. This condition is more common in older women than in older men, and it can lead to broken bones. You can take steps now to help prevent osteoporosis. These steps include getting plenty of exercise and eating foods that are rich in calcium.

Alzheimer's disease generally affects people over the age of 65. Alzheimer's disease leads to memory loss and thinking problems. Scientists are currently researching the causes of Alzheimer's disease. They hope to learn how to cure or prevent this condition.

Some conditions, such as heart disease and osteoporosis, can be treated because of advances in medical technology. Technology, such as vaccines, surgical techniques, and medications, has improved the quality of life for many people. These technologies have also increased the length of time that people live. ⭐ 8.A; 8.B

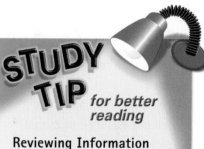

STUDY TIP *for better reading*

Reviewing Information
After reading through this lesson, find a partner and summarize the reading. Your partner should listen and add anything you omitted. Switch roles. Then discuss with your partner any parts of the lesson that the two of you did not understand.

Figure 13 Common Causes of Death

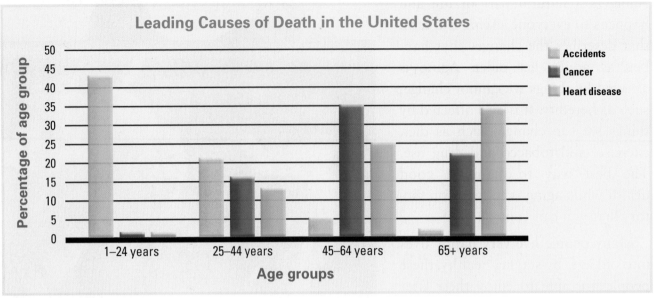

Leading Causes of Death in the United States

Source: Centers for Disease Control and Prevention.

Death and Grief

The end of life, or when all necessary life functions stop, is called **death.** Every living thing on Earth, including humans, dies. The average age of death, or the *life expectancy,* in the United States is 74 years for men and almost 80 years for women. Figure 14 shows common causes of death in the United States.

Sooner or later all of us will lose a loved one. When someone dies or a tragedy happens, it is normal to feel grief. **Grief** is a feeling of deep sadness about a loss. Most people go through the following five stages in dealing with grief:

1. **Denial** The person refuses to accept that their loved one is dead.

2. **Anger** The person is angry about the death of their loved one.

3. **Bargaining** The person wishes the loved one were still alive and tries to find a way to get their loved one back.

4. **Despair** The person is extremely sad about the loss of their loved one.

5. **Acceptance** The person comes to terms with the death and begins to move on with his or her life.

Sometimes people can stay in one stage for a long time without moving on. Most often, these people stay in despair. This despair can be harmful to their health. ★ 10.E

Health Journal

Describe a time when you have felt grief. An example could be when a friend or relative has died or moved away, when you lost a pet, or any other loss. Explain how you dealt with the grief.

★ 10.E

Dealing with Grief

Dealing with the death of someone you love is always difficult. But you can get through the pain by dealing with grief in a healthy way. The following list contains some ways to deal with grief: ⭐ 10.E

- Talk with your parents, trusted adults, and your friends about what you are going through. Don't try to handle grief alone. ⭐ 11.A

- Go to the funeral. Paying your last respects can help you accept your loss. Funerals also allow you to talk to others about what that person meant to you.

- Avoid focusing on your grief. You must grieve adequately, but you must also continue to live your life. Continue to fulfill your responsibilities at school and home. Maintain your relationships with your friends and family.

- Watch for signs of unhealthy grieving. Some signs are being unable to eat or sleep, feeling despair or overwhelming sadness, or feeling a desire to harm yourself or others. If you notice any of these problems, talk to a parent, a counselor, or another trusted adult immediately.

Figure 14 After the September 11 tragedy in 2001, much of the United States grieved by setting up memorials to the victims.

Lesson Review

Using Vocabulary

1. Define *adulthood*.

Understanding Concepts

2. Describe development during adulthood. ⭐ 2.A

3. Name and describe three conditions associated with aging. ⭐ 2.A

4. List and describe the stages of grief. ⭐ 10.E

Critical Thinking

5. Analyzing Ideas Life expectancy in the United States has changed over the last several decades. How has medical technology helped people live longer? ⭐ 8.A; 8.B

6. Making Inferences Why is it important for people to grieve the death of a loved one? ⭐ 10.E

Chapter Summary

■ Reproductive health is an important part of overall health. ■ A new cell forms when a sperm fertilizes an egg. This cell develops into a fetus. The developing fetus goes through many changes while inside the mother's uterus. After 9 months, an infant is born. ■ Children develop at different rates, but they all go through the same stages during childhood. ■ Adolescence is a time of physical, emotional, mental, and social changes. ■ The physical changes of adolescence are caused by the actions of hormones. ■ Rates of development are different for everyone. ■ Adulthood is the stage of life when humans are physically mature. ■ All living things get older and eventually die. ■ People grieve when someone dies. Grieving is a natural process.

Using Vocabulary

To complete the sentences, choose the correct term from the following word bank:

death   fertilization
infancy   puberty
childhood

❶ A new cell is formed in the process of ___, in which two sex cells combine.

❷ The stage of development known as ___ is the period between birth and age 1.

❸ The period of time between infancy and adolescence is called ___.

❹ All necessary life functions stop when ___ occurs.

❺ During ___, hormones make the reproductive system develop and mature.

For each pair of terms, describe how the meanings of the terms differ.

❻ egg/ovary

❼ adolescence/puberty

❽ testes/sperm

Understanding Concepts

❾ What is the function of the male reproductive system? Explain how the system performs this function. ⭐ 2.A; 2.B

❿ List four ways males can protect their reproductive system. List four ways females can protect their reproductive system. ⭐ 1.C; 2.A; 3.A; 5.I

⓫ What are three factors that affect the health of both the mother and fetus?
⭐ 1.A; 5.D

⓬ Summarize the growth and development of a fetus before birth.

⓭ What skills does an infant learn as it grows from birth to age 1?

⓮ In what age range do most children learn to connect different ideas?

⓯ How can some of the changes you go through during puberty lead to unhealthy behavior? ⭐ 1.C; 5.B; 5.D; 5.I

⓰ Why will you probably live to an older age than your grandparents?

⓱ List three conditions associated with aging. ⭐ 2.A

Critical Thinking

Analyzing Ideas

18 How might going through the stages of grief help someone deal with a loss? ⭐ 10.E

19 Why do mental and emotional changes accompany the physical changes of puberty? ⭐ 2.A; 2.B; 2.C

20 The life expectancy in the United States is 74 years for males and 80 years for females. Do you think other countries have this same life expectancy? Why or why not?

Making Good Decisions

21 You agree to baby-sit the 8-month-old baby of your parents' friends. While you are playing with the baby on the floor, the telephone rings down the hall. What do you do with the infant while you answer the phone? Explain your answer.

22 Within the last few months, you have started to feel awkward. Your body seems to be changing almost daily. Your emotions are also changing quickly. You feel happy one day and sad the next day. You are starting to feel that you are different from your classmates—like you don't fit in. What should you do? ⭐ 2.A; 2.B; 2.C

23 Your friend's grandmother recently died. Your friend hasn't seemed the same since the funeral. He stopped talking to you, and his grades are falling. Yesterday, you noticed he had little cut marks on his hand. When you ask him about the cuts, he gets angry and tells you to mind your own business. Do you tell someone about the cuts? If so, who do you tell and why? If not, why don't you tell? ⭐ 10.E; 11.A

Interpreting Graphics

Growth Pattern in Humans

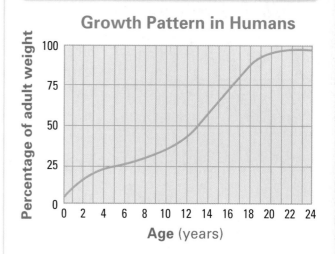

Use the figure above to answer questions 24–27. ⭐ M: 6.10D; 6.11A

24 The graph above shows the average growth pattern of humans. At what age do humans reach about half of their adult weight?

25 In what age range do humans grow the fastest?

26 Why do you think growth slows considerably around age 18?

27 If this graph were separated into male and female growth patterns, how might the male growth pattern differ from the female growth pattern?

Reading Checkup

Take a minute to review your answers to the Health IQ questions at the beginning of this chapter. How has reading this chapter improved your Health IQ?

Coping

At times, everyone faces setbacks, disappointments, or other troubles. To deal with these problems, you have to learn how to cope. Coping is dealing with problems and emotions in an effective way. Complete the following activity to develop your coping skills.

Frank's Falsetto

ACT 1

Setting the Scene

Frank's voice is changing. He'll be talking, and midsentence his voice cracks. It often happens while he is answering a question in class. And it always results in the entire class laughing. If that's not embarrassing enough, now a group of kids makes fun of him every day at lunch.

The 5 Steps of Coping

1. Identify the problem.
2. Identify your emotions.
3. Use positive self-talk.
4. Find ways to resolve the problem.
5. Talk to others to receive support.

Guided Practice

Practice with a Friend

Form a group of three. Have one person play the role of Frank and another person play the role of Frank's parent or a trusted friend. Have the third person be an observer. Walking through each of the five steps of coping, role-play Frank coping with the teasing. The observer will take notes, which will include observations about what the person playing Frank did well and suggestions of ways to improve. Stop after each step to evaluate the process. ★ 2.A; 2.B

Check Yourself

After you have completed the guided practice, go through Act 1 again without stopping at each step. Answer the questions below to review what you did.

1. What other emotions besides embarrassment could the teasing cause Frank to feel?

2. What are some positive things that Frank could tell himself to help him cope with the situation? ⊛ 2.A; 2.B; 2.C

3. Explain why talking with a parent or a trusted friend could help Frank cope. ⊛ 11.A

4. Describe a time in which you were teased. How did it make you feel, and how did you cope?

On Your Own

Frank's voice still cracks, but he doesn't worry about it as much anymore. Also, the kids have stopped teasing him. However, Frank has to give a speech in his social studies class next week. He's really nervous about talking in front of the class. Draw a comic strip showing how Frank could use the five steps of coping to deal with the event.

Controlling Disease

Check out
Current Health
articles related to this chapter by
visiting **go.hrw.com**. Just type in
the keyword **HD4CH10**.

> **"**I have **type 1 diabetes**. At first, I was **worried** that diabetes would mess up my life. Now, I go to my **doctor** for regular checkups. And I control my diabetes with medicine and my diet. As a result, I can do anything that anybody else can do.**"**

Health IQ

Disease and Your Body

Jasmine had the flu. She took medicine to reduce her aches and pains; she stayed in bed and drank a lot of fluid. Jasmine was well a few days later.

Many years ago, Jasmine might have had a different experience. In the years 1918 and 1919, there was a worldwide outbreak of the flu that killed between 20 million and 50 million people, including millions of healthy young people.

Disease

Influenza (IN floo EN zuh), also known as the flu, is a disease. A **disease** is any harmful change in the health of your body or mind. Many diseases, such as the flu and strep throat, are caused by pathogens. A **pathogen** is anything, especially a virus or microorganism, that causes disease. A *microorganism* (MIE kroh OR guhn IZ uhm) is a living thing so small that a microscope is needed to see it. Microorganisms include bacteria, fungi, and protozoa. Most viruses and microorganisms are harmless, but some are pathogens that cause serious diseases.

Other diseases are not caused by pathogens. Some diseases, such as muscular dystrophy (DIS truh fee), are inherited. In some diseases, such as one kind of arthritis, the body attacks its own tissues. Still other diseases, such as some forms of asthma, are triggered by something in the environment. And some diseases, such as hepatitis, have more than one cause. Alcohol abuse, infections, or exposure to certain chemicals or drugs may cause hepatitis. Finally, some diseases, such as Alzheimer's (AHLTS HIE muhrz) disease, do not have a known cause. ✪ 3.A; 3.C

What You'll Do

- **Describe** the difference between infectious and noninfectious diseases. ✪ 3.A; 3.C
- **Describe** how the human body fights diseases. ✪ 2.A

Terms to Learn

- disease
- pathogen
- infectious disease
- noninfectious disease
- immune system

Start Off
Write

What are some ways the human body protects itself against disease?

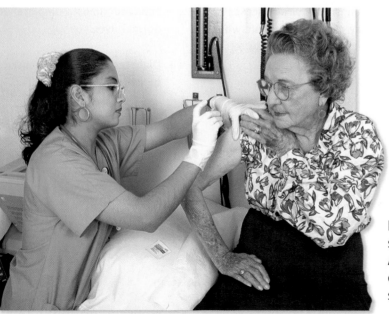

Figure 1 The flu virus can be spread from person to person. A flu shot is one way a person can be protected against the spread of this disease.

Figure 2 Examples of Infectious and Noninfectious Diseases

Infectious Diseases

▸ **Common cold** (virus)— head, nose, throat, lungs, muscles

▸ **Influenza** (virus)— throat, lungs, muscles

▸ **Chickenpox** (virus)— skin

▸ **Hepatitis** (virus)— liver

▸ **Strep throat** (bacteria)— throat

▸ **Tuberculosis** (bacteria)— lungs
⭐ 3.A

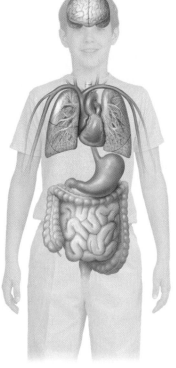

Noninfectious Diseases

▸ **Sickle cell disease**— red blood cells

▸ **Cystic fibrosis**— lungs and digestive tract

▸ **Muscular dystrophy**— muscles

▸ **Type 2 diabetes**— kidneys and other organs

▸ **Allergies**— lungs, skin, eyes

▸ **Cerebral palsy**— brain and nerves, muscles
⭐ 3.C

Infectious diseases can affect many parts of your body. For example, the flu directly affects your nose, throat, and lungs. But the flu's effects can also make asthma attacks and some heart conditions worse.

Noninfectious diseases, such as high blood pressure and cancer, can affect many parts of your body. Other noninfectious diseases strike only one organ or body system.

Infectious and Noninfectious Diseases

The flu, strep throat, and malaria are infectious (in FEK shuhs) diseases. An **infectious disease** is any disease that is caused by pathogens that invade the body. For example, viruses cause the flu. Bacteria cause strep throat. Tiny organisms called *protozoa* (PROHT oh ZOH uh) cause malaria. Some infectious diseases are *communicable* (kuh MYOO ni kuh buhl), which means that they can be passed directly from one person to another person. The flu is a communicable disease. The virus that causes the flu is easily passed from one person to another person. Malaria is not communicable. The pathogen that causes malaria is carried by certain kinds of mosquitoes.

Asthma, many cancers, and a wide variety of other diseases are not caused by pathogens. These diseases are called noninfectious diseases. A **noninfectious disease** is a disease that is not caused by a pathogen. Noninfectious diseases include diseases of specific body systems and nutritional disorders. Common noninfectious diseases include most types of heart disease, type 1 and type 2 diabetes, and Down syndrome. Injuries from accidents may also cause diseases. Many noninfectious diseases are chronic. A *chronic disease* is a disease that lasts a long time.
⭐ 3.A; 3.C

SOCIAL STUDIES ACTIVITY

Research the flu epidemic of 1918. Make a bulletin board that includes a timeline showing how the flu spread around the world. Include on your bulletin board news headlines and news stories that tell the story of the spread of the flu, the number of people affected, and the efforts made to stop the spread of the killer disease.

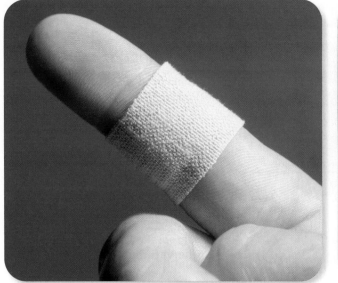

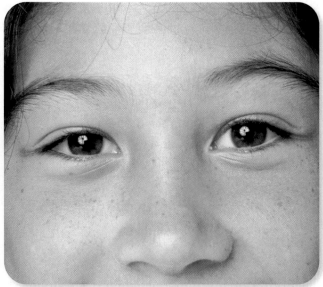

Figure 3 Your body has several defenses against disease, including your skin, nose hairs, eyelashes, and tears.

Defenses Against Disease

Your body's first lines of defense against infectious diseases include the following:

- **Skin** Your skin acts as a protective wall to keep organisms out. This wall includes the tiny hairs in your nose and your eyebrows and eyelashes.

- **Mucous Membranes** Mucous (MYOO kuhs) membranes produce *mucus*, a sticky fluid that traps pathogens. These tissues line your mouth, nose, eyes, throat, and other parts of your body.

- **Sweat, Saliva, and Tears** These body fluids contain chemicals that kill bacteria.

- **Stomach Acid** Sometimes pathogens enter your body through the food you eat or the liquids you drink. Most of the pathogens that enter your body in this way are killed by acid in your stomach.

- **Helpful Microorganisms** Most microorganisms are harmless to humans. Some microorganisms are even helpful. For example, helpful bacteria in your mouth take up most of the space and use up most of the food that invading bacteria could use. Harmful bacteria cannot live without food or space. And without the bacteria in your intestines, you couldn't completely digest your food.

Your body defenses keep out most viruses, bacteria, and other pathogens that can make you sick. But sometimes these invaders get through. Then, your immune system goes to work. ⊛ 2.A; 3.A; 3.C

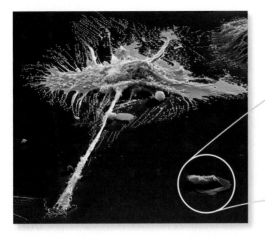
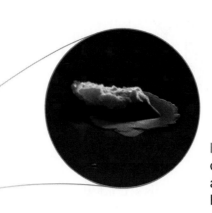

Figure 4 This white blood cell (large brown body) is attacking a bacterium (inset). Eventually, the white blood cell will destroy the bacterium.

The Immune System

The tissues, organs, and cells that fight pathogens make up your **immune system.** Your immune system consists of white blood cells and several organs, such as the *spleen*. White blood cells (WBCs) protect you against pathogens. One kind of WBC produces chemicals that stick to pathogens so that the pathogens cannot attack normal body cells. A second type of WBC either attacks pathogens directly or stimulates other WBCs to attack pathogens. A third kind of WBC, found in body tissues, surrounds and digests invading pathogens.

Your spleen also helps protect your body against pathogens. The spleen contains large numbers of WBCs. As blood flows through your spleen, WBCs remove pathogens in your blood and kill them. And the spleen releases WBCs into your blood to fight pathogens that may be in other parts of your body.

You must protect your immune system. The best way to take care of your immune system is to eat a healthy diet, get plenty of rest and exercise, and reduce stress as much as you can.

⭐ 1.A; 1.B; 1.C; 1.F; 2.A

Lesson Review

Using Vocabulary

1. Define *disease*. ⭐ 3.A; 3.C

Understanding Concepts

2. What is the difference between infectious and noninfectious diseases? ⭐ 3.A; 3.C

3. What are pathogens, and how does the body fight them? ⭐ 2.A; 3.A; 3.C

Critical Thinking

4. **Making Inferences** Why is your blood an important part of your immune system? ⭐ 2.A

5. **Drawing Conclusions** Explain why you must maintain good health to protect yourself against disease. ⭐ 1.C; 1.G; 2.A; 3.C

🔲 internet connect

www.scilinks.org/health
Topic: Cardiovascular and Cancer Research in Texas
HealthLinks code: HHTX003

HEALTH LINKS™ Maintained by the National Science Teachers Association

Infectious Diseases

Luis has a cold, so his mother won't let him play with his baby sister. Luis's mother is afraid that Luis will give his cold to his little sister.

Luis's cold is caused by a virus that can be passed to other people. The virus may not make Luis feel too bad, but it could make his baby sister very sick.

Viruses

Viruses cause some common infectious diseases. A **virus** is a tiny, disease-causing particle that invades a healthy cell and instructs that cell to make more viruses. Viruses are not living things. Viruses are so small they can only be seen with an electron microscope.

Some viruses, such as herpes, are spread by direct person-to-person contact, such as shaking hands or kissing. Other viruses are spread by indirect contact. For example, sneezing can allow viruses to move through the air from one person to another person. Flu and cold viruses are often spread this way. Viruses can also pass indirectly when a person uses a drinking glass or other object that has been used by someone with the virus. Some viruses, such as the West Nile virus, are spread indirectly by insects.

Some viruses are harmless. Other viruses cause diseases, such as AIDS and severe acute respiratory syndrome (SARS). Some viral diseases, such as mumps and measles, can be prevented with vaccines. A *vaccine* (vak SEEN) is medicine that contains killed or weakened pathogens and is given to protect you against a particular disease. Vaccines stimulate your immune system to produce *antibodies*. An antibody is a chemical that your body produces to fight invading pathogens. Each type of antibody fights a particular pathogen.

⊛ 3.A; 3.C

What You'll Do

- **Identify** four causes of infectious diseases. ⊛ 3.A

- **Explain** how the spread of common infectious diseases can be prevented. ⊛ 1.C; 3.A; 3.C

Terms to Learn

- virus
- bacteria
- protozoa
- fungi

Start Off
Write

How can you keep from catching a cold?

Figure 5 These people are victims of the flu virus that spread around the world in 1918 and 1919. Millions of people died from the flu in those 2 years.

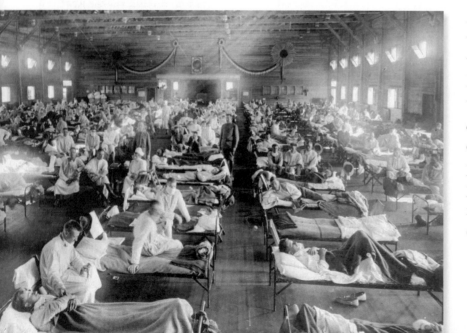

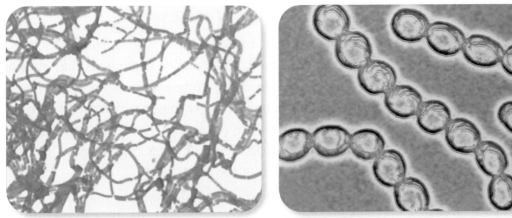

Figure 6 Bacteria come in a variety of shapes. Some types of bacteria cause diseases.

Bacteria

Bacteria are living things and are more complex than viruses. **Bacteria** are extremely small, single-celled organisms that do not have a nucleus. Most bacteria can live on their own. And they live everywhere. Bacteria spread the same way viruses do— through direct and indirect contact as well as through air, water, and soil. Most bacteria are harmless to humans. Several types of bacteria, such as those that live in your intestines, are helpful to humans. In fact, humans could not live without bacteria. But some kinds of bacteria cause serious illness.

Bacteria cause a wide range of diseases in humans. Some major bacterial diseases are whooping cough, cholera (KAHL uhr uh), anthrax, and tooth decay. Bacteria also cause some kinds of food poisoning and some kinds of ulcers.

You can control the spread of bacteria by washing your hands, by keeping your kitchen clean, by not sharing drinking glasses or eating utensils with someone who is sick, and by getting treatment for an illness before it spreads to other people. If the water supply has harmful bacteria in it, boiling the water or treating it with certain chemicals will help stop the spread of the bacteria.

Most bacterial diseases can be treated with antibiotics. An *antibiotic* is a medicine used to stop the growth of or to kill bacteria or other microorganisms. If you are ill, your doctor can tell you if you have a bacterial infection. If bacteria are the cause of your illness, your doctor may prescribe an antibiotic. Sometimes, your doctor may tell you that the best treatment is to get plenty of rest. ✪ 1.C; 1.G; 3.A; 3.C

Antibiotics and viruses

Antibiotics and antibacterial soaps do not kill the viruses that cause many infectious diseases, such as the common cold. Antibiotics only work against bacteria and other living organisms. ✪ 3.C

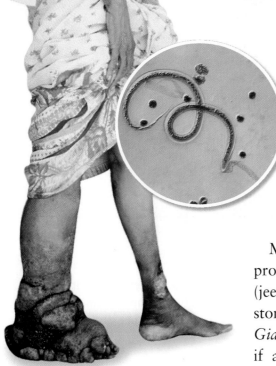

Protozoa and Parasites

Protozoa (PROHT oh ZOH uh) cause some diseases. **Protozoa** are small, single-celled organisms that have a nucleus. They are more complex than bacteria. Most protozoa can be seen only through a microscope. Some kinds of protozoa are parasites. A *parasite* is an organism that gets its food from another organism, called the *host*, without killing the host.

Most protozoa are harmless to humans. But there are a few protozoa that cause illness. For example, the parasite *Giardia* (jee AHR dee uh) is found in water supplies. *Giardia* can cause stomach upset, stomach cramps, and diarrhea in humans. *Giardia* outbreaks are relatively rare in the United States, but if a water supply becomes contaminated with *Giardia,* the outbreak usually makes the news.

Another parasite, *Plasmodium* (plaz MOH dee uhm), causes malaria in humans. *Plasmodium* protozoa are carried by certain kinds of mosquitoes. A person bitten by one of these mosquitoes may become ill with malaria. Malaria is usually found in tropical countries and is not common in the United States.

You cannot see protozoa with the naked eye. This is one reason campers treat water from streams before drinking it. And travelers to other countries may get parasites from an insect bite, or by eating contaminated food or by drinking contaminated water. Fortunately, antibiotics and other drugs are available to treat most diseases caused by protozoa and other parasites.

✪ 3.A; 3.C

Figure 7 Tiny parasitic worms cause fluid to build up in parts of the body, which makes limbs swell to many times their normal size.

Hands-on ACTIVITY

INFECTIOUS DISEASES

1. Go to the library or to the Internet and look up "infectious diseases."

2. Select one infectious disease and do research on it. Your research should include the name of the disease, where in the world the disease is found, what causes it, how it is transmitted, what its symptoms are, and what the treatment for it is.

3. Make a poster that displays the results of your research.

Analysis

1. Combine the results of your research with your classmates' results to make a map of the world showing where infectious diseases are most common.

2. Using a computer or graph paper, make a pie chart or bar graph showing the five most common ways that infectious diseases are spread.

✪ 1.C; 3.A

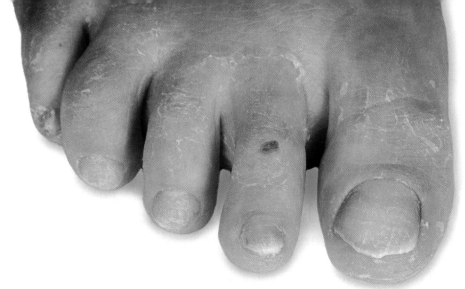

Figure 8 The areas of redness and flaking skin are caused by athlete's foot, one of the most common diseases caused by a fungus.

Fungi

Some diseases are caused by fungi (FUHN JIE). **Fungi** (singular *fungus*) are complex organisms that cannot make their own food. Fungi break down other substances and absorb the nutrients from them. Fungi are everywhere—there are over 100,000 species of fungi. Most fungi are harmless to humans. Some fungi, such as yeast and edible mushrooms, are useful to humans. But some fungi cause diseases in humans. The most common fungal diseases are athlete's foot and yeast infections.

Some fungal diseases are spread by person-to-person contact. Other diseases are spread by fungal spores in the air, water, or soil. Most fungal diseases can be treated with medicines applied to the skin. For example, athlete's foot may be treated with antifungal creams or powders. To get rid of some fungal infections, such as toenail fungus, you must take medicine by mouth. ⊛ 1.C; 3.A; 3.C

Lesson Review

Using Vocabulary

1. Identify and define four causes of infectious diseases. ⊛ 3.A; 3.C

Understanding Concepts

2. What is an antibiotic? ⊛ 3.C

3. Why does your doctor need to know that the illness you have is caused by a virus? ⊛ 3.A; 3.C

Critical Thinking

4. **Making Inferences** In tropical countries, malaria kills 1 million to 2 million people every year. Why do you think it is so hard to stop this disease? ⊛ 3.A; 3.C

5. **Analyzing Ideas** Pathogens are all around you. How can you prevent the spread of common infectious diseases? ⊛ 1.C; 3.A; 3.C

▣ internet connect

www.scilinks.org/health
Topic: Infectious Disease Detection and Prevention in Texas
HealthLinks code: HHTX011

HEALTH LINKS₅ Maintained by the National Science Teachers Association

Controlling Infectious Diseases

What You'll Do

- **Discuss** two ways to protect yourself from infectious diseases. ★ 1.B; 1.C; 3.A; 3.C

- **Identify** two ways to control the spread of infectious diseases. ★ 3.A; 3.C

Start Off
Write

Why should you know basic ways to stop the spread of infectious disease?

Sandy's class visited a laboratory where scientists research antibiotics. The class learned that finding useful antibiotics is a very long and expensive process.

Sandy also learned that some of the best ways to stop the spread of infectious diseases do not involve antibiotics or vaccines. Sometimes, controlling infectious diseases is a matter of using common sense and good personal hygiene.

Protecting Yourself

One way to avoid pathogens is to stay away from people who are sick. Another way to avoid pathogens is to wash your hands. Washing with warm, soapy water will help protect you from colds and the flu. You can also help your body fight pathogens by maintaining a healthy diet and getting plenty of rest and exercise.

Vaccines provide protection against some infectious diseases. Many infants and children receive vaccinations against a variety of diseases. Most vaccinations are given to children between birth and six years of age. The following diseases are commonly prevented by vaccines:

- hepatitis B (HEP uh TIET is BEE)
- diphtheria (dif THIR ee uh), tetanus, and whooping cough
- poliomyelitis (POH lee OH MIE uh LITE is)
- measles, mumps, and rubella
- chickenpox ★ 1.B; 3.A; 3.C

Figure 9 These children are getting shots of polio vaccine, which was introduced in the 1950s. Polio vaccines have since stopped the spread of polio.

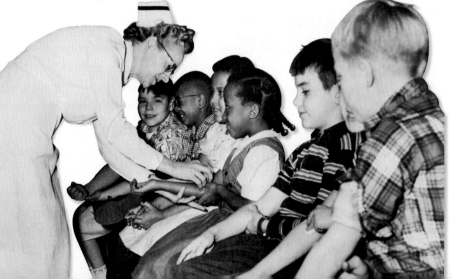

SPREAD OF PATHOGENS

1. Some students will be given surgical masks to wear during the activity.

2. Your teacher will spray some air freshener. The air freshener represents pathogens in a sneeze.

3. Using a seating chart and a stopwatch, record how much time it takes for each student to smell the air freshener.

Analysis

1. Using the data you collected with the seating chart and the stopwatch, draw a diagram showing the spread of the pathogens in the classroom.

2. What is the purpose of the surgical masks? Were they effective?

Protecting Others

After you have done what you can to protect yourself against pathogens, what can you do to protect others? Remember that pathogens usually spread by direct, person-to-person contact, by indirect contact with another person, through contaminated food or water, and through contact with insects and other animals.

The same steps you take to protect yourself from pathogens will also help protect other people. If you get a vaccination that protects you from a pathogen, you will not spread that pathogen to other people.

Communities take steps to stop the spread of pathogens. Some communities offer free flu shots before flu season. Many communities have vaccination programs for preschool children. And most communities have a health department that warns people when a disease outbreak is coming.

Public health officials sometimes use animals, such as chickens, to track the spread of diseases carried by insects. Often, these animals become infected before people do. By observing the animals, officials can tell when pathogens have reached a community.

⊛ 1.C, 3.A; 6.A

Figure 10 This scientist is testing a sentinel chicken for infectious diseases.

Lesson Review

Understanding Concepts

1. Describe two ways to protect yourself from infectious diseases.
⊛ 1.B; 1.C; 3.A; 3.C

2. Identify two ways to control the spread of infectious diseases.
⊛ 3.A

Critical Thinking

3. Making Predictions If the health department announced that your neighborhood was in the path of a disease carried by fleas, what steps would you take to protect yourself?
⊛ 1.C; 3.A; 3.C; 6.A

Lesson 4

Sexually Transmitted Diseases

What You'll Do

- **Describe** how HIV attacks the immune system. ⭐ 2.A; 3.B
- **Identify** five common STDs. ⭐ 3.A
- **Describe** how to avoid getting STDs. ⭐ 5.I

Terms to Learn

- sexually transmitted disease (STD)
- AIDS
- abstinence

Start Off Write

What causes AIDS?

Misaki's cousin Takumi has tested positive for HIV. Misaki is worried about him.

Human immunodeficiency (im MYOO noh di FISH uhn see) virus, or HIV, is the virus that causes AIDS. AIDS is a sexually transmitted disease. A **sexually transmitted disease,** or STD, is a disease that can be spread from person to person during sexual contact. ⭐ 3.A

HIV and the Immune System

HIV is generally spread by sexual contact, from a mother to her baby, or from a contaminated blood product, usually from a needle shared by drug users.

HIV causes **AIDS,** or **acquired immune deficiency syndrome,** a deadly disease that weakens the body's ability to fight pathogens. A person whose immune system has been weakened by AIDS cannot fight off other diseases, such as some types of pneumonia and cancer. A person who has AIDS usually dies from a disease that a healthy immune system would resist.

A person infected with HIV may not develop AIDS for 10 years or more. But even if an HIV-infected person shows no signs of AIDS, he or she can spread the virus to other people. ⭐ 3.A; 3.B; 5.I

Figure 11 Like other viruses, the HIV invades healthy cells and instructs them to make more copies of the HIV.

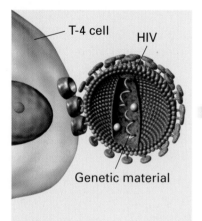

The HIV attaches to an immune system cell called a T-4 cell. The HIV then enters the T-4 cell.

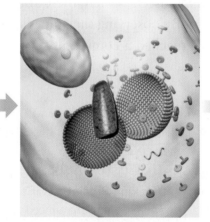

Once inside, the HIV breaks apart and releases its genetic material. This material instructs the T-4 cell to make new HIV.

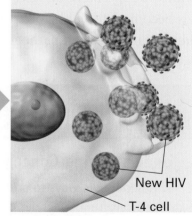

The new HIV leave the T-4 cell and look for more T-4 cells to infect. Each T-4 cell can produce many HIV. ⭐ 3.B

224 | **Chapter 10** Controlling Disease

STDs: More Than Just AIDS

You might think that HIV is the only STD or is the most common one. Herpes, chlamydia (kluh MID ee uh), genital warts, gonorrhea (GAHN uh REE uh), and trichomoniasis (TRIK uh muh NIE uh sis) are STDs that are more common among teens than HIV is. These common STDs are caused by a variety of pathogens. Bacteria cause chlamydia, syphilis (SIF uh lis), and gonorrhea. Viruses cause herpes, genital warts, and AIDS.

Each STD has specific symptoms. For example, the symptoms of chlamydia—for men and women—include a clear discharge, frequent urination, or burning when urinating. But people infected with chlamydia often do not have any symptoms. These people may not realize they have an STD. Even so, if a person with an STD has sexual contact with someone else, the STD can be spread.

Someone who suspects that he or she has an STD should see a doctor immediately. Viral STDs cannot be cured, but some can be treated. Bacterial STDs can be cured with antibiotics, and treatment should begin as soon as possible after infection. Often, drugs used to treat STDs, especially drugs used to treat HIV and AIDS, have unpleasant physical side effects. These side effects are one more reason to avoid STDs. ✪ 3.A; 5.I

Myth & Fact

Myth: You can always tell when you or someone else has an STD.

Fact: No, you can't! Some STDs have no obvious symptoms. Anyone who has sexual contact with a person who has an STD can be infected by an STD. The only way to be sure you do not have an STD is to practice abstinence. ✪ 5.I

TABLE 1 Common Sexually Transmitted Diseases

Disease (cause)	Symptoms	Treatment
Chlamydia (bacteria)	burning during urination; discharge; may show no symptoms, but bacteria can still be spread	antibiotics are a cure
Genital herpes (virus)	fever; painful, itchy genital sores; burning feeling during urination	medicine can relieve symptoms; no cure
Genital warts (virus)	painless warts in genital area; warts usually appear 3 weeks to 6 months after infection; virus remains in body	warts can be removed by surgery or freezing; no cure
Gonorrhea (bacteria)	unusual discharge from penis or vagina; pain or burning feeling during urination; sometimes no symptoms, but bacteria can still be spread	antibiotics are a cure (but some types of gonorrhea bacteria are drug resistant)
Trichomoniasis (protozoa)	yellowish, foul-smelling discharge (females); itching (females); may have no symptoms (males)	antibiotics are a cure
Syphilis (bacteria)	moist, painless, red sores where bacteria enter body; rash; flulike symptoms; may cause brain damage	antibiotics are a cure ✪ 3.A

Figure 12 When you choose activities that do not put your health at risk, your life will be a lot more fun.

Abstinence and Preventing STDs

Disease control and prevention are important because no one wants to be sick. Some diseases are mild, other diseases are much more deadly. Infections caused by STDs can be especially painful and unpleasant. Some STDs, such as HIV and herpes, cannot be cured. You have to live with them forever. Some STDs, such as untreated syphilis and HIV that develops into AIDS, can kill you.

But the spread of STDs is easily prevented. In fact, there is one way you can be absolutely sure that you will not get an STD. The only way to avoid STDs is called *abstinence*. **Abstinence** is refusing to take part in any activity or behavior that puts your health and the health of other people at risk. Sexual activity is risky behavior. It puts you and other people in danger of becoming infected with an STD. Abstinence from sexual activity—making the decision not to take part in sexual activity—eliminates that danger.

Why is abstinence the best prevention? Most STDs are transmitted only by direct contact with other people's body fluids. These body fluids include saliva, blood, semen, and vaginal fluid. You can avoid other people's body fluids—and STDs—by

- not using alcohol or drugs, because people who are under the influence of alcohol or drugs are more likely to engage in sexual activity

- not sharing needles, because people who share a needle with an HIV-infected person expose themselves to HIV

- not having sexual contact

Abstinence has other benefits, too. These benefits include respecting yourself and being happy, being able to reach your personal goals, avoiding the risks of pregnancy, and respecting your parents. ✪ 3.A; 5.I

Figure 13 Myths and Facts About STDs

★ 3.A; 5.I

Lesson Review

Using Vocabulary

1. Define *STD*, and list five common STDs. ★ 3.A

2. What is AIDS?

Understanding Concepts

3. Describe how HIV attacks the immune system. ★ 3.A; 3.B

4. Describe ways to avoid getting an STD. ★ 5.I

Critical Thinking

5. **Making Inferences** A small number of people have been infected with HIV for 10 years or more and still show no symptoms of AIDS. Does this mean that these people do not have to worry about infecting another person? Explain your answer. ★ 3.A

6. **Analyzing Ideas** How can two people show affection for each other and still practice abstinence? ★ 10.D

Noninfectious Diseases

Hunter has Down syndrome. He has the facial features, learning disabilities, and characteristics of most people who have Down syndrome. Hunter was born with Down syndrome, and he can't do anything to change it.

Hunter's condition, Down syndrome, is one of many noninfectious diseases and disorders that affect people. A **noninfectious disease** is a disease or disorder that is not caused by a virus or living organism.

Causes of Noninfectious Diseases

Noninfectious diseases include some immune system disorders, diseases of specific organ systems, and nutrition disorders. Some noninfectious diseases, called *genetic and congenital diseases*, are present at birth. A **genetic disease** is a disease or disorder that is caused entirely or partly by genetic information passed on to a child from one or both parents. Hunter's condition, Down syndrome, is a genetic disorder. A **congenital disease** is a disease or disorder that is present at birth but is not a genetic disease. For example, some people are born with defects in parts of their heart. This condition is congenital heart disease.

Some noninfectious diseases are related to lifestyle choices. For example, using tobacco may cause heart disease or lung cancer. Other noninfectious diseases are related to factors in a person's surroundings. For example, air pollution may trigger asthma attacks or cause lung cancer.
✪ 3.C; 5.D

What You'll Do

- **Explain** the difference between genetic disease and congenital disease.
  ✪ 3.A; 3.C
- **Identify** three common noninfectious diseases. ✪ 3.C

Terms to Learn

- noninfectious disease
- genetic disease
- congenital disease

Start Off Write

What is the difference between an infectious disease and a noninfectious disease?

Figure 14 Having a noninfectious disease doesn't have to stop you from having a happy life.

▶ **All over**—Cancer is a group of about 100 diseases that can affect any tissue or organ in the body.

▶ **Liver**—Liver disease, often the result of alcohol abuse, may be fatal.

▶ **Red blood cells**—Sickle cell disease damages red blood cells and it causes anemia and extreme pain.

▶ **Joints**—Arthritis causes joints to swell, which makes movement painful.

▶ **Muscles**—Muscular dystrophy is a group of diseases that weaken muscles, especially heart and skeletal muscles.

▶ **Brain**—Alzheimer's disease causes memory loss and behavior changes. Down syndrome causes mild mental retardation.

▶ **Heart**—Congenital heart disease may cause damage to heart valves or other parts of the heart. Other heart diseases, such as high blood pressure and arterial disease, may cause heart attacks and heart failure.

▶ **Lungs**—Emphysema, allergies, and asthma cause breathing difficulties.

▶ **Kidneys**—Type 1 and type 2 diabetes may cause severe kidney damage.

Figure 15 Noninfectious diseases affect many parts of the body.

Common Noninfectious Diseases

Some common noninfectious diseases include the following:

- **Heart Disease** High blood pressure, heart attacks, strokes, and artery diseases are types of heart disease. Heart disease is the leading cause of death in the United States.

- **Diabetes** Diabetes is a disease in which the body is not able to use sugar properly.

- **Cancer** Cancer is a group of diseases in which cells grow uncontrollably and invade and destroy healthy tissues. Cancer can attack any part of the body.

- **Allergy** An allergy is an overreaction of the immune system to something in your surroundings that is harmless to most people.

- **Asthma** Asthma is a breathing disease that can be triggered by allergies, infections, exercise, changes in weather, and smoke.

- **Alzheimer's disease** Alzheimer's disease is an incurable brain disease that causes a gradual and permanent loss of memory and other brain functions. ✪ 3.B; 3.C

Brain Food

There are several types of congenital heart disease. Some types affect the valves in the heart. Other types affect the walls between parts of the heart. Still other types affect the aorta or other blood vessels of the heart.

Health Journal

What would you do if someone in your family had Down syndrome and other people picked on that family member? How would you react? What could you tell those people about your family member's condition that might help them understand the condition and your family member better? Write your answers in your Health Journal.

⭐ 10.A; 10.B

Some noninfectious diseases are serious or even fatal, while others have few effects. Some noninfectious diseases can be cured. For example, a congenital heart condition that affects a heart valve can usually be repaired with surgery. Even noninfectious diseases that cannot be cured can usually be treated. For example, heart disease caused by lifestyle choices can be managed by eating a healthy diet, not using tobacco, and getting plenty of exercise. Type 2 diabetes, a genetic disease, can often be controlled with exercise and proper diet.

A person living with a noninfectious disease may have to eat a special diet, take medicine, avoid certain activities, or have special medical care. But living with these diseases does not mean that person has to live an unhappy life or be alone. In fact, most people with these diseases lead relatively normal lives.

Every disease has both physical and mental effects. A person who has a noninfectious disease may be embarrassed by his or her condition. But, in fact, most people who have noninfectious diseases can live relatively normal, happy, and exciting lives. Even so, these people may sometimes be the target of teasing or insults. Teasing someone because he or she has a noninfectious disease is like teasing someone because he or she has a cold. Teasing is mean, and it is wrong. ⭐ 3.C

Figure 16 Having a noninfectious disease doesn't have to stop you from becoming an outstanding athlete—or anything else!

TABLE 2 Controlling Noninfectious Diseases

Disease	Description	Control or treatment
Allergies	an overreaction by the body to things that are usually harmless	avoiding things to which you are allergic; taking medicine to relieve symptoms
Asthma	a disease of the respiratory system that causes shortness of breath, coughing, and wheezing	avoiding triggers, such as cigarette smoke; taking medicine to open airways
High blood pressure	a disease in which blood exerts too much force on walls of blood vessels	having a healthy diet; getting plenty of exercise; taking medicine to help reduce blood pressure
Cancer	a group of diseases that cause uncontrolled cell growth; can attack any tissue or organ	not using alcohol or tobacco, limiting exposure to the sun, and eating a healthy diet (prevention); chemotherapy, surgery, radiation therapy, and taking medicine (treatment)
Type 1 diabetes	a disease in which the body does not make enough insulin, so the body cannot use sugars from food for energy	taking daily insulin injections; having a healthy diet
Type 2 diabetes	a disease in which the body makes insulin, but cannot use it properly, so the body cannot use sugars from food for energy	controlling weight; getting plenty of exercise; having a healthy diet; taking medicine may help the body use insulin
Arthritis	a group of diseases that cause swelling and severe pain in the joints	taking medicine to control swelling and reducing pain; exercising to keep joints flexible; using heat or cold to reduce pain

Lesson Review

Using Vocabulary

1. Compare and contrast genetic and congenital diseases. ⊛ 3.C

2. What is a noninfectious disease? ⊛ 3.A; 3.C

Understanding Concepts

3. Name three common noninfectious diseases and the way in which each can be treated or controlled. ⊛ 3.C

4. Why is it unfair to tease someone who was born with a genetic disorder? ⊛ 3.C; 10.A

Critical Thinking

5. **Making Inferences** Explain why someone who has asthma would want to avoid a friend who has an infectious disease such as the flu. ⊛ 2.A; 3.A; 3.C

6. **Analyzing Ideas** Why might it be more difficult to treat a genetic disease than to treat a case of athlete's foot? ⊛ 3.A; 3.C

Chapter Summary

■ Infectious diseases are caused by pathogens. ■ Pathogens are viruses, bacteria, protozoa and parasites, and fungi. ■ Noninfectious diseases are not caused by pathogens. ■ Your body has ways to protect against infectious diseases. ■ Antibiotics are drugs that kill bacteria or slow the growth of bacteria. ■ One of the easiest ways to protect yourself against infectious diseases is to wash your hands thoroughly. ■ HIV is not the most common STD. ■ Abstinence is the only way to be sure you will not get an STD. ■ Common noninfectious diseases include heart disease, diabetes, cancer, allergies and asthma. ■ Many noninfectious diseases cannot be cured, but they can often be treated.

Using Vocabulary

For each pair of terms, describe how the meanings of the terms differ.

1 infectious disease/noninfectious disease

2 bacteria/virus

3 AIDS/HIV

4 genetic disease/congenital disease

For each sentence, fill in the blank with the proper term from the word bank provided below.

HIV	antibiotic
genetic disease	pathogen
fungi	heart disease
influenza	abstinence

5 A drug that kills bacteria or slows the growth of bacteria is called a(n) ___.

6 A disease caused by genetic information passed to a child from his or her parents is a(n) ___.

7 The leading cause of death in the United States is ___.

Understanding Concepts

8 How can coughing or sneezing spread infectious diseases? ⭐ 3.A

9 Why is your skin part of your defenses against diseases? ⭐ 2.A; 3.A

10 What is your immune system, and why is it important? ⭐ 2.A; 3.A

11 Do all people who have an STD get sick or show symptoms? Explain. ⭐ 3.A

12 How does washing your hands and washing your drinking glasses help stop the spread of disease? ⭐ 1.C; 3.A

13 Why should you stay home from school if you have the flu or a bad cold? ⭐ 1.C; 3.A

14 What are two differences between communicable diseases and noninfectious diseases? ⭐ 3.A; 3.C

15 Explain what abstinence is and discuss why it is an important way to fight STDs. ⭐ 5.I

Applying Concepts

16 If your doctor tells you that you are allergic to peanuts, what are two ways to control your allergy? ⊛ 3.C

17 Does everybody infected with HIV also have AIDS? Explain. ⊛ 3.B

18 Why are children often vaccinated against a variety of childhood diseases? ⊛ 3.A

Making Good Decisions

19 A doctor speaks to your school about HIV. During her speech, she tells everybody that she is HIV positive, meaning that she is infected with HIV. After the speech, you want to shake the doctor's hand, but you are concerned that you might catch HIV. Should you shake the doctor's hand or not? Explain. ⊛ 3.A

20 Your little sister has asthma. During your summer vacation, you want to take her to the park to spend the afternoon playing. You hear on the news that pollen levels and air pollution levels will be high during the day. Should this news affect your decision to take your sister to the park? Explain. ⊛ 3.C

21 You go to the doctor with a sore throat and the doctor prescribes an antibiotic for you to take. The instructions for the medicine say that you should take it until it is gone. You take the antibiotic for a few days, and then you start feeling better. Do you think it is safe to stop taking the antibiotic as soon as you feel all better, even if the instructions say to take all of it? Explain. ⊛ 3.A

Interpreting Graphics

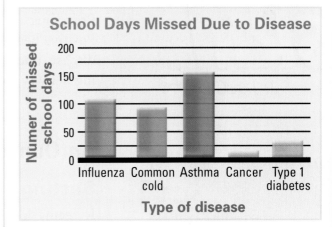

School Days Missed Due to Disease

The graph above shows the number of missed days at Braintree Middle School that were caused by each of five different diseases. Use this graph to answer questions 22–25.

22 Which disease caused almost 100 missed days of school?

23 Approximately how many fewer days were lost to type 1 diabetes than to influenza?

24 Which disease caused the most missed school days?

25 More students at the school caught common colds than had influenza, yet influenza caused more total missed days of school. What might the reason be?

Reading Checkup

Take a minute to review your answers to the Health IQ questions at the beginning of this chapter. How has reading this chapter improved your Health IQ?

Practicing Wellness

Practicing wellness means practicing good health habits. Positive health behaviors can help prevent injury, illness, disease, and even premature death. Complete the following activity to learn how you can practice wellness.

An Ounce of Prevention

ACT 1

Setting the Scene

It seems like almost everybody in Ken's math class is sick. Some people are staying home with the flu, while others are coming to school because they do not want to fall behind in their classes. Ken just doesn't want to get sick. He's going to be a starter at next week's basketball game, and he doesn't want to miss it because he's sick.

⭐ 1.C; 3.A

The **4** Steps of Practicing Wellness

1. Choose a health behavior you want to improve or change.
2. Gather information on how you can improve that health behavior.
3. Start using the improved health behavior.
4. Evaluate the effects of the health behavior.

Guided Practice

Practice with a Friend

Form a group of two. Have one person play the role of Ken, and have the second person be an observer. Walking through each of the four steps of practicing wellness, role-play Ken avoiding getting sick. Ken may speak to a doctor about what he can do to avoid getting sick. The observer will take notes, which will include observations about what the person playing Ken did well and suggestions of ways to improve. Stop after each step to evaluate the process.

Independent Practice

Check Yourself

After you have completed the guided practice, go through Act 1 again without stopping at each step. Answer the questions below to review what you did.

1. What are three things Ken can do to avoid getting sick? What are some health behaviors Ken may want to improve? ⊛ 1.C

2. Beside talking to his doctor, where else can Ken get information about staying healthy?

3. How can Ken evaluate the effects of his health behaviors?

ACT 2 | On Your Own

Ken avoids getting sick and gets to start in the basketball game. Because Ken wants to start in other games, he practices every day. After a few weeks, Ken's shins start hurting all the time. Make a flowchart that shows how Ken can use the four steps of practicing wellness to help him get on the road to recovery.

Lessons

Check out
Current Health
articles related to this chapter by visiting **go.hrw.com**. Just type in the keyword **HD4CH11**.

> **"My family** lives pretty close to my school. So, I usually **walk** to school. Walking is **good exercise** and helps me stay fit. I usually walk with my friends. So, walking to school is also a great way to catch up with my friends. **"**

PRE-READING

Answer the following multiple-choice questions to find out what you already know about physical fitness. When you've finished this chapter, you'll have the opportunity to change your answers based on what you've learned.

1. Physical fitness can prevent which of the following?
a. shortness of breath
b. soreness
c. feeling very tired
d. all of the above ⭐ 1.F

2. Which of the following is NOT a component of physical fitness?
a. flexibility
b. endurance
c. fitness goal
d. muscular strength

3. Which of the following is an example of exercise?
a. running
b. raking the leaves
c. walking to school
d. all of the above

4. Which of the following is NOT a warning sign of injury?
a. swelling
b. muscle soreness
c. bruises
d. sharp pain

5. Which of the following is a benefit of exercise?
a. improving physical fitness
b. managing stress
c. meeting new friends
d. all of the above ⭐ 1.F

6. Which of the following activities can help you prevent injury?
a. warming up until you sweat lightly
b. cooling down until your heart beats slower
c. stretching
d. all of the above ⭐ 1.F

ANSWERS: 1. d; 2. c; 3. d; 4. b; 5. d; 6. d

What Is Physical Fitness?

What You'll Do

- **Describe** the relationship between fitness and exercise. ⭐ 1.B; 1.F

- **List** the four parts of physical fitness. ⭐ 2.A

- **Describe** the physical benefits of exercise. ⭐ 1.F

- **Explain** the mental, emotional, and social benefits of exercise. ⭐ 1.F

Terms to Learn

- physical fitness
- exercise
- strength
- endurance
- flexibility

Start Off
Write

What are some benefits of exercise?

> Javier likes to skateboard. He and his friends try new tricks almost every day. They don't think of themselves as athletes. But they are in good shape.

You may not think of skateboarding as a sport. But it can improve your physical fitness. **Physical fitness** is the ability to do daily physical activities without becoming short of breath, sore, or very tired.

Physical Fitness and Exercise

Physical fitness means different things to different people. For children, it may mean playing without getting tired. For some people, it may mean being able to do chores. An athlete might think that physical fitness is being able to play his or her best. In any case, physical fitness helps you do the things you need to do every day.

Sometimes, people spend too much time watching TV or using the computer. As a result, their physical fitness suffers. People need to exercise to improve their physical fitness. **Exercise** is any physical activity that maintains or improves your physical fitness. Chores, such as raking the leaves or mowing the lawn, are exercise. Playing at the park with friends is exercise. Physical education class and walking to school are also exercise. For Javier, skateboarding is exercise. If you start exercising now, you're more likely to keep exercising as you get older. Regular exercise can help you stay healthy throughout your life. ⭐ 1.B; 1.F

Figure 1 If you start good fitness habits now, you can benefit from lifelong health.

Figure 2 Different activities use different parts of physical fitness. Here are some examples.

Four Parts of Physical Fitness

There are four basic parts of physical fitness: strength, endurance (en DOOR uhns), flexibility (FLEK suh BIL uh tee), and body composition (KAHM puh ZISH uhn).

Strength is the amount of force muscles apply when they are used. This force can be measured as the amount of weight you can lift. Strength helps support bones and makes joints stronger. It can also keep you from getting hurt if you fall. You use strength when you are lifting, pushing, and pulling.

Endurance is the ability to do activities for more than a few minutes. There are two kinds of endurance. Muscular endurance is the ability of the muscles to work over time. It lets you repeat an activity without losing the strength to keep going. For example, you use muscular endurance when you lift something several times. The second type of endurance is heart and lung endurance. It is the ability of your heart and lungs to work efficiently during exercise. Heart and lung endurance helps you run, walk, and bicycle without becoming short of breath.

Flexibility is the ability to bend and twist joints easily. Flexibility helps you move. It also helps keep you from getting hurt. You use flexibility when you bend, turn, and reach.

Body composition compares the weight of your fat to the weight of your muscles, bones, and joints. Fat is important to your health. But too much fat can make staying fit hard.

⊛ 1.B; 1.F; 2.A

> **Health Journal**
> Make a list of the physical activities you do for fun and the physical activities that you do at home, such as yardwork. Describe which parts of physical fitness you use for each activity.

Physical Benefits of Exercise

Exercise is important for physical fitness. Poor fitness can make doing everyday tasks hard. Regular exercise can make the following happen:

- Your strength and muscular endurance improve. Muscles become stronger.

- Your endurance improves. The heart gets stronger. The lungs can take in more air.

- Your flexibility improves. When you exercise, you stretch the muscles around your joints.

- Your coordination improves. Coordination is the ability to use your body to make difficult movements.

- Your body burns more fat. Burning fat by exercising can help you improve body composition.

Different physical activities benefit different parts of fitness. Some activities improve endurance. Other activities improve strength or flexibility. The figure below lists some of the activities that can improve strength, endurance, and flexibility.

⭐ 1.B; 1.F; 2.A

Figure 3 Activities That Benefit Parts of Fitness

Strength

weight lifting
rock climbing
wrestling

Endurance

swimming
cycling
soccer
skating

Flexibility

yoga
dancing
martial arts
gymnastics

Figure 4 Exercise gives you a chance to meet new people.

Other Benefits of Exercise

Exercise doesn't just make you more fit. Exercise also has mental, emotional, and social benefits.

- **Mental** Physical activity improves blood flow to the brain. So, you feel more awake. You can also think more clearly.

- **Emotional** Exercise can improve your self-esteem. Exercise can also help you deal with stress. It gives you a chance to release the tension caused by stress.

- **Social** You will most likely exercise with other people. Exercise gives you a chance to make new friends. So, you can also work on your social skills while you exercise. ✪ 1.B; 1.F; 1.H

Lesson Review

Using Vocabulary

1. Describe the relationship between physical fitness and exercise. ✪ 1.B; 1.F

Understanding Concepts

2. Compare muscular endurance and heart and lung endurance. ✪ 1.F; 2.A

3. List the four parts of fitness. Which part do you use when you bend down? when you carry your books? ✪ 1.B; 1.F; 2.A

Critical Thinking

4. **Making Predictions** Ben and Greg joined the track team. How might their fitness improve?

5. **Identifying Relationships** Since Sofia started skating after school, she has felt more alert in class and has felt better about herself. How would you explain how she feels? ✪ 1.F; 1.H; 2.A

☑ internet connect

www.scilinks.org/health
Topic: Health Benefits of Sports
HealthLinks code: HD4050

HEALTH LINKS™ Maintained by the National Science Teachers Association

Your Fitness and Goals

What You'll Do

- **Explain** why you should visit the doctor before starting a fitness program. ⭐ 1.B; 1.F
- **List** physical fitness standards for your age group.
- **Describe** two things you should consider when choosing activities. ⭐ 1.B; 1.F
- **List** two influences on physical fitness goals. ⭐ 1.B; 1.C; 11.A

Terms to Learn

- sports physical
- fitness goal

Start Off Write

When should you change your fitness goals?

Nicole had to visit the doctor before her first season on the school basketball team. She was very nervous. But the visit wasn't bad. The doctor and nurse did some simple tests and told her everything was OK.

Nicole visited her doctor because she was starting a new sport. Nicole wanted to make sure that she could play basketball safely.

Visiting the Doctor

Everyone should go to the doctor regularly, especially when starting a new exercise program. Ask your parents to make an appointment for you. One of your parents will need to go with you. The doctor will have questions about your health history. He or she will want to know about any illnesses and shots you've had. The doctor will also want to know about your past injuries. Your parents can help you answer these questions.

Many schools ask students to see a doctor before they can play sports. A **sports physical** is a medical checkup that is required before playing with a sports team. The doctor will check your height, weight, heart rate, and blood pressure. The doctor may also test your reflexes. Sometimes, the doctor asks for blood and urine samples. The doctor wants to make sure you can play sports safely. ⭐ 1.B; 1.F

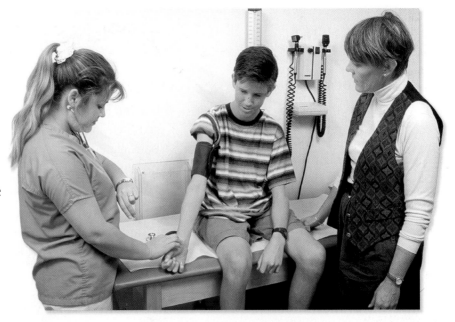

Figure 5 This student is getting his blood pressure checked as part of a sports physical.

Figure 6 The sit-and-reach test checks flexibility. A ruler on the box shows how far you reach. If your flexibility is healthy, you will be able to reach farther than the standard for your age group.

Testing Your Fitness

Maybe you don't want to play sports. You should still know your fitness strengths and weaknesses. There are simple tests for each part of physical fitness. Pull-ups and curl-ups test your strength and muscular endurance. The 1-mile run tests your heart and lung endurance. The sit-and-reach test checks your flexibility. Your teacher or coach can help you test your fitness.

Physical fitness standards are different for different people. For example, someone who plays sports usually has to meet higher standards. If you don't play sports, you should try to meet healthy standards. Table 1 shows the healthy fitness zones for your age group. If you don't meet these standards, you should try to exercise more.

Brain Food

In 2001, Alan Webb set the high school record for the 1-mile run. He ran the mile in 3 minutes and 53.43 seconds!

TABLE 1 Healthy Fitness Zones for Ages 11 to 13				
Activity		**11**	**12**	**13**
Pull-ups	Boys	1–3	1–3	1–4
	Girls	1–2	1–2	1–2
Curl-ups	Boys	15–28	18–36	21–40
	Girls	15–29	18–32	18–32
1-mile run (minutes and seconds)	Boys	11:00–8:30	10:30–8:00	10:00–7:30
	Girls	12:00–9:00	12:00–9:00	11:30–9:00
Sit and reach (inches)	Boys	8	8	8
	Girls	10	10	10

Source: *FITNESSGRAM.*

LIFE SKILLS ACTIVITY

SETTING GOALS

Draw a table with five columns. In column one, list your fitness goals. What part of your fitness do you want to improve? In column two, list the activities that will help you reach your fitness goals. In column three, describe how each activity you listed in column two will help you reach your fitness goals. Use column three to help you decide which activities you want to try. List those activities in column four. Do these activities for 4 weeks. Then, describe your progress in column five. ⭐ 1.F

Choosing Your Activities

After testing your physical fitness, you may want to improve your fitness. Use your interests and your goals to choose physical activities. If you try many different activities, you will find some that you enjoy. If you choose activities you like, you're more likely to keep doing them. Do not limit yourself to one sport or activity. As shown in Figure 7, even professional athletes play other sports.

Some people set fitness goals before choosing an activity. A **fitness goal** is a goal to improve your physical fitness. When you set fitness goals, choose activities that will help you meet your goals. For example, if your goal is to improve your flexibility, you might take yoga or martial arts classes. If your goal is to improve your endurance, try running or bicycling. ⭐ 1.B; 1.F

Figure 7 Even professional athletes play other sports. Michael Jordan played golf to relax between basketball seasons.

Influences on Your Goals

You should pick your goals carefully. Set goals that are reasonable. Ask your parents or teacher to help you with your goals. Set short-term goals to help you meet a long-term goal. Meeting your short-term goals will help you feel good about yourself. Also, don't be afraid to change your goals. You can change your goals if they're unreasonable or if you don't like the results.

Many things will affect your fitness goals. One is the risk of injury. You're more likely to get hurt while doing certain activities. Maybe your fitness goals include risky activities, such as mountain biking. Before doing these activities, talk to someone who knows how to do them. He or she can tell you what to expect. Your values and the values of the people around you also affect your goals. If people around you think physical fitness is important, you are more likely to meet your fitness goals. This is especially true if good physical fitness is also important to you. ★ 1.B; 1.C; 11.A

Figure 8 These students have set short-term goals that will help them meet their long-term goal of running in a 5-kilometer race.

Lesson Review

Using Vocabulary

1. What is a sports physical? Why should you see your doctor? ★ 1.B; 1.F

2. What is a fitness goal?

Understanding Concepts

3. What two things affect the activities you try? ★ 1.B; 1.F

4. Why should you try many different activities?

5. What are two influences on your fitness goals? ★ 1.B; 1.C; 11.A

Critical Thinking

6. Applying Concepts Andrea is 12 years old. She can do 2 pull-ups and 20 curl-ups. She runs a mile in 13 minutes and reaches 9 inches on the sit-and-reach test. Is Andrea meeting healthy fitness standards? If not, what does she need to improve? ★ 1.B

Meeting Your Goals

What You'll Do

- **List** three things you can change to meet personal fitness goals. ⍟ 1.B; 1.C
- **Describe** how resting heart rate and recovery time change as fitness improves. ⍟ 1.F

Terms to Learn

- resting heart rate (RHR)
- recovery time

Start Off
Write

What can you do to make sure your fitness improves?

Shari read about an Olympic training program in a sports magazine. She couldn't understand why anyone would want to train so much. Some of the athletes trained for more than 6 hours each day!

Olympic athletes don't start out by training 6 hours a day. They start with shorter workouts. Then, they slowly increase the length of their workouts. This helps Olympic athletes improve.

Frequency, Intensity, and Time

When you exercise, you can change three things to improve your fitness. They are frequency (FREE kwuhn see), intensity (in TEN suh tee), and time, or FIT.

- **Frequency** is how often you exercise. The more often you exercise, the more your fitness can improve.
- **Intensity** is how hard you work out. When you increase intensity, your body works harder. Your fitness can also improve more.
- **Time** is how long you work out. Olympic athletes work out longer to become better at their sports.

To avoid getting hurt, do not increase more than one part of FIT at a time. Also, don't increase any part too much. Keep a fitness log to describe how you use FIT. A *fitness log* is a notebook you can use to record your progress. ⍟ 1.C; 1.F

Figure 9 Keeping a fitness log is one way to keep yourself working toward your goals.

Fitness Log

Sunday May 6	Played soccer at the park. We played pretty hard. I was tired when we were done, but I had a good time.	*1 hour*
Monday May 7	I didn't do anything today.	
Tuesday May 8	We played basketball in PE today. I got pretty hot, but our team won!	*40 minutes*
Wednesday May 9	We learned some new forms in Karate class tonight. They were pretty hard. I'm going to practice them to get better.	*1 hour*

Checking Your Heart Rate

One way to measure your physical fitness is to check your heart rate. You can use your resting heart rate to see if your fitness has improved. **Resting heart rate (RHR)** is the number of beats your heart makes per minute when you are not exercising. Your RHR decreases as your physical fitness improves. You can check your heart rate, or pulse, on your neck and wrist. To find your pulse, place your index and middle fingers under your jaw and in front of your ear. You can also put your fingers on the thumb-side of your wrist. Do not use your thumb to check your pulse.

To improve your endurance, you need to exercise at a higher heart rate. For example, a 12-year-old should exercise at a rate between 125 and 177 beats per minute. This range is called a *target heart rate zone*. The amount of time your heart takes to return to RHR after exercise is called **recovery time.** As your physical fitness improves, your recovery time gets shorter.

Hands-on ACTIVITY

CHECKING YOUR PULSE

1. Find your pulse. Count beats for 10 seconds. Multiply the number of beats by 6 to find your RHR.
2. Jog for 3 minutes.
3. As you finish jogging, check your pulse to see if you reached your target heart rate zone.
4. Check your pulse each minute for the next 10 minutes. Record your results.

Analysis
1. How long was your recovery time after you jogged?
2. If you increase the amount of physical activity you do, what do you think will happen to your recovery time?

Figure 10 This student is checking his pulse by placing two fingers on his neck.

Lesson Review

Using Vocabulary

1. What are resting heart rate and recovery time? How do they change as fitness improves? ★ 1.C

Understanding Concepts

2. What is FIT? ★ 1.B; 1.C; 1.F

Critical Thinking

3. Making Predictions If you do the same workout for several weeks, what will happen to your fitness? ★ 1.B; 1.F

Lesson 4

Sports

What You'll Do

- **Compare** individual and team sports.
- **Describe** six benefits of sports. ⭐ 1.F

Terms to Learn

- individual sport
- team sport
- competition

Start Off
Write

What are some benefits of competition?

Stefan wants to join the wrestling team. But he doesn't understand why it's called a team. Everyone wrestles individually. Why would his school have a wrestling team if no one competes together?

Although wrestlers work on their own, they can still be part of a team. The team members work out together. And the scores for each of the team members are combined for a team score during wrestling matches.

Types of Sports

Wrestling is an example of an individual sport. An **individual sport** is a sport in which athletes play alone against other players. You may want to try individual sports if you like one-on-one games. Or maybe you want to focus on personal goals. Individual sports include track and field, swimming, and gymnastics. Many individual sports have teams. Players can practice their sport with a group. These groups are different from team sports. **Team sports** are sports in which two or more people work together against another team. Team sports let you share your skills with others. Team sports include soccer, basketball, and ice hockey.

You can play sports for fun with your friends, with a group in your community, or with a school team. Many people also play sports because they like competition. **Competition** is a contest between two or more individuals or teams. Competition gives you a chance to test your skills. It also helps some people improve their fitness. ⭐ 1.F

Figure 11 These are just two examples of the many kinds of individual and team sports.

Figure 12 Each person on this field hockey team leads by taking responsibility for her position.

Benefits of Sports

Sports are a fun way to exercise. When you play sports, the following may happen:

- You can improve your fitness.
- You can manage your weight.
- You can work on social skills and make friends.
- You can improve your self-esteem.
- You can learn teamwork. Being part of a team helps you learn to work with other people.
- You can learn leadership. *Leadership* is the ability to guide other people in an organized and responsible way. Leadership can help you make decisions that are good for the whole team. ⭐ 1.C; 1.F

Lesson Review

Using Vocabulary

1. Compare individual and team sports.

Understanding Concepts

2. List three examples of individual and team sports other than those in the text.

3. If you join a sports team, how will your fitness change? ⭐ 1.C

Critical Thinking

4. Applying Concepts Brian has a hard time working with others and making decisions. He wants to play baseball. How do you think playing baseball can help Brian learn how to make decisions? How can it help him work with other people? ⭐ 1.F

Injury

Lanny really likes to play soccer. He read a magazine article about soccer players who got injured. They pushed themselves too hard or played while they were hurt. Lanny doesn't want that to happen to him.

You might get hurt when you do physical activity. This risk doesn't mean you should avoid activity. But you should know the warning signs of injury.

Warning Signs of Injury

The day after hard exercise, you might feel uncomfortable. This feeling is called *muscle soreness*. It usually goes away the next time you exercise. Muscle soreness is caused by hard exercise. It is not a sign of injury. However, the following are warning signs of injury:

- **Sharp Pain** The area may hurt more when you touch it. You may also feel sharp pain when trying to use an injured body part.

- **Swelling** Swelling often starts right after the injury happens. Swelling is usually painful.

- **Bruises** The injured area may bruise right after an accident. Bruises may also take a few days to appear. They can cover a large area. Bruising and swelling often happen together.
  ⊛ 5.G

What You'll Do

- **Identify** three warning signs of injuries. ⊛ 5.G

- **Compare** muscle soreness and the warning signs of injury. ⊛ 5.G

- **Describe** the steps of RICE.
  ⊛ 5.F; 5.G

- **Describe** strains, sprains, and fractures.

Terms to Learn

- strain
- sprain
- fracture

Start Off
Write

How do you know if you have an injury?

Figure 13 Injuries are often painful. Some injuries cause swelling and bruising.

First Aid for Injury

If you think you are injured, tell your parents or teacher right away. You may need to see a doctor. You may also need to take the following steps:

- **Rest** Stop playing. Rest keeps the injury from getting worse. Keep the injured body part still until you can find out how badly you are hurt.

- **Ice** Put ice or a cold pack on the injury to reduce swelling and pain. Don't put ice on your bare skin. Wrap the ice in a towel first.

- **Compression** Wrap the injury with an elastic bandage or athletic tape. This reduces swelling and keeps the injured area from moving. Don't wrap too tightly. You may cut off blood flow if you do.

- **Elevation** Raise the injured body part. This helps bring down swelling. Don't elevate the injury if doing so makes the injury hurt more.

It may help you recall these steps if you remember that the first letters of the words spell *RICE*.

Injuries heal best when you get plenty of rest and eat right. Take your doctor's advice about exercising again. If you exercise too soon, you may hurt yourself again. When you begin activity again, slowly increase exercise until you regain your fitness. ★ 5.F; 5.G

STUDY TIP *for better reading*

Organizing Information
An acronym is a word formed from the first letters or the first few letters of a series of words. Acronyms such as RICE are good ways to help you remember information.

Figure 14 An elastic bandage will reduce swelling in an injured knee.

Figure 15 Can you identify the parts of RICE in this photo? The student is using ice and elevation to take care of his ankle.

Myth: No pain, no gain.

Fact: Pain that doesn't go away or gets worse is a sign of injury.

Strains

Maybe you've heard someone say that he or she pulled a muscle or tendon. A *tendon* attaches a muscle to a bone. When someone has a pulled muscle or tendon, he or she has a strain. A **strain** is a muscle or tendon that has been stretched too far or torn. Signs of a strain may include pain and weakness in the injured area. Strains can be caused by doing too much exercise. Sometimes, a muscle is stretched too far or too quickly. Mild muscle strains can take as little as a week to heal. Some strains need surgery.

Sprains

A *ligament* attaches one bone to another bone in a joint. A **sprain** is an injury that happens when a joint is twisted suddenly and the ligaments in the joint are stretched too far or torn. Sprains often happen when a joint is twisted in a way that it does not normally move. A sprain is often painful. Also, it may be hard to move a sprained joint. Sprained joints often swell and bruise. A sprained ankle or knee can make it hard to stand. Many sprains heal in about 2 to 6 weeks. Some sprains need surgery to repair the torn ligaments.

Fractures

Have you ever broken a bone? If not, maybe someone you know has. A **fracture** (FRAK chuhr) is a cracked or broken bone. Fractures can cause pain, swelling, bruising, and weakness in the injured area. Sometimes, a body part with a fracture doesn't move the way it should. You should see a doctor if you think you have a fracture.

There are many different kinds of fractures. The treatment depends on the kind and location of the fracture. The damage to the area around a fracture may also affect how the fracture is treated. A cast is often used to keep the bone or joint still while the fracture heals. However, some fractures are only wrapped or braced. Many fractures take 4 to 12 weeks to heal. Some fractures need surgery to help them heal.

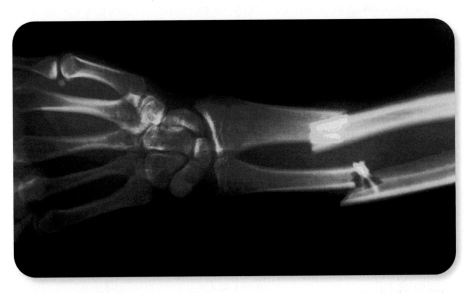

Figure 16 This photo shows an X-ray image of a broken forearm. You can see that both bones are broken.

Lesson Review

Using Vocabulary

1. Describe strains, sprains, and fractures. ⍟ 5.F

Understanding Concepts

2. List three warning signs of injury. Compare the warning signs of injury with muscle soreness. ⍟ 5.G

3. Describe the steps of RICE. ⍟ 5.F

Critical Thinking

4. **Identifying Relationships**
Swelling is the body's response to injury. Swelling actually helps keep an injured body part from moving. If this is the case, why do people use ice, compression, and elevation to reduce swelling? ⍟ 2.A; 5.F

🖳 internet connect ≣≣≣
www.scilinks.org/health
Topic: Sports Injury
HealthLinks code: HD4093

HEALTH
LINKS. Maintained by the National Science Teachers Association

Avoiding Injury While Exercising

Rosa has a friend who complains about stretching before practice. Rosa doesn't understand why. She knows stretching can help keep her friend from pulling a muscle.

What You'll Do

- **Explain** why you should warm up, cool down, and stretch each time you exercise. ✪ 1.B; 1.F; 5.G

- **Describe** eight basic stretches. ✪ 5.G

Terms to Learn

- warm-up
- cool-down
- stretching

Start Off
Write

What does a cool-down do?

Rosa is right. Injuries can happen easily when you play sports. But you can avoid most injuries by warming up, cooling down, and stretching every time you exercise. Read on to find out more!

Warming Up

You should warm up before you exercise. A **warm-up** is any activity you do to get your body ready for exercise. A warm-up increases your heart rate and the blood flow in your body. It loosens muscles so that they move easily. A warm-up also slightly raises your body temperature. A fast walk or a slow jog is a good warm-up. You should warm up until you're sweating lightly. This usually takes about 15 to 20 minutes. By taking time to warm up, you can prevent injuries, such as strains.

You may also want to do some exercises similar to the activity you will be doing. For example, you can throw and catch before playing baseball or pass and serve before playing volleyball. These exercises aren't just a good way to warm up. Warming up can also help you work on your skills. ✪ 1.B; 1.F; 5.G

Figure 17 An easy jog is one way to warm up for a soccer game.

Cooling Down

Cooling down after an activity is as important as warming up. A **cool-down** is any activity that helps your body return to the way it was before exercising. A cool-down helps the heart return to its resting heart rate. Cooling down can also keep your muscles from getting tight and sore. A good cool-down is often a slow activity, such as jogging or walking.

You may have noticed that runners don't stop moving after a race is over. The runners walk or keep running at a slower pace. This cool-down helps their bodies return to normal.

A cool-down is also a good time to work on your flexibility. So, you can stretch as part of your cool-down. Stretching during a cool-down makes it less likely that you will feel sore later.

⭐ 1.B; 1.F; 5.G

Figure 18 A slow jog after a hard workout gives the heart a chance to recover slowly.

LIFE SKILLS ACTIVITY

BEING A WISE CONSUMER

1. Work in small groups. Take a look at popular fitness, health, and fashion magazines. Look for articles about short workouts.

2. Discuss each of the workouts with your group. What do the workouts have in common? What is different?

3. Do the workouts have warm-ups and cool-downs? Why do you think some workouts have warm-ups and cool-downs and others don't?

4. If a workout doesn't have a warm-up and cool-down, would you still do it? Explain your answer.

5. Make a short workout in your group. What is the shortest workout you can make that includes a warm-up and cool-down? Does it improve physical fitness?

6. Describe your workout on a poster, and present it to the class. ⭐ 1.F

Figure 19 Some Easy Stretches

▶ Standing quadriceps stretch
Put your right hand on the wall for balance. With your left hand, grab the ankle of your left foot. Pull the heel of your foot up until you feel a stretch in your thigh. Don't lean forward while stretching. Repeat the stretch for your right leg.

◀ Calf stretch
Lean forward, and place your hands against the wall. Place your right foot near the wall. Slowly move your left foot away from the wall until you feel a stretch in your left calf muscle. Repeat for your right calf.

▲ Back stretch
On your hands and knees, slowly lift your back toward the ceiling to stretch your upper back.

▶ Groin stretch
Sit with the soles of your feet together. Hold your ankles, and rest your elbows on the inside of your knees. Slowly lean forward and push your knees down with your elbows. Keep your back straight.

Stretching

Stretching is an important part of physical activity. **Stretching** is any activity that loosens muscles and increases flexibility. Also, stretching may help prevent injury. Stretch only after a warm-up or during a cool-down. Stretching muscles that haven't been warmed up can cause injury. Stretch slowly and without bouncing. Bouncing can also cause injury. Stretch until you feel a pull in your muscles. Don't hold a stretch that hurts. Hold your stretch about 10 to 30 seconds.

Stretches must be done correctly. If you stretch incorrectly, you can hurt yourself. Ask your coach or teacher to show you how to stretch correctly. Figure 19 shows some examples of stretches.

⭐ 1.F; 5.G

◄ Shoulder stretch
Extend your right arm in front of your body. Use your left arm to pull the arm toward your body while keeping your right arm straight. Repeat for your left arm.

◄ Trunk twist stretch
Put your left leg straight in front of you while seated. Bend your right leg, and put your right foot on the outside of your left knee. Put your right arm behind you. With your left arm on the outside of your right leg, twist your body toward your right until you feel a stretch in your right side. Repeat for your left side.

▲ Sitting hamstring stretch
Sit with your feet together. With your knees slightly bent, reach toward your toes until you feel a stretch in the back of your legs. Keep your back straight while bending.

◄ Forearm stretch
Extend your left arm with your palm up. With your right hand, pull the fingers of your left arm down and back toward your body. Repeat for your right arm.

✪ 1.F; 5.G

Lesson Review

Using Vocabulary

1. Use each of the following terms in a sentence: *warm-up*, *stretching*, and *cool-down*. ✪ 1.B; 1.F; 5.G

Understanding Concepts

2. Which four stretches would you do to stretch your legs? Which four stretches would you use for your arms and upper body? ✪ 1.B; 5.G

Critical Thinking

3. Making Predictions Diego plays basketball for his school's team. Diego warms up, but he doesn't cool down at the end of practice. What do you think may happen to Diego if he keeps playing without cooling down? Explain your answer. ✪ 1.B; 1.F; 5.G

Safety Equipment

What You'll Do

- **Explain** why you should use safety equipment. ⭐ 5.G
- **List** six examples of sports safety equipment. ⭐ 5.G

Terms to Learn

- safety equipment

Start Off
Write

Describe safety equipment for a sport.

Xavier likes to ride his bicycle. Some of his friends give him a hard time because he always wears his helmet, even if he is just going down the block. But Xavier knows the helmet could save his life.

Xavier's helmet is an example of safety equipment. **Safety equipment** is equipment that helps prevent injury. Many physical activities can be unsafe if you don't use safety equipment.

Why Use Safety Equipment?

Safety equipment helps protect you from injury. In sports such as football and hockey, you run into other players during games. So, players wear helmets and pads to protect themselves. Skateboarders and in-line skaters often fall while they work on tricks. They use helmets, elbow pads, and knee pads to stay safe. You should use safety equipment when you play a sport in which you may run into other people or fall.

Safety equipment doesn't just protect you from injury. It also makes sports more fun. You can enjoy sports more when you don't have to worry as much about getting hurt. And some activities wouldn't be possible without safety equipment. For example, rock climbers would not be able to climb mountains without ropes and harnesses. And helmets help keep rock climbers from getting hurt. So, rock climbers can have more fun. ⭐ 1.B; 5.G

Figure 20 Skateboarders use helmets and pads to protect themselves from injury.

Figure 21 Many activities have special safety equipment to prevent injury.

Examples of Safety Equipment

Over time, improvements in safety equipment have made some sports safer. For example, until the mid 1970s, many bicyclists used hockey helmets or helmets made of leather strips. These helmets were often big and uncomfortable. Some of these helmets didn't provide much protection. Today, bicyclists wear helmets that are lightweight and wind resistant. These helmets also protect bicyclists' heads better.

There is safety equipment for almost every sport. Soccer players wear shin guards. Skaters use helmets, knee pads, and elbow pads. Helmets, harnesses, and ropes protect rock climbers. Gymnasts use soft mats. Safety equipment must be used correctly. And make sure you use the right equipment for your sport. ⭐ 5.G

Brain Food

Bicycle helmets should always be replaced after an accident in which you hit your head. Bicycle helmets are made with a special foam that crushes on impact. After the foam is crushed, the helmet no longer protects your head.

Lesson Review

Using Vocabulary

1. What is safety equipment? ⭐ 5.G

Understanding Concepts

2. List two examples of safety equipment other than those described in the text. Why are they used? ⭐ 5.G

Critical Thinking

3. Making Good Decisions Imagine there is a new sport. The players in this sport tackle each other and kick a ball into a goal to score. Would players need safety equipment? Explain your answer. ⭐ 5.G

Chapter Summary

■ Physical fitness is the ability to do everyday activities without becoming short of breath, sore, or tired. ■ Four parts of physical fitness are muscular strength, endurance, flexibility, and body composition. ■ Exercise is any activity that maintains or improves physical fitness. ■ Interests and goals influence your selection of physical activities. ■ Increasing frequency, intensity, and time of exercise improves physical fitness. ■ Recovery time is the amount of time the heart takes to resume its resting heart rate after exercise. ■ The warning signs of injury are sharp pain, swelling, and bruising. ■ Warming up, cooling down, and stretching prevent injury. ■ Equipment that prevents injury is called *safety equipment*.

Using Vocabulary

For each sentence, fill in the blank with the proper word from the word bank below.

strain	strength
resting heart rate	exercise
physical fitness	flexibility
stretching	sprain
recovery time	fitness goal

① ___ is the ability to do everyday activities.

② ___ improves or maintains your physical fitness.

③ You use ___ when you lift and carry a backpack full of books.

④ If you plan to run a 5-kilometer race next month, you have set a(n) ___.

⑤ ___ is the number of beats your heart makes per minute when you are not exercising.

⑥ ___ is the amount of time your heart takes to return to its resting heart rate.

⑦ A(n) ___ happens when the ligaments in a joint are stretched too far or are torn.

⑧ ___ is an activity that increases the flexibility of a joint.

Understanding Concepts

⑨ Describe the four parts of physical fitness. ★ 2.A

⑩ Describe the physical benefits of exercise. ★ 1.B; 1.F; 2.A

⑪ How can exercise improve mental, emotional, and social health? ★ 1.B; 1.F

⑫ Why should you warm up, cool down, and stretch every time you exercise? ★ 1.F; 5.G

⑬ Why should you visit a doctor before starting a fitness program? ★ 1.B; 1.G; 5.G

⑭ List the healthy fitness zones for pull-ups, curl-ups, and the 1-mile run for your age group.

⑮ What two things should you keep in mind when choosing a new physical activity? ★ 1.F; 2.A; 5.G

⑯ List six benefits of sports. ★ 1.F; 2.A

⑰ What four steps are used to treat sports injuries? ★ 5.F; 5.G

⑱ List examples of sports safety equipment for five sports.

Critical Thinking

Making Inferences

19 Kaya has been exercising with the swim team for 6 weeks. When she started, she noticed that her heart beat very quickly when she swam. Now, it doesn't seem to beat so quickly, and it doesn't take as long to slow down when she's finished. What do you think made Kaya's heart rate change? ⭐ 1.C; 1.F; 2A

20 Tanya wants to play soccer. Her friend Keith doesn't want to play soccer, but he wants to stay fit. How might Tanya's and Keith's values affect their fitness goals?

21 Ranjan likes to challenge himself when he tries a physical activity. He always tries to do better than he did last time. He also likes to focus on his fitness goals. What type of sport do you think Ranjan would prefer? Explain your answer. ⭐ 1.B; 1.F

Making Good Decisions

22 Imagine you are practicing for a running race. After working out for over a month, you have met your first goal of running a mile in less than 10 minutes. However, you notice that you aren't improving anymore. What do you think you need to do to keep getting faster? ⭐ 1.F; 2.A

23 Imagine that you notice a sharp pain in your knee. When you look at it, the knee is a little swollen. It doesn't hurt too badly, and you want to keep exercising. What should you do? ⭐ 5.G

Interpreting Graphics

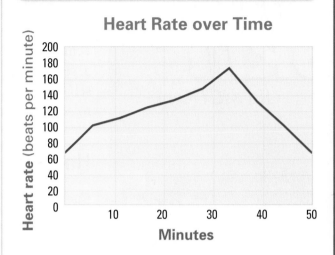

Heart Rate over Time

Use the graph above to answer questions 24–26. ⭐ M: 6.10D

24 What is this person's resting heart rate (RHR)?

25 The maximum heart rate for a person is estimated by subtracting the person's age from 220. This person is 11 years old. What is her maximum heart rate?

26 To improve physical fitness, a person should make sure his or her heart rate falls within a target heart rate zone during exercise. The target heart rate zone for an 11-year-old is 125 to 178 beats per minute. Did this person reach his or her target heart rate zone? If so, how long was he or she in the target heart rate zone?

Reading Checkup

Take a minute to review your answers to the Health IQ questions at the beginning of this chapter. How has reading this chapter improved your Health IQ?

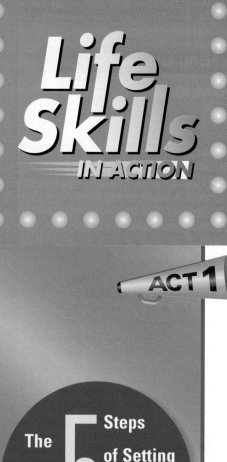

Life Skills IN ACTION

The 5 Steps of Setting Goals

1. Consider your interests and values.
2. Choose goals that include your interests and values.
3. If necessary, break down long-term goals into several short-term goals.
4. Measure your progress.
5. Reward your success.

Setting Goals

A goal is something that you work toward and hope to achieve. Setting goals is important because goals give you a sense of purpose and achieving goals improves your self-esteem. Complete the following activity to learn how to set and achieve goals.

Hayley's Goal

ACT 1

Setting the Scene

Hayley is in OK physical condition, but she doesn't exercise as much as she probably should. One day, Hayley's physical education teacher announces to the class that they will take a physical-fitness test called the *President's Challenge* in 3 months. Last year, Hayley's older sister, Tia, took the same test and won a Presidential Physical Fitness Award. Hayley wants to win an award, too.

Guided Practice

Practice with a Friend

Form a group of three. Have one person play the role of Hayley and another person play the role of Tia. Have the third person be an observer. Walking through each of the five steps of setting goals, role-play Hayley working toward her goal of winning a Presidential Physical Fitness Award. Tia should offer advice and support as Hayley works toward her goal. The observer will take notes, which will include observations about what the person playing Hayley did well and suggestions of ways to improve. Stop after each step to evaluate the process.

Check Yourself

After you have completed the guided practice, go through Act 1 again without stopping at each step. Answer the questions below to review what you did.

1. What are some values that Hayley might consider before setting her goal?

2. Hayley's long-term goal is to win a Presidential Physical Fitness Award. What are some short-term goals that will help her achieve this long-term goal?

3. How can Hayley measure her progress toward her long-term goal?

4. What is one of your long-term goals? What short-term goals will help you reach your long-term goal?

ACT 2 On Your Own

Three months later, Hayley takes the President's Challenge and wins the Presidential Physical Fitness Award. Her physical education teacher congratulates her and tells her about another award she could try to earn. The award is the Presidential Active Lifestyle Award. Hayley's teacher suggests that she read about it on the Internet. Make a pamphlet that explains how Hayley could use the five steps of setting goals to earn a Presidential Active Lifestyle Award. You will need to research the requirements of the award on the Internet.

Nutrition

Check out
Current Health
articles related to this chapter by
visiting go.hrw.com. Just type in
the keyword **HD4CH12**.

" My **friends** buy **chips** and **soft drinks** from the vending machine **every day** after school.

My mom lets me buy a snack only on Fridays. She says that eating too much food from the vending machine is unhealthy. "

PRE-READING

Answer the following true/false questions to find out what you already know about nutrition. When you've finished this chapter, you'll have the opportunity to change your answers based on what you've learned.

1. You get the energy you need for your daily activities from the food you eat. ⊛ 1.B

2. You need to drink only two glasses of water every day. ⊛ 1.A

3. Your nutrition affects your overall health. ⊛ 1.F

4. To be healthy, you have to cut all the fat from your diet. ⊛ 1.A

5. The Nutrition Facts label shows you how much of each food you should eat.

6. The food you eat must be broken down into a different form before your body can use it.

7. Practicing good nutrition means that you can eat one type of food every day as long as the food is healthy. ⊛ 1.A

8. You get all the water you need by drinking one soft drink each day. ⊛ 1.B

9. The Food Guide Pyramid shows you if a food is a good source of nutrients. ⊛ 1.B

10. There are four food groups. ⊛ 1.A

11. The Dietary Guidelines are a set of suggestions you can follow to develop a healthy lifestyle. ⊛ 1.A

12. A small amount of fat in your diet is good for your body. ⊛ 1.B

13. The meat, poultry, fish, dry beans, eggs, and nuts group is the largest group on the Food Guide Pyramid. ⊛ 1.B

ANSWERS: 1. True; 2. False; 3. True; 4. False; 5. False; 6. True; 7. False; 8. False; 9. False; 10. False; 11. True; 12. True; 13. False

Nutrition and Your Health

What You'll Do

- **Describe** how nutrition affects your overall health. ⭐ 1.B
- **Explain** how your body uses food. ⭐ 1.A; 2.A

Terms to Learn

- nutrient

Start Off *Write*

How does nutrition affect your daily activities?

What do you think food does for your body? You know that you need to eat when you are hungry, but why do you need food?

You need food because food contains substances that your body uses to work properly. Many of these substances provide your body with the energy it needs to grow, heal, and keep its systems working.

What Is Nutrition?

The substances in food that promote normal growth, maintenance, and repair in your body are called **nutrients** (NOO tree uhnts). Because your body gets nutrients from food, the food you eat can affect your overall health. Nutrition is the study of how our bodies use the food we eat to keep us healthy. Your nutrition affects the way your body carries out normal body functions. It also affects your growth and the way your body repairs itself.

In general, eating too much or not eating enough food is not healthy. Also, eating the right combination of healthy foods is important. When you do this, you are practicing good nutrition.

Your nutrition affects your daily activities. Practicing good nutrition gives you the energy you need to play with your friends, to study for school, and to be physically active. ⭐ 1.A; 1.B

Figure 1 Practicing good nutrition helps your body stay active and gives you the nutrients you need to grow.

How Your Body Uses Food

Like a car, your body needs fuel for the energy it needs to run. If you do not use the right kind of fuel for your car, your car may break down. Your body needs the right kind of fuel to run properly. You can think of food as fuel for your body. Your body cannot use food directly for energy. Your body has to break down food into nutrients. *Digestion* is the process in which your food is broken down into a form that your body can use for energy.

Imagine that you are having a peanut butter and jelly sandwich for lunch. When you chew your sandwich, you break it into smaller chunks. When you swallow, the sandwich goes down a tube, called your *esophagus,* and into your stomach. In your stomach, the sandwich is mixed with strong stomach juices. These juices break the sandwich into even smaller parts. The sandwich is now like a thick milkshake. This liquid food passes from your stomach into your intestines. In your intestines, your sandwich is broken down into nutrients.

The nutrients are absorbed into your blood and delivered to tissues throughout your body. Finally, your body can use some of the nutrients for energy. Your body uses the other nutrients to maintain your health. For example, some nutrients are used to build strong bones and teeth. Some are used to keep your hair, skin, and nails healthy. ✪ 1.A; 1.B; 2.A

◄ The nutrients in carrots help your eyesight.

◄ The nutrients in milk help you build strong teeth.

Figure 2 Your body uses the nutrients in food to stay healthy.

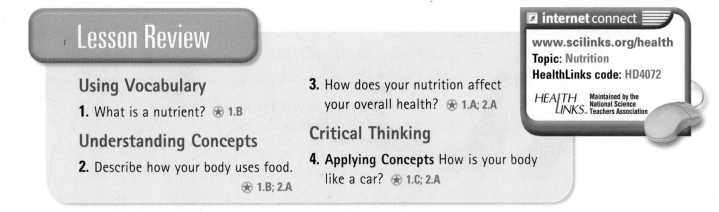

Lesson Review

Using Vocabulary

1. What is a nutrient? ✪ 1.B

Understanding Concepts

2. Describe how your body uses food.
✪ 1.B; 2.A

3. How does your nutrition affect your overall health? ✪ 1.A; 2.A

Critical Thinking

4. Applying Concepts How is your body like a car? ✪ 1.C; 2.A

internet connect

www.scilinks.org/health
Topic: Nutrition
HealthLinks code: HD4072

HEALTH LINKS Maintained by the National Science Teachers Association

The Nutrients You Need

Your body needs the nutrients in food to grow and to stay healthy. There are many different nutrients, and each one helps your body in a different way. But what are these nutrients, and what do they do for you?

What You'll Do

- **Describe** each of the six classes of essential nutrients. ⊛ 1.A
- **Identify** foods that are good sources of each nutrient. ⊛ 1.A; 1.B

Terms to Learn

- Calorie
- carbohydrate
- protein
- fat
- vitamin
- mineral

Start Off
Write

How much fat does your body need to stay healthy?

Your body can make some of the nutrients you need. But, most of the nutrients you use come from the food you eat. Your body cannot work properly without these nutrients. So, they are called the *essential nutrients*. There are six classes of essential nutrients.

The Six Classes of Essential Nutrients

The six classes of essential nutrients are *carbohydrates* (CAHR boh HIE drayts), *proteins* (PROH TEENZ), *fats*, *vitamins* (VIET uh minz), *minerals (*MIN uhr uhlz), and *water*. Carbohydrates, proteins, and fats are nutrients that give your body energy. The energy you get from these nutrients is measured in units called **Calories.** The number of Calories in food is how much energy that food provides. Vitamins, minerals, and water do not have any Calories. Instead, these nutrients help your body use the other nutrients. For example, water is important because it helps control your body temperature and transports other nutrients through your body. Together, these nutrients help your body work properly. Because the essential nutrients come from different foods, you should eat a variety of foods each day. This will help you get all the nutrients you need. ⊛ 1.A

Figure 3 Have you ever been confused about the essential nutrients in your cereal? These nutrients are good for you, and you can get them only from food!

Carbohydrates

Carbohydrates give you energy to be physically active. A **carbohydrate** is a chemical that is made up of one or more sugars chained together. The two kinds of carbohydrates are sugars and starches. Sugars are found in foods such as table sugar, honey, and fruits. Foods that have sugars are usually sweet. Starches are made up of many sugars chained together. Your body breaks down starches into sugars. Starches are found in foods such as rice, bread, and pasta. Some starches are good sources of fiber. Fiber is a part of a healthy diet and can be found in whole grain foods such as brown rice and whole wheat bread.
⭐ 1.A; 1.B

Carbohydrates

Proteins

Nutrients that help build and heal body tissues are called **proteins.** Proteins also help build strong muscles. Proteins are made up of smaller parts called *amino acids* (uh MEE noh AS idz). Your body breaks down the proteins you eat into amino acids. Think of amino acids as building blocks. Your body uses these building blocks to form new proteins. Your body uses the proteins to build and repair your tissues. Chicken, fish, pork, and beef are sources of protein. You can also get proteins from beans, nuts, tofu, cheese, eggs, and soy milk. ⭐ 1.A; 1.B

Proteins

Fats

Your body needs a small amount of fat to stay healthy. **Fats** are energy-storage nutrients that help the body store some vitamins. Fats also help your body produce hormones (HAWR MOHNZ). Fats are the substances that make many foods smell and taste good. Fats provide a lot of energy. But your body needs only a small amount of fat to work properly. Some fats are liquid, while others are solid. Liquid fats are found in cooking oils and salad dressings. Solid fats are found in foods such as butter, sour cream, and cream cheese. Solid fats are also found in meats such as beef and pork. Fried foods, ice cream, creamy dips, potato or corn chips, and most desserts are high in fats. ⭐ 1.A; 1.B

Fats

Figure 4 Here are some examples of foods that are sources of carbohydrates, proteins, and fats.

Vitamins

Without vitamins, your body will not be able to function properly. **Vitamins** are organic compounds that control several body functions. Vitamins help your body use the energy provided by other nutrients. Your body needs only a very small amount of vitamins each day. There are many types of vitamins. Vitamin C helps your body fight germs. Vitamin D helps your body build strong bones. Vitamin A helps keep your eyes healthy. One type of vitamin B can help with your memory and concentration. As you can see, vitamins are necessary for good health. Almost all foods contain some vitamins; whole grains, meats, fruits, vegetables, and dairy products are good sources of vitamins.
⭐ 1.A; 1.B

Minerals

Like vitamins, your body needs minerals to stay healthy. **Minerals** are elements that are necessary for good health. However, you need only a small amount every day to stay healthy. Examples of minerals include iron, calcium (KAL see uhm), sodium, and potassium (poh TAS ee uhm). Iron helps your blood transport oxygen through your body. Calcium is important for building and keeping strong bones. Sodium and potassium help regulate blood pressure. Minerals can be found in many kinds of foods, such as those shown in Table 1. ⭐ 1.A; 1.B

Did you know that minerals such as iron and calcium are elements found in nature? You may have learned about these elements in science class. The Periodic Table lists all the elements. You can find a Periodic Table in a science book or science classroom. Locate the minerals listed in this chapter on the Periodic Table. Then research to find out what foods are good sources of each mineral.

TABLE 1 Good Sources of Some Important Vitamins and Minerals

Name		What It Does For Your Body	Where You Get It
Vitamin A		necessary for healthy eyes and skin	carrots, sweet potatoes, squash
Vitamin C		helps your body fight germs that cause illness	orange juice, broccoli, papaya
Vitamin B-12		aids in concentration, memory, and balance	fish, milk and milk products, eggs, meat, poultry
Calcium		necessary for healthy, strong bones and teeth	milk; cheese; yogurt; leafy, green vegetables, such as spinach, broccoli, and turnip greens
Iron		necessary for healthy blood; prevents tiredness	tofu, spinach, blackeyed peas, red meat

⭐ 1.A; 1.B

Water

If you don't have water for a couple of days, you may die! More than half of your body is made of water. Why does your body need so much water? Your body needs the water for many different functions. You need water to help you digest your food and to get rid of waste. Water helps your body transport the nutrients you get from other foods. Finally, water helps your body keep a steady temperature. For example, imagine you have been playing outside and are now hot and sweaty. The sweat is made of water. The sweat dries on your skin, and as a result it cools off your body.

Your body loses water when you sweat and when you use the bathroom. You have to replace the water that you lose each day. To do this, you should drink about 8 to 10 glasses of water every day. If you are very active, play sports, or dance, you should drink even more water. If you don't replace the water your body loses, you run the risk of drying out. This is called *dehydration* (DEE hie DRAY shuhn). If you dehydrate, your body cannot function properly. So, make sure to drink enough water! ★ 1.A; 1.B

PRACTICING WELLNESS

Think of five ways to drink more water every day. Make a small poster that lists your ideas. Hang the poster in your locker or your room to help remind yourself to drink more water! ★ 1.A

Figure 5 Replacing the water you have lost will help keep you from drying out.

🖳 **internet** connect

www.scilinks.org/health
Topic: Edible/Medicinal Plants; Foods Grown in Texas
HealthLinks code: HHTX005; HHTX007

HEALTH LINKS™ Maintained by the National Science Teachers Association

Lesson Review

Using Vocabulary

1. What are vitamins?

2. What are carbohydrates?

Understanding Concepts

3. Explain what proteins do for your body. Give two examples of foods that are sources of protein. ★ 1.A; 1.B

4. Why is water such an important nutrient? ★ 1.A; 1.B

5. What are fats, and what do they do for your body? ★ 1.A; 1.B

Critical Thinking

6. **Analyzing Ideas** Why is it important to eat a variety of foods? ★ 1.A; 1.B

Eating for Life

You always hear about eating the right foods. But what does that mean? And how do you know how much of the right foods to eat?

Three guides can help you make healthy food choices every day. These guides are the Food Guide Pyramid, the Nutrition Facts label, and the Dietary Guidelines for Americans.

The Food Guide Pyramid

The Food Guide Pyramid is shown on the next page. The **Food Guide Pyramid** is a tool that shows you which foods to eat and how much of each type of food you should eat every day. The pyramid is made up of six food groups. A food group is made up of foods that contain similar nutrients. Each food group has its own block. Each block is a different size. The size of each block shows you how much food from that food group you should eat. The larger the block, the more food from that food group you should eat. The number of servings for each group tells you how much food from that food group you should eat daily. A serving is the amount of food that is considered healthy to eat. ⭐ 1.A; 1.B

What You'll Do

■ **Identify** the food groups shown on the Food Guide Pyramid. ⭐ 1.A; 1.B

■ **Explain** how to read a Nutrition Facts label. ⭐ 1.A; 1.B

■ **Describe** the Dietary Guidelines for Americans. ⭐ 1.A; 1.B

Terms to Learn

• Food Guide Pyramid
• Nutrition Facts label
• Dietary Guidelines for Americans

Start Off
Write

Why is eating plenty of fruits and vegetables important?

Figure 6 The Food Guide Pyramid can help you make healthy food choices wherever you choose to eat.

Figure 7 The Food Guide Pyramid ⊛ 1.A

Fats, oils, and sweets
Use sparingly

Meat, poultry, fish, dry beans, eggs, and nuts
2 to 3 servings

• 2 to 3 oz of cooked poultry, fish, or lean meat
• 1/2 cup of cooked dry beans
• 1 egg

Milk, yogurt, and cheese
2 to 3 servings

• 1 cup of milk or yogurt
• 1 1/2 oz of natural cheese
• 2 oz of processed cheese

Fruits
2 to 4 servings

• 1 medium apple, banana, or orange
• 1/2 cup of chopped, cooked, or canned fruit
• 3/4 cup of fruit juice

Vegetables
3 to 5 servings

• 1/2 cup of chopped vegetables
• 1 cup of raw, leafy vegetables
• 3/4 cup of vegetable juice

Topic: **Food Guide Pyramid**
Go To: **go.hrw.com**
Keyword: **HOLT PYRAMID**
Visit the HRW Web site for updates on the Food Guide Pyramid.

Bread, cereal, rice, and pasta
6 to 11 servings

• 1 slice of bread
• 1 oz of ready-to-eat cereal
• 1/2 cup of rice or pasta
• 1/2 cup of cooked cereal

Hands-on ACTIVITY

LET THE PYRAMID BE YOUR GUIDE

1. Write down everything that you eat in 1 day.

2. Compare what you ate to the Food Guide Pyramid.

Analysis

1. Make a chart showing how many servings of each food group you ate.

2. Did you get enough servings of each food group? If not, which food groups did you miss? Write down three ideas that will help you meet your daily servings of each food group.

⊛ 1.A; 1.B

The Nutrition Facts Label

The Nutrition Facts label is a good source of nutrition information. The **Nutrition Facts label** is a label found on the outside packages of food that states the number of servings in the container, the number of Calories in each serving, and the amount of nutrients in each serving.

The Nutrition Facts label provides information about the nutrients in the food. You can tell if the food is a good source of a nutrient by looking at the percent daily value of the nutrient. The daily value of a nutrient is the amount of your daily nutrient need that the food contains. A daily value of 5 percent or less means that the food is low in that nutrient. A daily value of 20 percent or more means that the food is high in that nutrient. You can use this information to make healthy food choices.

⭐ 1.A; 1.B

Health Journal

Save the Nutrition Facts labels from one of your favorite snacks. In your Health Journal, write down the amount of carbohydrates, fats, and proteins you are eating. Is your snack helping you get the right amount of these nutrients?

Figure 8 The Nutrition Facts Label

Serving information

Number of Calories per serving

Percentage of daily value of nutrients per serving

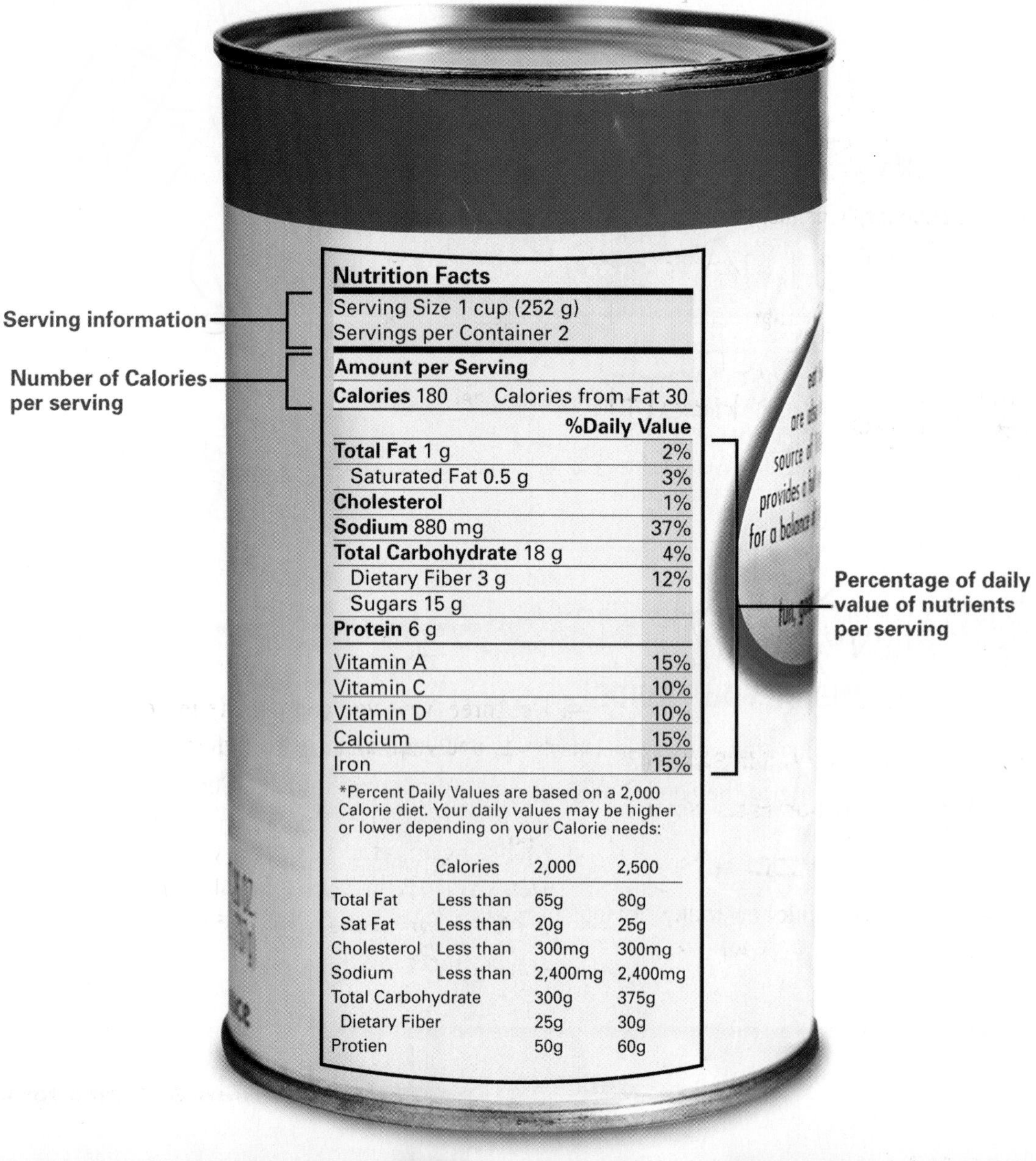

Nutrition Facts

Serving Size 1 cup (252 g)
Servings per Container 2

Amount per Serving

Calories 180   Calories from Fat 30

	%Daily Value
Total Fat 1 g	2%
Saturated Fat 0.5 g	3%
Cholesterol	1%
Sodium 880 mg	37%
Total Carbohydrate 18 g	4%
Dietary Fiber 3 g	12%
Sugars 15 g	
Protein 6 g	
Vitamin A	15%
Vitamin C	10%
Vitamin D	10%
Calcium	15%
Iron	15%

*Percent Daily Values are based on a 2,000 Calorie diet. Your daily values may be higher or lower depending on your Calorie needs:

	Calories	2,000	2,500
Total Fat	Less than	65g	80g
Sat Fat	Less than	20g	25g
Cholesterol	Less than	300mg	300mg
Sodium	Less than	2,400mg	2,400mg
Total Carbohydrate		300g	375g
Dietary Fiber		25g	30g
Protien		50g	60g

Guidelines for Good Nutrition

The Dietary Guidelines for Americans are another tool that you can use to make healthy food choices. The **Dietary Guidelines for Americans** are a set of tips that help you practice good nutrition and form a healthy lifestyle. The guidelines suggest that you aim to be physically active each day. So, you should try to take part in activities that make you move your body. Activities can include playing sports, playing outside, riding bikes, dancing, or in-line skating. Also, choose healthy foods by using the Food Guide Pyramid. Eat plenty of whole grains, fresh fruits, and vegetables. If you are not getting enough fruits and vegetables every day, look at Table 2 for some suggestions. Choose foods that are low in salt, sugar, and fat. Make sure your food is fully cooked. Store foods properly by keeping cold foods cold and by refrigerating hot foods soon after you are finished with them. Following the Dietary Guidelines for Americans will help you develop healthy eating habits. ✷ 1.A; 1.B

Sneaky Servings

It may seem that there aren't many grams of fat or many Calories in that bag of corn chips. But take a closer look, because the number of servings per container may be twice as much as you thought! The information on the label is for one serving, but one small bag of corn chips may contain up to 2.5 servings! ✷ 1.B

TABLE 2 Ideas for Eating More Fruits and Vegetables

Snack on raw, crunchy vegetables such as carrot or celery sticks.

Add sliced peaches, bananas, or berries to your breakfast cereal.

Drink a glass of fruit juice or tomato juice each day.

Eat a salad made of dark, leafy greens and chopped vegetables with dinner every night.

Include fresh fruit in your dessert. For example, try eating gelatin or yogurt with fresh fruit.

Lesson Review

Using Vocabulary

1. What is the Food Guide Pyramid? ✷ 1.A

2. What is a Nutrition Facts label? ✷ 1.A

Understanding Concepts

3. Why is it a good idea to follow the Dietary Guidelines for Americans? ✷ 1.A; 1.B

4. List three ways you can include more fruits and vegetables in your diet. ✷ 1.A; 1.B

Critical Thinking

5. Analyzing Ideas Explain how you would use a Nutrition Facts label to decide on which snack to eat before playing soccer. ✷ 1.A; 1.B

12 CHAPTER REVIEW

Chapter Summary

■ Nutrients are the substances in food that your body needs for normal growth, maintenance, and repair. ■ Because your body cannot make some nutrients, you have to get these nutrients from the food you eat. These nutrients are called the *essential nutrients*. ■ Carbohydrates, fats, and proteins are the essential nutrients that provide your body with energy. ■ Vitamins and minerals control many body functions and help your body use the other essential nutrients. ■ Water is used to transport nutrients and regulate body temperature. ■ The Food Guide Pyramid shows you which foods to eat and how much of each food you should eat each day. ■ The Nutrition Facts label shows you how many servings of food are in a package and how many Calories and nutrients are found in each serving. ■ The Dietary Guidelines for Americans are a set of suggestions that can help you make healthy food choices.

Using Vocabulary

For each sentence, fill in the blank with the proper word from the word bank provided below.

Dietary Guidelines for Americans	vitamins
	fats
nutrients	Nutrition Facts label
Food Guide Pyramid	proteins
minerals	carbohydrates
Calories	

1 The substances in food that your body needs for normal growth, maintenance, and repair are called ___.

2 The energy provided by carbohydrates, proteins, and fats is measured in units called ___.

3 Nutrients called ___ help build healthy body tissues.

4 Chemicals made of one or more sugars chained together, or ___, give you energy to be physically active.

5 ___ store energy and some vitamins.

6 If you want to plan a menu for a day, you can use the ___ to help you make healthy food choices.

7 You can find the number of servings of a food and how many Calories and nutrients are in each serving by looking at the ___.

Understanding Concepts

8 Explain the process of digestion. ⍟ 2.A

9 What do proteins do for your body? ⍟ 1.A

10 What are the Dietary Guidelines for Americans, and why are they important? ⍟ 1.A; 1.B

11 How can you use the Nutrition Facts label to find out if a food is high in calcium? ⍟ 1.A; 1.B

12 Describe minerals, and give three examples of foods that are good sources of minerals. ⍟ 1.A; 1.B; 2.A

13 List the six classes of essential nutrients. List two foods that are good sources of each. ⍟ 1.A; 1.B

14 Identify the food groups shown on the Food Guide Pyramid.

Analyzing Ideas

15 Explain how you would use the Food Guide Pyramid to plan a menu for 1 day. ⭐ 1.A; 1.B

16 Should you eat one kind of food every day? Explain your answer. ⭐ 1.A; 1.B

17 Most packaged foods have a Nutrition Facts label on the outside of the package. Why should you look at the number of servings per container? ⭐ 1.A; 1.B

18 Meat, chicken, and fish are considered sources of protein. However, many people do not eat these foods. What other sources of protein can a person choose? ⭐ 1.A

Making Good Decisions

19 Imagine that you are at a restaurant and you have two choices for lunch. The first choice is a cheeseburger, french fries and a soda. The second choice is a grilled chicken sandwich, a plate of fresh fruit, and a glass of fruit juice. According to the Dietary Guidelines for Americans, which meal should you choose? Explain your answer. ⭐ 1.A; 1.B

20 You are on your way to soccer practice, and you are looking for a snack. Your dad packed an extra apple in your lunch bag. However, you realize that you have some pocket change. You have enough money to buy chips from the vending machine. Which snack should you choose—the apple or the chips? Explain your answer. ⭐ 1.A; 1.B

Interpreting Graphics

Nutrition Facts	
Serving Size 8 fl oz (240 mL)	
Servings per Container 2.5	
Amount per Serving	
Calories 100	
	% Daily Value
Total Fat 0 g	0%
Cholesterol 0 mg	0%
Sodium 35 mg	1%
Carbohydrates 27 g	9%
Protein 0 g	
Vitamin A	0%
Vitamin C	0%
Calcium	0%
Iron	0%

Use the Nutrition Facts label for a soft drink above to answer questions 21–25.

21 How many Calories are in the container of this soft drink?

22 Is this soft drink high in carbohydrates? Explain your answer.

23 Although this soft drink contains no fat, is it a healthy food? Explain your answer.

24 How many grams of carbohydrate are in the container of this soft drink?

25 How many ounces of the soft drink are in the container?

Reading Checkup

Take a minute to review your answers to the Health IQ questions at the beginning of this chapter. How has reading this chapter improved your Health IQ?

Life Skills IN ACTION

Being a Wise Consumer

Going shopping for products and services can be fun, but it can be confusing, too. Sometimes, there are so many options to choose from that finding the right one for you can be difficult. Being a wise consumer means evaluating different products and services for value and quality. Complete the following activity to learn how to be a wise consumer.

Snack Bar Shopping

Setting the Scene

Tonight, Keiko is spending the night at her friend Mica's house. Mica's parents drive the two teens to the grocery store so they can buy snack bars to eat during the sleepover. Keiko and Mica start looking at all of the choices. They both want to eat something healthy that is also tasty. ✪ 1.A; 1.B

Purple Mountain Granola Bar

Nutrition Facts	
Serving Size: 1 bar	
Amount per Serving	
Calories 140	
	% Daily Value
Total Fat 4 g	6%
Cholesterol 0 mg	0%
Sodium 110 mg	5%
Carbohydrates 24 g	8%
Sugars 15 g	

Amber Grain Granola Bar

Nutrition Facts	
Serving Size: 1 bar	
Amount per Serving	
Calories 110	
	% Daily Value
Total Fat 2 g	3%
Cholesterol 0 mg	0%
Sodium 80 mg	3%
Carbohydrates 23 g	8%
Sugars 10 g	

ACT 1

The 5 Steps of Being a Wise Consumer

1. List what you need and want from a product or a service.
2. Find several products or services that may fit your needs.
3. Research and compare information about the products or services.
4. Use the product or the service of your choice.
5. Evaluate your choice.

Guided Practice

Practice with a Friend

Form a group of three. Have one person play the role of Keiko and another person play the role of Mica. Have the third person be an observer. Walking through each of the five steps of being a wise consumer, role-play Keiko and Mica's selection of snack bars. Keiko and Mica should discuss the kinds of snacks they like to eat. When you get to step 3, look at the Nutrition Facts labels above to compare the nutritional value of two snack bars. The observer will take notes, which will include observations about what the people playing Keiko and Mica did well and suggestions of ways to improve. Stop after each step to evaluate the process.

Independent Practice

Check Yourself

After you have completed the guided practice, go through Act 1 again without stopping at each step. Answer the questions below to review what you did.

1. What specific things could Keiko and Mica look for in their snack bars? (Think of things like the ingredients or the amount of fat in the snack bars.)

2. Which snack bar is healthier? Use the Nutrition Facts labels to explain your answer.

3. After eating their snack bars, how could Keiko and Mica evaluate their choice?

4. What do you consider when you are selecting food at the grocery store? ⊛ 1.A; 1.B

ACT 2

On Your Own

After eating their dinners, Keiko and Mica decide that they want to go shopping. Mica's parents drive them to the mall. Keiko wants to buy a new cell phone so the two of them go to the electronics store and start looking at different phones. Keiko tells Mica that she wants to get a small cell phone that is not too expensive. Make a flow-chart showing how Keiko could use the five steps of being a wise consumer as she shops for a cell phone.

Understanding Drugs

Lessons

Check out **Current Health**® articles related to this chapter by visiting go.hrw.com. Just type in the keyword HD4CH13.

" I have never been as **scared** as I was **when I saw** my friend Chris faint from **inhaling glue fumes.**

He blacked out right away, and I couldn't tell if he was breathing. I had to tell his parents what happened so that they could call an ambulance. I didn't know if Chris was going to live or die. **"**

Health IQ

PRE-READING

Answer the following multiple-choice questions to find out what you already know about drugs. When you've finished this chapter, you'll have the opportunity to change your answers based on what you've learned.

1. Which of the following is NOT a drug?
  a. caffeine
  b. alcohol
  c. medicine
  d. water

2. Prescription medicines
  a. are not drugs.
  b. can be bought only with a doctor's written order.
  c. can be bought without a doctor's permission.
  d. are illegal for teens.

3. A drug can
  a. change how the mind works.
  b. change how the body works.
  c. damage human health.
  d. All of the above ⭐ 2.A

4. Who can get addicted to drugs?
  a. adults who take drugs
  b. criminals who take drugs
  c. teens who take drugs
  d. all of the above ⭐ 5.C

5. Which of the following is NOT a form of drug abuse?
  a. taking an illegal drug
  b. taking too much of a medicine on purpose
  c. taking medicine as recommended by a doctor
  d. taking someone else's prescription medicine ⭐ 5.C

6. Which of the following statements is true?
  a. Teens can help each other avoid drugs.
  b. If you refuse drugs, you have to give an explanation.
  c. Most teens do drugs.
  d. Drugs can improve a person's social life. ⭐ 5.E

ANSWERS: 1. d; 2. b; 3. d; 4. d; 5. c; 6. a

Facts About Drugs

What You'll Do

- **Explain** how drugs affect people. ⭐ 2.A; 5.D

- **Describe** how reactions to a drug can vary. ⭐ 2.A; 5.D

Terms to Learn

- drug

Start Off
Write

Why is it important to know how drugs can affect people?

Have you ever felt different after drinking caffeinated soda, coffee, or tea? Some people feel more alert after drinking something that has caffeine in it. These drinks affect the mind and body because caffeine is a drug.

Drugs Change the Mind and Body

A **drug** is any substance that changes how the mind or body works. Food and water are not drugs because the body needs them every day in order to function properly. Drugs are not usually needed on a daily basis. And unlike food, drugs do not give the body nutrients. Certain drugs, such as cough syrup, can affect the body in healthy ways. But drugs can also affect your body in unhealthy ways. In fact, even cough syrup can be dangerous. Any drug may change the mind or body in unexpected and possibly harmful ways.

Because drugs can be dangerous, people have rules about drugs. These rules say when and how each kind of drug can be used. Many drugs are never legal for anyone. Some drugs are legal only for adults. Other drugs require a doctor's permission for someone to use them. By following rules about drugs, people can avoid many health risks caused by taking drugs.
⭐ 1.C; 2.A; 5.D

Figure 1 There are several different kinds of drugs.

Different Kinds of
DRUGS

Drugs That Are Legal for Everyone	**Drugs That Are Legal for Adults**	**Medicines**	**Illegal Drugs**
Coffee, tea, and soda	Tobacco and alcohol	Prescription medicines and over-the-counter medicines	Marijuana, stimulants, hallucinogens, and opiates

Drugs Are Unpredictable

Predicting how drugs will affect a person is often hard. Different people can react differently to the same drug. And the same person can react differently to the same drug at different times. How a person responds to a drug depends on many things. Table 1 lists several things that affect how people respond to drugs.

Body weight plays a major part in determining a drug's effects. A person with low body weight usually needs less of a drug than a larger person does to feel the same effects. Young people usually weigh less than adults do. Because of this lower weight, drugs can have strong effects on young people. This is one reason that some drugs are legal only for adults.

The amount of a drug taken also affects a person's response to the drug. Taking a large amount of a drug at one time causes a strong reaction. Taking a small amount of the drug causes a weaker reaction. Medicines come with instructions that explain how much of the drug can be taken safely at once. Taking too much of a drug can be very dangerous—even fatal.

Unpredictable effects are only one of many risks from taking drugs. Taking drugs can put relationships and lives at risk. It can also affect your responsibilities. Before using any drug, you should make sure you know the risks. Then you will be able to make an informed decision about using it. You can ask a parent or trusted adult for help in finding information about the risks of taking drugs. ⭐ 2.A; 4.B; 5.A; 5.D; 6.A

TABLE 1 Factors that Affect a Person's Reaction to Drugs

Weight	A lighter person needs less of a drug to feel the same effects that a heavier person feels from a drug.
Mood	Drugs can intensify your mood.
Food	Having food in the stomach can decrease the strength of some drugs.
Mixing	Mixing different drugs can change how they affect the mind and body.
Amount	Taking more of a drug causes a stronger reaction.
Allergies	Some people have allergies to certain drugs, causing unexpected and dangerous reactions to the drug.

⭐ 5.A

Lesson Review

Using Vocabulary

1. Define *drug* in your own words.

Applying Concepts

2. Explain how drugs affect people. ⭐ 2.A; 5.D

3. How can individual reactions to a drug vary? ⭐ 2.A; 5.D

Critical Thinking

4. Making Inferences When people eat a lot of sugar, they sometimes feel full of energy. Why might some people think of sugar as a drug? Why might others not consider sugar a drug? ⭐ 2.A; 4.B; 5.A

🔲 **internet** connect ▤▤▤

www.scilinks.org/health
Topic: Drugs
HealthLinks code: HD4030

HEALTH LINKS. Maintained by the National Science Teachers Association

Medicine

Mike's older brother, Jay, had some pain-killers left over from his oral surgery. Now, Jay wants to take some of the pills for fun. Mike is worried. What would happen if Jay took too many pills at once?

Any drug—even one that is supposed to help people stay healthy—can be dangerous. Taking painkillers when they aren't needed can even cause death. Understanding the risks can help you use medicines safely.

What Is a Medicine?

A **medicine** is a drug that is used to cure, treat, or prevent pain, disease, and illness. When used correctly, medicines can save lives. However, improper use of medicines can cause health problems. For example, taking too much of a medicine can lead to sickness or death. Other examples of improper use include taking medicine when it is not needed or taking medicine with other drugs. Even accidentally taking the wrong medicine can make people sick. Following instructions from your doctor or pharmacist or on the medicine's label will help you use medicines safely. ⭐ 4.A

What You'll Do

- **Compare** the terms *drug* and *medicine*. ⭐ 4.A
- **Explain** the difference between prescription and over-the-counter medicines. ⭐ 4.A; 5.A
- **List** three things you can do to use medicines safely. ⭐ 4.A; 5.A

Terms to Learn

- medicine
- over-the-counter (OTC) medicine
- prescription medicine

Start Off
Write

What advice would you give to a friend about how to use medicine safely?

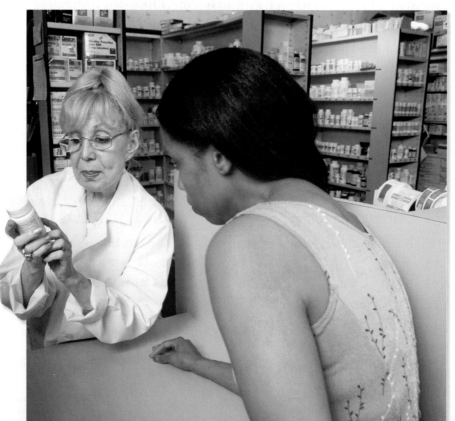

Figure 2 Advice from professionals helps people use medicine safely.

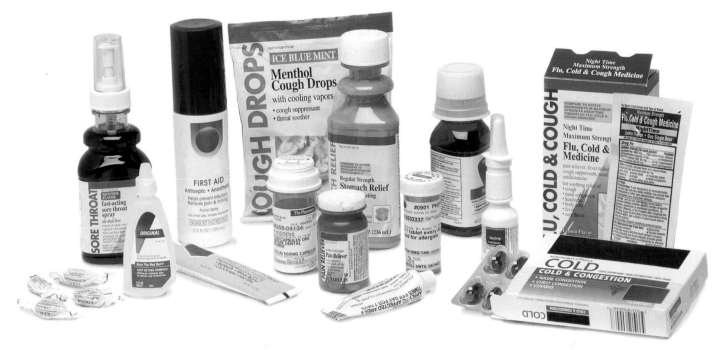

Figure 3 Medicines come in many forms.

Different Forms of Medicine

Medicines come in many forms. Medicine can take the form of a pill, liquid, syrup, cream, or spray. Some medicines can be swallowed, inhaled, or injected. Others are rubbed into the skin or dripped into the eyes, nose, or ears. How people take a medicine influences the effects of the medicine. For example, drugs that are inhaled reach the blood very quickly. Drugs that are swallowed take longer to reach the blood. So, a medicine that is helpful when swallowed might be dangerous when inhaled. It is important to take a medicine exactly as directed by a doctor or by the medicine's label. ⭐ 4.A

Over-the-Counter Medicines

Over-the-counter (OTC) medicines are medicines that can be bought without a doctor's written order. People can buy OTC medicines at drugstores and grocery stores. These drugs are used for minor problems, such as headaches or sore throats. They are not used to cure serious illnesses. OTC medicines usually have few side effects. *Side effects* are unexpected changes in the body or mind that are caused by medicines. One example of a side effect is feeling tired. If OTC medicines are not used properly, they can be dangerous. People who use OTC medicines should follow the label's instructions carefully.

⭐ 4.A; 5.A

The labels of over-the-counter pain relievers list how many pills a person feeling pain should take. Suppose a label says that an adult should take 1 to 2 pills every 4 to 6 hours while the pain lasts, but no more than 6 pills in a 24-hour period. What is the highest number of pills an adult can take if the pain lasts for 2 days?

⭐ 4.A; M: 6.2C

Prescription Medicines

Prescription medicines (pree SKRIP shuhn MED ı suhnz) are medicines that can be bought only with a written order, or *prescription*, from a doctor or other licensed professional. These drugs are used to treat, prevent, or cure serious medical problems. Sometimes, these medicines have strong side effects. Common side effects from prescription medicines include headaches, nausea, and tiredness. However, a medicine's health benefits usually make up for any uncomfortable side effects.

People should never take a prescription medicine unless a doctor recommends it. Prescription medicines are strong enough to fight serious health problems. They have powerful effects on the mind and body. If they are not used correctly, they can be dangerous. Taking too much of some prescription medicines can even be deadly. ✪ 5.A

Reading a Medicine Label

Reading medicine labels can help you use medicines safely. Both OTC medicines and prescription medicines have detailed instructions on their labels. The labels state how much of the medicine to take at one time and how often to take the medicine. This amount can vary depending on a person's age. The labels also tell you when a medicine is too old to use. A medicine may no longer work properly after this date. The labels also warn you of any possible side effects. If serious side effects occur, you should talk to a doctor.

Prescription labels contain some extra information. They show the patient's name and the doctor's name. Labels for prescription medicines may list special directions for individual patients. ✪ 4.A; 4.B

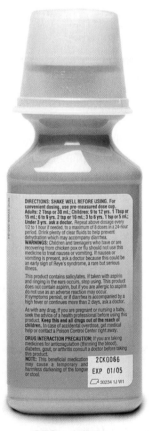

OTC medicine

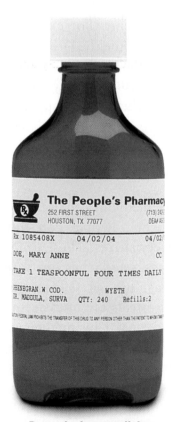

Prescription medicine

Figure 4 Both OTC and prescription medicines have instructions on the label.

Figure 5 Always check to see how much of a medicine you should take.

Using Medicines Safely

Following directions from doctors and on medicine labels helps make using medicine safe. But there are other things to know about medicine safety. One rule is never to mix drugs unless a doctor tells you to. Taking a medicine with another drug—even another medicine—can change the effects of the drugs. Another part of medicine safety is to be aware of allergies. Some people have sensitive reactions, or allergies, to certain medicines. If you react strangely to a drug, you should tell a doctor. If you know that you have a drug allergy, you can carry a card that says so. The card will keep people from giving you that drug in an emergency.

Medicine is not always the best way to solve or prevent health problems. For example, if you have a headache you may need water. If you feel bad, make sure to get enough food, exercise, sleep, and water. If you get enough of these things, then medicine may help you feel better. Ask an adult before taking any medicine.
★ 4.A; 5.A

LIFE SKILLS ACTIVITY

MAKING GOOD DECISIONS

In a small group, discuss how to know whether you need medicine for a health problem. Imagine that you have a sore throat, and decide what to do about it. Is an OTC medicine always the best way to get rid of a sore throat? ★ 4.A

Lesson Review

Using Vocabulary

1. What makes medicine a drug? ★ 4.A
2. What is the difference between over-the-counter medicine and prescription medicine? ★ 4.A; 5.A

Understanding Concepts

3. What are three things you can do to use a medicine safely? ★ 4.A; 5.A

Critical Thinking

4. **Applying Concepts** Suppose that you spent a day hiking outside in strong sunlight. You ran out of water before you finished the hike. That night, you got a headache that really bothered you. How should you try to get rid of the headache? Is medicine the best solution in this case? ★ 4.B

internet connect

www.scilinks.org/health
Topic: Medicine Safety
HealthLinks code: HD4066

HEALTH LINKS. Maintained by the National Science Teachers Association

Illegal Drugs

> Rose's friend Becky inhaled fumes from a can of paint last week. Becky just laughed when Rose told her that inhaling fumes was dangerous.

Inhaling poisonous fumes is no laughing matter. These drugs are very dangerous, and can be fatal. Taking dangerous drugs can damage your physical, social, and mental health.

Marijuana

Marijuana (MAR i WAH nuh) is one of the most commonly used illegal drugs. This drug has many names, such as pot, grass, bud, and weed. People who abuse marijuana usually smoke parts of the dried plant. The drug is often smoked from a rolled-up paper, called a *joint*. Smoking marijuana can make people nervous and can raise their heart rate. Marijuana can harm the immune system, increasing a person's risk of developing infections. The drug also makes it hard to pay attention. Marijuana can affect short-term memory and the ability to judge time and distance. Marijuana is considered to be a gateway drug. A **gateway drug** is a drug that introduces people to drug use, increasing the risk that they will try stronger drugs.

Long-term use of marijuana can damage the lungs. Tar and chemicals build up in the lungs when marijuana is smoked. Problems similar to those caused by smoking tobacco may develop, such as cancer. In fact, five joints can contain as many cancer-causing chemicals as seven packs of cigarettes do.

★ 1.C; 5.D; 6.A

What You'll Do

- **Describe** the dangerous effects of marijuana. ★ 1.C; 5.D; 6.A
- **List** six health problems caused by inhalants. ★ 1.C; 2.A; 6.A
- **Explain** why anabolic steroids are dangerous. ★ 6.A

Terms to Learn

- gateway drug
- stimulant
- depressant
- hallucinogen

Start Off *Write*

What would you tell a friend who wanted to try marijuana?

Figure 6 Marijuana is used in many different forms.

Figure 7 Effects of Inhalants on the Body

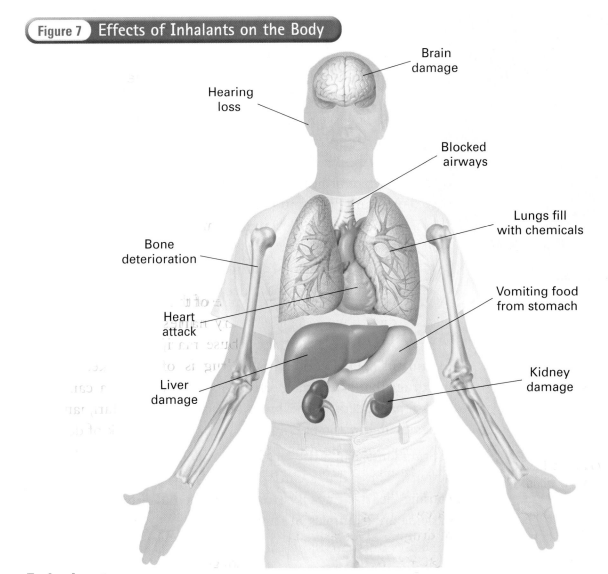

Brain damage

Hearing loss

Blocked airways

Lungs fill with chemicals

Bone deterioration

Vomiting food from stomach

Heart attack

Liver damage

Kidney damage

Inhalants ⭐ 1.C; 5.C

Inhalants (in HAYL uhnts) are chemical products that have strong fumes, or odors. Examples include nail polish remover and paint. Breathing fumes from such products makes a person feel lightheaded. Some people abuse inhalants to feel this way for fun. However, inhalants also cause dizziness, nosebleeds, nausea, headaches, and, in some cases, death.

Serious effects can occur immediately after using inhalants. Breathing these products can make the heart stop beating within a few minutes. Inhalants can also keep a person from getting enough air. If chemicals fill the lungs, there is no room for fresh air. If the drug causes nausea, vomit can also prevent air from reaching the lungs. Using inhalants can lead to death.

Death is the most serious danger of using inhalants, but there are other dangers. Inhalants can cause brain damage and hearing loss. They can also damage the kidneys, the liver, and bones.

WARNING!

A Chemical Smell

Accidentally inhaling a chemical product can be just as dangerous as inhaling one on purpose. If you are having a strong reaction to a chemical smell in your home, get fresh air immediately by opening all of the windows or by going outside.

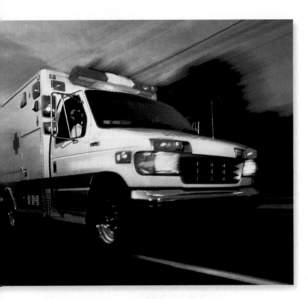

Figure 8 It is estimated that cocaine is involved in 29 percent of drug-related trips to the emergency room.

Anabolic Steroids

Anabolic steroids (A nuh BAH lik STER OIDZ) are drugs that are abused to build muscles. Steroids can be used legally when they are prescribed by a doctor. However, some people illegally abuse steroids to improve their athletic ability. Steroids cause fast weight gain and muscle growth. But these drugs also increase one's risk of having a stroke or heart attack. Other effects include high blood pressure, liver and kidney tumors, serious acne, and dangerous behavior. Young people who abuse steroids also risk stunting their growth. Steroids can cause enlarged breasts and genital shrinking in men. These drugs can cause facial hair and a deeper voice in women.

★ 1.C; 5.C; 5.D

Stimulants and Depressants

Stimulants (STIM yoo luhnts) and depressants (dee PRES uhnts) are drugs that affect the body in opposite ways. **Stimulants** are drugs that speed up the brain and the heart. **Depressants** are drugs that slow the body down.

Stimulants can raise heart rate, blood pressure, and brain activity. These drugs can speed up body processes too much, causing heart attacks, strokes, or even death. Cocaine and caffeine are examples of stimulants.

Depressants can slow the body processes so much that it is hard for the body to pump blood or get enough oxygen. Low breathing and heart rates can cause breathing failure, a coma, and, in some cases, death. Alcohol and sleeping pills are examples of depressants. ★ 1.C; 5.C; 5.D

Hands-on ACTIVITY

DRUG AND CHEMICAL SAFETY

1. Examine empty boxes and containers from household chemical products and medicines provided by your teacher.

2. Make a table with columns for

(1) the name of each product

(2) chemicals in each product

(3) dangers of each chemical or product, and

(4) first-aid responses for exposure to each product.

3. Fill in the table by using the information on the labels of the chemical product containers.

Analysis

1. What are some dangers of these common household products? Are these dangers similar to the dangers of using illegal drugs?

2. What should you do if you accidentally breathe, swallow, or touch these products?

Other Illegal Drugs

Some illegal drugs can change how a person's senses work. **Hallucinogens** (huh LOO si nuh juhnz) are strong drugs that can make people see and hear things that do not exist. This can cause people to do dangerous things that they otherwise would not do. Hallucinogens also cause anxiety and depression.

Opiates (OH pee its) are a group of drugs that are made from poppy flowers. Some opiates are used as medicine to treat severe pain. All opiates slow heart rate, breathing, and brain activity. Heroin (HER oh in) is an illegal opiate that is very dangerous. In large amounts, heroin or other opiates can be fatal.

Illegal drugs are very dangerous. The government monitors foods and legal drugs for our safety. Nobody monitors illegal drugs. Illegal drugs can be mixed with unknown chemicals that change the drugs' effects. A person can never know the strength of an illegal drug before taking the drug. There is never a good reason to risk taking an illegal drug. ⊛ 5.C; 5.D

teen talk

Teen: What is ecstasy?

Expert: Ecstasy (EK stuh see) is an illegal drug that is both a stimulant and a hallucinogen. It can cause severe dehydration, which sometimes leads to death. It raises a person's heart rate and blood pressure, which can lead to a heart attack. Ecstasy also causes brain damage.

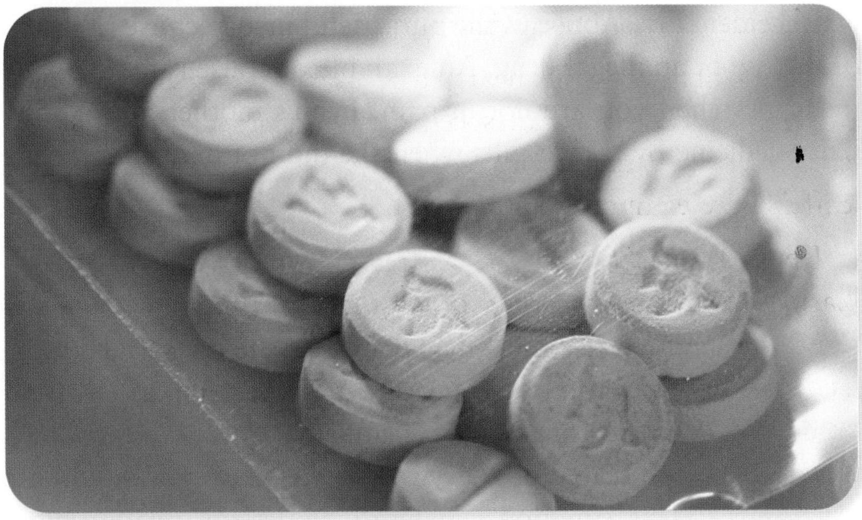

Figure 9 Illegal drugs do not have labels. People who take these drugs never know exactly what ingredients they contain.

Lesson Review

Using Vocabulary

1. Why is marijuana a gateway drug? ⊛ 1.C; 5.C; 5.D

2. What is a hallucinogen? ⊛ 2.A; 5.D

Applying Concepts

3. Why are anabolic steroids dangerous? ⊛ 1.C; 5.C; 5.D

4. What are six health problems caused by using inhalants? ⊛ 2.A; 5.C; 5.D

Critical Thinking

5. Applying Concepts Marijuana has no warning labels. Design a label that warns people about the dangers of marijuana. ⊛ 2.A; 5.C; 5.D

🖵 **internet** connect

www.scilinks.org/health
Topic: Anabolic Steroids
HealthLinks code: HD4009

HEALTH LINKS. Maintained by the National Science Teachers Association

Drug Abuse

Lynn knew that her mom used medicine for her back pain. But lately her mom seemed to take more pills more often. Lynn noticed that her mom got cranky and nervous whenever she ran out of the medicine.

What You'll Do

- **Explain** the difference between misuse and abuse. ✪ 5.A; 5.C; 5.D
- **Discuss** the costs of abusing drugs. ✪ 5.A
- **Describe** how drugs affect one's ability to make decisions. ✪ 2.A; 5.A

Terms to Learn

- misuse
- abuse

Start Off
Write

How could drug abuse damage a person's relationships?

✪ 5.A

If used correctly, medicines can help people. But Lynn's mother was not using her pain medicine correctly. Using too much of a drug—even a medicine—can cause serious problems.

Misuse and Abuse

Using drugs is not always dangerous. Most adults can control their use of alcohol to drink it safely. And medicine can cure disease. Drugs become dangerous when they are misused or abused. **Misuse** is the accidental incorrect use of a drug. An example of misuse is taking an extra pill of prescription medicine accidentally. **Abuse** is the purposeful incorrect use of drugs or the use of an illegal drug. An example of abuse is taking pain medicine when you are not in pain. Lynn's mother abused her pain medicine by taking pills when she did not need them.
✪ 5.A; 5.C; 5.D

The Cost of Abusing Drugs

Abusing drugs is very costly. People who abuse drugs risk more than damaging their physical health. They also risk losing their friends, families, and jobs. Friends and family members of drug abusers may feel scared or angry when a loved one abuses drugs. This situation can harm or destroy relationships. Drug abuse can also keep people from concentrating on responsibilities. As a result, drug abusers may lose their jobs or do poorly in school.

In addition to its social costs, drug abuse has high financial costs. Using a drug frequently can make a person want more of the drug. Buying so much of a drug becomes expensive. ✪ 5.A

Figure 10 People caught using illegal drugs can go to prison.

Drug Abuse Affects Decisions

Drugs change the way your mind works. For this reason, making healthy decisions while abusing drugs is difficult. Drug abuse can have terrible effects on social decisions. For example, drugs may influence a person's decisions about having sex. Sex can result in diseases, pregnancy, and confusing emotions. A person should never make such important decisions while influenced by drugs.

Drug abuse can also influence how people decide to spend their time. When people abuse drugs, they may forget about things that were once important to them. Drug abusers may neglect relationships with friends or family. They may neglect healthy activities, such as exercise. They spend their time using drugs or finding ways to get more drugs.

Avoiding drugs helps you focus on what is important to you. Without drugs, you can make healthy decisions. That way, you can be successful in reaching your goals. ★ 5.A; 5.D

Health Journal

Some drug abusers spend $2,500 a month on drugs! In your Health Journal, write a paragraph describing how you would spend $2,500 a month if you had that much money.

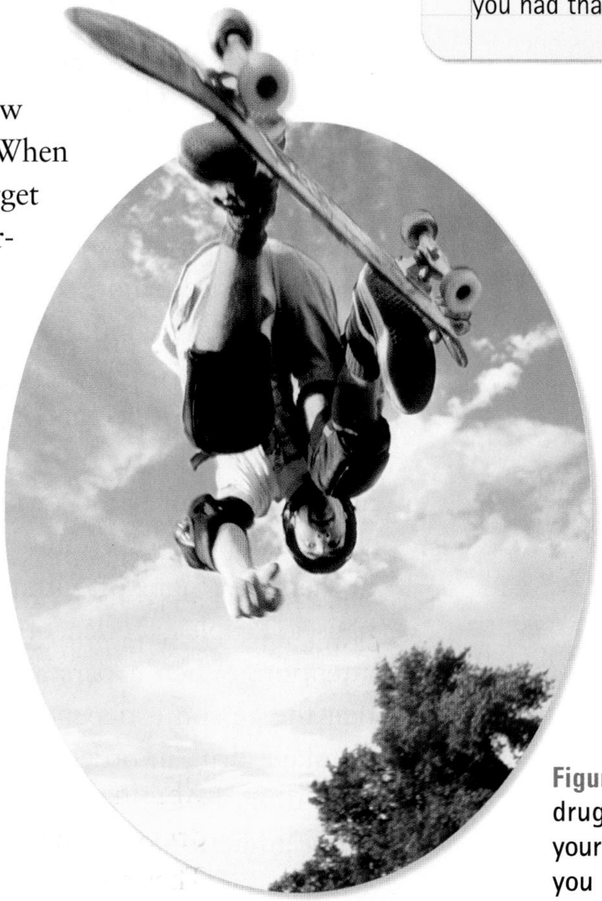

Figure 11 Avoiding drugs will help you do your best at whatever you like to do.

Lesson Review

Using Vocabulary

1. What is the difference between misusing and abusing a drug? ★ 5.A; 5.C; 5.D

Applying Concepts

2. How can abusing drugs affect a person's friendships? ★ 5.A; 7.A
3. What are the costs of abusing drugs? ★ 5.A; 5.D

Critical Thinking

4. **Making Inferences** Depressants are drugs that slow down the body's functions. How do you think depressants could change the way a person's mind works? How could these changes affect a person's ability to make decisions? ★ 2.A; 5.A

Drug Addiction

Eduardo knew that Uncle Dave was trying to quit using drugs. He had tried to quit before but had not succeeded. Why was it so hard for Uncle Dave to quit?

When people take strong drugs or take drugs for a long time, quitting can be very difficult. The body gets so used to drugs that a person feels uncomfortable without them.

Becoming Addicted

Suppose that a person takes a drug many times. Eventually, the body will need more of the drug to feel the original effect. **Tolerance** is a condition in which a person needs more of a drug to feel the original effects of the drug. When a person takes more of a drug to feel its original effect, the problem gets worse. The person may begin to feel uncomfortable without the drug and suffer from withdrawal (with DRAW uhl). **Withdrawal** is the body's reaction to not having a drug that is usually present in the body. Signs of withdrawal include headaches, chills, and nausea. People experiencing withdrawal may have trouble paying attention. When a person experiences withdrawal, it is a sign that the person is dependent on a drug. *Dependence* is the need to take a drug in order to feel normal. If a person is dependent on a drug, he or she craves it every day and has an addiction. **Drug addiction** is the failure to control one's use of a drug. The best way to avoid drug addiction is never to start abusing drugs. ✷ 5.C

What You'll Do

- **Explain** how people can form a drug addiction. ✷ 5.C
- **Describe** how difficult it is to quit using drugs once a person is addicted. ✷ 5.C

Terms to Learn

- tolerance
- withdrawal
- drug addiction

Start Off
Write

How does a person become addicted to drugs? ✷ 5.C

Figure 12 This is an example of how drug abuse can lead to dependence on the drug.

Takes pain killers when he has no headache

Needs many pills to relieve the pain of a headache

Takes pills all the time—without them, he would have a headache

Recovery

Recovering from a drug addiction is very hard. Addicted people who stop using drugs go through a tough period of time. Withdrawal from an addiction can be painful and even dangerous. Withdrawal is painful because the body has been used to large amounts of a drug. When a person stops taking the drug, a major change in body chemistry takes place. Withdrawal from some drugs, such as alcohol, can require medical help.

Unfortunately, withdrawal makes it hard for a person to stop using a drug. People who try to quit may start using drugs again to avoid the painful symptoms. However, the extreme discomfort of withdrawal will go away. The time needed to recover from withdrawal depends on the kind of drug addiction. With support, a person can recover from drug addiction and live a healthy life. ✪ 5.B; 5.C

STUDY TIP *for better reading*

Reviewing Information
Look at the introductory story about Eduardo and his uncle, Dave. Using the words *tolerance*, *withdrawal*, and *addiction*, write a few sentences to answer Eduardo's question. Why was it hard for Dave to quit if he really wanted to stop using drugs? ✪ 5.C

Figure 13 Support groups can help people get through the tough process of ending a drug addition.

Lesson Review

internet connect
www.scilinks.org/health
Topic: Drug Addiction
HealthLinks code: HD4028
HEALTH LINKS Maintained by the National Science Teachers Association

Using Vocabulary

1. How do tolerance and withdrawal contribute to forming a drug addiction? ✪ 5.C

Understanding Concepts

2. Why is it difficult for a person who has a drug addiction to stop using drugs? ✪ 5.C

Critical Thinking

3. Applying Concepts A friend who just quit smoking tells you that she can't think clearly without cigarettes and may start smoking again. Use your knowledge of withdrawal to encourage the friend to avoid cigarettes a little longer. ✪ 5.B; 5.C

Refuse to Abuse

What You'll Do

■ **Explain** how avoiding drug environments can help you stay drug free. ★ 5.E

■ **List** four ways to deal with problems without using drugs. ★ 5.E

■ **Describe** how you could refuse an offer to try drugs. ★ 5.E; 7.B; 7.D

Start Off
Write

How could friends help you refuse to try drugs?

Angela knew that some older teens at her cousin's party would be smoking marijuana. She didn't want to try marijuana and felt nervous just knowing it would be at the party. What could she do?

Angela has many options for avoiding drugs. She could practice refusing drugs. Or, she could stay home from the party and avoid drugs completely. Planning a way to avoid drugs ahead of time can help you stay drug free.

Avoiding Drug Environments

One way to avoid drugs is to stay away from places where they are used. For example, if you think drugs will be used at a party or activity, do not go. Remember that you can still be social while avoiding drug environments. If someone invites you to a party where drugs may be used, you can suggest going somewhere else. Many fun things do not involve drugs. By filling your time with drug-free activities in drug-free places, you can avoid a lot of social pressure to use drugs. ★ 5.B; 5.E; 5.H

Drug-Free Coping

Some people use drugs to cope, or deal with problems. This makes quitting very difficult. It is important to find drug-free ways to deal with problems. Talking to a friend, parents, or trusted adult can be a good first step to coping. Even if talking to someone does not solve a problem, that person may suggest other sources of help. The person might suggest that you speak to a counselor, see a doctor, or call a teen hotline. ★ 5.B; 5.E

Figure 14 Talking to a trusted adult can help you solve problems without using drugs.

Refusing Offers

If you were offered drugs, would you know how to refuse? Thinking about ways to refuse drugs ahead of time can be helpful. Then, if you ever face that situation, you'll know what to do. Simply saying, "No, thanks," is usually enough. But you may be more comfortable giving a reason why you don't want to do drugs. Or you may want to suggest another idea, such as getting ice cream. Another way to escape uncomfortable situations is to leave. Walking away from an offer sends a clear message that you do not want to try drugs.

Remember that most teens do not do drugs. Friends that share your ideas about drug abuse can help you avoid drugs. These friends can set examples of how to refuse drugs. They can support you when you act on your decisions about drugs. And most important, these friends can enjoy doing drug-free activities with you. ★ 5.B; 5.E; 5.H; 7.B; 7.D

Figure 15 The Red Ribbon Campaign helps people stay drug free. It honors Kiki Camarena, who was killed while working for the U.S. Drug Enforcement Agency.

PRACTICING WELLNESS

Make a list of 10 fun, drug-free things that you like to do. Then, meet with other students in small groups to exchange ideas. Add other students' ideas to your list if those ideas sound like fun to you. Keep this list in a safe place at school or at home. Look at the list when you feel bored or if you are tempted to try drugs. As a class, make one huge poster that lists every idea that was mentioned. Put this poster up in the classroom or in a place where everyone at school can look at it to get ideas for alternatives to using drugs. ★ 5.E; 5.H

Lesson Review

Applying Concepts

1. How can avoiding drug environments help you stay drug free?
★ 5.E; 5.H

2. What are four ways to deal with personal problems without using drugs? ★ 5.E; 5.H

Critical Thinking

3. Using Refusal Skills Suppose that you are at a party with a friend. An older teen offers your friend some drugs. How could you use refusal skills to help your friend get out of an uncomfortable situation? ★ 5.E; 7.B; 7.D

Chapter Summary

■ Drugs change how the mind and body work. These changes can be dangerous. ■ Some drugs can be used as medicine to cure, treat, and prevent disease. Medicine can be dangerous if it is not used correctly. ■ Some people illegally abuse marijuana, inhalants, steroids, stimulants, and depressants. ■ Abusing drugs is very costly—financially, physically, and socially. ■ Drug abuse can also affect decision making. ■ Drug addiction can ruin relationships with friends and family. ■ Ending an addiction is very difficult. ■ Refusal skills, such as saying "No, thanks," leaving uncomfortable situations, or suggesting alternatives, can help you refuse drugs.

Using Vocabulary

For each pair of terms, explain how the meanings of the terms differ.

1 drug/medicine

2 misuse/abuse

3 prescription medicine/OTC medicine

For each sentence, fill in the blank with the proper word from the word bank provided below.

medicine	tolerance
drug addiction	gateway drug
drug	withdrawal

4 Marijuana is considered a(n) ___ because it may lead users to try other drugs.

5 When a drug user can't control the need for a drug, the drug user has a(n) ___.

6 Headaches, chills, and nausea are often signs of ___.

7 The need to take more of a drug to feel the original effects is called ___.

Understanding Concepts

8 Why is it difficult to recover from a drug addiction? ✪ 5.C

9 What should you do if you experience strange side effects after taking a drug? ✪ 5.A

10 Why is it dangerous to take a drug that does not have a label? ✪ 4.A

11 What are four ways to refuse an offer of drugs? ✪ 5.E

12 What are six health problems caused by inhalants? ✪ 5.A

13 What are three social costs of abusing drugs? ✪ 5.D

14 How can a person build up a tolerance to a drug? ✪ 5.C

15 Why are foods not considered to be drugs?

16 How does the amount of a drug taken affect a person's reaction to the drug? ✪ 5.A

17 What can you do to ensure that you are never given a drug that you are allergic to? ✪ 4.A; 5.E

Critical Thinking

Applying Concepts

18 Suppose you have a friend on the football team. You notice that he has recently gained a lot of weight and has bulked up with muscles. He has also been very aggressive lately. What do you think could be causing these changes? ⭐ 5.A

19 If one of your friends started using drugs, what kind of changes might you notice in your friend? ⭐ 5.A; 5.C

20 What do you think is the biggest danger for each of the following kinds of drugs: marijuana, inhalants, anabolic steroids, stimulants, and depressants. Support your answer with specific reasons.
⭐ 2.A; 5.C; 5.D; 6.A; 7.A

Making Good Decisions

21 Imagine that your friend is very sad. This friend suggests going to a party and doing drugs to forget his or her problems. What could you suggest as an alternative solution? ⭐ 5.B; 5.E; 5.H

22 A friend of yours tells you that she has a drug addiction. Your friend says that she has entered a drug treatment program but that it will be difficult to recover. What can you do to help your friend recover? ⭐ 5.B; 5.E

23 Suppose you need to get home from a party. You could take a bus, walk, get a ride from a friend, or call your parents to ask for a ride. How might drugs affect your ability to make this decision? What could happen if you made the wrong decision while influenced by drugs? ⭐ 5.B

24 A friend tells you that he is worried that his brother has a drug addiction. Your friend asks you where he could find help for his brother. What could you tell your friend? ⭐ 5.B; 5.E

Interpreting Graphics

People Who Use Illegal Drugs Monthly

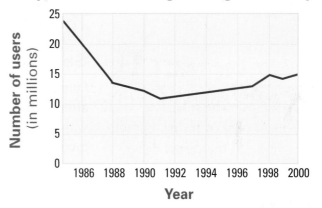

Use the figure above to answer questions 25–28. ⭐ M: 6.10D

25 What was the trend in monthly illegal drug use between 1985 and 2000?

26 How many fewer monthly drug users were there in 2000 than in 1986?

27 During which years was the decline in monthly illegal drug use the greatest?

28 In what year was monthly illegal drug use the lowest?

Reading Checkup

Take a minute to review your answers to the Health IQ questions at the beginning of this chapter. How has reading this chapter improved your Health IQ?

Life Skills IN ACTION

Making Good Decisions

You make decisions every day. But how do you know if you are making good decisions? Making good decisions is making choices that are healthy and responsible. Following the six steps of making good decisions will help you make the best possible choice whenever you make a decision. Complete the following activity to practice the six steps of making good decisions.

The Way Home

Setting the Scene

ACT 1

Guillermo walks home from school every afternoon. He always hurries because he wants to get home in time to watch his favorite TV show. On his way home the last few days, Guillermo has been stopped by some older teens. The older teens always pressure him to try some drugs. Guillermo doesn't like talking to the older teens, but he knows that he would have to take a longer way home to avoid them. Guillermo goes to talk with his friend Steve about his problem.

✪ 5.B; 5.E;.5.H

The **6** Steps of Making Good Decisions

1. Identify the problem.
2. Consider your values.
3. List the options.
4. Weigh the consequences.
5. Decide, and act.
6. Evaluate your choice.

Guided Practice

Practice with a Friend

Form a group of three. Have one person play the role of Guillermo and another person play the role of Steve. Have the third person be an observer. Walking through each of the six steps of making good decisions, role-play Guillermo talking to Steve about his problem. Steve can help by brainstorming options with Guillermo. The observer will take notes, which will include observations about what the person playing Guillermo did well and suggestions of ways to improve. Stop after each step to evaluate the process.

Check Yourself

After you have completed the guided practice, go through Act 1 again without stopping at each step. Answer the questions below to review what you did.

1. What values could Guillermo consider as he makes his decision?

2. What options does Guillermo have in this situation?

3. What are the consequences of each of his options?

4. Which of the six steps of making good decisions is the most difficult for you? Explain your answer.

On Your Own

Guillermo now takes a longer way home to avoid meeting the older teens. He tries to run most of the way home so that he won't miss much of the TV show he enjoys watching. Yesterday, Guillermo sprained his ankle while running home. His ankle hurts a lot, so Steve gives him a prescription painkiller that Steve took after his tonsil surgery. Steve says that the medicine is safe because it was prescribed by a doctor. Guillermo is not sure if he should take the medicine. Draw a comic strip that shows how Guillermo could use the six steps of making good decisions to decide whether to take Steve's medicine.

⭐ 4.A; 4.B; 5.A; 5.E

The People's Pharmacy
Rx
252 FIRST STREET   (713) 242-2299
HOUSTON, TX 77077   DEA# AS 3455

Rx 1085408X   04/02/04   04/02/04

MUMFORD, STEVE   CC

TAKE 1 TABLET EVERY
FOUR HOURS FOR PAIN

Tylenol 4, WITH Codeine
DR. MADDULA, SURVA   QTY: 50   Re lls:0

CAUTION: FEDERAL LAW PROHIBITS THE TRANSFER OF THIS DRUG TO ANY PERSON OTHER THAN THE PATIENT TO WHOM IT WAS PRESCRIBED.

Keep out of reach of children.

The People's Pharma
Rx
Rx 1085408X   04/02/

                        CC

TAKE 1 TABLET EVERY
FOUR HOURS FOR PAIN

Tylenol 4, WITH Codeine
QTY: 50   Refills:0

CAUTION: FEDERAL LAW PROHIBITS THE TRANSFER OF THIS DRUG TO ANY PERSON OTHER THAN THE PATIENT TO WHOM IT WAS PRESCRIBED.

Lessons

Check out
Current Health®
articles related to this chapter by
visiting **go.hrw.com**. Just type in
the keyword **HD4CH14**.

> ❝ I never **understood** why my dad was so **angry** about catching me **smoking cigarettes** until I met my great aunt.
>
> She had to breathe through a hole in her throat, and she had to hold a little machine to her neck to speak. My dad told me that she got throat cancer from smoking for many years. ❞

Health IQ

PRE-READING

Answer the following multiple-choice questions to find out what you already know about tobacco and alcohol. When you've finished this chapter, you'll have the opportunity to change your answers based on what you've learned.

1. Alcohol can cause
a. emphysema.
b. cirrhosis.
c. gum disease.
d. shortness of breath. ⭐ 5.C

2. Which of the following drugs is illegal for some or all teens?
a. caffeine
b. tobacco
c. alcohol
d. tobacco and alcohol ⭐ 5.D

3. Advertisements for tobacco and alcohol products
a. always tell the truth.
b. demonstrate how drugs can improve your life.
c. don't show the negative effects of drugs.
d. help teens understand what doing drugs is like. ⭐ 8.A

4. Tobacco smoke
a. can increase asthma symptoms.
b. cannot hurt a nonsmoker.
c. cannot cause cancer.
d. harms only smokers. ⭐ 2.A

5. Why is it so difficult to quit using tobacco once an addiction has formed?
a. The body is dependent on carbon monoxide.
b. The body is dependent on nicotine.
c. The body is dependent on environmental tobacco smoke.
d. The body is dependent on tar. ⭐ 5.E

ANSWERS: 1. b; 2. d; 3. c; 4. a; 5. b

Tobacco and Alcohol as Drugs

What You'll Do

■ **Explain** why tobacco and alcohol are drugs. ✪ 5.C

Terms to Learn

● tobacco
● alcohol

Start Off
Write

What is dangerous about tobacco and alcohol?

Have you ever watched someone smoke a cigarette or drink a glass of wine? Did you notice a change in that person's behavior? How was he or she affected?

Using cigarettes and wine may make people feel energetic, relaxed, or out of control. Any kind of tobacco or alcohol can cause these short-term effects in the mind and body. Tobacco and alcohol also cause a variety of long-term health effects. Because they affect the mind and body, tobacco products and alcohol are drugs. ✪ 5.C

Affecting the Mind and Body

Tobacco is a plant with leaves that can be dried and mixed with chemicals to make products such as cigarettes, smokeless tobacco, and cigars. When people use tobacco, their bodies and minds feel different. Sometimes, their minds seem to work faster. Other times, they feel more relaxed. Because tobacco causes these effects, it is considered to be a drug.

Alcohol is a liquid that can affect the way people think and act when they drink it. Alcohol causes body functions to slow down. For example, it lowers the heart rate and breathing rate. Alcohol also makes the mind slow down. When the mind works more slowly, a person takes longer to think. Alcohol can change how people react in a situation. Because it causes these changes, alcohol is classified as a drug. ✪ 2.A; 5.C; 5.D

Figure 1 Tobacco and alcohol are not legal for everyone.

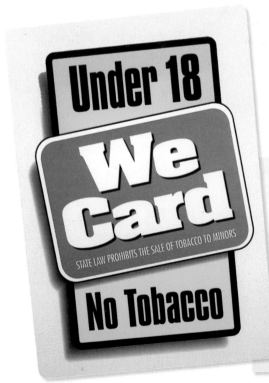

Tobacco and Alcohol Are Unpredictable

Predicting how people will react to a drug is difficult. People do not always react to drugs in the same way. Alcohol's effects are especially dependent on individual characteristics. For example, body weight plays a role in determining alcohol's effects. A person who has a low body weight usually reacts to alcohol more than a heavier person does. Another factor in a person's response to alcohol is how much food is in the stomach. Food slows the rate at which the blood absorbs alcohol.

Another difference in how people react to tobacco or alcohol is how much they have used the drug in the past. People who frequently use a drug react differently than people who try a drug for the first time. The first time a person smokes a cigarette, he or she might feel dizzy or sick. But after the person smokes for a few weeks, the sick feelings get weaker.

Because tobacco and alcohol cause unpredictable changes in the mind and body, people who use these drugs must be careful. Mixing one of these drugs with another drug can change either drug's effects. For example, drinking alcohol while taking certain medicines, such as painkillers, can cause serious liver damage. Mixing alcohol with other drugs can even cause body functions to slow down so much that a person may die. ⭐ 2.A; 5.C; 5.D

Health Journal
Drugs can affect a person differently at different times. In your Health Journal, write about how you think a person might respond to alcohol differently at the following times: after a big meal or in the morning before breakfast.

Figure 2 Mixing alcohol with other drugs is very dangerous.

Lesson Review

Using Vocabulary

1. What is tobacco?

2. What is alcohol?

Understanding Concepts

3. Why are tobacco and alcohol classified as drugs? ⭐ 5.C; 5.D

4. How can tobacco and alcohol affect a person's mind and body? ⭐ 2.A; 5.C; 5.D

Critical Thinking

5. Analyzing Ideas Why do you think tobacco and alcohol are legal for adults but illegal for young people? Remember that the effects of drugs are unpredictable. ⭐ 5.D

6. Applying Concepts Some medicines must be taken with food. How could food change how the medicine affects people? ⭐ 2.A

Tobacco Products

Erin just started going to a new school. She met some girls that she likes, but they keep inviting her to smoke with them after school. She doesn't want to smoke, but she wants to be friends with these girls.

At some point, you may have to face a problem like Erin's. Deciding not to use tobacco products is important because tobacco is very bad for your health. To be able to make a healthy decision, you need to know the facts about tobacco.

Chemicals in Tobacco Products

Tobacco products are made with hundreds of chemicals. Most of the chemicals in tobacco products are dangerous to the human body. One dangerous chemical found in all tobacco products is nicotine (NIK uh TEEN). **Nicotine** is an addictive drug. Nicotine's addictive properties cause people to want more tobacco.

When tobacco products are burned, even more chemicals form. Cigarette smoke contains thousands of chemicals, such as carbon monoxide (KAR buhn muh NAHKS IED) and tar. *Carbon monoxide* is a dangerous gas. When smoke is inhaled, the lungs absorb carbon monoxide. This gas keeps the body from getting enough oxygen. *Tar* is a black, sticky substance that coats the lungs. This coating can lead to serious diseases. Tar can also keep the body from filtering out harmful particles in air. ⭐ 5.C

What You'll Do

- **Describe** early effects of smoking. ⭐ 5.C
- **Discuss** health problems caused by smokeless tobacco. ⭐ 5.C
- **Describe** two diseases caused by long-term use of tobacco products. ⭐ 5.C

Terms to Learn

- nicotine
- environmental tobacco smoke (ETS)
- cancer

Start Off *Write*

How can tobacco smoke harm a nonsmoker?

Figure 3 Cigarette smoke contains some surprising ingredients.

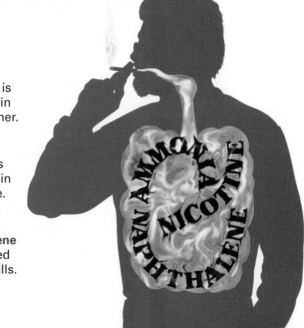

▶ **Ammonia** is also used in toilet cleaner.

▶ **Nicotine** is also used in insecticide.

▶ **Naphthalene** is also used in mothballs.

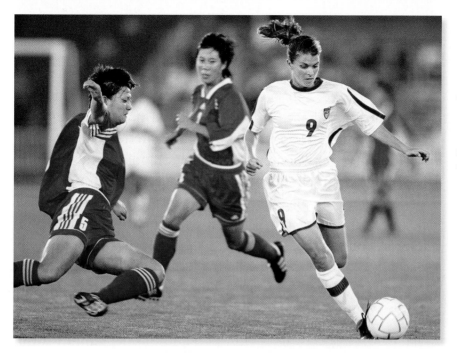

Figure 4 Smoking would make these athletes get short of breath more quickly. Most professional athletes do not smoke so that they can do their best.

Early Effects of Cigarettes

Even the first cigarette someone smokes is harmful. Just one puff leaves chemicals in the mouth, throat, and lungs. Smoke can make hair and clothes smell bad. Every time a smoker has a cigarette, more chemicals build up in the smoker's body. Chemicals coating the mouth and throat can cause bad breath and dulled taste buds. Eventually, these chemicals can even stain a smoker's teeth yellow. In addition, chemicals that keep smokers from getting enough oxygen can eventually cause skin to wrinkle.

Smoking cigarettes affects more than a person's appearance. When a person does not get enough oxygen, he or she cannot stay active. When tar and carbon monoxide coat and fill the lungs, oxygen cannot enter the bloodstream as easily. Less oxygen in the blood causes smokers to breathe faster to get more oxygen. When people have difficulty breathing, it is harder for them to exercise or play sports. ✪ 5.C; 5.D

Brain Food

Bidis (BEE deez) are flavored, unfiltered cigarettes. Bidis are flavored with chocolate, strawberry, mango, or mint, which makes them seem less dangerous than regular cigarettes. In fact, they have very high levels of nicotine. As a result, bidis are even more hazardous to your health than regular cigarettes are.

LIFE SKILLS ACTIVITY

COMMUNICATING EFFECTIVELY

Write and illustrate a short story that demonstrates some effects of using tobacco products. Draw any visible effects of tobacco use, and explain other effects in your story. Mention health problems related to cigarettes. Write two endings to your story—one happy and one sad. Some tobacco users could decide to quit, while others might suffer from tobacco-related health problems. ✪ 5.D

Environmental Tobacco Smoke

Cigarette smoke can also be dangerous for nonsmokers. **Environmental tobacco smoke (ETS)** is a mixture of exhaled smoke and smoke from the ends of lit cigarettes. ETS is sometimes called *secondhand smoke*. People standing near someone who is smoking cannot avoid breathing smoke from the air around them. Someone who breathes ETS may cough and feel sick or short of breath. ETS can even increase symptoms of allergies and asthma in some people—especially children. Nonsmokers who often breathe ETS can build up chemicals in their lungs. Eventually, nonsmokers can have the same health problems that smokers do. ⭐ 5.D

Smokeless Tobacco

Smokeless tobacco comes in two forms. *Snuff* is powdered tobacco that can be sniffed into the nose or put inside the mouth under the lips. *Chewing tobacco,* also called *spit tobacco* or *chew,* is made from chopped tobacco leaves that are chewed or tucked under the lips. Snuff and chew form a brown slime when mixed with saliva in the mouth. People who put smokeless tobacco in their mouth must spit often to get rid of this mixture.

But the brown slime is not the worst thing about smokeless tobacco. Smokeless tobacco is just as harmful as cigarettes are. Like cigarettes, chew and snuff cause yellow teeth and bad breath. They can cause cuts and sores in the mouth when they are tucked under the lips or chewed. These products often contain sugar, which causes tooth decay. If snuff is sniffed frequently, it can destroy the ability to smell and taste. Snuff can even cause the inside of the nose to decay. Each of these problems gets worse the longer a person uses smokeless tobacco. ⭐ 5.D

Figure 5 This man had his lower jaw removed because it was destoyed by using smokeless tobacco.

Tobacco-Related Disease and Death

Using tobacco products over many years causes serious health problems. The longer a person uses tobacco, the higher his or her risk of getting serious diseases.

Smoking can lead to emphysema (EM fuh SEE muh). *Emphysema* is a disease in which the lungs get so damaged that they cannot absorb enough oxygen. People with emphysema usually need machines to help them breathe. Eventually, emphysema can cause death.

Tobacco products also increase a person's risk of getting cancer. **Cancer** is a disease in which groups of cells grow uncontrollably. These abnormal cells destroy healthy body tissues. Smoking tobacco can lead to lung and throat cancer. Smokeless tobacco can lead to cancer of the mouth, throat, or stomach. Sometimes, these cancers harm a person's ability to speak or eat. Cancer can also lead to death. ⭐ 5.C; 5.D

SOCIAL STUDIES ACTIVITY

Each year, more Americans die as a result of using tobacco than as a result of using all other drugs combined. As a class, collect data about how tobacco affects the health of people in your state. Prepare a poster to present your data.

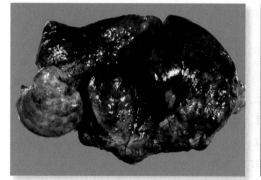 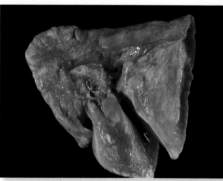

Figure 6 The lung on the left was damaged by emphysema. The lung on the right belonged to a healthy person.

Lesson Review

Using Vocabulary

1. Use the term *environmental tobacco smoke* in a sentence. ⭐ 5.D

Understanding Concepts

2. List three early effects of smoking. ⭐ 5.C; 5.D
3. Name two health problems caused by smokeless tobacco. ⭐ 5.D

4. What are two diseases caused by using tobacco for many years? ⭐ 5.C

Critical Thinking

5. **Making Inferences** Emphysema can be deadly because the lungs do not get enough oxygen. Can you find similarities between emphysema and any of the early effects of smoking? Explain your answer. ⭐ 5.C; 5.D

🔲 **internet** connect

www.scilinks.org/health
Topic: Tobacco
HealthLinks code: HD4101

HEALTH LINKS. Maintained by the National Science Teachers Association

Alcohol

What You'll Do

- **Discuss** the effects of intoxication. ✪ 2.A; 5.D

- **Name** two health problems caused by long-term alcohol abuse. ✪ 5.C; 5.D

- **Describe** how alcohol impairs the ability to drive. ✪ 2.A; 5.D

Terms to Learn

- intoxication
- blood alcohol concentration (BAC)
- cirrhosis
- fetal alcohol syndrome (FAS)

Start Off
Write

How does alcohol affect a person's behavior?

Sebastian's best friend, Liam, was hanging out with a new group of guys. Liam drank beer with his new friends every weekend. Liam always invited Sebastian, but going with them seemed risky to Sebastian.

Deciding how to deal with pressures to drink alcohol is an important decision for teens. Knowing the facts about alcohol will help you make a healthy decision.

Early Effects of Alcohol

Alcohol enters the blood through the stomach and small intestine. The blood carries alcohol through the body. When alcohol reaches the brain, thoughts and actions become less controlled. A person who drinks a small amount of alcohol might feel light-headed and warm. With more alcohol, the person could feel dizzy or tired. The person may act strangely and make poor decisions.

As even more alcohol is consumed, the body's response gets stronger. The body reacts to too much alcohol the same way it reacts to a poison. People may vomit if they take in too much alcohol. Vomiting prevents more alcohol from passing into the blood. Sometimes the body gets so overwhelmed by alcohol that the person passes out. In some cases, body functions slow down so much that the person dies of alcohol poisoning. ✪ 2.A; 5.D

Figure 7 The amount of alcohol in each of these drinks is the same. One beer is as strong as one glass of wine or one shot of liquor.

Blood Alcohol Concentration

People often use terms such as *drunk* or *wasted* to describe someone who is intoxicated. **Intoxication** (in TAHKS i KAY shuhn) is the state of being affected by alcohol. It is possible to measure a person's level of intoxication by measuring the amount of alcohol in the blood. The percentage of alcohol in a person's blood is called the **blood alcohol concentration (BAC)**. As the BAC rises, a person's behavior becomes less controlled. A very high BAC can lead to death. Table 1 shows the effects of some BACs.

The amount of alcohol that reaches the blood depends on how much alcohol a person drinks. Drinking five beers causes more alcohol to enter the blood than drinking one beer does. A person's body weight also affects BAC. Drinking one beer would cause a higher BAC in a lighter person than in a heavier person.

⭐ 5.D

STUDY TIP *for better reading*

Reviewing Information
To better understand blood alcohol concentration, teach this concept to a friend or family member. Be sure to explain what can increase a person's BAC. Also explain how a high BAC can affect a person.

TABLE 1 Blood Alcohol Concentration	
BAC	**Effects**
0.02%	feeling lightheaded
0.05%	slowed reaction time, feeling relaxed
0.08%	poor judgment, illegal to drive in many states
0.15%	memory loss, poor balance and movement
0.20%	vomiting, loss of control
0.30%	loss of consciousness
0.40%	coma, death ⭐ 2.A; 5.D

Hands-on ACTIVITY

UNDERSTANDING BLOOD ALCOHOL CONCENTRATION

Set up two medium glasses, one small glass, and one large glass. Fill each with water colored by red food coloring. Add one drop of blue food coloring to a medium glass and three drops to each of the other glasses. Observe the color changes.

Analysis

1. If the blue food coloring was alcohol and the red water was blood, which glass would have the highest BAC? Which would have the lowest?

2. How does the size of the glass affect the BAC?

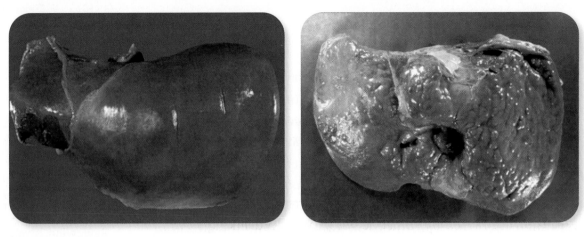

Figure 8 The liver on the left is from a healthy person. The liver on the right is from a person who had cirrhosis.

Long-Term Effects of Alcohol

If people drink large amounts of alcohol over many years, health effects can build up. The body breaks down alcohol in the liver. If the liver tries to break down too much alcohol, the liver can be damaged, causing cirrhosis (suh ROH sis). **Cirrhosis** is a disease that causes the liver to stop working properly. When the liver stops working, toxins build up in the body. These toxins can cause pain, fever, tiredness, low blood pressure, and even death.

Long-term alcohol abuse affects other organs, too. Alcohol can cause *ulcers,* or open sores, in the stomach's lining. The brain can begin to work more slowly when exposed to long-term alcohol abuse. Alcohol abuse can cause some parts of the brain to stop working altogether. Alcohol can also increase the risk of high blood pressure, heart disease, and stroke.

Much of the body's development happens during the teen years. For example, important brain development continues during the teen years. Drinking alcohol as a teen may affect this brain development and cause changes that are hard to overcome. For example, drinking alcohol as a teen makes it more likely that a person will become addicted to alcohol.

⭐ 2.A; 5.C; 5.D

Alcohol and Pregnancy

If a pregnant woman drinks alcohol, her child may be born with health problems. The food a mother eats provides nutrients for her unborn baby. If the mother drinks alcohol, the alcohol also reaches the baby. **Fetal alcohol syndrome (FAS)** is a group of birth defects that can occur when an unborn baby is exposed to alcohol. FAS affects how an unborn baby develops. Babies born with FAS can have a low birth weight. They may also have abnormal physical features, behavioral problems, and mental disabilities. ⭐ 2.A; 5.D

Teen Risks

Because teen minds and bodies are growing and developing, drugs have the potential to do serious damage to teens. A drug can keep a teen from developing normally and cause permanent damage.

Drunk Driving

Driving when even slightly intoxicated is very dangerous. It risks the lives of the driver and anyone near the automobile. Also, driving when intoxicated is illegal. Because cars move at such high speeds, driving requires the ability to react quickly. Alcohol slows down a person's ability to react and make responsible decisions. A drunk driver cannot respond as quickly as he or she normally would. That is why drunk drivers cause so many accidents. Never get into a car driven by someone who has been drinking.

It is not safe to drive any vehicle while influenced by alcohol. Boats, snowmobiles, and even bicycles are dangerous when operated by a drunk driver. These vehicles may not be used as often as cars are, but they can still cause deadly accidents. ✮ 5.D

Health Journal

In your Health Journal make a list of reasons not to drive drunk. Then list reasons not to ride in a car driven by a drunk person. Finally, make a list of ways to avoid riding with a drunk driver.

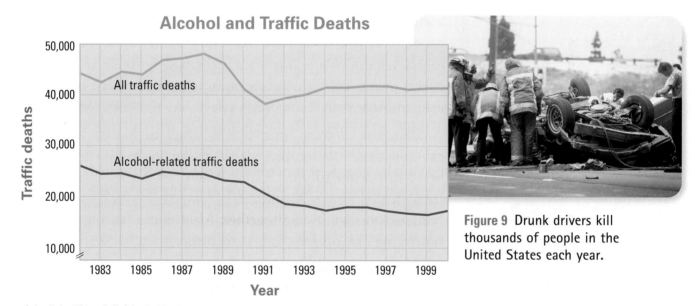

Source: National Highway Traffic Safety Administration.

Figure 9 Drunk drivers kill thousands of people in the United States each year.

Lesson Review

Using Vocabulary

1. What is *intoxication*? ✮ 2.A; 5.D

Understanding Concepts

2. Name two health problems caused by long-term alcohol abuse. ✮ 5.C; 5.D
3. How can alcohol affect a person's ability to drive? ✮ 2.A; 5.D

Critical Thinking

4. **Analyzing Ideas** An unborn baby can be seriously hurt by an amount of alcohol that hardly affects the mother. Remember how body size relates to BAC. Explain why the effects on the unborn baby are so strong. ✮ 2.A; 5.D

☐ internet connect ▤

www.scilinks.org/health
Topic: Blood Alcohol Concentration
HealthLinks code: HD4016

Topic: Drunk Driving
HealthLinks code: HD4032

HEALTH LINKS™ Maintained by the National Science Teachers Association

Addiction

Charles's grandmother was very sick, but she wouldn't stop drinking alcohol. Charles knew alcohol was bad for her, and he couldn't understand why she kept drinking.

Alcohol is a powerful drug that can cause physical changes in the brain. If someone has been drinking for many years, that person may need alcohol to feel normal. It is very hard for people in this situation to stop drinking alcohol.

Becoming Addicted

Tobacco and alcohol cause mental and physical changes. The body reacts to these changes just as it reacts to changes caused by other drugs. Over time, the body builds up a tolerance to tobacco and alcohol. *Tolerance* is the body's ability to resist the effects of a drug. Tolerance causes a person to need more of a drug in order to feel the drug's effects. As the body gets used to a drug, a person feels uncomfortable without the drug. The person may use the drug more often to avoid this discomfort. Eventually, the person needs the drug to feel normal. A person who cannot control his or her use of a drug has a *drug addiction*.

A person can become addicted without realizing it. Most people are not aware of their tolerance to tobacco or alcohol until they are already dependent on the drug. Once a person is dependent on one of these drugs, it is very hard to quit using the drug. ⊛ 5.C

What You'll Do

■ **Explain** how alcoholism affects the alcohol user and his or her family. ⊛ 5.C

■ **Describe** how difficult it is to quit using drugs once a person is addicted. ⊛ 5.C

Terms to Learn

• alcoholism

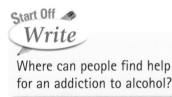

Start Off *Write*

Where can people find help for an addiction to alcohol?

When Columbus arrived in the Americas in 1492, the native people greeted him with gifts of dried tobacco leaves. Columbus and his crew did not know what tobacco leaves were used for, so they threw them away.

Success in Quitting Smoking

y-axis: Percentage of smokers (0, 10, 20, 30, 40, 50, 60, 70, 80, 90, 100)

x-axis: Smokers — Want to quit, Permanently quit each year

Figure 10 Smokers have a hard time quitting—even when they want to quit.

Alcoholism

Alcoholism is a disease caused by physical and psychological dependence on alcohol. Alcohol takes over a person's life, and it can be deadly. When people develop alcoholism, they have difficulty carrying out their duties. People who have alcoholism cannot make decisions well. They may have strange reactions to normal events. Job performance may suffer. They may also neglect family and friends.

Alcoholism can be very painful for families. Children may not understand how alcohol can have such power over a parent. Parents affected by alcoholism may not realize how their behavior changes while they are intoxicated. Support programs can help both people who have alcoholism and their families. Alcoholics Anonymous (AL kuh HAWL iks uh NAHN uh muhs) is one group that helps people recover. Al-Anon offers families a place to talk about living with a person who has alcoholism. Alateen offers support specifically for teens. With help, people who have alcoholism can rebuild their lives. ✪ 5.C; 9.B

Figure 11 Teens can find support for dealing with family members who suffer from alcoholism.

Recovering from Addiction

Once a person is addicted, it is extremely difficult to stop using a drug. Smokers who want to quit often try many times before they succeed. Quitting an addiction to alcohol can even be dangerous. The body can become so dependent on alcohol that it physically needs the drug to function. Suddenly stopping the supply of alcohol can even be fatal. In such cases, hospital care helps a person quit safely. When people who suffer from addiction take action and refuse to give up, they can recover. ✪ 5.B; 5.C

Lesson Review

Using Vocabulary

1. What is the relationship between addiction and alcoholism? ✪ 5.C

Understanding Concepts

2. How could alcoholism affect the family and friends of an alcoholic? ✪ 5.B; 9.B

Critical Thinking

3. **Analyzing Ideas** You learned that it can be deadly for an alcoholic to suddenly quit abusing alcohol. If quitting suddenly could be fatal, why should the person quit using the drug? ✪ 5.C; 5.D

🖅 **internet** connect

www.scilinks.org/health
Topic: Teens, Drugs, and Alcohol in Texas
HealthLinks code: HHTX015

Topic: Alcoholism
HealthLinks code: HD4007

HEALTH LINKS Maintained by the National Science Teachers Association

What You'll Do

- **Describe** how friends, family, and role models pressure teens to try tobacco and alcohol.
  ⭐ 5.B; 6.A; 7.A
- **Explain** how peer pressure can be positive or negative.
  ⭐ 5.B; 11.C
- **Discuss** how the media can influence teens about drugs.
  ⭐ 5.B; 8.A

Terms to Learn

- peer pressure

Start Off ✏️
Write

Why might a person try alcohol or tobacco?

Feeling Pressure

Gillian's older brother, Will, just started chewing tobacco. Whenever Gillian bugged him about it, Will said that his favorite baseball star chewed tobacco, so it couldn't be that bad. Gillian knew Will was wrong.

People try tobacco, alcohol, or other drugs for many reasons. Even seeing a baseball star use tobacco can pressure a teen to try tobacco. Being aware of such pressures can help you make wise decisions to resist tobacco and other drugs. ⭐ 5.H

Pressure from Other People

Pressure to try tobacco, alcohol, or other drugs can come from many places. Identifying the pressures to try drugs is the first step to resisting drugs. People who smoke or drink alcohol are a major source of pressure. These people can make smoking and drinking seem safe, fun, or cool. But tobacco and alcohol are dangerous—especially for teens.

Some pressure may come from friends. **Peer pressure** is influence from a friend or a group of friends. For example, another student might offer you a cigarette or a beer. Or you might feel pressure from simply seeing others use drugs. Seeing a group of friends use drugs can give the false idea that drugs help people make friends. But drugs can get in the way of friendships. Drugs can cause people to act strangely. Also, people who use drugs may cause friends who don't use drugs to feel uncomfortable. Luckily, peer pressure can also be positive. Good friends can help you avoid drugs by supporting your decision not to use drugs.

Family members and celebrities who use drugs can also place pressure on teens. Parents, famous athletes, and movie stars can make drugs seem safe. But we rarely see the negative health effects of drug use on a famous person's life. And a drink that hardly affects an adult can be dangerous for a teen.
⭐ 5.B; 5.H; 6.A; 7.A; 8.A; 11.C

Figure 12 Pressure to use drugs can come from celebrities who use drugs and make drugs seem safe or cool.

Advertisements

Another source of pressure to use tobacco and alcohol comes from advertisements. Magazines and billboards make tobacco and alcohol users look glamorous or cool. Some people falsely think that if they use alcohol or tobacco, they will look like the people in advertisements. But in fact, alcohol can cause people to act foolish and make poor decisions. Tobacco can cause skin to wrinkle and teeth to turn yellow. These things are not glamorous.

Advertisements do not show the negative parts of drug use. People in magazines and on billboards seem to use tobacco and alcohol without suffering any negative consequences. These images give a false idea of the experience of doing drugs. ⊛ 8.A

Health Journal

Write three sources of pressure to try drugs across the top of a page in your Health Journal. Under each source, brainstorm at least three reasons to resist each of these pressures.

Getting Through Rough Times

Some people abuse tobacco or alcohol as an escape from thinking about problems. People who are sad or stressed out sometimes take advantage of how drugs affect the mind. People think drugs will help them forget about their problems. However, drugs never solve problems. Drugs may even make problems worse. A drug's effects on a person's social, mental, and physical health can be very destructive.

When people need help with problems that cause sadness or stress, they can find drug-free help. Talking to friends, parents, or trusted adults can help. Counselors or doctors can also help solve problems.

⊛ 5.B; 5.H

Figure 13 Talking to friends can help teens solve problems without using drugs.

Lesson Review

Using Vocabulary

1. How can peer pressure be positive or negative? ⊛ 5.B; 11.C

Understanding Concepts

2. How can friends, family, and celebrities pressure teens to try drugs? ⊛ 6.A; 7.A; 11.C

3. How do advertisements influence teens about tobacco and alcohol? ⊛ 5.B; 8.A; 11.C

Critical Thinking

4. Making Good Decisions Suppose that a friend told you that alcohol is a great way to feel better. What would you tell your friend about how to cope with sadness? ⊛ 5.H

Refusing Tobacco and Alcohol

What You'll Do

- **Discuss** ways to refuse tobacco or alcohol.
  ⭑ 5.H; 7.B; 7.D
- **Describe** drug-free ways to be social. ⭑ 5.H

Start Off
Write

What can you do to resist an offer of tobacco or alcohol?

Imagine that you are at a friend's house. You walk into the kitchen and find your friend's sister taking alcohol from a liquor cabinet. She asks you if you want a drink.

Pressure to use drugs can come at unexpected times. Thinking ahead can help you know how to react in these situations.

Ways to Refuse

You never need to make excuses for refusing to do drugs. If someone offers you a cigarette or a drink, it may be easiest to say, "No, thanks." Usually, people will leave you alone when they know you are not interested. You can also give a reason for refusing if it feels more comfortable to do so. For example, you could say, "No, I have a dance recital tomorrow. I want to be in really good shape." You could even say, "No way—it's illegal."

Figure 14 Suggesting a different activity is a powerful way to refuse drugs.

If someone continues to pressure you after you have said no, you can be more clear. You can refuse more firmly or simply leave. Walking away from situations in which drugs are available is a good way to avoid danger. And if someone pressures you to try drugs, it is a good idea to question your relationship with that person. Why would another person want you to try drugs? True friends will always respect your decision to refuse drugs. ⭑ 5.H; 7.B; 7.D

Providing Alternatives

Sometimes, you may not be comfortable giving reasons for refusing drugs. In these cases, you can change the subject to get out of an uncomfortable conversation. Suggesting a fun activity to do instead of doing drugs can often relieve pressure. For example, imagine that a friend asks if you want to drink a beer. You could suggest getting a soda instead. There are many drug-free choices. ⭑ 5.H

Build an Active Social Life

Some people feel that they need drugs in order to be social. However, drugs are not necessary for having fun or meeting people. In fact, drugs can make it harder to be social when they cause confusion and tiredness. Think of all the times that you have had fun without drugs. If you ever wonder whether you need to use drugs to have fun, you can remember those times.

You can find drug-free ways to make friends. If you have an interest in a hobby or activity, join a group that shares that interest. You could join a sports team, a music group, a science club, a theater group, or a volunteer program. Joining a group will help you meet people. It might be easy to get to know people in these groups because you share a common interest. You will also be spending time doing something that you enjoy. ✪ 5.H

Figure 15 There are many drug-free ways to have fun and make friends.

Lesson Review

Understanding Concepts

1. List three ways to refuse an offer of tobacco or alcohol. ✪ 5.H

2. List ten ways teens can have fun without using drugs. ✪ 5.H

3. What can you do if someone continues to pressure you to try drugs after you have said no? ✪ 5.H; 7.B; 7.D; 10.B

Critical Thinking

4. **Using Refusal Skills** Suppose that you were with a group of teens when a stranger offered your friend a cigarette. If your friend looked uncomfortable with the offer, how could you use your knowledge of refusal skills to help your friend? ✪ 11.B; 11.C

Chapter Summary

■ Tobacco and alcohol are drugs because they cause changes in the mind and body.
■ Tobacco products contain nicotine, which is an addictive chemical. ■ Using tobacco causes diseases such as emphysema and cancer. ■ Alcohol causes intoxication, which makes it unsafe for a person to drive and hard for a person to make decisions.
■ Drinking alcohol can lead to cirrhosis or brain damage. ■ Addiction to alcohol is called *alcoholism*. ■ Pressure to use tobacco and alcohol can come from friends, family, advertisements, or an attempt to escape problems. ■ You can refuse tobacco and alcohol by saying, "No, thanks," walking away, or providing alternatives.

Using Vocabulary

For each pair of terms, describe how the meanings of the terms differ.

1 addiction/alcoholism

2 nicotine/tobacco

For each sentence, fill in the blank with the proper word from the word bank provided below.

cirrhosis	peer pressure
emphysema	tar
environmental	tobacco
tobacco smoke	blood alcohol
nicotine	concentration

3 Cigarettes and cigars are made from a plant called ___.

4 Tobacco products contain a drug called ___.

5 Cigarettes cause a black, sticky substance called ___ to build up in a person's air passages.

6 ___ is a disease caused by long-term use of tobacco products.

7 A nonsmoker inhales ___ from exhaled smoke and the ends of burning cigarettes.

8 ___ is a disease that affects the liver.

Understanding Concepts

9 Why are tobacco products and alcohol considered to be drugs? ⭐ 5.C; 5.D

10 Describe the effects of intoxication. ⭐ 2.A; 5.D

11 Why do people with high blood alcohol concentration vomit? ⭐ 2.A; 5.D

12 What are two health problems caused by long-term alcohol abuse? ⭐ 5.C

13 Describe how alcohol impairs the ability to drive. ⭐ 2.A; 5.D

14 Why is it difficult to quit using tobacco or alcohol once a person is addicted? ⭐ 5.C

15 What are the effects of smoking one cigarette?

16 Is using smokeless tobacco safer than smoking? ⭐ 5.C; 5.D

17 What is the difference between positive and negative peer pressure? ⭐ 11.C

Critical Thinking

Applying Concepts

18 Many restaurants separate smoking sections from nonsmoking sections. How could sitting in a smoking section affect your health? What might decrease the benefits of sitting in a nonsmoking section? ⭐ 5.D; 5.E

19 You have learned about fetal alcohol syndrome resulting from a pregnant mother's alcohol use. Cigarette packages print a warning from the Surgeon General that says that pregnant women should not smoke. How do you think smoking could harm an unborn baby? ⭐ 2.A

20 Suppose that you have a friend whose father suffers from alcoholism. How do you think your friend, his father, his mother, and his entire family would be affected? ⭐ 5.C; 9.B

21 What different pressures to try using tobacco or alcohol could come from the following sources: friends, family, role models, and advertisements? ⭐ 5.B; 7.A; 8.A; 11.C

22 Suppose that a friend wants to smoke and drink alcohol. She insists that she doesn't think she can have as much fun without these drugs. What drug-free ways to be social and have fun could you describe to her? ⭐ 5.E

Making Good Decisions

23 A classmate smuggled a flask of rum into school and offers you a drink at lunch. What are three possible ways you could refuse this alcohol? ⭐ 7.B; 7.C; 7.D; 11.B

24 Suppose that you go to a New Year's Eve party with your 25-year-old brother, who drives you to the party. At the party, he becomes intoxicated. How could the two of you return home safely? ⭐ 9.A; 9.B

25 Use what you have learned in this chapter to set a personal goal. Write your goal, and make an action plan by using the Health Behavior Contract for tobacco and alcohol. You can find the Health Behavior Contract at go.hrw.com. Just type in the keyword HD4HBC04.

Name _____ Class _____ Date _____

Health Behavior Contract
Tobacco and Alcohol

My Goals: I, _____, will accomplish one or more of the following goals:
I will not use tobacco or alcohol.
I will find out where to go for help if a friend becomes an alcoholic.
I will use refusal skills if alcohol and tobacco are offered to me.
Other: _____

My Reasons: By abstaining from tobacco and alcohol and using refusal skills if someone offers tobacco or alcohol to me, I will protect my health. By knowing how to deal with alcoholism, I will be prepared to help my friends and family.
Other: _____

My Values: Personal values that will help me meet my goals are
_____
_____
_____

My Plan: The actions I will take to meet my goals are
_____
_____

Evaluation: I will use my Health Journal to keep a log of actions I took to fulfill this contract. After 1 month, I will evaluate my goals. I will adjust my plan if my goals are not being met. If my goals are being met, I will consider setting additional goals.

Signed _____
Date _____

Reading Checkup

Take a minute to review your answers to the Health IQ questions at the beginning of this chapter. How has reading this chapter improved your Health IQ?

Life Skills IN ACTION

Evaluating Media Messages

You receive media messages every day. These messages are on TV, the Internet, the radio, and in newspapers and magazines. With so many messages, it is important to know how to evaluate them. Evaluating media messages means being able to judge the accuracy of a message. Complete the following activity to improve your skills in evaluating media messages. ⭐ 5.C; 8.A

ACT 1

The Cigarette Ad

Blake and his friend Diana are looking through some magazines. In one magazine, Blake finds a cigarette ad showing several attractive young adults having fun in a nightclub. Blake says that he wants to smoke the brand of cigarettes shown in the ad when he is older so that he can be cool like the people in the picture. Diana is surprised by his comment and asks if he read the Surgeon General's warning at the bottom of the ad. ⭐ 4.B

SURGEON GENERAL'S WARNING: Smoking Causes Lung Cancer, Heart Disease, Emphysema, And May Complicate Pregnancy.

The **5** Steps of Evaluating Media Messages

1. Examine the appeal of the message.

2. Identify the values projected by the message.

3. Consider what the source has to gain by getting you to believe the message.

4. Try to determine the reliability of the source.

5. Based on the information you gather, evaluate the message.

Guided Practice

Practice with a Friend

Form a group of three. Have one person play the role of Blake and another person play the role of Diana. Have the third person be an observer. Walking through each of the five steps of evaluating media messages, role-play a conversation between Blake and Diana. In their conversation, the two should evaluate the ad shown above. The observer will take notes, which will include observations about what the people playing Blake and Diana did well and suggestions of ways to improve. Stop after each step to evaluate the process.

Independent Practice

Check Yourself

After you have completed the guided practice, go through Act 1 again without stopping at each step. Answer the questions below to review what you did.

1. Why do you think the cigarette company used young adults in their ad?

2. What values are projected by the cigarette ad?

3. Do you think the ad is a reliable source? Explain your answer.

4. Describe a time when you purchased a product based on information you saw in an ad. Did the product do what the ad said it would do? ⊛ 8.A

On Your Own

After thinking about the cigarette ads, Blake is convinced that smoking will not make him popular. A few days later, Blake sees a report on an Internet site that claims that taking a certain mixture of herbal supplements will make a person taller and stronger. The site is owned by a company that sells herbal supplements. Write a short story in which Blake uses the five steps of evaluating media messages to analyze the Internet site.

⊛ 4.B; 8.A

Health and Your Safety

Lessons

Check out
Current Health
articles related to this chapter by
visiting go.hrw.com. Just type in
the keyword **HD4CH15**.

> **"** My **family** goes on a **rafting trip** every summer. We always wear our **life jackets**. You never know when you **might fall out** of the boat! **"**

Health IQ

PRE-READING

Answer the following multiple-choice questions to find out what you already know about safety. When you've finished this chapter, you'll have the opportunity to change your answers based on what you've learned.

1. **When getting into shallow water, the best way to stay safe is to**
   a. dive head first.
   b. lower yourself in.
   c. jump in feet first.
   d. None of the above ⭐ 5.G

2. **Which of the following actions will help keep you safe while you are cycling?**
   a. wearing a helmet
   b. going with friends
   c. wearing bright clothing
   d. all of the above ⭐ 5.G

3. **People younger than 12 should sit in**
   a. the back seat of a car.
   b. a child safety seat.
   c. the front seat of a car.
   d. None of the above ⭐ 5.G

4. **Which type of burn is dark colored and deep?**
   a. first-degree burn
   b. second-degree burn
   c. third-degree burn
   d. none of the above ⭐ 5.G

5. **What should you NOT do while trying to save a drowning person?**
   a. get in the water
   b. use a long pole to reach the person
   c. throw the person a life preserver
   d. call for help ⭐ 5.G

6. **Which of the following is NOT an important part of a fire escape plan?**
   a. It includes two ways out of the building from each room.
   b. It includes a safe place for your family to meet outside of the building.
   c. It explains how to put the fire out.
   d. Your family practices it regularly. ⭐ 5.G

ANSWERS: 1. b; 2. d; 3. a; 4. c; 5. a; 6. c

Safety Around Home

Ravi's little sister leaves her toys on the stairs. Ravi always picks up after her. Ravi knows that if he didn't put the toys away, someone may trip on them. Someone could have an accident.

What You'll Do

- **Describe** three accidents that happen at home. ⭐ 5.G
- **Describe** five ways to stay safe when you cycle or skate. ⭐ 5.G
- **List** three ways to stay safe in a vehicle. ⭐ 5.G

Terms to Learn

- accident
- smoke detector
- fire extinguisher

Write

How can you stay safe while you are skating?

An **accident** is an unexpected event that may lead to injury. Falls, fires, and electrical shock are three common accidents.

Falls

Have you ever tripped and fallen? Almost everyone has. Most of the time, people aren't hurt. But falls cause many of the injuries seen in an emergency room. Some people trip over objects on the stairs. Other people fall when they use a chair instead of a ladder to reach something high. Have you ever spilled something on the floor and forgotten to wipe it up? People can slip on a wet floor and fall. You can prevent falls by doing the following things:

- Don't leave objects on the stairs or floors. Help younger children put their toys away.
- Use a ladder instead of a chair to get items that are out of reach.
- Wipe up spills right away.
- To protect small children, put safety gates in front of stairways. Watch out for other hazards, such as open windows. ⭐ 5.G

Figure 1 Can you see the potential accidents in this picture? Toys on the stairs and a wet floor could cause a fall. The boy should use a ladder instead of a wheeled stool.

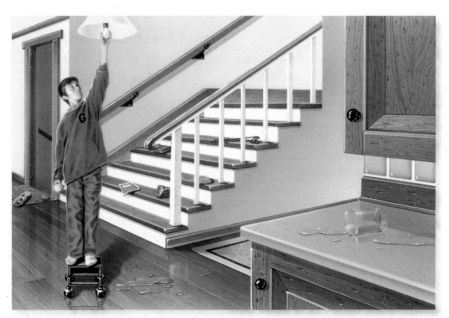

Fires

Fires can cause burns, and inhaling smoke can injure lungs. Open flames, frayed electrical cords, and overloaded power outlets can cause fires. Some chemicals can start a fire, also.

Ask your parents to put smoke detectors in each room of your home. A **smoke detector** is a small, battery-operated alarm that detects smoke from a fire. Check your smoke detectors once a month to make sure they are working. You can also ask your parents to buy a fire extinguisher. A **fire extinguisher** is a device that releases chemicals to put out a fire.

Make an escape plan with your family in case there is a fire. You should know two ways out of the house from each room. Also, choose a place where everyone can meet outside. Your family should practice your escape plan regularly. ★ 5.G

Putting Out Grease Fires

Never use water to put out a grease fire. Water will make the fire spread. Always use a fire extinguisher, baking soda, or salt. When in doubt, leave the building and call for help from a neighbor's home.

PRACTICING WELLNESS

In groups, draw a picture of a home or room that has 10 accident risks. You could include things that cause falls, fires, or other accidents. Trade your picture with other groups, and identify the risks that are in each picture. Describe how each risk can be fixed. ★ 5.G

ACCIDENTS AT HOME

1. In groups, write down five accidents that happened in your home last week. How often did each happen?

2. Make a bar graph of your results. The graph should show the kinds of accidents and how often they happen.

Analysis

1. Which type of accident is the most common? Which type is the least common?

2. What can you do to prevent the accidents you listed from happening?

Electrical Shock

Has anyone ever told you to be careful around electrical outlets? If you aren't careful, you could be shocked. *Electrical shock* is an accident in which electricity passes through the body. Electrical shock can stop a victim's heart. Also, the victim may stop breathing. Many victims have burns and internal injuries. Do the following to avoid electrical shock:

- Don't touch bare electrical wires.
- Avoid putting too many plugs into an outlet.
- Put safety covers on outlets if small children are in the home.
- Keep small appliances, such as hairdryers, away from water.
  ✪ 5.G; 6.B

Cycling and Skating Safety

Cycling and skating are fun. But they can also be risky. Thousands of teens are hurt each year while cycling and skating. Many of these injuries can be avoided.

Wearing your safety gear is very important. Wear a bicycle helmet every time you ride your bike. A helmet lowers your chances of a head injury. You should also use a helmet for skateboarding and in-line skating. Elbow pads, knee pads, and wrist guards also keep skaters from getting hurt.

The following can help keep you safe when you cycle or skate:

- Pay attention to traffic, and avoid busy areas.
- Follow the rules of the road.
- Wear bright clothes, and don't ride or skate after dark.
- Don't cycle or skate alone. ✪ 5.G; 6.B

Figure 3 Safety gear keeps you safe when you skateboard.

Vehicle Safety

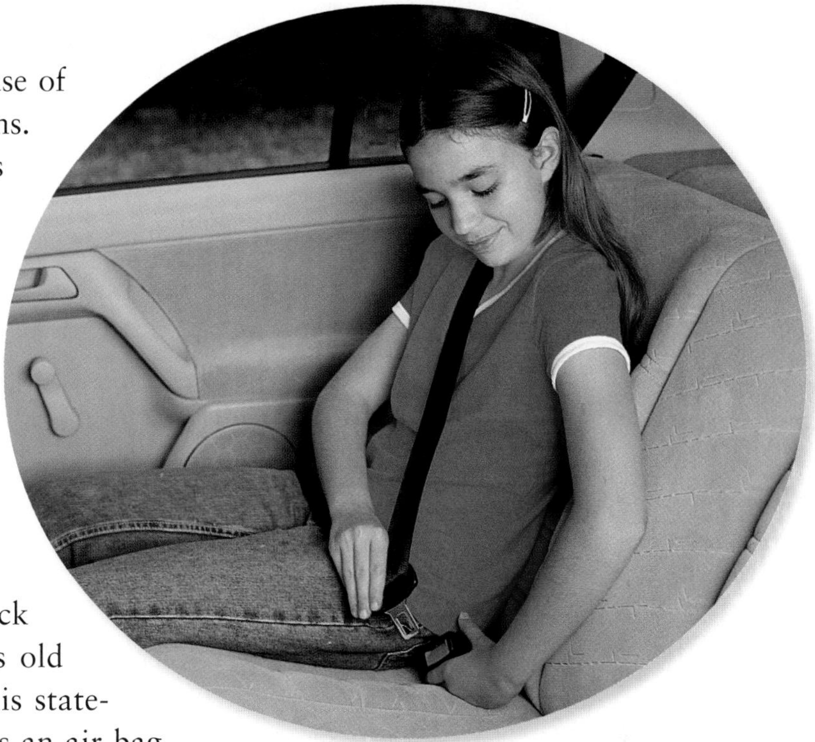

Figure 4 If you buckle your seat belt every time you get in the car, you are less likely to get hurt during an accident.

Vehicle accidents are the leading cause of injury and death for children and teens. Many of these children and teens were not wearing their seat belts. Seat belts can keep you from getting hurt during an accident.

A seat belt must be worn correctly for it to help you. Younger children should use a child safety seat or booster seat. Teens and adults should use both shoulder belts and lap belts.

The safest part of a car is the back seat. People younger than 12 years old should not sit in the front seat. This statement is especially true if the car has an air bag. Air bags are meant to protect larger people. They can injure smaller people. If you have to sit in the front seat, move your seat as far back as possible. Doing so gives you more protection from injury.

The driver of a car or bus has a lot of responsibility. It is important not to distract him or her. If you're on a bus, stay in your seat. Bus rides can be very bumpy, and you could be thrown if you are standing. Know where the emergency exits are. If there is an accident, follow the bus driver's instructions.

5.G; 6.A

Lesson Review

Using Vocabulary

1. What is an accident?

Understanding Concepts

2 List three common accidents.

3. What are three ways to stay safe during a fire? 5.G

4. Name four things other than wearing safety equipment that you can do to stay safe when cycling or skating. 5.G

5. What are three ways to stay safe in a vehicle? 5.G

Critical Thinking

6. Applying Concepts Fire extinguishers should be put in areas where fires are a risk. What are three areas in your home where you could put a fire extinguisher? Explain your answer. 5.G; 6.A

internet connect

www.scilinks.org/health

Topic: Safety

HealthLinks code: HD4084

HEALTH LINKS Maintained by the National Science Teachers Association

Safety at School

A student at Elfia's school was caught with a knife in his backpack. The student was expelled. But it was still scary. Elfia wondered why anyone would take a knife to school.

What You'll Do

■ **List** five causes of violence. ✪ 5.H

■ **List** four ways to avoid violence in school. ✪ 5.H

Terms to Learn

• violence

• gang

Start Off
Write

How can you avoid violence at school?

When people think of violence at school, they often think of guns or knives. **Violence** (VIE uh luhns) is using physical force to hurt someone or cause damage. The student in Elfia's school might have used the knife he brought to school to hurt someone.

Violence

Why does violence happen at school? Many things can lead to violence. The following are some examples:

• **Anger** Everyone gets angry. Most people can handle their anger. People who can't control their anger may become violent.

• **Stress** Students may be stressed by things at home or at school. Stress causes frustration. Some people take out their frustration on other people.

• **Illegal Drugs** When people use illegal drugs, they act differently. Some people want drugs so much that they will hurt other people to get drugs. Some people hurt other people while they are on drugs.

• **Prejudice** Forming an opinion about other people because they are different is called *prejudice*. Prejudice can cause some people to dislike and to try to hurt others.

• **Negative Peer Pressure** Sometimes, people are violent because they want to fit in or someone else pressured them to be violent. Some students may join a gang. A **gang** is a group of people who often use violence.
✪ 5.H; 10.F

Figure 5 Uncontrolled anger can lead to violence.

Figure 6 Community service, such as a beach cleanup, can help you stay away from violent situations.

Staying Safe

You hear about school violence on the news. Maybe you have read a magazine article about school violence. What can you do to avoid violence? There are many things you can do. If you don't feel safe at school, talk to your parents or school counselor. If you know about a violent situation, tell an adult. You're protecting not only yourself but also other people. Brush up on your refusal skills, and learn conflict management skills. These skills can keep you out of a dangerous situation.

Finally, to avoid violence, find a positive way to spend your time. Joining sports teams or school clubs is a great way to avoid violence. You can also volunteer in your community. These activities can keep you out of violent situations. They also provide you with positive influences. So, you're less likely to be around violence. ✪ 5.G; 5.H; 6.A

USING REFUSAL SKILLS

Make a poster showing ways to use refusal skills to avoid violence in school. You could draw cartoons or use magazine clippings to make your poster exciting.

Lesson Review

Using Vocabulary

1. Use the terms *violence* and *gang* in a sentence. ✪ 5.H

Understanding Concepts

2. What are five causes of violence?

3. List four ways to avoid violence in school. ✪ 5.G; 5.H; 6.A

Critical Thinking

4. Using Refusal Skills One of Claudia's friends wants her to join a gang. How could Claudia use her refusal skills to tell her friend that she won't join a gang? ✪ 5.H; 7.B; 7.D; 7.E

Seven Ways to Protect Yourself

What You'll Do

- **List** seven ways to protect yourself from accidental injury. ⊛ 5.G; 7.B; 7.E

- **Describe** how the seven safety rules protect you from injury. ⊛ 5.G

Start Off
Write

How does knowing your limits keep you safe?

Liza's brother never seems to think about what he is doing before he does it. He is always doing crazy stunts on his skateboard. Last time he tried something, he had to go to the emergency room. He was OK. But it still worried Liza.

Accidents happen all the time. But you can avoid many of them. Liza's brother should have thought about the consequences of his actions. He might have avoided a trip to the emergency room.

Think Before You Act

Imagine that you have been invited to go swimming. Do you know how to swim? Will there be a lifeguard? Could you get hurt? These are just some of the questions you may want to ask yourself before you go swimming. Thinking about the risks of your actions will help you avoid injuries. Ask yourself if what you're going to do is dangerous. Avoid doing anything that might hurt you or another person. ⊛ 5.G

Pay Attention

Take a look around you. Do you see any risky situations? Chances are, you probably do. Pay attention to what's around you. This is one of the best ways to keep from getting hurt. When you pay attention, you know about accidents that could happen. For example, there could be something in your path that could make you trip and fall. Maybe there's a fire risk. Keep your eyes open. If you stay aware, you can be safer. ⊛ 5.G

Figure 7 Paying attention when crossing a busy street is important.

Know Your Limits

Have you ever played a sport before? If so, you may already know that there are limits to what you can do physically. Know your limits, and stay within those limits. Don't do an activity you know you aren't ready to do. You will be less likely to get hurt.

You can also have limits based on your values. If something is important to you, you probably won't do anything to put it at risk. For example, you may want to make good grades in school. Getting caught cheating could ruin your grades. So, you won't cheat to make good grades. ⍟ 5.G

Practice Refusal Skills

Have you ever had a friend ask you to do something that might get you hurt? What did you do? Did you use your refusal skills? Don't be afraid to say no. It may seem hard to say no to your friends. You may be afraid of what they will think. But is doing what they want you to do worth getting hurt?

You can practice your refusal skills with your parents and friends. Make up situations that are hard to refuse. Then, think of different ways to say no. And learn how to sound like you mean it when you tell someone no. Remember that you can always walk away. Using your refusal skills in risky situations can keep you from getting hurt. ⍟ 5.G; 7.B; 7.E

Figure 8 Should you try the hard slope or the easy slope? Knowing when something is too hard for you can keep you from getting hurt.

Health Journal
Write about a time when you didn't do something because you weren't ready for it.

Figure 9 Safety goggles protect your eyes during science experiments.

Use Safety Equipment

Safety equipment may not keep you from having an accident. But it can keep you from getting hurt when you do. There are many different kinds of safety equipment. Rubber gloves protect your hands from dangerous chemicals. Goggles protect your eyes. You can avoid burns by using potholders to pick up hot pans.

Safety equipment is very important for sports and outdoor activities. Be sure to use the right safety equipment for your activity. Don't ride your bike without wearing a helmet. Wear a helmet, elbow pads, and knee pads when you go skating. Wear a life jacket when you go boating. When you use safety equipment, you can avoid getting hurt. ⭐ 5.G

Change Risky Behavior

Do you sometimes forget to close cabinet doors? Do you ride in a car without using your seat belt? These habits are examples of risky behavior. Risky behavior can lead to an accident. If you want to stay safe, try to change your risky behaviors. Ask your family or your friends to help you identify your risky behaviors. Then, the next time you catch yourself doing something risky, you can remind yourself to stop.

Maybe a friend or someone in your family has a risky behavior. Let him or her know about it. Together, you can work on changing risky behavior. ⭐ 5.G

Change Risky Situations

Maybe you've changed your risky behavior. But there may still be risky situations. Take a look around you. Do you see anything that may cause an accident? For example, you may see an overloaded outlet, which could cause a fire. Or you may see a spill on the floor, which could cause a fall. So, what can you do about these risky situations? You can change them! Tell an adult about the danger. Or if you won't get hurt, you can change the risky situation yourself. For example, you can wipe up that spill.

If you see a risky situation outside your home, let your parents know. Even if you can't fix it, letting someone know about a risky situation helps. You may keep someone from having an accident. ★ 5.G

Figure 10 Taking an active part in preventing accidents is one way to avoid injuries.

Lesson Review

Understanding Concepts

1. What are seven ways to avoid injury? ★ 5.G; 7.B; 7.E

2. List three examples of risky behaviors other than those listed in the text. ★ 5.G

3. How are risky behaviors and risky situations different? ★ 5.G

Critical Thinking

4. Making Inferences You have been asked to go to a party at a friend's house. What are some risks you may think about before you go? ★ 5.G

Safety in the Water

Horatio's mom makes Horatio wear a life jacket when they go boating. He doesn't like to wear it. But he knows it may save his life.

A **life jacket** is a vest that keeps you floating in the water. Horatio wears his life jacket in case there is an accident while he is boating. A life jacket will keep Horatio's head above water so he can breathe.

Boating Safely

Have you ever gone rafting or canoeing? Or do you know someone who has a motor boat? Boating can be a lot of fun. But it can also be risky. You should wear a life jacket when you're boating. In fact, many states have laws about life jackets. These states often require that everyone in a boat has a life jacket. The following can also make boating safe and fun.

- Always go with an experienced person.
- Don't stand in a boat. The boat might tip over, or you may fall out.
- Avoid boating in bad weather.
- Avoid rough water unless you know how to handle it. If you're white-water rafting, wear a helmet to protect your head.
  ⊛ 5.G

What You'll Do

- **Explain** why you should wear a life jacket while boating. ⊛ 5.G
- **List** seven ways to stay safe while swimming. ⊛ 5.G
- **Describe** diving safety. ⊛ 5.G
- **List** fours ways to avoid drowning. ⊛ 5.G
- **Explain** how you can rescue someone who is drowning.
- **Describe** the water survival float. ⊛ 5.G

Terms to Learn

- life jacket

Start Off Write

Why shouldn't you jump in the water to save someone who is drowning?

Figure 11 Life jackets can keep you safe when you're boating.

Figure 12 There are many different kinds of warning signs near water. To stay safe, be sure to follow them.

Swimming Safely

Swimming is a great way to cool down on a hot day. It is also great exercise. But it is important to stay safe when you go swimming. Keep the following tips in mind the next time you go swimming:

- Learn how to swim.

- Don't swim alone.

- Obey posted safety warnings. Signs around swimming areas let you know about safety risks.

- Swim in designated areas. Avoid areas that don't have a lifeguard on duty.

- Watch out for boats. Boaters often can't see swimmers.

- Don't swim away from shore. Swim parallel to shore. That way you can get back to shore if you get tired.

- Avoid swimming in rough water and in bad weather. ✪ 5.G

Diving Safely

Diving can be fun, but it can also be dangerous. If you are going to dive, make sure that you know how deep the water is. Also, make sure the bottom is free of obstacles, such as rocks and debris. Diving into shallow or unknown water is dangerous. You may hit your head on the bottom or on a rock. The impact can cause paralysis or even death. If you are unsure of the water's depth or of what obstacles the water may contain, you should slowly enter feet first. ✪ 5.G

LIFE SKILLS ACTIVITY

COMMUNICATING EFFECTIVELY

Imagine you are a radio announcer. In groups, create a public service announcement (PSA) that promotes safe swimming and diving. Perform your PSA for the class.

Figure 13 Taking a swim class can help you avoid drowning.

Brain Food

Drowning is second only to car accidents for accidental death in children under 15 years old. More than 4,000 people drown each year. Of those, more than one-third were less than 14 years old.

Avoid Drowning

Thousands of people drown each year. Drowning is an accident you can avoid. Swimming alone, improper diving, and horseplay increase your chances of drowning. Changing these behaviors can keep you safe. Obeying warning signs and wearing a life jacket can also keep you safe in the water. You should swim in areas that have a lifeguard on duty. Lifeguards are trained to save you. ★ 5.G

Saving a Drowning Person

Sometimes a lifeguard isn't around to help. You may have to help someone who is in trouble. If you see someone drowning, yell or call for help first. Try to find an adult. If you can't get help right away, try to rescue the victim from shore or the side of the pool. Use a pole or another long object to reach the person. You can also throw a life preserver to the victim.

You should never get into the water to save someone unless you have been trained to do so. Rescuing a drowning person can be dangerous. A drowning person will panic and may drag the rescuer under water. Even strong swimmers are at risk when they try to save a drowning person. Once the drowning person is out of the water, he or she may need medical care. Call for help right away. ★ 5.G

Water Survival

Have you ever been scared while swimming? Did the water seem too deep? Or did you feel tired? If you are ever in such a situation again, don't panic. Staying calm is the most important thing you can do in the water. If you are having trouble, yell or wave your hands to get help. While you're waiting for help, use the water survival float shown in the figure below to stay afloat.

⭐ 5.G

Figure 14 Water Survival Float

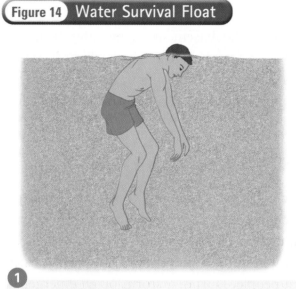

1 Inhale deeply, and hold your breath. Lie face down in the water, and relax your body. Let arms and legs dangle below your body. Move as little as possible while you float. Staying still keeps you from using up your oxygen. Rest in this position until you need to breathe.

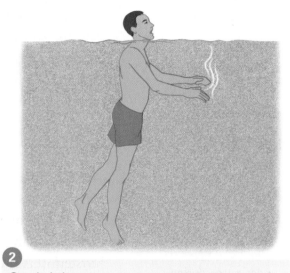

2 Gently bring your arms up, and slowly push down against the water. Meanwhile, gently kick your legs like you're riding a bicycle. Extend your body, and bring your head above water to breathe. After you take a breath, resume the resting position until you need to breathe again.

Lesson Review

Using Vocabulary

1. What is a life jacket? ⭐ 5.G

Understanding Concepts

2. What are seven ways to stay safe while swimming? ⭐ 5.G

3. Describe safe diving. ⭐ 5.G

4. What are four ways to avoid drowning? ⭐ 5.G

5. How can you rescue someone who is drowning? ⭐ 5.G

6. Describe the water survival float. ⭐ 5.G

Critical Thinking

7. Making Good Decisions Imagine you see a person drowning in a pool. There's no lifeguard. What should you do? ⭐ 5.G

Weather Emergencies and Natural Disasters

Figure 15 While it may look beautiful, lightning is very dangerous.

Natalia's parents woke her up in the middle of the night once. A storm warning was on the radio. Natalia and her family spent the rest of the night in the basement. That night was frightening.

Natalia's family stayed in the basement to be safer from the storm. Storms that cause a lot of damage are natural disasters. A **natural disaster** is a natural event that causes widespread injury, death, and property damage. Most storms don't become natural disasters.

Recognizing Weather Emergencies

Bad weather can be dangerous. How will you know when the weather has become dangerous? Turn on the radio or TV. Your local radio and TV stations will let you know if a storm has gotten worse. Radio and TV stations will use the Emergency Alert System (EAS) to warn people. During a storm or an emergency, the EAS sends a tone through your TV or radio. The tone is followed by instructions about how you can stay safe. Some communities use emergency sirens or fire-station sirens to let people know about weather emergencies. Storms cause power outages. Have a battery-operated radio in case the power goes out. Then, you can find out about how to stay safe in bad weather.
⊛ 5.G

Thunderstorms

Have you ever been scared by a thunderstorm? **Thunderstorms** are heavy rainstorms that have strong winds, lightning, and thunder. Thunderstorms happen when warm, moist air rises quickly. Tall, dark clouds form as the air cools. Within these clouds, electrical energy begins to gather. But the cloud can hold only a certain amount of electrical energy. The cloud releases the excess electrical energy as lightning. Lightning transfers the energy to the air. The air expands and sends out sound waves. These sound waves are called *thunder*.

Lightning is one of the most dangerous parts of a thunderstorm. Lightning is attracted to tall objects. If you are outside, stay away from trees. Lightning may strike the tree you are hiding under and knock it down. If you are in an open field, lie down. Otherwise, you're the tallest object in the area! You should also stay away from bodies of water. If lightning hits water while you are in it, you could be hurt or die. ✪ 5.G

Almost 75 percent of the world's tornadoes happen in the United States. If 1,250 tornadoes happen worldwide each year, how many happen in the United States? ✪ M: 6.2C

Figure 16 Many tornadoes are smaller than the one in this picture. Tornadoes can cause a lot of damage.

Tornadoes

A tornado happens in about 1 percent of thunderstorms. A **tornado** is a spinning column of air that has high wind speed and touches the ground. Some tornadoes are strong enough to pick up trees, cars, or houses.

Because of advances in weather forecasting, knowing about tornadoes before they happen is usually possible. Weather forecasters use watches and warnings to let people know about tornadoes. A *watch* is a weather alert that lets people know that a tornado may happen. A *warning* is a weather alert that lets people know that a tornado has been spotted. Thunderstorms also have watches and warnings.

If there is a tornado warning for your area, find shelter. The best place to go is a basement or cellar. If you don't have a basement or cellar, go to a windowless room, such as a closet, in the center of the building. If you are caught outside, try to find shelter indoors. Otherwise, lie down in a large, open field or a deep ditch. ✪ 5.G

Figure 17 The people in this picture are preparing for a hurricane. The wooden boards help protect their windows from the high winds of a hurricane.

Hurricanes

Hurricanes form over warm, tropical areas of the ocean. A **hurricane** is a large, spinning tropical weather system that has wind speeds of at least 74 miles per hour. Hurricanes can last several days. Wind speeds of most hurricanes reach 74 to 93 miles per hour. Some wind speeds reach about 190 miles per hour. Hurricanes can also produce major rains and heavy surf.

If there is a hurricane, the weather service will give a warning. Sometimes, people living on the shore are asked to move inland to wait out the storm. ✪ 5.G

Floods

Some storms produce a lot of rain. Other storms cause hail and snow that melt into water. Where does all of this water go? Sometimes, an area gets so much rain that it begins to flood. A **flood** is an overflowing of water into areas that are normally dry. Floods tend to happen near rivers or creeks. Flooding also happens around lakes and the ocean. For example, hurricanes can cause large waves that flood the coast.

Like thunderstorms and tornadoes, floods also have watches and warnings. In areas where flooding is common, there is often plenty of warning about floods. However, sometimes there isn't much warning. A *flash flood* is a flood that rises and falls with very little warning. Flash floods are often caused by very heavy rainfall in a short amount of time or by the failure of a dam.

The best thing to do during a flood is to find a high place to wait out the flood. Stay out of floodwaters. Even shallow water can be dangerous if it is fast moving. Some floodwater moves so quickly that it can pick up cars. ✪ 5.G

Earthquakes

What's that shaking? It could be an earthquake! An **earthquake** is a shaking of the Earth's surface caused by movement along a break in the Earth's crust. Earthquakes last only a few seconds, but they can cause a lot of damage. Earthquakes can damage buildings and other structures. You may lose electricity and water. They can also cause landslides.

If you are inside during an earthquake, kneel or lie face down under a heavy table or desk. Stay away from windows, and cover your head. If you are outside, find an open area. Avoid buildings, power lines, and trees. Lie down, and cover your head. If you are in a car, have the driver stop the car in an open area. Stay inside the car until the earthquake is over. ★ 5.G

Health Journal

Describe a time when you were caught in severe weather or a natural disaster.

Lesson Review

Using Vocabulary

1. List and describe five events that may cause a natural disaster.

Understanding Concepts

2. What are three ways to learn about a weather emergency? ★ 5.G

3. What is the difference between a watch and a warning?

Critical Thinking

4. **Making Inferences** One way to protect yourself after an earthquake is to keep an emergency kit. If an earthquake caused power and water outages, injuries, and road damage, what would you need in your emergency kit? ★ 5.G

Lesson 6

Dealing with Emergencies

Hannah's older brother just finished a special class. He learned how to take care of people who have been hurt in an accident.

Hannah's brother was learning how to give first aid. **First aid** is emergency medical care for someone who has been hurt or who is sick. First aid is given to someone until professional medical care is possible. First aid is used to save someone's life. It is also used to care for minor injuries.

When to Give First Aid

When should you give first aid? Someone who is unconscious, not breathing, or in pain needs first aid. But before you give first aid, you need to learn the right way to do it. You can take a first-aid class to learn how to care for someone who is hurt. You should not give first aid unless you have taken a first-aid class. If you give first aid incorrectly, you may hurt the victim more.

Don't give first aid if you are in danger. For example, if a victim is in a burning house, you should not go inside the house. Make sure that whatever caused the victim's accident won't also hurt you. Then, call for help right away. When you find someone who is hurt, check the area around the victim. You can also look for clues about what happened. The figure below lists some of the things you should check before giving first aid. ⊛ 5.F; 5.G

What You'll Do

- **Describe** when you should give first aid. ⊛ 5.F; 5.G
- **List** five things you should tell an operator during an emergency phone call. ⊛ 5.G

Terms to Learn

- first aid

Start Off Write

What information should you give during an emergency phone call?

Figure 19 The rescuer in this photo is checking to see if the victim is breathing.

Things to Look For

▶ Is the victim conscious?

▶ Are there any obvious injuries?

▶ Is the victim breathing?

▶ Does the victim have a pulse?

▶ Are there any bottles or boxes which indicate poisoning?

▶ Does the victim have any preexisting health problems?

Making Emergency Phone Calls

If you see an emergency, call for help. In most areas, you can call 911. If your community doesn't use 911, be sure you know the local emergency numbers. In fact, many people keep an emergency phone number list next to the phone. Most emergency phone number lists include the police department, the fire department, and poison control. Also, a list can include numbers for your parents at work, your doctor, your neighbors, and other people in your family.

Stay calm when making an emergency phone call. When you call for help, you will need to give the following information:

- your name
- your location
- the type of emergency
- the condition of the victim if someone is hurt
- what you have done to care for a victim

If you call for help, don't hang up right away. The operator may have more questions for you. The operator can also help you through the emergency.

Your safety always comes first. Get away from danger before you call for help. If you are by yourself and you find someone who is hurt, call for help before giving first aid. If you are with someone else, one person should stay with the victim while the other calls for help. ⍟ 5.F; 5.G

Figure 20 Making an emergency phone call can save someone's life.

Health Journal

In your Health Journal, create an emergency phone number list for your family.

Lesson Review

Using Vocabulary

1. What is first aid? ⍟ 5.F

Understanding Concepts

2. What are five things you need to tell an operator when you make an emergency phone call? ⍟ 5.F; 5.G

Critical Thinking

3. Making Good Decisions Imagine that you see a house on fire. You know that someone lives in the house. What should you do? ⍟ 5.G

Giving First Aid

You may have wondered why some restaurants have posters about choking. These posters show people how to give abdominal thrusts to a choking person.

What You'll Do

- **Explain** how to give abdominal thrusts to an adult. ⭐ 5.F
- **Describe** rescue breathing. ⭐ 5.F
- **Describe** how to treat a victim of poisoning. ⭐ 5.F
- **Describe** how to treat wounds. ⭐ 5.F
- **Compare** the three types of burns. ⭐ 5.F

Terms to Learn

- abdominal thrust
- rescue breathing

Start Off *Write*

How can you help someone who is choking?

An **abdominal thrust** (ab DAHM uh nuhl THRUHST) is the process of applying pressure to a choking person's stomach to force an object out of the throat. An abdominal thrust pushes air out of the lungs. This air dislodges the object that is choking the victim. ⭐ 5.F; 5.G

Giving Abdominal Thrusts

Before you give abdominal thrusts, you need to make sure that the victim is choking. A victim who can speak or cough can still breathe. Don't give abdominal thrusts if a person can still breathe. Keep the victim calm. Let him or her cough until the object comes loose or help arrives. A person who needs abdominal thrusts cannot speak or breathe. He or she will probably hold his or her throat.

Before you give abdominal thrusts, call for help. If the victim is an adult, stand behind the victim. Place the thumb side of your fist against the victim's stomach. Your fist should be between the victim's belly button and breastbone. Cover your fist with your other hand. Quickly thrust inward and upward on the victim's stomach. Thrust five times in a row or until the object comes loose. ⭐ 5.F; 5.G

Figure 21 Learning how to give abdominal thrusts can help you save a choking person's life.

Figure 22 Rescue Breathing for Adults | FIRST AID | Certification required

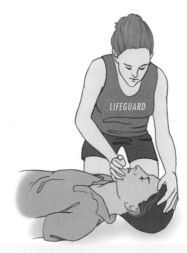

1 First, open the victim's airway. Push down on the forehead, and gently lift the chin up to tilt the victim's head back. Clear any objects out of the victim's mouth. Look at the victim's chest for movement, listen for sounds of breathing, and feel for breath on your cheek.

2 If the person is not breathing, give two slow rescue breaths. With your mouth, make a tight seal around the victim's mouth. Pinch the victim's nose shut. Breathe out, into the victim's mouth. Look to see if the victim's chest is moving up and down while you breathe.

Giving Rescue Breathing

Sometimes, accident victims stop breathing on their own. One way to save someone who isn't breathing is to give rescue breathing. **Rescue breathing** is an emergency technique in which a rescuer gives air to someone who is not breathing. You should not give rescue breathing unless you have been trained in it.

Before giving rescue breathing, call for help. Don't move the victim unless you are sure it is safe to do so. Lay the victim on his or her back. The victim should be on the ground or a hard, flat surface. Start rescue breathing by opening the victim's airway. Tilt the victim's head back, and lift his or her chin. Clear any objects out of the victim's mouth. Look, listen, and feel for breathing. If the victim is not breathing, pinch his or her nose shut. Put your mouth over the victim's mouth. Give two, slow full breaths into the victim's mouth. Watch to make sure the victim's chest is rising. If not, the victim has something stuck in his or her airway. Give abdominal thrusts, or wait until more help arrives. Continue rescue breathing until the victim starts breathing again or help arrives.

Rescue breathing for small children and infants is similar to rescue breathing for adults. However, you should place your mouth over the child's nose as well as his or her mouth. And give infants smaller, faster breaths. ⭐ 5.F; 5.G

Brain Food

Some diseases are spread by saliva. When you give rescue breathing to a victim, you can use a breathing mask to protect you from disease.

Caring for Victims of Poisoning

Many things around your home can cause poisoning. Cleaning products, pesticides, and car fluids are just a few of these things. Some medicines cause poisoning if too much is taken. If you find someone who has been poisoned, ask the victim what he or she ate. If the victim isn't awake, check out the area around the victim. Look for clues about the poison. Is there a bottle or box nearby? Is there a smell that you recognize? You can also look at the victim for clues. Call 911. Then, call your local poison control center for help. An operator will ask you questions and tell you what to do. ✪ 5.F; 5.G

Figure 23 Many common household products can cause poisoning.

Treatment for Bleeding

When treating someone who is bleeding, you should use sterile gloves to prevent the spread of disease.

Treating Wounds

Have you ever scraped your knee? Or have you ever cut your hand? Scrapes and cuts are usually easy to treat. Some scrapes and cuts can be very serious. Deep cuts can be life threatening.

When you help someone treat a cut, wear sterile gloves. Doing so keeps the injury clean. It also protects you from disease. Then, you should try to stop the bleeding. Cover the injury with gauze. Do not remove the gauze. Add more gauze as you need it. Use your hands to put pressure on the cut. This slows down the flow of blood from the cut. Remember that cuts on your head and hands may bleed a lot even if the cut is not large. You can also elevate the injured area. But don't elevate it if doing so makes the injury worse. If bleeding doesn't slow down or stop within a few minutes, call for help. For deep cuts, go to the emergency room even if bleeding has stopped. The cut may need stitches. The table below describes how to take care of cuts and scrapes. ✪ 5.F; 5.G

TABLE 1 Treating Cuts, Scrapes, and Deep Wounds	
Ask yourself . . .	**If your answer is yes, then you should . . .**
Is the scrape or cut minor?	Clean the cut with mild soap and water. Put some antibacterial cream on the cut or scrape. Cover the cut or scrape with a bandage.
Is the cut deep?	Cover the cut with clean gauze. Apply pressure to the cut. Continue to apply pressure until the bleeding stops. If the bleeding doesn't stop quickly, call for help. If the cut is very deep, go to the emergency room. You may need stitches.
Is there a lot of bleeding?	Call for help. Cover the wound with gauze. Apply pressure until help arrives. Add more pieces of gauze if the bleeding continues. Don't lift the gauze from the cut. Raise the injured area to help stop the bleeding.

✪ 5.F; 5.G

Treating Burns

Open flames, hot water or objects, chemicals, and the sun all cause burns. The three kinds of burns are as follows:

- A *first-degree burn* is red, mild, and not very deep. For example, a mild sunburn is usually a first-degree burn.

- *Second-degree burns* are deeper than first-degree burns. They cause blisters and are very painful.

- *Third-degree burns* are dark in color and deeper than second-degree burns. These burns destroy pain receptors, so these burns usually aren't as painful as second-degree burns.

⭐ 5.F; 5.G

Figure 24 Caring for Burns

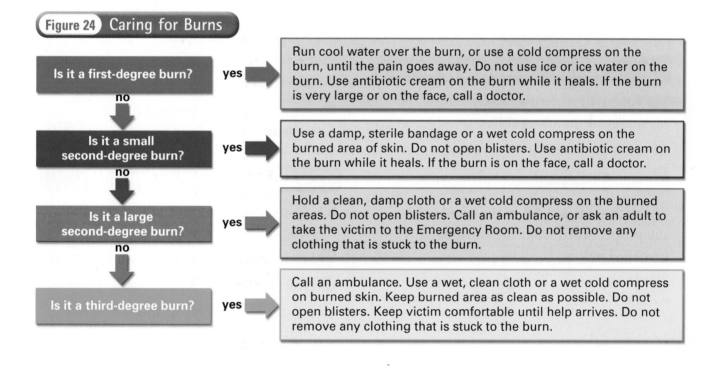

Is it a first-degree burn? **yes** → Run cool water over the burn, or use a cold compress on the burn, until the pain goes away. Do not use ice or ice water on the burn. Use antibiotic cream on the burn while it heals. If the burn is very large or on the face, call a doctor.

no ↓

Is it a small second-degree burn? **yes** → Use a damp, sterile bandage or a wet cold compress on the burned area of skin. Do not open blisters. Use antibiotic cream on the burn while it heals. If the burn is on the face, call a doctor.

no ↓

Is it a large second-degree burn? **yes** → Hold a clean, damp cloth or a wet cold compress on the burned areas. Do not open blisters. Call an ambulance, or ask an adult to take the victim to the Emergency Room. Do not remove any clothing that is stuck to the burn.

no ↓

Is it a third-degree burn? **yes** → Call an ambulance. Use a wet, clean cloth or a wet cold compress on burned skin. Keep burned area as clean as possible. Do not open blisters. Keep victim comfortable until help arrives. Do not remove any clothing that is stuck to the burn.

Lesson Review

Using Vocabulary

1. What is an abdominal thrust?
⭐ 5.F

Understanding Concepts

2. How should you take care of a victim of poisoning? ⭐ 5.F; 5.G

3. What are the three types of burns?

4. How do you care for deep cuts?
⭐ 5.F; 5.G

Critical Thinking

5. Making Good Decisions Imagine that you found someone unconscious on the floor. The victim doesn't have any visible injuries. You notice a funny smell in the air. What should you do?
⭐ 5.F; 5.G

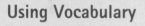

🔲 **internet** connect

www.scilinks.org/health
Topic: First Aid
HealthLinks code: HD4042

HEALTH LINKS. Maintained by the National Science Teachers Association

Chapter Summary

■ An accident is an unexpected event that may lead to injury. ■ Violence is using physical force to hurt someone or cause damage. ■ Use a pole or life preserver to save someone who is drowning. ■ Examples of weather emergencies and natural disasters are thunderstorms, tornadoes, hurricanes, floods, and earthquakes. ■ First aid is emergency medical care for someone who is hurt or sick. ■ Do not give first aid if you are in danger or are not trained. ■ An abdominal thrust is the process of applying pressure to a choking person's stomach to force an object out of the throat. ■ Rescue breathing is an emergency technique in which air is given to someone who is not breathing.

Using Vocabulary

For each pair of terms, describe how the meanings of the terms differ.

1 smoke detector/fire extinguisher

2 abdominal thrust/rescue breathing

For each sentence, fill in the blank with the proper word from the word bank provided below.

thunderstorm	earthquake
first aid	natural disaster
flood	violence
tornado	hurricane
accident	

3 An overflowing of water into areas that are normally dry is called a(n) ___.

4 A(n) ___ is an unexpected event that may cause injury.

5 A(n) ___ is a shaking of the Earth's surface.

6 A spinning column of air that has high winds and touches the ground is a(n) ___.

7 Using physical force to hurt someone or cause damage is called ___.

8 A(n) ___ is a natural event that causes widespread damage.

9 ___ is emergency medical care for someone who is hurt or sick.

Understanding Concepts

10 How can you prevent falls, fires, and electrical shock? ✪ 5.G

11 List five ways to stay safe while skating. ✪ 5.G

12 How can you avoid violence? ✪ 5.H

13 List the seven ways to stay safe from injury. ✪ 5.G

14 What are five ways to stay safe while boating? ✪ 5.G

15 Describe the water survival float. ✪ 5.G

16 Why should you get into water feet first if you don't know how deep it is? ✪ 5.G

17 When should you give first aid? ✪ 5.F

18 What five things do you need to tell a 911 operator during an emergency? ✪ 5.G

19 Describe abdominal thrusts and rescue breathing. ✪ 5.F

Applying Concepts

20 Smoke detectors should be installed in every room of your home. You should also check smoke detectors once a month to make sure they are still working. Why is it so important to take these two steps? ⭐ 5.G

21 In the last 50 years, the number of people killed during weather emergencies has gotten smaller. What could explain this trend?

22 During the water survival float, a swimmer doesn't move much. In fact, the less a swimmer moves, the better. Why is it so important to keep movement to a minimum during the water survival float? ⭐ 5.G

23 When you give rescue breathing to a small child or infant, you should put your mouth over the victim's mouth and nose. Why don't you cover only the victim's mouth? ⭐ 5.F

Making Good Decisions

24 Lauren doesn't feel safe. A gang has been giving her a hard time. Most of the time, she can avoid the gang, but sometimes doing so is pretty hard. What should Lauren do to stay safe? ⭐ 5.H; 7.B; 7.E

25 Pablo learned to skate a few weeks ago. He's been having a good time, and he's learned a lot. Now, his friends want him to try some tricks that he hasn't learned yet. What should Pablo do? ⭐ 5.G; 7.E

26 Tony is eating at a restaurant. Someone at the next table starts choking. The person is coughing and pointing to his throat. What should Tony do? ⭐ 5.F

Interpreting Graphics

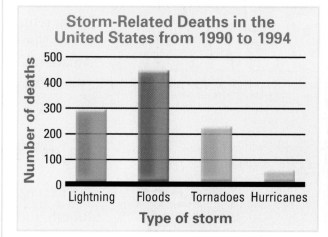

Use the figure above to answer questions 27–31. ⭐ M: 6.10D; 6.11A

27 Which weather emergency causes the most deaths? Which causes the least?

28 How many people were killed by tornadoes? by floods?

29 If lightning killed 3,200 people in 1940, how many fewer people were killed between 1990 and 1994?

30 What could explain why floods kill more people than other types of storms do?

31 Fewer people died in tornadoes between 1990 and 1994 than died in tornadoes in 1940. What could explain this?

Reading Checkup

Take a minute to review your answers to the Health IQ questions at the beginning of this chapter. How has reading this chapter improved your Health IQ?

Using Refusal Skills

Using refusal skills is saying no to things you don't want to do. You can also use refusal skills to avoid dangerous situations. Complete the following activity to develop your refusal skills.

Rajesh's Refusal

Setting the Scene

ACT 1

Rajesh and his family are camping in a state park. One afternoon, Rajesh goes to swim in the lake that borders the park. At the lake, he meets a group of teens. A teen named Kyle suggests jumping off steep rocks into the water. All of the other teens want to try, but Rajesh doesn't think it is a good idea. Kyle and the other teens start calling Rajesh a chicken. ✬ 5.G; 7.B

The 5 Steps of Using Refusal Skills

1. Avoid dangerous situations.
2. Say "No."
3. Stand your ground.
4. Stay focused on the issue.
5. Walk away.

Guided Practice

Practice with a Friend

Form a group of three. Have one person play the role of Rajesh and another person play the role of Kyle. Have the third person be an observer. Walking through each of the five steps of using refusal skills, role-play Rajesh responding to Kyle. Kyle should try to convince Rajesh to jump from the rocks. The observer will take notes, which will include observations about what the person playing Rajesh did well and suggestions of ways to improve. Stop after each step to evaluate the process.

Independent Practice

Check Yourself

After you have completed the guided practice, go through Act 1 again without stopping at each step. Answer the questions below to review what you did.

1. What is dangerous about the situation that Rajesh is in?

2. Which refusal skills are the most effective in this situation? Explain your answer.

3. What could Rajesh say to the other teens when he is standing his ground? ⭐ 7.B; 7.E

4. Why could it be difficult for you to say no in a peer pressure situation? ⭐ 11.C

ACT 2 — On Your Own

Rajesh was able to talk some of the other teens out of jumping from the rocks. As they walk away from the river, one of the teens suggests going on a hike. Rajesh says that he needs to tell his parents where he is going, but the other teens don't want to waste time walking back to Rajesh's campsite. Write a skit about the conversation between Rajesh and the other teens. Be sure to stress the five steps of using refusal skills in your skit. ⭐ 7.B; 7.E

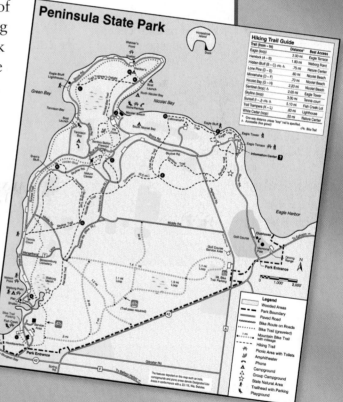

Appendix

Topic: Food Guide Pyramid
Go To: go.hrw.com
Keyword: HOLT PYRAMID
Visit the HRW Web site for updates on the Food Guide Pyramid.

The Food Guide Pyramid

Do you know which foods you need to eat to stay healthy? How much of each food do you need to eat? The Food Guide Pyramid is a tool you can use to make sure you're eating healthfully. Each of the major food groups has its own block on the pyramid. The larger the block, the more you need to eat from that food group. The smaller the block, the less you need to eat from that food group. Use the Food Guide Pyramid as a guide for choosing a healthy diet!

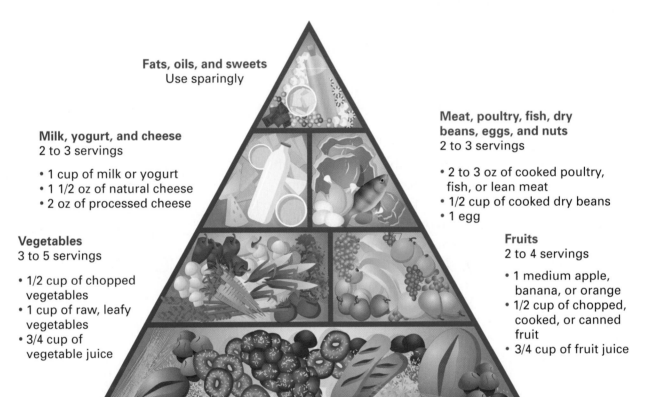

Fats, oils, and sweets
Use sparingly

Milk, yogurt, and cheese
2 to 3 servings

• 1 cup of milk or yogurt
• 1 1/2 oz of natural cheese
• 2 oz of processed cheese

Meat, poultry, fish, dry beans, eggs, and nuts
2 to 3 servings

• 2 to 3 oz of cooked poultry, fish, or lean meat
• 1/2 cup of cooked dry beans
• 1 egg

Vegetables
3 to 5 servings

• 1/2 cup of chopped vegetables
• 1 cup of raw, leafy vegetables
• 3/4 cup of vegetable juice

Fruits
2 to 4 servings

• 1 medium apple, banana, or orange
• 1/2 cup of chopped, cooked, or canned fruit
• 3/4 cup of fruit juice

Bread, cereal, rice, and pasta
6 to 11 servings

• 1 slice of bread
• 1 oz of ready-to-eat cereal
• 1/2 cup of rice or pasta
• 1/2 cup of cooked cereal

Alternative Food Guide Pyramids

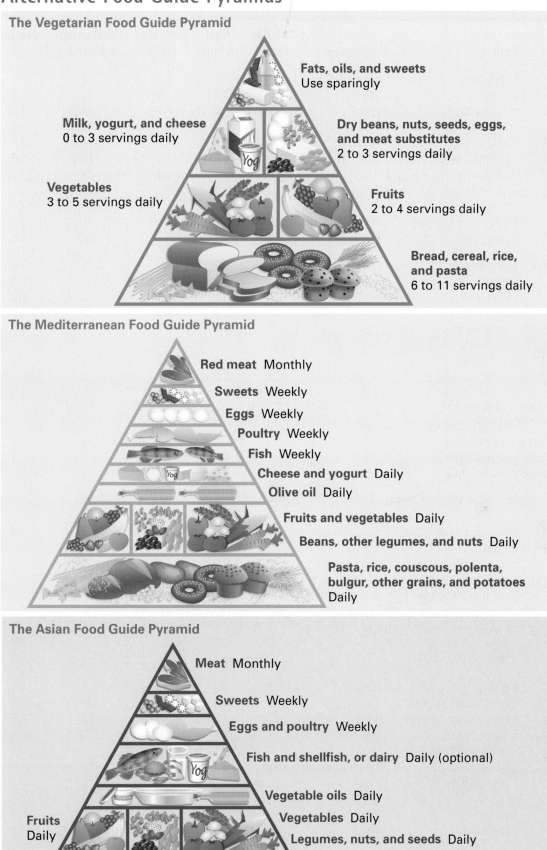

The Vegetarian Food Guide Pyramid

Fats, oils, and sweets
Use sparingly

Milk, yogurt, and cheese
0 to 3 servings daily

Dry beans, nuts, seeds, eggs, and meat substitutes
2 to 3 servings daily

Vegetables
3 to 5 servings daily

Fruits
2 to 4 servings daily

Bread, cereal, rice, and pasta
6 to 11 servings daily

The Mediterranean Food Guide Pyramid

Red meat Monthly

Sweets Weekly

Eggs Weekly

Poultry Weekly

Fish Weekly

Cheese and yogurt Daily

Olive oil Daily

Fruits and vegetables Daily

Beans, other legumes, and nuts Daily

Pasta, rice, couscous, polenta, bulgur, other grains, and potatoes Daily

The Asian Food Guide Pyramid

Meat Monthly

Sweets Weekly

Eggs and poultry Weekly

Fish and shellfish, or dairy Daily (optional)

Vegetable oils Daily

Vegetables Daily

Fruits Daily

Legumes, nuts, and seeds Daily

Rice, noodles, breads, corn, and other grains Daily

TABLE 1 Calorie and Nutrient Content of Common Foods

Food group	Food	Serving size	Calories (kcal)	Total fat (g)	Saturated fat (g)	Total carbo-hydrate (g)	Protein (g)
Bread, cereal, rice and pasta	bagel, plain	1 bagel	314	1.8	0.3	51	10.0
	biscuit	1 biscuit	101	5.0	1.2	13	2.0
	bread, white	1 slice	76	1.0	0.4	14	2.0
	bread, whole wheat	1 slice	86	1.0	0.3	16	3.0
	matzo	1 matzo	111	0.2	0.0	22	3.5
	pita bread, wheat	1 pita	165	1.0	0.1	33	5.0
	rice, brown	1/2 cup	110	1.0	0.2	23	2.0
	rice, white and enriched	1/2 cup	133	0.0	0.1	29	2.0
	tortilla, corn and plain	1 tortilla, 6 in.	58	0.7	0.1	12	2.0
	tortilla, flour	1 tortilla, 8 in.	104	2.3	0.6	18	3.0
Vegetables	broccoli, cooked	1 cup	27	0.0	0.0	5	3.0
	carrots, raw	1 baby carrot	4	0.0	0.0	1	0.0
	celery, raw	4 small stalks	10	0.1	0.0	2	0.5
	corn, cooked	1 ear	83	1.0	0.0	19	2.6
	cucumber, raw with peel	1/8 cup	25	0.1	0.0	6	0.6
	green beans, cooked	1 cup	44	0.4	0.0	10	2.4
	onions, raw, sliced	1/4 cup	11	0.0	0.0	3	0.3
	potatoes, baked with skin	1/2 cup	66	0.1	0.0	15	1.0
							1.4
	salad, mixed green, no dressing	1 cup	10	1.0	0.0	2	
							0.0
	spinach, fresh	1 cup	7	0.1	0.0	1	0.9
Fruits	apple, raw, with skin	1 medium apple	81	0.1	0.1	21	0.2
	banana, fresh	1 medium banana	114	1.0	0.2	27	1.0
	cherries, sweet, fresh	1 cup, with pits	84	0.3	0.0	19	1.4
	grapes	1/2 cup	62	0.1	0.0	16	0.6
	orange, fresh	1 large orange	85	0.0	0.0	21	1.7
	peach, fresh	1 medium peach	37	0.0	0.0	9	1.0
	pear, fresh	1 medium pear	123	1.0	0.0	32	0.8
	raisins, seedless, dry	1 cup	495	0.2	0.0	131	5.3
	strawberries, fresh	1 cup	46	0.0	0.0	11	0.9
	tomatoes, raw	1 cup	31	0.5	0.0	7	1.3
	watermelon	1/2 cup	26	0.0	0.0	6	0.0
Meat, poultry, fish, dry beans, eggs, and nuts	bacon	3 pieces	109	9.0	3.3	0	6.0
	beans, black, cooked	1/2 cup	114	0.0	0.1	20	7.6
	beans, refried, canned	1/2 cup	127	1.0	0.1	23	8.0
	chicken breast, fried meat and skin	1 split breast	364	18.5	4.9	13	34.8
	chicken breast, skinless, grilled	1 split breast	142	3.0	0.9	73	27.0
	chorizo	1 link	273	23.0	8.6	1	14.5
	egg, boiled	1 large egg	78	5.3	1.0	0	6.0
	humus	1/4 cup	106	5.2	0.0	13	3.0

TABLE 1 Calorie and Nutrient Content of Common Foods *(continued)*

Food group	Food	Serving size	Calories (kcal)	Total fat (g)	Saturated fat (g)	Total carbo-hydrate (g)	Protein (g)
Meat, poultry, fish, dry beans, eggs, and nuts *(continued)*	peanut butter	2 Tbsp	190	16.0	3.0	7	8.0
	pork chop	3 oz	300	24.0	9.7	0	19.7
	roast beef	3 oz	179	6.5	2.3	0	28.1
	shrimp, breaded and fried	4 large shrimp	73	3.5	0.6	3	6.4
	steak, beef, broiled	6 oz	344	14.0	5.2	0	52.0
	sunflower seeds	1/4 cup	208	19.0	2.0	5	7.0
	tofu	1/2 cup	97	5.6	0.8	4	10.1
	tuna, canned in water	3 oz	109	2.5	0.7	0	20.1
	turkey, roasted	3 oz	145	4.2	1.4	0	24.9
Milk, yogurt, and cheese	cheese, American, prepackaged	1 slice	70	5.0	2.0	2	4.0
	cheese, cheddar	1 oz	114	9.0	6.0	0	7.1
	cheese, cottage, lowfat	1/2 cup	102	1.4	0.9	4	7.0
	cheese, cream	1 Tbsp	51	5.0	3.2	0	1.1
	milk, chocolate, reduced fat (2%)	1 cup	179	5.0	3.1	26	8.0
	milk, lowfat (1%)	1 cup	102	3.0	1.6	12	8.0
	milk, reduced fat (2%)	1 cup	122	5.0	2.9	12	8.1
	milk, skim, fat free	1 cup	91	0.0	0.0	12	8.0
	milk, whole	1 cup	149	8.0	5.1	11	8.0
	yogurt, lowfat, fruit flavored	1 cup	231	3.0	2.0	47	12.0
Fats, oils, and sweets	brownie	1 square	227	10.0	2.0	30	1.5
	butter	1 tsp	36	3.7	2.4	0	0.0
	candy, chocolate bar	1.3 oz	226	14.0	8.1	26	3.0
	soda, no ice	12 oz	184	0.0	0.0	38	0.0
	cheesecake	1 piece	660	46.0	28.0	52	11.0
	cookies, chocolate chip	1 cookie	59	2.5	0.8	8	0.6
	cookies, oatmeal	1 cookie	113	3.0	0.8	20	1.0
	gelatin dessert, flavored	1/2 cup	80	0.0	0.0	19	2.0
	ice-cream cone, one scoop regular ice cream	1 cone	178	8.0	4.9	22	3.0
	margarine, stick	1 tsp	34	3.8	0.7	0	0.0
	mayonnaise, regular	1 Tbsp	57	4.9	0.7	4	0.1
	pie, apple, double crust	1 piece	411	18.0	4.0	58	3.7
	popcorn, microwave, with butter	1/3 bag	170	12.0	2.5	26	2.0
	potato chips	1 oz	150	10.0	3.0	10	1.0
	pretzels	10 twists	229	2.1	0.5	48	5.5
	tortilla chips, plain	1 oz	140	7.3	1.4	18	2.0

APPENDIX

The Physical Activity Pyramid

How often do you exercise during the week? Do you think you get enough exercise to stay fit? Take a look at the Physical Activity Pyramid to find out if you're exercising enough to stay fit!

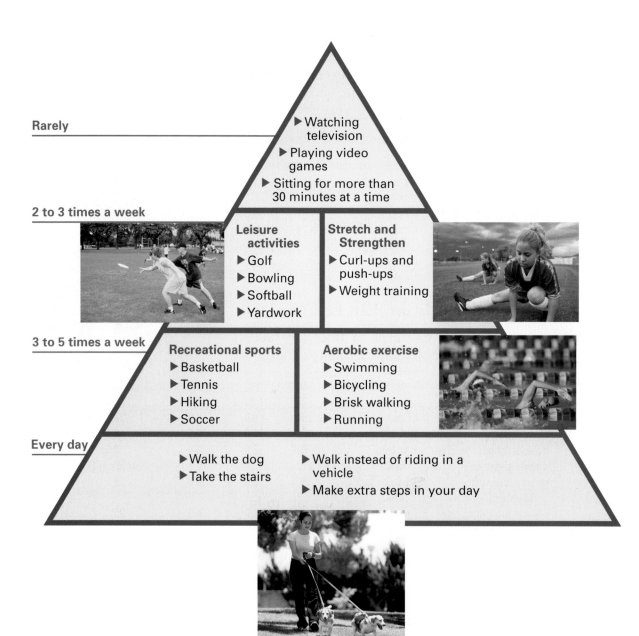

Rarely
- Watching television
- Playing video games
- Sitting for more than 30 minutes at a time

2 to 3 times a week

Leisure activities
- Golf
- Bowling
- Softball
- Yardwork

Stretch and Strengthen
- Curl-ups and push-ups
- Weight training

3 to 5 times a week

Recreational sports
- Basketball
- Tennis
- Hiking
- Soccer

Aerobic exercise
- Swimming
- Bicycling
- Brisk walking
- Running

Every day
- Walk the dog
- Take the stairs
- Walk instead of riding in a vehicle
- Make extra steps in your day

Target Heart Rate Zone

What Is the Target Heart Rate Zone?

When you exercise, you need to exercise hard enough to reach your target heart rate zone. The target heart rate zone is a heart rate range that you should exercise in to ensure that your fitness improves.

The target heart rate zone is based on maximum heart rate (MHR). MHR is the maximum number of times that your heart can beat per minute when you exercise. MHR is different for everyone, and it usually lowers as you get older. You need to see a fitness specialist to find your actual MHR, but a formula can be used to estimate your MHR.

After you know your MHR, you can calculate your target heart rate zone. Generally, the target heart rate zone is 60 to 85 percent of your MHR. But the target heart rate zone may vary according to a person's fitness goals. For example, athletes may have a target heart rate zone that is as high as 90 percent of their MHR.

How Do You Calculate Your Target Heart Rate Zone?

You need to see a fitness specialist to find your actual MHR, but you can use the following formula to estimate your MHR:

$$MHR = 220 - your\ age$$

So, a 12-year-old would have an estimated MHR of 208.

$$MHR = 220 - 12 = 208$$

After you know your estimated MHR, use the following equations to calculate your target heart rate zone:

$$60\ percent\ of\ MHR = MHR \times 0.6$$

$$85\ percent\ of\ MHR = MHR \times 0.85$$

For a 12-year-old, the calculations would be as follows:

$$60\ percent\ of\ MHR = 208 \times 0.6 = 125$$

$$85\ percent\ of\ MHR = 208 \times 0.85 = 177$$

So, a 12-year-old's target heart rate zone is 125 to 177 heartbeats per minute.

Being Safe

Fire Safety

Every year, thousands of homes and other buildings are destroyed by fire. Many people suffer burns and smoke injuries. Do you know what to do if a fire happens in your home?

Fires are dangerous. But you can take steps to prevent fires and to escape them if they happen. To ensure your safety and the safety of your family, you can do the following:

- With your family, make a fire evacuation plan by drawing a map of your home and marking escape routes from every room. Make sure everyone has at least two ways to leave the building. Don't forget to mark a meeting place outside and away from the building. Then, schedule times to practice your fire evacuation plan. If you practice your plan, you'll be able to get out of your home more quickly during a fire.

- Ask your parents to put smoke detectors in every large room or hallway. A smoke detector will sound an alarm if smoke is in the air. So, if you're asleep when a fire starts, a smoke detector can save your life by waking you up. You should also test your smoke detectors once a month and replace the batteries at least once a year or as necessary.

- Keep fire extinguishers in areas where fires are likely to start, such as the kitchen or garage. A fire extinguisher releases chemicals that put a fire out. There are different types of fire extinguishers, so make sure you have the right one for your home. Also, read the instructions on the fire extinguisher so you know how to use it. Fire extinguishers can be used to put out most fires. Sometimes, you can use water to put out a fire. However, never use water on grease fires. For these fires, you can use a fire extinguisher, pan lid, salt, or baking soda to smother the fire.

- Always remember that putting out a fire is dangerous. You should never do so if your safety is at risk. Leave the area and call for help from another location. While you are waiting for help, remember that you should never go back into a burning building. Your safety should always come first.

Hot Weather Safety

Do you drink enough water on a hot day? Not drinking enough water on a hot day can cause injury to your body.

On a hot day, your body uses water when you sweat to stay cool. If you don't drink enough water to replace the water you lose through sweat, you can get heat exhaustion. Heat exhaustion is an injury caused by too much water loss. People with heat exhaustion have a headache, feel dizzy and sick to their stomach, and have clammy skin. If you have these symptoms, you should find a cool, shady place and drink plenty of fluids. If symptoms don't improve, call for help immediately.

Another heat injury is heatstroke. Heatstroke is a severe and sometimes life-threatening injury that results from the body's failure to regulate, or control, its temperature. People with heatstroke can't sweat, so their body temperature rises. Victims sometimes collapse and have seizures. Heatstroke victims should be taken to the emergency room immediately.

Cold Weather Safety

Have you ever noticed that you shiver on a cold day? Shivering helps your body stay warm. Sometimes, people who have been exposed to the cold for a long time can't stop shivering. Not being able to stop shivering is a sign of hypothermia. Hypothermia is a below-normal body temperature. In addition to shivering, hypothermia victims feel sleepy, have slurred speech, and seem confused. Victims of hypothermia should be kept warm. Remove any wet clothing, and wrap the victim in dry blankets. Call for medical help right away.

Another cold injury is frostbite. Frostbite is damage to skin and tissues that is caused by extreme cold. It usually affects the fingers, toes, ears, and nose. The affected area will be pale, stiff, and numb. For frostbite victims, call for medical help. Place the affected area in lukewarm water until help arrives.

You can avoid cold injuries by dressing in layers on a cold day. Also, wear gloves and a hat to protect your hands and ears. Limit your exposure to the outdoors on extremely cold days, and go inside if you start shivering. If you get wet on a cold day, go inside immediately and put on dry clothes.

Emergency Kit

A disaster can happen anytime and anywhere. During a disaster, people lose power, gas, and water. Sometimes, people are not able to get help for a few days. You can prepare for disasters by making an emergency kit. There are six basic things you should keep stocked in your emergency kit.

1. **Water** Store water in plastic containers. You'll need water for drinking, food preparation, and cleaning. Store a gallon of water per person per day. Have at least three days' worth of water in your kit.

2. **Food** Store at least three days' worth of nonperishable food. These foods include canned foods, freeze-dried foods, canned juices, and high-energy foods, such as nutrition bars. You should also keep vitamins in your emergency kit.

3. **First–Aid Kit** Someone may get hurt, so you'll want to have plenty of first-aid supplies. Include the following supplies in your first-aid kit:

   - self-adhesive bandages
   - gauze pads
   - rolled gauze
   - adhesive tape
   - antibacterial ointment and cleansers
   - thermometer
   - scissors, tweezers, and razor blades
   - sterile gloves and breathing mask
   - over-the-counter medicines

4. **Clothing and Bedding** An emergency kit should include at least one complete change of clothing and shoes per person. You should also store blankets or sleeping bags, rain gear, and thermal underwear.

5. **Tools and Supplies** Always keep your emergency kit stocked with a flashlight, battery-operated radio, and extra batteries. Also, include a can opener, cooking supplies, candles, waterproof matches, fire extinguisher, tape, and hardware tools. You should also store emergency signal supplies, such as signal flares, whistles, and signal mirrors.

6. **Special Items** Be sure to remember family members who have special needs. For example, store formula, baby food, and diapers for infants. For adults, you might keep contact lens supplies, special medications, and extra eyeglasses in your emergency kit.

Staying Home Alone

It is not unusual for teens to spend time home alone after school. Their parents may still be at work. Or they may be running errands. If you spend time at home alone, remember the following safety tips:

- Lock the doors and make sure your windows are locked.

- Never let anyone who calls or comes to your door know that you are home alone.

- Don't open the door for anyone you don't know or for anyone that isn't supposed to be at your home. If the visitor is delivering a package, ask him or her to leave it at the door. If the visitor wants to use the phone, send him or her to a phone booth. If the visitor is selling something, you can tell him or her through the door, "We're not interested."

- If a visitor doesn't leave or you see someone hanging around your home, call a trusted neighbor or the police for help.

- If you answer the phone, don't tell the caller anything personal. Offer to take a message without revealing you're alone. If the call becomes uncomfortable or mean, hang up the phone and tell your parents about it when they get home. You can also avoid answering the phone altogether when you're alone. Then, the caller can leave a message on the answering machine.

- Keep an emergency phone number list next to every phone in your home. If there is an emergency, call 911. Don't panic. Follow the operator's instructions. If the emergency is a fire, immediately leave the building and go to a trusted neighbor's home to call for help.

- Find an interesting way to spend your time. Time passes more quickly when you're not bored. Get a head start on your homework, read a book or magazine, clean your room, or work on a hobby. Avoid watching television unless your parents have given you permission to watch a specific program.

- Consider having a friend stay with you. But do so only if your parents have given you permission to have your friend over. That way, you won't be alone and you will have someone to pass the time with you.

- Remember your safety behaviors. By practicing them, you can make sure you stay safe.

☑ Think before you act.　☑ Use safety equipment.
☑ Pay attention.　☑ Change risky behavior.
☑ Know your limits.　☑ Change risky situations.
☑ Practice refusal skills.

Computer Posture

You know that computers can be both fun and helpful. You can play games on a computer, research and write a paper, and e-mail your friends. But sitting in front of a computer for hours at a time can also strain your eyes, neck, wrists, spine, and hands. So, it is important to practice good posture when using a computer. To help prevent injuries related to using a computer, follow the tips listed below.

Tips for Good Computer Posture

- Make sure your entire body faces the computer screen and keyboard.
- Position the computer screen so that you have to look slightly down to see it. The screen should be 18 to 24 inches from your eyes.
- Keep your feet flat on the floor.
- Make sure your thighs are parallel to the floor. You may have to adjust your chair height.
- Keep your shoulders and neck relaxed.
- Keep your back straight, and make sure you have good lower back support.
- Keep your wrists straight while you are typing. Do not flex your wrists up or down.
- Your arms should be bent at a 90° angle.
- Take breaks every 30 minutes to an hour. Stretch, and walk around.

▶ Entire body faces the computer screen and keyboard

▶ Computer screen is slightly below eye level

▶ Feet flat on the floor

▶ Thighs parallel to the floor

▶ Shoulders and neck relaxed

▶ Back straight

▶ Wrists straight

▶ Arms bent at a 90° angle

Internet Safety

The Internet is a wonderful tool. It allows you to communicate with people, access information, and educate yourself. You can also use it to have fun. But when using any tool, there are certain precautions or safety measures you must take. Using the Internet is no different. Listed below are some rules to follow to make sure you stay safe when you are using the Internet.

Rules for Internet Safety

- Set up rules with your parents or another trusted adult about what time of day you can use the Internet, how long you can use the Internet, and what sites you can visit on the Internet. Follow the rules that have been set.

- Do not give out personal information, such as your address, telephone number, or the name and location of your school.

- If you find any information that makes you uncomfortable, tell a parent or another trusted adult immediately.

- Do not respond to any messages that make you uncomfortable. If you receive such a message, tell your parents or another trusted adult immediately.

- Never agree to meet with anyone before talking to your parents or another trusted adult. If your parents give you permission to meet someone, make sure you do so in a public place. Have an adult come with you.

- Do not send a picture of yourself or any other information without first checking with your parents or a trusted adult.

Baby Sitter Safety

Baby-sitting is an important job. You're responsible for taking care of another person's children. You have to make decisions not only for yourself but also for other people. So, you have to make good decisions. Keep the following tips in mind when you baby-sit.

Before You Baby-Sit

- Take a baby-sitting course or a first-aid class.

- Find out what time you should arrive and arrange for your transportation to and from the home.

- Ask the parents how long they plan to be away.

- Find out how many children you will be caring for and what your responsibilities are.

- Settle on how much the parents will pay you for your work.

- Consider visiting the family while the parents are home so you can get to know the children a few days before you baby-sit.

When You Arrive

- Arrive early so the parents can give you information about caring for the children. Ask the parents about the children's eating habits, TV habits, and bedtime routine.

- Find out where the parents are going. Write down the address and phone number for where they will be and put it next to the phone. Find out when they plan to return. If the parents have a cellular phone, be sure to get that number, too.

- Know where the emergency numbers are posted. Also, make sure you have the address for the home so that you can give it to an operator in the event of an emergency.

- If you are watching toddlers or infants, find out where their formula and diaper supplies are stored.

- Learn where the family keeps their first-aid supplies. If the children need any medicine while you care for them, make sure you know how to give it to them. Remember that you shouldn't give children medicine unless you have the parents' permission to do so.

- Ask if the children have any special needs. For example, some children are diabetic or asthmatic. Make sure you know what to do if they have any trouble.

While You Are Baby-Sitting

- Never leave a child alone, even for a short time.

- Don't leave an infant alone on a changing table, sofa, or bed.

- Check on the children often, even when they're sleeping.

- Don't leave children alone in the bathtub or near a pool.

- Keep breakable and dangerous objects out of the reach of children.

- Keep the doors locked. Unless the parents have given you permission, do not open the door for anyone.

- If the phone rings, take a message. Do not let the caller know that you are the baby sitter and that the parents are not home.

- If the child gets hurt or sick, call the parents. Don't try to take care of it yourself. In case of a serious emergency, call 911. Then, call the parents.

FUN THINGS YOU CAN DO WHILE YOU BABY-SIT

Baby-sitting is a huge responsibility. But it is also very rewarding. Children love it when you pay attention to them and when you play with them. Don't be afraid to get down on the floor with them. They like you to play at their level. Consider doing the following fun activities, but remember to always get the parents' permission, first!

- Take children outside or to a local park to play.

- Read stories to each other. Let the children pick their favorite story.

- Go to story time at the local library.

- Draw pictures or color in coloring books. Take this a step further and pretend you have an art gallery in the house. Hang up the pictures and pretend to be visiting the gallery.

- Pretend you are at a restaurant during mealtimes. Have the children make up menus and pretend to be waiters.

- Plan a scavenger hunt.

- Bring some simple craft items for the children, and let them get creative.

- Play board games or card games.

Promises for Great Health

Have you ever made a promise to yourself? Maybe you promised yourself that you would make better grades or that you would exercise more. Making promises to yourself and keeping them is a good way to improve your health and overall wellness. Here are some other promises you can make to achieve wellness.

Assessing Your Health

▶ I promise to assess all four parts of my health to identify my strengths and my weaknesses.

▶ I promise to list the major stressors in my life and to find ways to manage them.

▶ I promise to evaluate my nutritional habits and to adjust my eating habits if needed.

▶ I promise to evaluate my self-esteem and to use strategies for building healthy self-esteem.

▶ I promise to monitor my heart rate as I exercise so that I can track my fitness level.

▶ I promise to evaluate my organizational skills and to improve them if necessary.

Making Good Decisions

▶ I promise to protect my personal safety during emergencies.

▶ I promise to make healthy decisions about food when making meals at home and eating out.

▶ I promise to make good decisions that are not influenced by negative peer pressure.

▶ I promise to consider my values before making any decision.

▶ I promise to weigh the consequences of each option before making a decision.

Setting Goals

▶ I promise to set a goal of making my home safer.

▶ I promise to make a plan to build healthy self-esteem and a healthy body image.

▶ I promise to make a plan to practice better nutrition and manage my weight healthfully.

▶ I promise to pay attention to the news so that I can stay aware of what is happening in the world and can learn from other people's experiences.

▶ I promise to set realistic and challenging goals for myself.

▶ I promise to set short-term goals that will help me meet my long-term goals.

Using Refusal Skills

▶ I promise to use refusal skills to avoid violence at school.

▶ I promise to refuse to ride with anyone who has been drinking.

▶ I promise to practice using refusal skills so that I will know how to respond if I am ever offered drugs.

▶ I promise to help my younger siblings refuse drugs by setting a good example and discussing the consequences of drug abuse with him or her.

▶ I promise to form a support group with my friends and family to help me deal with negative peer pressure.

▶ I promise to talk to a trusted adult if I need help walking away from a dangerous situation.

▶ I promise to abstain from sexual activity.

Communicating Effectively

▶ I promise to find healthy ways to express my emotions.

▶ I promise not to use violence to express my emotions.

▶ I promise to use good listening skills when talking with others.

▶ I promise to be aware of my body language and the body language of others.

▶ I promise to think before I speak and to choose my words carefully.

Coping

▶ I promise to find positive ways to deal with an injury or illness.

▶ I promise to manage my stress by prioritizing my activities and schoolwork.

▶ I promise to use healthy means of coping, such as talking with parents and friends.

▶ I promise to use positive self-talk.

Evaluating Media Messages

▶ I promise to be aware of the media's influence on my body image and self-esteem.

▶ I promise to look at advertisements for tobacco and other drugs with the understanding that the advertisements do not show the negative effects of drugs.

▶ I promise to read the fine print in advertisements for medicines to learn about dangerous side effects.

▶ I promise to compare information from different media sources to determine which source is most objective.

▶ I promise to be aware of the messages that the media presents about violence and dating relationships.

Practicing Wellness

▶ I promise to learn about any history of noninfectious diseases in my family and to take steps to avoid the risk factors of these diseases.

▶ I promise to schedule free time for myself every day.

▶ I promise to take care of my body by drinking water, getting enough sleep, exercising, and eating healthy foods.

▶ I promise to take care of my emotional health by talking with people when I have emotional problems.

▶ I promise to visit a doctor regularly for physical checkups.

▶ I promise to maintain good posture.

▶ I promise to practice behaviors that ensure my safety and the safety of my family.

▶ I promise to develop my refusal skills, my conflict-management skills, and my negotiation skills so that I can avoid violent or dangerous situations.

Being a Wise Consumer

▶ I promise to buy and use only well-fitting and appropriate safety gear for my sports activities.

▶ I promise to conserve resources by buying products that have little packaging or packaging that can be reused or recycled.

▶ I promise to research products before purchasing them and to evaluate them after using them.

▶ I promise to find services that can help me deal with the physical, mental, emotional, and social changes of adolescence.

▶ I promise to evaluate sources of information for bias.

Glossary

A

abdominal thrusts (ab DAHM uh nuhl THRUHSTS) the act of applying pressure to a choking person's stomach to force an object out of the throat (346)

abstinence (AB stuh nuhns) the refusal to take part in an activity that puts your health or the health of others at risk (103, 226) (See also *sexual abstinence*.)

abuse (uh BYOOS) the harmful or offensive treatment of one person by another person; the purposeful incorrect use of drugs or the use of an illegal drug (92, 292)

accident an unexpected event that may lead to injury or death (326)

acne an inflammation of the skin that happens when pores of the skin become clogged with dirt and oil (144)

adolescence (AD'l ES'ns) the stage of development during which humans grow from childhood to adulthood (200)

adulthood the period of life that follows adolescence and that ends at death (204)

affection a feeling of liking or fondness (89, 102)

AIDS acquired immune deficiency syndrome (uh KWIERD im MYOON dee FISH uhn see SIN DROHM), an illness that is caused by HIV infection and that makes an infected person more likely to get unusual forms of cancer and infection because HIV attacks the body's immune system (224)

alcohol a liquid that can affect the way people think and act when they drink it (304)

alcoholism a disease caused by addiction to alcohol; a physical and psychological dependence on alcohol (315)

anger a strong negative feeling toward someone or something that is caused by a sense of being hurt or wronged (120)

anorexia nervosa (AN uh REKS ee uh nuhr VOH suh) an eating disorder that involves self-starvation, an unhealthy body image, and extreme weight loss (74)

artery a blood vessel that carries blood away from the heart (176)

assertiveness defending one's views in a positive manner (30)

attitude the way in which you act, think, or feel that causes you to make particular choices (10)

B

bacteria extremely small, single-celled organisms that do not have a nucleus; single-celled microorganisms that are found everywhere (219)

behavior the way that a person chooses to respond or act (84)

binge eating disorder an eating disorder in which a person has difficulty controlling how much food he or she eats (75)

blood alcohol concentration (BAC) the percentage of alcohol in a person's blood (311)

blood pressure the force that blood exerts on the inside walls of a blood vessel (176)

body image the way that you see yourself and imagine your body (62)

body language a way of communicating by using facial expressions, hand gestures, and posture (83)

body system a group of organs that work together to complete a specific task in the body (166)

bone a living organ of the skeletal system that is made of bone cells, connective tissues, and minerals (170)

bone marrow the soft tissue inside a bone (170)

brain the major organ of the nervous system; the mass of nervous tissue that is located inside the skull (180)

brainstorming the act of thinking of all of the ways to carry out a decision (25)

bulimia nervosa (boo LEE mee uh nuhr VOH suh) an eating disorder in which a person eats a large amount of food and then tries to remove the food from his or her body (74)

C

calcium (KAL see uhm) a mineral that makes bones strong and healthy (183)

Calorie a unit used to measure the amount of energy that the body gets from food (268)

cancer a disease in which cells grow uncontrollably and invade and destroy healthy tissues (309)

capillary (KAP uh LER ee) a tiny blood vessel that carries blood between arteries and veins (176)

carbohydrate (KAHR boh HIE drayt) a chemical composed of one or more simple sugars; includes sugars, starches, and fiber (269)

cardiac muscle muscle that forms the heart (172)

cavity a hole that is in a person's tooth and that is made by acids (149)

cell the simplest and most basic unit of all living things (166)

childhood the stage of development between infancy and adolescence (199)

cirrhosis (suh ROH sis) a deadly disease that replaces healthy liver tissue with useless scar tissue; most often caused by long-term alcohol abuse (312)

cochlea (KAHK lee uh) a tiny, snail-shaped, fluid-filled part of the inner ear that is involved in hearing (154)

collaboration (kuh LAB uh RAY shuhn) a solution to a conflict in which both parties get what they want without having to give up anything important (114)

communication the ability to exchange information and the ability to express one's thoughts and feelings clearly (82)

competition a contest between two or more individuals or teams (248)

compromise (KAHM pruh MIEZ) a solution to a conflict in which both sides give up things to come to an agreement (114)

conflict any situation in which ideas or interests go against one another (110)

congenital disease a disease or disorder that is present at birth but that is not a genetic disease (228)

consequence a result of one's actions and decisions (23)

cool-down any activity that helps the body return to the way it was before exercising (255)

cooperation (koh AHP urh AY shuhn) the act of working with others to reach a goal (100)

cornea (KAWR nee uh) the protective, clear structure at the front of the eye (152)

cuticle (KYOOT i kuhl) a thin flap of skin around the nail (147)

dandruff (DAN druhf) flaky clumps of dead skin cells (146)

death the end of life or the stopping of all necessary life functions (206)

dermis (DUHR mis) the living layer of skin under the epidermis (144)

diaphragm a muscle that separates the chest from the abdomen and that aids in breathing (179)

Dietary Guidelines for Americans a set of suggestions designed to help people develop healthy eating habits and increase physical activity levels (275)

digestion the process of breaking down food into a form that the body can use (174)

disease any harmful change in the state of health of the body or mind (214)

drug any chemical substance that causes a change in a person's physical or psychological state (282)

drug addiction the condition in which a person can no longer control his or her need or desire for a drug (294)

E

earthquake a shaking of the Earth's surface that is caused by movement along a break in the Earth's crust (343)

eating disorder a disease in which a person has an unhealthy concern for his or her body weight and shape (73)

egg the sex cell made by females (194)

empathy (EM puh thee) sharing and understanding another person's feelings (85, 113)

endurance (en DOOR uhns) the ability to do activities for more than a few minutes (239)

environment all of the living and nonliving things around you (9)

environmental tobacco smoke (ETS) the mixture of exhaled smoke and smoke from the ends of burning cigarettes (308)

epidermis (EP uh DUHR mis) the outer layer of skin (144)

exercise any physical activity that maintains or improves your physical fitness (238)

external conflict conflict that happens with another person or another group of people (111)

F

family conflict any clash of ideas or interests within a family (91)

fats an energy-storage nutrient that helps the body store some vitamins (269)

fertilization (FUHR t'l uh ZAY shuhn) the reproductive process in which one sperm and one egg come together to form a new cell and the genes of the mother and father combine (196)

fetal alcohol syndrome (FAS) a group of birth defects that affect an unborn baby that has been exposed to alcohol (312)

fetus (FEET uhs) the developing cells in a woman's uterus, from the start of the ninth week of pregnancy until birth (196)

fire extinguisher a device that releases chemicals to put out a fire (327)

first aid emergency medical care for someone who has been hurt or who is sick (344)

fitness goal a goal to improve one's physical fitness (244)

flexibility (FLEK suh BIL uh tee) the ability to bend and twist joints easily (239)

flood an overflowing of water into areas that are normally dry (342)

Food Guide Pyramid a tool for choosing what kinds of foods to eat and how much of each food to eat every day (272)

fracture (FRAK chuhr) a crack or break in a bone (253)

friendship a relationship between people who enjoy being together, who care about each other, and who often have similar interests (94)

fungi (FUHN JIE) complex organisms that cannot make their own food (221)

G

gang a group of people who often use violence (330)

gateway drug a drug that makes people want to try drugs whose effects are stronger (288)

genetic disease a disease or disorder that is caused entirely or partly by defective genetic information passed on to a child from one or both parents (228)

goal something that someone works toward and hopes to achieve (32)

good decision a decision in which a person carefully considers the outcome of each choice (22)

grief a feeling of deep sadness about a loss (206)

hallucinogen (huh LOO si nuh juhn) any drug that causes the user to see or hear things that are not real (291)

head lice small insects that live on the scalp and suck blood (146)

health a condition of physical, emotional, mental, and social well-being (4)

healthcare consumer (kuhn SOOM erh) anyone who pays for healthcare products or services (156)

healthcare provider any professional who helps people stay healthy (158)

heredity the passing down of traits from parents to their biological child (8)

hormone (HAWR MOHN) a chemical made in one part of the body that is released into the blood, that is carried through the bloodstream, and that causes a change in another part of the body; controls growth and development and many other body functions (200)

hurricane a large, spinning tropical weather system that has wind speeds of at least 74 miles per hour (342)

immune system (i MYOON SIS tuhm) a combination of the physical and chemical defenses that your body has to fight infection; the tissues, organs, and cells that fight pathogens (217)

individual sport a sport in which athletes play alone against other players (248)

infancy the stage of development between birth and 1 year of age (198)

infectious disease any disease that is caused by an agent or pathogen that invades the body (215)

interest something that one enjoys and wants to know more about (36)

internal conflict conflict with oneself (110)

intoxication (in TAHKS i KAY shuhn) the physical and mental changes produced by drinking alcohol (311)

iris (IE ris) the colorful part of the eye (152)

joint a place where two or more bones meet in the body (170)

leadership the ability to guide others in a responsible way (99)

lens the structure in the eye that focuses light on the retina (152)

life jacket a vest that keeps you floating in the water (336)

life skills tools that help you deal with situations that can affect your health (12)

lifestyle a set of behaviors by which you live your life (10)

lungs large, spongelike organs in which oxygen and carbon dioxide pass between the blood and the air (178)

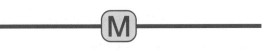

medicine a drug that is used to cure, prevent, or treat pain, disease, or illness (284)

menstruation (MEN STRAY shuhn) the monthly breakdown and shedding of the lining of the uterus during which blood and tissue leave the woman's body through the vagina (194)

mentor a person who can give you valuable advice (37)

mineral (MIN uhr uhl) an element that is essential for good health (270)

misuse the accidental incorrect use of a drug (292)

natural disaster a natural event that causes widespread injury, death, and property damage (340)

neglect (ni GLECKT) the failure of a parent or other responsible adult to provide for basic needs, such as food, clothing, or love (92)

nerve a bundle of cells that conducts electrical signals from one part of the body to another (180)

nicotine (NIK uh TEEN) a highly addictive drug that is found in all tobacco products (306)

noninfectious disease a disease that is not caused by a pathogen (215, 228)

nutrient a substance in food that the body needs in order to work properly (174, 266)

Nutrition Facts label a label that is found on the outside packages of food and that states the number of servings in the container, the number of Calories in each serving, and the amount of nutrients in each serving (274)

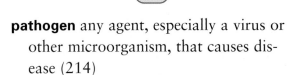

option a choice that you can make (25)

organ two or more tissues that work together to perform a special function (166)

ovary one of the two organs of the female reproductive system that make eggs and the hormones estrogen and progesterone (194)

over-the-counter (OTC) medicine any medicine that can be bought without a prescription (285)

pathogen any agent, especially a virus or other microorganism, that causes disease (214)

peer pressure a feeling that you should do something because your friends want you to (28, 316)

GLOSSARY

physical fitness the ability to perform daily physical activities without becoming short of breath, sore, or overly tired (238)

plaque (PLAK) a mixture of bacteria, saliva, and food particles found on teeth (148)

prescription medicine (pree SKRIP shuhn MED ı suhn) a medicine that can be bought only with a written order from a doctor (286)

preventive healthcare taking steps to prevent illness and accidents before they happen (11)

protein (PROH TEEN) a nutrient that supplies the body with energy for building and repairing tissues and cells (269)

protozoan (PROHT oh ZOH uhn) a small, single-celled organism that has a nucleus (220)

puberty the period of time during adolescence when the reproductive system becomes mature (201)

pupil (PYOO puhl) a hole in the iris that controls the amount of light that enters the eye (152)

recovery time the amount of time that the heart takes to return to the resting heart rate after exercise (247)

reflex an automatic response to stimuli that occur outside the body (181)

refusal skill a strategy to avoid doing something that you don't want to do (28)

relationship an emotional or social connection between two or more people (82)

rescue breathing an emergency technique in which a rescuer gives air to someone who is not breathing (347)

resource something that can be used to meet a need or achieve a goal (37)

resting heart rate (RHR) the number of times that the heart beats per minute while the body is at rest (247)

retina (RET'n uh) the part of the eye that contains millions of light-sensitive cells that detect the energy from light (152)

safety equipment equipment that helps prevent injury (258)

self-concept a measure of how you see and imagine yourself as a person (50)

self-esteem a measure of how much you value, respect, and feel confident about yourself (33, 46)

sexually transmitted disease (STD) any of a number of infections that are spread from one person to another by sexual contact (224)

skeletal muscle muscle that attaches to bones (172)

sleep a period of reduced awareness during which many body systems rest or slow down (184)

smoke detector a small, battery-operated alarm that detects smoke from a fire (327)

smooth muscle muscle that forms some internal organs (172)

sound wave vibrations that travel through solids, water, or air (154)

sperm the sex cell made by males (192)

spinal cord a bundle of nervous tissue that is about a foot and a half long and that is surrounded by the backbone; carries messages to and from the brain (180)

sports physical a medical checkup that is required before a person can play with a sports team (242)

sprain an injury in which the ligaments in a joint are stretched too far or are torn (252)

strain an injury in which a muscle or tendon has been stretched too far or has torn (252)

strength the amount of force that muscles can apply when they are used (239)

stress the combination of a new or possibly threatening situation and the body's natural response to the situation (128)

stretching any activity that loosens muscles and increases flexibility (256)

success the achievement of one's goals (34)

support the act of helping when help is needed (89)

support system a group of people, such as friends and family, who will stand by you and encourage you when times get hard (31)

team sport a sport in which two or more people work together against another team (248)

testes (TES TEEZ) the male reproductive organs that make sperm and the hormone testosterone (192)

thunderstorm a heavy rainstorm that has strong winds, lightning, and thunder (341)

tissue a group of similar cells that work together to perform a single function (166)

tobacco a plant whose leaves can be dried and mixed with chemicals to make products such as cigarettes, smokeless tobacco, and cigars (304)

tolerance the ability to overlook differences and to accept people for who they are (85); a condition in which a person needs more of a drug to feel the original effects of the drug (294)

tornado a spinning column of air that has high wind speed and that touches the ground (341)

trachea (TRAY kee uh) the pipe that carries air deep into the body (178)

unit price the cost of an item divided by the amount of the item (157)

V

values beliefs that one considers to be of great importance (25)

vein a blood vessel that carries blood toward the heart (176)

violence (VIE uh luhns) physical force that is used to harm people or damage property (120, 330)

virus a tiny, disease-causing particle that consists of genetic material and a protein coat and that invades a healthy cell and instructs that cell to make more viruses (218)

vitamin (VIET uh min) an organic compound that controls many body functions and that is needed in small amounts to maintain health and allow growth (270)

W

warm-up any activity that gets the body ready for exercise (254)

wellness a state of good health that is achieved by balancing physical, emotional, mental, and social health (7)

withdrawal (with DRAW uhl) uncomfortable physical and psychological symptoms produced when a person who is physically dependent on drugs stops using drugs (294)

Spanish Glossary

A

abdominal thrust/empuje abdominal acción de aplicar presión al estómago de una persona atragantada para lograr que un objeto salga por la garganta (346)

abstinence/abstinencia decisión de no participar en una actividad que ponga en riesgo la salud propia o la de otros (103, 226) (Ver también *abstencia sexual*)

abuse/abuso tratamiento dañino u ofensivo de una persona hacia otra; el uso indebido e intencional de drogas o el uso de una droga ilegal (92, 292)

accident/accidente acontecimiento inesperado que puede provocar lesión o muerte (326)

acne/acné inflamación de la piel que se forma cuando los poros de la piel se tapan con suciedad y grasa (144)

adolescence/adolescencia etapa del desarrollo en la que los seres humanos pasan de la infancia a la edad adulta (200)

adulthood/edad adulta período de la vida que sigue a la adolescencia y termina con la muerte (204)

affection/afecto sentimiento de agrado o cariño (89, 102)

AIDS/SIDA síndrome de inmunodeficiencia adquirida, enfermedad producida por la infección del VIH que hace que una persona infectada tenga más posibilidades de contraer formas poco comunes de cáncer e infecciones debido a que el VIH ataca al sistema inmunológico del cuerpo (224)

alcohol/alcohol líquido que al beberlo puede afectar la forma de pensar y actuar de una persona (304)

alcoholism/alcoholismo enfermedad ocasionada por la adicción al alcohol; dependencia física y psicológico al alcohol (315)

anger/enojo sentimiento negativo intenso hacia alguien o algo, provocado por la percepción de haber sido lastimado u ofendido (120)

anorexia nervosa/anorexia nerviosa trastorno alimenticio en el que la persona deja de comer, tiene una percepción enferma de su cuerpo y sufre una pérdida de peso extrema (74)

artery/arteria vaso sanguíneo que transporta la sangre desde el corazón (176)

assertiveness/aserción acción de defender la opinión propia de forma correcta (30)

attitude/actitud forma particular de actuar, pensar o sentir de una persona (10)

B

bacteria/bacteria organismos unicelulares extremadamente pequeños que no tienen núcleo; microorganismos de una sola célula que se encuentran en todas partes (219)

behavior/conducta la forma en la que una persona decide reaccionar o actuar (84)

binge eating disorder/trastorno alimenticio compulsivo trastorno alimenticio en el que una persona tiene dificultad para controlar cuánto come (75)

blood alcohol concentration (BAC)/ concentración de alcohol en la sangre (CAS) porcentaje de alcohol en la sangre de una persona (11)

blood pressure/presión arterial fuerza que la sangre ejerce contra el interior de las paredes de un vaso sanguíneo (176)

body image/imagen corporal forma en que piensas en ti mismo y en tu cuerpo (62)

body language/lenguaje corporal forma de comunicarse utilizando expresiones de la cara, gestos con la mano y la postura del cuerpo (83)

body system/sistema corporal grupo de órganos que trabajan juntos para cumplir una función específica en el cuerpo (166)

bone/hueso órgano vivo del sistema esquelético formado por células óseas, tejidos conectivos y minerales (170)

bone marrow/médula ósea capa de tejido blando que está en el centro de muchos huesos (170)

brain/cerebro órgano principal del sistema nervioso; masa de tejido nervioso que se encuentra dentro del cráneo (180)

brainstorming/lluvia de ideas acción de pensar en todas las maneras posibles de llevar a cabo una decisión (25)

bulimia nervosa/bulimia nerviosa trastorno alimenticio en el que una persona come una gran cantidad de alimentos y luego intenta eliminar la comida del cuerpo (74)

C

calcium/calcio mineral que hace que los huesos se mantengan sanos y fuertes (183)

Calorie/Caloría unidad que se utiliza para medir la cantidad de energía que el cuerpo obtiene de los alimentos (268)

cancer/cáncer enfermedad caracterizada por el crecimiento anormal de las células (309)

capillary/capilar pequeño vaso sanguíneo que transporta sangre entre las arterias y las venas (176)

carbohydrate/carbohidratos sustancia química compuesta por uno o más azúcares simples; incluye azúcares, féculas y fibras (269)

cardiac muscle/músculo cardíaco músculo que forma el corazón (172)

cavity/caries orificio en la dentadura de una persona producido por ácidos (149)

cell/célula unidad más simple y básica de todos los elementos vivientes (166)

childhood/niñez etapa del desarrollo entre la infancia y la adolescencia (199)

cirrhosis/cirrosis enfermedad mortal que reemplaza los tejidos sanos del hígado por tejidos cicatrizados inservibles; en la mayoría de los casos está causada por el abuso de alcohol durante un largo período de tiempo (312)

cochlea/cóclea porción pequeña del oído interno, con forma de caracol y llena de líquido, que participa en la audición (154)

collaboration/colaboración solución a un problema en el que ambas partes obtienen lo que desean sin tener que renunciar a nada importante (114)

communication/comunicación capacidad de intercambiar información y de expresar los pensamientos y los sentimientos propios con claridad (82)

competition/competencia enfrentamiento entre dos o más personas o equipos (248)

compromise/convenio solución a un problema en el que ambas partes renuncian a ciertas cosas para lograr un acuerdo (114)

conflict/conflicto toda situación en la que las ideas o los intereses se enfrentan (110)

congenital disease/enfermedad congénita enfermedad o trastorno presente al nacer pero hereditario (228)

consequence/consecuencia resultado de las acciones y las decisiones de una persona (23)

cool-down/enfriamiento toda actividad que le permite al cuerpo recuperar el estado previo al ejercicio (255)

cooperation/cooperación acción de trabajar con otros para alcanzar una meta (100)

cornea/córnea estructura transparente y de protección que está en la parte delantera del ojo (152)

cuticle/cutícula pliegue delgado de piel alrededor de la uña (147)

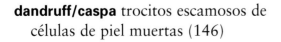

dandruff/caspa trocitos escamosos de células de piel muertas (146)

death/muerte final de la vida o interrupción de todas las funciones vitales necesarias (206)

dermis/dermis capa viva de la piel debajo de la epidermis (144)

diaphragm/diafragma músculo que separa el pecho del abdomen y ayuda en la respiración (179)

Dietary Guidelines for Americans/Guía alimenticia para los Estadounidenses conjunto de sugerencias diseñado para ayudar a las personas a crear hábitos alimenticios sanos y aumentar los niveles de actividad física (275)

digestion/digestión proceso de descomponer los alimentos de manera que el cuerpo pueda utilizarlos (174)

disease/enfermedad todo cambio dañino en el estado de salud del cuerpo o la mente (214)

drug/droga toda sustancia química que provoca un cambio en el estado físico o psicológico de una persona (282)

drug addiction/drogadicción estado en el que una persona ya no puede controlar el consumo de una droga (294)

earthquake/terremoto temblor de la superficie de la Tierra producido por un movimiento a lo largo de una ruptura en la corteza terrestre (343)

eating disorder/trastorno alimenticio enfermedad en la que una persona se preocupa de manera negativa por su silueta y su peso corporal (73)

egg/óvulo célula sexual elaborada por las mujeres (194)

empathy/empatía compartir y entender los sentimientos de otra persona (85, 113)

endurance/resistencia capacidad de realizar actividades durante más de unos pocos minutos (239)

environment/medio ambiente todos los seres vivos y elementos sin vida que rodean a una persona (9)

environmental tobacco smoke (ETS)/ humo de tabaco ambiental (HTA) mezcla del humo exhalado por los fumadores y el humo de los cigarrillos al consumirse (308)

epidermis/epidermis capa externa de la piel (144)

exercise/ejercicio toda actividad física que mantiene o mejora el estado físico (238)

external conflict/conflicto externo conflicto que se produce con otra persona u otro grupo de personas (111)

F

family conflict/conflicto familiar todo choque de ideas o intereses dentro de una familia (91)

fats/grasas nutriente que almacena energía y permite al cuerpo almacenar algunas vitaminas (269)

fertilization/fecundación proceso reproductivo mediante el cual un óvulo y un espermatozoide se unen para formar una célula nueva y los genes de la madre y el padre se combinan (196)

fetal alcohol syndrome (FAS)/síndrome de alcohol fetal (SAF) grupo de defectos de nacimiento que afectan a un bebé que estuvo expuesto al alcohol durante la gestación (312)

fetus/feto células en desarrollo en el útero de la madre, desde el inicio de la novena semana de embarazo hasta el nacimiento (196)

fire extinguisher/extintor dispositivo que libera sustancias químicas para apagar un incendio (327)

first aid/primeros auxilios atención médica de emergencia para una persona que se lastimó o está enferma (344)

fitness goal/meta de estado físico meta para mejorar el estado físico de una persona (244)

flexibility/flexibilidad capacidad de doblar y girar las articulaciones con facilidad (239)

flood/inundación exceso de agua en zonas normalmente secas (342)

Food Guide Pyramid/Pirámide alimenticia herramienta para escoger qué tipos de alimentos se deben comer y qué cantidad de cada alimento se debe comer cada día (272)

fracture/fractura fisura o rotura de un hueso (253)

friendship/amistad relación entre personas que disfrutan de estar juntas, se cuidan entre sí y suelen tener intereses similares (94)

fungi/hongos organismos complejos que no pueden elaborar su propio alimento (221)

G

gang/pandilla grupo de personas que suelen utilizar la violencia (330)

gateway drug/droga de inicio droga que hace que las personas sientan deseo de probar drogas más fuertes (288)

genetic disease/enfermedad genética enfermedad o trastorno provocado de manera total o parcial por información genética defectuosa transmitida de uno o ambos padres al hijo (228)

goal/meta algo por lo que una persona se esfuerza y que espera alcanzar (32)

good decision/buena decisión decisión que toma una persona luego de analizar sus consecuencias detenidamente (22)

grief/duelo sentimiento de profunda tristeza por una pérdida (206)

H

hallucinogen/alucinógeno cualquier droga que hace que el usuario vea u oiga cosas que no son reales (291)

head lice/piojos pequeños insectos que viven en el cuero cabelludo y chupan sangre (146)

health/salud condición de bienestar físico, emocional, mental y social (4)

healthcare consumer/consumidor de servicios de salud toda persona que paga para recibir productos y servicios del cuidado de la salud (156)

healthcare provider/proveedor de servicios de salud todo profesional que ayuda a las personas a mantenerse sanas (158)

heredity/herencia transmisión de rasgos de padres a hijos (8)

hormone/hormona sustancia química elaborada en una parte del cuerpo que se libera dentro de la sangre, se transporta a través del torrente sanguíneo y produce un cambio en otra parte del cuerpo; controla el crecimiento y el desarrollo y muchas otras funciones del cuerpo (200)

hurricane/huracán fenómeno del clima tropical que produce una masa grande y giratoria de vientos que se desplazan por lo menos a aproximadamente 74 millas por hora (342)

I

immune system/sistema inmunológico combinación de las defensas físicas y químicas que el cuerpo posee para combatir infecciones; los tejidos, los órganos y las células que combaten a los agentes patógenos (217)

individual sport/deporte individual deporte en el que los atletas se enfrentan solos a otros jugadores (248)

infancy/infancia etapa del desarrollo entre el nacimiento y el primer año de edad (198)

infectious disease/enfermedad infecciosa toda enfermedad causada por un agente o un patógeno que invade el cuerpo (215)

interest/interés algo que uno disfruta y desea conocer mejor (36)

internal conflict/conflicto interno conflicto con uno mismo (110)

intoxication/intoxicación cambios físicos y mentales producidos por beber alcohol (311)

iris/iris la parte del ojo que tiene color (152)

joint/articulación parte del cuerpo en la que dos o más huesos se encuentran (170)

leadership/liderazgo capacidad de guiar a otros con responsabilidad (99)

lens/cristalino estructura en el ojo que enfoca la luz en la retina (152)

life jacket/chaleco salvavidas chaleco que te permite flotar en el agua (336)

life skills/destrezas para la vida herramientas que te ayudan a manejarse en situaciones que pueden afectar tu salud (12)

lifestyle/estilo de vida conjunto de conductas que marcan tu forma de vivir (10)

lungs/pulmones órganos grandes con aspecto de esponja en los que se produce el intercambio de oxígeno y dióxido de carbono entre el aire y la sangre (178)

medicine/medicamento toda droga utilizada para curar, prevenir o tratar enfermedades o molestias (284)

menstruation/menstruación proceso mensual de desprendimiento del recubrimiento interior de la matriz durante el que la sangre y los tejidos salen del cuerpo de la mujer a través de la vagina (194)

mentor/mentor persona capaz de proporcionarte un consejo valioso (37)

mineral/mineral elemento esencial para una buena salud (270)

misuse/uso indebido uso incorrecto no intencional de una droga (292)

natural disaster/desastre natural acontecimiento natural que causa muchas lesiones, muertes y daños a propiedades (340)

neglect/negligencia incumplimiento de un padre u otro adulto responsable en su deber de satisfacer las necesidades básicas, tales como comida, ropa o amor (92)

nerve/nervio conjunto de células nerviosas (neuronas) que transmiten señales eléctricas desde una parte del cuerpo a otra (180)

nicotine/nicotina droga altamente adictiva que se encuentra en todos los productos con tabaco (306)

noninfectious disease/enfermedad no infecciosa enfermedad que no es causada por un agente patógeno (215, 228)

nutrient/nutriente sustancia en los alimentos que el cuerpo necesita para funcionar correctamente (174, 266)

Nutrition Facts label/etiqueta de Valores nutricionales etiqueta que se encuentra en el exterior de los envases de alimentos y en la que se informa el número de porciones que incluye el envase, el número de calorías que contiene cada porción y la cantidad de nutrientes que aporta cada porción (274)

O

option/opción elección que puedes realizar (25)

organ/órgano dos o más tejidos que trabajan juntos para llevar a cabo una función especial (166)

ovary/ovario uno de los dos órganos del aparato reproductor femenino que produce los óvulos y las hormonas estrógeno y progesterona (194)

over-the-counter (OTC) medicine/ medicamentos de venta sin receta (VSR) todo medicamento que se puede comprar sin receta médica (285)

P

pathogen/patógeno todo agente, especialmente un virus u otro microorganismo, que provoca una enfermedad (214)

peer pressure/presión de pares sensación de que debes hacer algo que tus amigos quieren que hagas (28, 316)

physical fitness/buen estado físico capacidad de realizar actividades físicas todos los días sin sentir falta de aire, dolor o cansancio extremos (238)

plaque/placa mezcla de bacterias, saliva y partículas de alimentos que se deposita en los dientes (148)

prescription medicine/medicamento recetado medicamento que se puede comprar sólo con una orden escrita del médico (286)

preventive healthcare/cuidado preventivo de la salud medidas para prevenir enfermedades y accidentes antes de que ocurran (11)

protein/proteína nutriente que suministra energía al cuerpo para construir y reparar tejidos y células (269)

protozoan/protozoario pequeño organismo unicelular que tiene núcleo (220)

puberty/pubertad período de tiempo durante la adolescencia en el que se produce la maduración del aparato reproductor (201)

pupil/pupila orificio en el iris que controla la cantidad de luz que entra al ojo (152)

R

recovery time/tiempo de recuperación cantidad de tiempo que el corazón necesita para volver al índice cardíaco de descanso después de realizar ejercicios (247)

reflex/reflejo respuesta automática a estímulos que se producen fueran del cuerpo (181)

refusal skill/habilidad de negación estrategia para evitar hacer algo que no quieres hacer (28)

relationship/relación conexión emocional o social entre dos o más personas (82)

rescue breathing/respiración de rescate técnica de emergencia mediante la cual una persona le proporciona aire a la que no respira (347)

resource/recurso algo que se puede utilizar para satisfacer una necesidad o alcanzar una meta (37)

resting heart rate (RHR)/índice de pulsaciones en reposo (IPR) número de veces que el corazón late por minuto mientras el cuerpo está en reposo (247)

retina/retina parte del ojo que contiene millones de células sensibles capaces de detectar la energía de la luz (152)

safety equipment/equipo de seguridad equipo que ayuda a prevenir lesiones (258)

self-concept/autoconcepto medición de cómo una persona se ve y se imagina a sí misma como individuo (50)

self-esteem/autoestima medición de cuánto se valora, respeta y cuánta confianza en sí misma tiene una persona (33, 46)

sexually transmitted disease (STD)/ enfermedad de transmisión sexual (ETS) cualquiera de un número de infecciones que se transmiten de una persona a otra a través del contacto sexual (224)

skeletal muscle/músculo esquelético músculo que se sujeta a huesos (172)

sleep/sueño período de actividad reducida durante el que muchos aparatos y sistemas del cuerpo descansan o funcionan más lentamente (184)

smoke detector/detector de humo alarma pequeña que funciona con pilas utilizada para detectar el humo de un incendio (327)

smooth muscle/músculo liso músculo que constituye algunos órganos internos (172)

sound wave/onda de sonido vibraciones que se desplazan a través de materia sólida, agua o aire (154)

sperm/espermatozoide célula sexual elaborada por los hombres (192)

spinal cord/médula espinal acumulación de tejido nervioso que mide aproximadamente un pie y medio de largo y está rodeado por la columna vertebral; transmite mensajes hacia y desde el cerebro (180)

sports physical/revisión médica examen médico que se le requiere a una persona antes de permitirle jugar con un equipo deportivo (242)

sprain/esguince lesión en la que los ligamentos de una articulación se estiran demasiado o se desgarran (252)

strain/distensión lesión en la que un músculo o un tendón se estiró demasiado o se desgarró (252)

strength/fuerza cantidad de fuerza empleada por los músculos al utilizarlos (239)

stress/estrés combinación de una situación nueva o posiblemente amenazante y la respuesta natural del cuerpo a esa situación (128)

stretching/elongación toda actividad que afloje los músculos y aumente la flexibilidad (256)

success/éxito logro de las metas propuestas (34)

support/apoyar acción de ayudar cuando se necesita ayuda (89)

support system/sistema de apoyo grupo de personas, por ejemplo, amigos y familiares, que estarán a tu lado y te apoyarán en momentos difíciles (31)

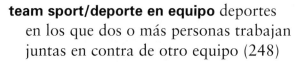

T

team sport/deporte en equipo deportes en los que dos o más personas trabajan juntas en contra de otro equipo (248)

testes/testículos órganos reproductores masculinos que producen espermatozoides y la hormona testosterona (192)

thunderstorm/tormenta eléctrica tempestad con vientos fuertes, relámpagos y truenos (341)

tissue/tejido grupo de células similares que trabajan juntas para cumplir una única función (166)

tobacco/tabaco planta cuyas hojas se secan y mezclan con sustancias químicas para hacer productos tales como cigarrillos, tabaco rapé y puros (304)

tolerance/tolerancia capacidad de aceptar a las personas por lo que son a pesar de las diferencias (85); condición en la que una persona necesita más cantidad de una droga para sentir sus efectos originales (294)

tornado/tornado columna giratoria de aire que tiene vientos de alta velocidad y cuyo extremo toca el suelo (341)

trachea/tráquea tubo que transporta aire hacia adentro del cuerpo (178)

U

unit price/precio unitario costo de un producto dividido por la cantidad de unidades del producto (157)

V

values/valores creencias que uno considera de mucha importancia (25)

vein/vena vaso sanguíneo que transporta la sangre hacia el corazón (176)

violence/violencia fuerza física que se utiliza para dañar a una persona o una propiedad (120, 330)

virus/virus partícula pequeña, capaz de causar enfermedades, formada por material genético y un revestimiento de proteína que invade a una célula sana y le indica que produzca más virus (218)

vitamin/vitamina compuesto orgánico que controla muchas funciones del cuerpo y que es necesario en pequeñas cantidades para mantener la salud y permitir el crecimiento (270)

W

warm-up/calentamiento actividad que prepara al cuerpo para realizar ejercicios (254)

wellness/bienestar estado de buena salud que se logra mediante el equilibrio de la salud física, emocional, mental y social (7)

withdrawal/supresión síntomas psicológicos y físicos molestos que se producen cuando una persona que tiene dependencia a una droga deja de consumirla (294)

SPANISH GLOSSARY

Index

Note: Page references followed by *f* refer to figures. Page references followed by *t* refer to tables. Boldface page references refer to the primary discussion of the term.

Acknowledgments continued from page iv.

Teacher Reviewers

Dan Aude
Magnet Programs Coordinator
Montgomery Public Schools
Montgomery, Alabama

Judy Blanchard
District Health Coordinator
Newtown Public Schools
Newtown, Connecticut

David Blinn
Secondary Sciences Teacher
Wrenshall School District
Wrenshall, Minnesota

Johanna Chase, C.H.E.S.
Health Educator
California State University
Dominguez Hills, California

JeNean Erickson
Sports Coach, Physical Education and Health Teacher
New Prague Middle School
New Prague, Minnesota

Stacy Feinberg, L.M.H.C.
Family Counselor for Autism
Broward County School System
Coral Gables, Florida

Arthur Goldsmith
Secondary Sciences Teacher
Hallendale High School
Hallendale, Florida

Jacqueline Horowitz-Olstfeld
Exceptional Student Educator
Broward County School District
Fort Lauderdale, Florida

Kathy LaRoe
Teacher
St. Paul School District
St. Paul, Nebraska

Regina Logan
Sports Coach, Physical Education and Health Teacher
Dade County Middle School
Trenton, Georgia

Alyson Mike
Sports Coach, Science and Health Teacher
East Valley Middle School
East Helena, Montana

Elizabeth Rustad
Sports Coach, Life Science and Health Teacher
Centennial Middle School
Yuma, Arizona

Rodney Sandefur
Principal
Nucla Middle School
Nucla, Colorado

Helen Schiller
Science and Health Teacher
Northwood Middle School
Taylor, South Carolina

Gayle Seymour
Health Teacher
Newtown Middle School
Newtown, Connecticut

Bert Sherwood
Science and Health Specialist
Socorro Independent School District
El Paso, Texas

Beth Truax, R.N.
Science Teacher
Lewiston-Porter Central School
Lewiston, New York

Jenny Wallace
Science Teacher
Whitehouse Middle School
Whitehouse, Texas

Kim Walls
Alternative Education Teacher
Lockhart Independent School District
Lockhart, Texas

Alexis Wright
Principal, Middle School
Rye Country Day School
Rye, New York

Joe Zelmanski
Curriculum Coordinator
Rochester Adams High School
Rochester Hills, Michigan

Teen Advisory Board

Teachers

Melissa Landrum
Physical Education Teacher
Hopewell Middle School
Round Rock, Texas

Stephanie Scott
Physical Education Teacher
Hopewell Middle School
Round Rock, Texas

Krista Robinson
Physical Education Teacher
Hopewell Middle School
Round Rock, Texas

Hopewell Middle School Students

Efrain Nicolas Avila

Darius T. Bell

Micki Bevka

Kalthoom A. Bouderdaben

La Joya M. Brown

Jennafer Chew

Seth Cowan

Mariana Diaz

Marcus Duran

Timothy Galvan

Megan Ann Giessregen

Shane Harkins

Ryan Landrum

Maria Elizabeth Ortiz Lopez

Travis Wilmer

Staff Credits

Editorial

Robert Todd, *Associate Director, Secondary Science*
Debbie Starr, *Managing Editor*

Senior Editors

Leigh Ann García
Kelly Rizk
Laura Zapanta

Editorial Development Team

Karin Akre
Shari Husain
Kristen McCardel
Laura Prescott
Betsy Roll
Kenneth Shepardson
Ann Welch
David Westerberg

Copyeditors

Dawn Marie Spinozza, *Copyediting Manager*
Anne-Marie De Witt
Jane A. Kirschman
Kira J. Watkins

Editorial Support Staff

Jeanne Graham
Mary Helbling
Shannon Oehler
Stephanie S. Sanchez
Tanu'e White

Editorial Interns

Kristina Bigelow
Erica Garza
Sarah Ray
Kenneth G. Raymond
Kyle Stock
Audra Teinert

Online Products

Bob Tucek, *Executive Editor*
Wesley M. Bain
Catherine Gallagher
Douglas P. Rutley

ACKNOWLEDGMENTS

Staff Credits *(continued)*

Production

Eddie Dawson,
Production Manager
Sherry Sprague,
Senior Production Coordinator
Mary T. King, *Administrative Assistant*

Design

Book Design

Bruce Bond, *Design Director*
Mary Wages, *Senior Designer*
Cristina Bowerman,
Design Associate
Ruth Limon, *Design Associate*
Alicia Sullivan, *Designer,
Teacher Edition*
Sally Bess, *Designer, Teacher Edition*
Charlie Taliaferro, *Design Associate, Teacher Edition*

Image Acquisitions

Curtis Riker, *Director*
Jeannie Taylor,
Photo Research Supervisor
Stephanie Morris,
Photo Researcher
Sarah Hudgens, *Photo Researcher*
Elaine Tate, *Art Buyer Supervisor*
Angela Parisi, *Art Buyer*

Design New Media

Ed Blake, *Design Director*
Kimberly Cammerata,
Design Manager

Media Design

Richard Metzger, *Director*
Chris Smith, *Senior Designer*

Graphic Services

Kristen Darby, *Director*
Jeff Robinson,
Senior Ancillary Designer

Cover Design

Bruce Bond, *Design Director*

Design Implementation and Page Production

Preface, Inc.,
Schaumburg, Illinois

Electronic Publishing

EP Manager

Robert Franklin

EP Team Leaders

Juan Baquera
Sally Dewhirst
Christopher Lucas
Nanda Patel
JoAnn Stringer

Senior Production Artists

Katrina Gnader
Lana Kaupp
Kim Orne

Production Artists

Sara Buller
Ellen Kennedy
Patty Zepeda

Quality Control

Barry Bishop
Becky Golden-Harrell
Angela Priddy
Ellen Rees

New Media

Armin Gutzmer,
Director of Development
Melanie Baccus,
New Media Coordinator
Lydia Doty,
Senior Project Manager
Cathy Kuhles, *Technical Assistant*
Marsh Flournoy, *Quality Assurance
Project Manager*
Tara F. Ross, *Senior Project Manager*

Ancillary Development and Production

General Learning Communications, Northbrook,
Illinois

Illustration and Photography Credits

Abbreviations used: (t) top,
(c) center, (b) bottom, (l) left,
(r) right, (bkgd) background

Illustrations

All work, unless otherwise noted, contributed by Holt, Rinehart & Winston.

Chapter One: L1: Page 7 (c), Argosy; L2: 9 (tl),(tr), Mark Heine; REV: 17 (tr), Leslie Kell.

Chapter Two: L2: Page 24 (b), Argosy; 27 (c), Argosy; L3: 28 (bc), Marty Roper/Planet Rep; L4: 32 (b), Marty Roper/Planet Rep; L5: 37 (b), Rita Lascaro; 39 (c), Argosy; FEA: 42, Laura Bailie.

Chapter Three: L1: Page 49 (t), Marty Roper/Planet Rep; L3: 53 (tr), Argosy; REV: 57 (tr), Leslie Kell.

Chapter Four: L1: Page 62 (b), Marty Roper/ Planet Rep.

Chapter Five: L1: Page 84 (b), Leslie Kell; L3: 93 (c), Argosy; L5: 99 (b), Argosy.

Chapter Six: L2: Page 112 (b), Rita Lascaro; 113 (tr), (cr), (br), Argosy; L4: 121 (br), Mark Heine; L5: 124 (b), Argosy; REV: 139 (tr), Leslie Kell.

Chapter Seven: L1: Page 144 (b), Christy Krames; L3: 148 (b), Christy Krames; 149 (b), Christy Krames; L4: 152 (b), Christy Krames; L5: 154 (bl), Christy Krames.

Chapter Eight: L1: Page 166 (b), Christy Krames; 168 Christy Krames; L3: 172 (bl), Christy Krames; 173 (tl), Christy Krames; L4: 174 (b), Christy Krames; L5: 176 (bl), Christy Krames; 177 (tl), Christy Krames; L6: 178 (bl), (br), Christy Krames.

Chapter Nine: L1: Page 192 (b), Christy Krames; 194 (t), Christy Krames; 195 (t), Christy Krames; L3: 199 (tl), Leslie Kell; L4: 202 (t), Marcia Hartsock/The Medical Art Company; L5: 206 (t), Leslie Kell; REV: 209 (tr), Leslie Kell; FEA: 211, Marty Roper/Planet Rep.

Chapter Ten: L1: Page 215 (t), Christy Krames; L4: 224 (b), Stephen Durke/Washington Artists; 227 (t), Marty Roper/Planet Rep; REV: 233 (tr), Leslie Kell; FEA: 235, Rita Lascaro.

Chapter Eleven: L1: Page 240 (b), Argosy; L3: 246 (b), Argosy; REV: 261 (tr), Leslie Kell.

Chapter Twelve: L3: Page 273 (t), Argosy; 274 (c), Argosy.

Chapter Thirteen: L3: Page 289 (t), Christy Krames; L5: 294 (b) Marty Roper/Planet Rep; REV: 299 (tr), Leslie Kell; FEA: 301, Leslie Kell.

Chapter Fourteen: L2: Page 306 (b), Mark Heine; 313 (cl), Leslie Kell; L4: 314 (bc), Leslie Kell; FEA: 322, Rick Herman.

Chapter Fifteen: L1: Page 326 (b), Mark Heine; L3: 333 (t), Mark Heine; L4: 337 (t), Argosy; 339 (c), Marcia Hartsock/The Medical Art Company; L7: 347 (t), Marcia Hartsock/The Medical Art Company; 349 (c), Leslie Kell; REV: 351 (tr), Leslie Kell.

Appendix: Page 354 (c), Argosy; 355 (cl), (bl), (cr), Rick Herman; 358 (c), Rick Herman; 363 (br), Argosy.

Photography

Cover: Gary Russ/HRW

Table of Contents: v, Corbis; vi (t), Victoria Smith/HRW; (b), David Young-Wolff/PhotoEdit; vii (t), PhotoDisc, Inc.; (b), Gary Conner/PhotoEdit; viii (t), EyeWire; (b), David Young-Wolff/PhotoEdit; ix (t), PhotoDisc, Inc.; (b), Peter Van Steen/HRW; x (t), Victoria Smith/HRW; (c), SW Production/Index Stock; (b), David Kelly Crow/PhotoEdit; xi (t), PhotoDisc, Inc.; (b), Michael Newman/PhotoEdit; xii (t), Peter Van Steen/HRW; (bl), Myrleen Ferguson Cate/PhotoEdit; (br), Keith/Custom Medical Stock Photo; xiii (t), Jennie Woodcock; Reflections Photolibrary/Corbis; xiii (b), Reuters NewMedia

Illustration and Photography Credits *(continued)*

Inc./Corbis; xiv (t), Jim Cummins/Getty Images/FPG International; (b), Duomo/Corbis; xv (tl), PhotoDisc, Inc.; (tr), Burke/Triolo Productions/Getty Images/FoodPix; (b), Yoav Levy/Phototake; xvi (tl), Philip Gould/Corbis; (tr), Doug Mazell/Index Stock; xvii (t), Jim Cummins/Getty Images/FPG International; (b), EyeWire, Inc.; xviii (t), PhotoDisc, Inc.; (b), Stockbyte; xix (t), PhotoDisc, Inc.; (b), Barbara Haynor/Index Stock.

Chapter One: 2-3, Brad Wilson/Photonica; L1: 4, David Young-Wolff/PhotoEdit; 5, Bettmann/CORBIS; 6, Chuck Savage/CORBIS; L2: 8, Laura Dwight/CORBIS; 9, Sam Dudgeon/HRW; L3: 10 (all), Victoria Smith/HRW; 11, ARTHUR TILLEY/Getty Images/FPG International; L4: 12, David Young-Wolff/PhotoEdit; 14, Victoria Smith/HRW; 15, Lisette Le Bon/SuperStock; FEA: 18, Image Copyright ©2004 PhotoDisc, Inc.; 19, Bill Truslow/Getty Images/Stone.

Chapter Two: 20-21, ©Luc Beziat/Getty Images/Stone; L1: 22, Image Copyright © 2004 PhotoDisc, Inc.; 23, Index Stock/Omni Photo Communications Inc.; L2: 25, 26, Peter Van Steen/HRW; L3: 29, 30, 31, Peter Van Steen/ HRW; L4: 33 (r), Peter Van Steen/HRW; (l), Image Copyright ©2004 PhotoDisc, Inc./HRW; 34 (b), David Young-Wolff/Getty Images/Stone; (t), David Young-Wolff/PhotoEdit; 35, Index Stock/Network Productions; L5: 36, David Young-Wolff/Getty Images/Stone; 38, Gary Conner/PhotoEdit; FEA: 43, EyeWire.

Chapter Three: 44-45, Andrew Olnoy/Masterfile; L1: 46, Image Copyright ©2004 PhotoDisc, Inc.; 47, Jack Hollingsworth/CORBIS; 48, Peter Beck/Corbis Stock Market; L2: 50, Mary Kate Denny/PhotoEdit; 51, Index Stock/Barbara Haynor; L3: 52, Custom Medical Stock Photo/CMSP; 54, CLEO PHOTOG-RAPHY/PhotoEdit; 55, West Stock; FEA: 58, Peter Van Steen/HRW; 59, Victoria Smith/HRW.

Chapter Four: 60-61, Copyright © 1998-2001 EyeWire, Inc. All rights reserved.; L1: 63, Index Stock/Grantpix; 63, 64, Index Stock/Jon Riley; L2: 65 (all), Don Couch/HRW; 66, Index Stock/Myrleen Cate; 67, Peter Van Steen/HRW; 67 (TV screen), ©Moritz Steiger/Getty Images/The Image Bank; L3: 68, Sam Dudgeon/HRW; 69, Tom & Dee Ann McCarthy/CorbisStockMarket; 70, Michael Newman/PhotoEdit; 71, David Young-Wolff/ PhotoEdit; L4: 72, David Young-Wolff/PhotoEdit; 73, Peter Van Steen/HRW; 74, David Kelly Crow/PhotoEdit; FEA: 78, BARIL/RONCEN/ CORBIS KIPA; 79, PhotoDisc, Inc.

Chapter Five: 80-81, ©Randy Faris/CORBIS; L1: 82, 83 (all), Peter Van Steen/HRW; 85, Sonda Dawes/The Image Works; L2: 86 (l), David Young-Wolff/ PhotoEdit; (r), Myrleen Ferguson Cate/PhotoEdit; 87 (l), Benn Mitchell/Getty Images/The Image Bank; (r), RON CHAPPLE/Getty Images/FPG International; 88, Bob Daemmrich/Stock Boston; 89, EyeWire; L3: 90, Image Copyright ©2004 PhotoDisc, Inc.; 91, Michael Newman/PhotoEdit; 92, FLASH ! LIGHT/Stock Boston; L4: 94, Index Stock/Benelux Press; 95 (r), Syracuse Newspapers/The Image Works; (l), Michael Newman/PhotoEdit; 97, David K. Crow/PhotoEdit; L5: 98, Ellen Senisi/The Image Works; 100, Tony Freeman/PhotoEdit; 101, Nancy Richmond/The Image Works; L6: 102 (all), Peter Van Steen/HRW; 103, Image Copyright ©2004 PhotoDisc, Inc.; FEA: 106 (all), Image Copyright ©2004 PhotoDisc, Inc.; 107, Tom Stewart/Corbis Stock Market.

Chapter Six: 108-09, ©Gary Buss/Getty Images /FPG International; L1: 110 (all), Peter Van Steen/HRW; 111, David Young-Wolff/PhotoEdit; L2: 114, Skjold Photographs; 115, Peter Van Steen/HRW; L3: 116, Peter Van Steen/HRW; 117 (all), Charlie Fonville/ HRW; 118, Peter Van Steen/HRW; 119, David Young-Wolff/PhotoEdit; L4: 120 (t), David K. Crow/ PhotoEdit; (bl,c,br), Image Copyright ©2004 PhotoDisc, Inc.; (cl), Michael Newman/PhotoEdit; (br, cr), Philip Lee Harvey/Getty Images/Stone; 122, Image Copyright ©2004 PhotoDisc, Inc.; 123, Bonnie Kamin/PhotoEdit; L5: 125, Doug Martin/Photo Researchers, Inc.; 126, Tony Freeman/PhotoEdit; 127 (all), Peter Van Steen/HRW; L6: 128, Duomo/CORBIS; 129, Image Copyright ©2004 PhotoDisc, Inc.; 130, Mary Kate Denny/